INFANTRY COMBAT

INFANTRY COMBAT

The Rifle Platoon
An Interactive Exercise in Small-Unit Tactics and Leadership

John F. Antal

PRESIDIO

This is a work of fiction. Names, characters, places, and incidents are either fictional products of the author's imagination or are used fictionally. Any resemblance to actual events or locales or to persons living or dead is entirely coincidental. The views expressed in this book are those of the author and do not reflect official policies or positions of the Department of the Army, the Department of Defense, or the U.S. government.

Copyright © 1995 by John F. Antal

Published by Presidio Press
505 B San Marin Dr., Suite 300
Novato, CA 94945-1340

Library of Congress Cataloging-in-Publication Data

Antal, John F., 1955–
    Infantry combat the rifle platoon : an interactive exercise in small-unit tactics and leadership / John F. Antal.
       p. cm.
    ISBN 0-89141-536-X
    1. War games. 2. Infantry drill and tactics. I. Title.
U310.A573 1995
355.4'8—dc20
                                  95-30
                                  CIP

Typography by ProImage
Printed in the United States of America

*This book is dedicated to Captain David Kriecht,
U.S. Army (Ret). A superb infantry leader and a
proud warrior, Captain Kriecht was severely wounded
while training America's legions at the
National Training Center, Fort Irwin, California.
Dave, your legacy lives on.*

Battles are fought by platoons and squads.
Place emphasis on small unit combat instruction
so that it is conducted with the same precision
as close-order drill.

Gen. George S. Patton Jr.

Contents

Acknowledgments

Writing a book is a difficult undertaking, and writing an interactive fiction is particularly challenging. This book could not have been completed without the help of many people who deserve to be mentioned. First, special thanks to my good friend Mr. Bob Tate of Presidio Press for his insight, encouragement, and patience. Next to Mr. Richard Kane, Col. Dan Bolger, for their help and comments. Thanks also to Barbara Feller-Roth for her superb job of copy editing. Last, and most importantly, I want to thank my darling wife, Uncha, for her love, patience, and inspiration. Only with her help and constant encouragement was this effort possible.

Preface

Once more unto the beach, dear friends, once more;
Or close the wall up with our English dead!
In peace there's nothing so becomes a man
As modest stillness and humility;
But when the blast of war blows in our ears,
Then imitate the action of the tiger;
Stiffen the sinews, summon up the blood,
Disguise fair nature with hard-favor'd rage:
Then lend the eye a terrible aspect.
                                   Shakespeare, *Henry V*

The English victory over the French at Agincourt in northwest France on October 25, 1415, was a decisive triumph of infantry over cavalry. In Henry's day, battles were won or lost by the courage and determination of the common infantryman. At Agincourt, Henry's staunch yeomen and rapid-fire bowmen made mincemeat of the finest cavalry force in the world—a force that outnumbered the English five to one. Today, disciplined, well-trained infantrymen are still the backbone of an army. As at Agincourt, the deadliest weapon on the battlefield remains the individual soldier armed with a weapon he knows how to use.

The infantry is that part of an army consisting of armed foot soldiers, as distinguished from cavalry, armor, artillery, air, or sea forces. Since ancient times the infantryman has been the frontline fighting soldier. The infantry bear the brunt of offensive or defensive attack and usually suffers the greatest casualties. Often, because of the demands of combat, the infantry is asked to accomplish impossible tasks, as Henry's men were challenged at Agincourt.

This book is about modern infantry combat. Unlike the usual novel, this book is an interactive fiction. Designed both to entertain and to teach, *Infantry Combat* allows you to become an active participant in the battle. In this book, you are in command. You will be the leader of a platoon of U.S. Army light infantrymen in combat in

Preface

the Middle East. Your platoon will be placed in a deadly and desperate situation. At the end of each section you will be required to make a decision. Your skill, tactical knowledge, and luck will determine victory or defeat, life or death.

This book is a form of tactical decision game. It will challenge your leadership and decision-making abilities. It will test your tactical skills and military knowledge. You can face this challenge even if you have no military experience. To military readers, the book offers an opportunity to enhance their military education. To the general reader, it offers a unique insight into the difficult and deadly world of the combat soldier.

To play this tactical decision game and act in the role of the infantry platoon leader, you need three things: this book, a pair of six-sided dice, and all the tactical expertise you can muster! Each decision you make will influence the future course of the battle. Chance and the friction of war will also play their part against you. Plan your courses of action with boldness and determination. To assist you, pertinent historical quotations are strategically placed throughout the sections. Ponder these ideas from the great military theorists and leaders of the past and use their knowledge to help you make your decisions. Remember, your decisions determine the ending of this book. Unlike actual combat, if you select a section where you are killed or captured, you can simply start over from the beginning and use the knowledge of your past mistakes.

In this book, you are 2d Lt. Bruce Davis. You are twenty-three years old and recently commissioned as an officer in the U.S. Army from the U.S. Military Academy at West Point. After West Point you attended the demanding U.S. Army Airborne and Ranger courses. In addition, you graduated from the infantry Officer Basic Course at Fort Benning, Georgia. Eager to get into the "real" army, you look forward to taking over your first platoon and leading American soldiers.

Unfortunately, there is very little time for you to get to know your platoon and learn the tricks of the trade. Shortly after you are assigned to your unit, the peace is lost and the world explodes in conflict. A war erupts in Northeast Asia and focuses America's attention. Simultaneously, a crisis develops in the Middle East that forces the United States to rapidly deploy military forces. Light infantry forces are sent to the Middle East because they are the only ground force units that can get there in time to make a stand. Light infantry forces will have to hold the line until the heavier forces arrive. You will lead a platoon that is being sent to hold a part of that line.

Sound far-fetched? Actually, this kind of difficult situation has occurred several times before. The life and death trade-offs between strategic mobility and tactical capability are not new. Decision makers are often confronted with the choice of sending in light, rapidly deployable military units or not responding in time. Heavy forces, tanks, infantry fighting vehicles, and self-propelled artillery are the muscle of modern maneuver warfare but carry a significant strategic deployment penalty. Light forces, therefore, are an important part of a force-projection army. This dilemma can often place the light infantry in precarious tactical situations.

A classic example of this phenomenon occurred during the Korean War. On July 5, 1950, a force of 540 American infantrymen was ordered to stop the North Korean armored advance at a ridge north of the Korean town of Osan. In this battle, the lightly armed U.S. force, Task Force Smith, found itself outnumbered, outgunned, and outflanked by hordes of North Korean tanks. A more recent example of a situation where light infantry was ordered to hold the line against more heavily armed armored forces occurred during Operation Desert Shield in 1990.

On August 2, 1990, Saddam Hussein invaded Kuwait, capturing the entire country in less than forty-eight hours. The vital oil fields of Saudi Arabia were threatened. On August 6 Saudi Arabia requested U.S. assistance to stop the Iraqis. The United States immediately dispatched its most strategically deployable force, the 82d Airborne Division, to the sands of Saudi Arabia. The lead element of U.S. paratroopers arrived on August 9. Heavy forces—units with tanks, infantry fighting vehicles, and heavy artillery (the first of which were from the 24th Infantry Division [Mechanized])—didn't arrive until August 27. Between August 9 and August 27 the light infantry held the line against the fourth-largest army in the world. In the two weeks after the August 2 invasion, Iraq had deployed 8 divisions, 140,000 troops, 1,100 tanks, 610 artillery pieces, and 610 other armored vehicles along with engineers, air defense, and logistical support into the Kuwaiti theater of operations. On August 12 the only force in front of the Iraqis was one lone battalion of U.S. paratroopers. Luckily, Saddam blinked and didn't press on.

After the war, in testimony before Congress, Gen. Norman H. Schwarzkopf was asked if the paratroopers of the 82d Airborne Division could have withstood an Iraqi attack against such fierce odds. He replied: "It would not have been easy. I think we would have found ourselves in an enclave type of defense, the very toughest thing . . ." Remember Agincourt? On the morning of October 25, 1415, there were many English soldiers who feared defeat and wished for "only one ten- thousandth of those who slept in England" to reinforce their lines. My airborne friends who participated in Operation Desert Shield told me that they felt much the same way on the morning of August 12, 1990.

In *Infantry Combat,* you are faced with a different situation. The enemy is calling the bluff. This time, the enemy isn't going to hold back and wait for the United States to deploy and prepare full-strength combined-arms formations. This time, the enemy has learned a lesson from history. The very toughest thing is about to happen.

Are You Ready?

The duty of the soldiers assigned to light infantry squads and platoons is to kill the enemy in battle. To do this requires excellently trained riflemen and superb leadership. In this tactical decision game you will have an opportunity to test your tactical leadership.

The leadership and tactical principles that apply to a rifle platoon apply universally to almost all types of combat units. The right leadership gives purpose, direction, and motivation in combat. Confidence comes from knowing if your people, weapons, and tactics. The more you know about rifle platoon weapons and tactics, the more correct your decisions will be. The glossary and weapons data section at the end of this book will help you understand modern military terms, weapons, and tactics.

The conditions necessary for light infantry forces to hold against an armored attacker have not changed since the dawn of battle. Henry V's bowmen, the British squares at Waterloo, and the "Battling Bastards of the 101st Airborne at Bastogne" all accomplished three things to withstand a mounted armor attack. First, the defender must break the attacker's charge. Henry V did this by selecting a hill that had recently been plowed. The mud in front of his defensive position had the consistency of oatmeal. When the French attacked, riders and horses found themselves buried in goo up to their waists. Next, the defender must try to engage the enemy at long range before the armored force can overrun his positions. At Agincourt, Henry V's bowmen did a remarkably good job, knocking the slow-moving mounted knights out of the saddle and slaughtering the flower of French nobility. Last, the defender must have the discipline and courage to withstand the psychological shock of the rush of armor. Light infantrymen must have the same kind of faith in their weapons, leaders, and tactics as did the yeomen of Henry's army.

You are now in a shooting war. The stakes are high. The enemy is determined to kill you. You are outnumbered, and the odds are five to one against you. You will have to make up for your lack of numbers and firepower through superior leadership and expert tactical decision making. The fate of your platoon and the success of your unit depend on your decisions and your actions. Your challenge is to survive and win. Besides, if this situation was easy, the army wouldn't need lieutenants.

Once more unto the breach, dear friends, once more!

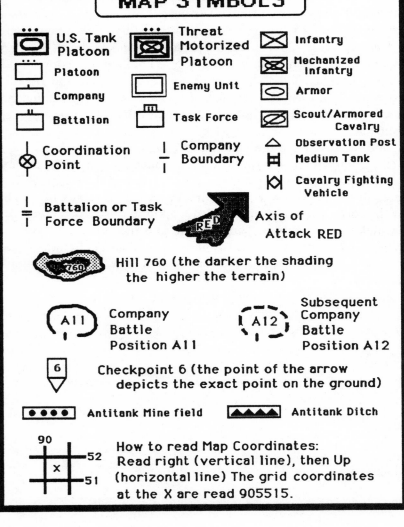

MAP SYMBOLS

U.S. Tank Platoon

Platoon

Company

Battalion

Threat Motorized Platoon

Enemy Unit

Task Force

Infantry

Mechanized Infantry

Armor

Scout/Armored Cavalry

Coordination Point

Company Boundary

Observation Post

Medium Tank

Cavalry Fighting Vehicle

Battalion or Task Force Boundary

Axis of Attack RED

Hill 760 (the darker the shading the higher the terrain)

Company Battle Position A11

Subsequent Company Battle Position A12

Checkpoint 6 (the point of the arrow depicts the exact point on the ground)

Antitank Mine field   Antitank Ditch

How to read Map Coordinates:
Read right (vertical line), then Up
(horizontal line) The grid coordinates
at the X are read 905515.

Prelude: The Scene of Battle

The United States will be forced to fight wars of policy during the balance of the century. This is inevitable, since the world is seething with disaffection and revolt . . . However repugnant the idea is to liberal societies, the man who will willingly defend the free world in the fringe areas is not the responsible citizen soldier. The man who will go where his colors go, without asking, who will fight a phantom foe in the jungle and mountain range, without counting, and who will suffer and die in the midst of incredible hardship, is still what he has always been, from Imperial Rome to sceptered Britain to democratic America. He is the stuff of which legions are made . . . If the free nations want a certain kind of world, they will have to fight for it, with courage, money, diplomacy—and legions.

T. R. Fehrenbach

The Situation

Vegetius, the Roman historian of the fourth century A.D., wrote: "Who desires peace, should prepare for war." A brief perusal of history reveals that the hard logic of this Roman sage has often been ignored. The United States of America, much like ancient Rome, has had to fight many wars to maintain its interests and sustain the peace. To accomplish this end, the nation relies on its trained, professional military.

The development of new technology has led many theorists, politicians, and political scientists to consider the style of twentieth-century warfare as obsolete. According to these theorists, conventional wars between the armies of opposing nations will be so rare as to bring about the rise of a fourth generation of warfare. These writers believe that future wars will be high-technology affairs, that conventional armies will be transformed into internal security forces, and that conventional military force will no longer matter.

Innovations in technology and doctrine are the harbingers of change in warfare. The hope that the United States has entered a new

1

era of high-technology, bloodless wars, however, is premature. Technology is an important element in fighting decisively, but trained, dedicated soldiers, proudly serving in disciplined units for a cause that they believe in, form the sinews of victory. The bloody proof of this truth was demonstrated by the seven hundred Purple Hearts that were issued to U.S. Army personnel from 1989 to 1994.

Although the nature of war is ever changing, the nature of man is not. Conventional war still prevailed during the last years of the twentieth century. Similar situations had brought about previous peacetime reductions in America's military strength. In the past, particularly after the First and Second World Wars, unilateral reductions had weakened the country's military capability and caused petty aggressors to become bold. The same thing happened at the end of the Cold War.

General George S. Patton Jr., answering the same argument on the obsolescence of conventional war made by a congressman visiting the battlefront during the Second World War, replied: "I told him that such statements since 2600 B.C. had signed the death warrant of millions of young men. He replied with the stock lie, 'Oh, yes, but things are different now.' My God! Will they never learn?"

The wars of the post–Cold War era began shortly after the collapse of Soviet communism. With the threat of nuclear annihilation reduced by the end of the Cold War, the frequency of conventional wars actually increased. The failure of democratic reforms, the rise of radical nationalism, age-old ethnic differences, fanned religious extremism, nuclear proliferation, and the transformation of old empires bred an emerging pattern of midintensity wars. With these rapid and significant changes the world's geopolitical framework underwent dramatic restructuring. As a result, a new era of brutal conflict emerged.

As the world suffered the effects of one bloody conflict after another, the United States continued the downsizing of its military forces, drastically reducing its conventional military options. As the force got smaller, however, the number of military commitments, treaties, and obligations increased. As the only world superpower, the United States was expected to lead the way in establishing peace. This required peacekeeping forces, nation building, humanitarian relief operations, and the serious commitment to stand firm against the destabilizing effects of nuclear proliferation.

These operations, called operations-other-than-war in the military's lexicon, occupied an ever-increasing part of the military budget and training focus. The shift from war fighting to operations-other-than-war drained the fighting power of the military. Training in conventional war fighting suffered from the increased importance of non-warfighting missions. It was only a matter of time until simultaneous world crises exposed severe shortcomings in an overextended military.

The Threat

History shows that changes of this scope, magnitude, and tempo increase global tension and disorder. In the wake of this tension and disorder follow crisis, conflict, and war. As America's military commitments grew, regional tyrants realized that anyone who could successfully oppose the United States could have his way in the world. Alarmingly, the most dangerous of these regional powers—among them North Korea, Iraq, and Iran—possessed large and dangerous conventional military forces.

Opposing the United States was a serious undertaking, no matter how overcommitted its military was. Potential adversaries studied Operation Desert Storm and learned two critical lessons. First, pick your objective carefully. Don't threaten America's vital interests unless you can fight decisively and quickly terminate the conflict with a political agreement. Second, never give the Americans time to build up conventional forces to fight a combined-arms campaign.

Fighting decisively requires excellent weapons, intensive training, and agile leadership. In the late 1990s regional powers took advantage of the glut of cheap Russian-made equipment and the hundreds of out of work ex-Soviet and Warsaw Pact soldiers and technicians to become better equipped and better trained. A new generation of sophisticated weapons was readily available for sale on the world arms markets. Regimes with cash secured new tanks, laser-guided munitions, and state-of-the-art air defense missiles. Intensive training and agile leadership were harder to come by, but by the late 1990s several regional powers possessed the means to win their objective by force of arms.

The second lesson dealt with timing. Fighting America required a quick conquest. Victory would depend on striking swiftly, before

Prelude

U.S. forces could be deployed in strength, and negotiating skillfully to consolidate conquered gains. Negotiations could be enhanced if the aggressor possessed an actual or perceived nuclear war capability. More importantly, it didn't take a very large or sophisticated nuclear capability to augment negotiations. Nations with regional ambitions, therefore, developed conventional military forces for conquest and pursued nuclear capability to consolidate their gains.

American Military Strategy in the Late 1990s

America's national military policy required the military to fight two wars almost simultaneously. By the late 1990s, due to excessive cuts and reduced training budgets, the U.S. military would have been severely strained to meet these requirements. Inaccurate analysis of the 1991 Gulf War led many to believe that high-tech wars could be fought without shedding American blood. War was dominated by technology, and America maintained clear technological superiority. The human factors, such as leadership, training, and unit cohesion, were dismissed as increasingly insignificant. As a result, the size of the U.S. Army was cut to a level that was less than the total U.S. ground forces in 1939.

The argument for a high-tech solution, emphasizing airpower, was very persuasive. It sold well to the American people and to the American business community. It also fit the American psyche. It made Americans feel superior to bomb an enemy from two thousand feet, especially since the enemy seldom had the means to shoot back. The operative strategy was to get in fast, bomb the hell out of the bad guy, and fly away at Mach 2. Surgical strikes became the watchword.

The hypnotic power of the words *airpower* and *air dominance* influenced a new generation of American policymakers with little actual experience of military affairs. High-tech air weapons were expected to win wars without costly ground campaigns. Presidents employed airpower more frequently and without consulting Congress. Dramatic air raids made presidents look decisive and gained points in the opinion polls. Pelting the nation's enemies with Tomahawk cruise missiles and Stealth bombers became an option of choice.

It also, however, made a lot of enemies without forcing a decision. From this hatred grew the desire for revenge.

Unfortunately for the United States, the airpower pundits had it wrong. Decisive action is the first demand of war. Airpower has the ability to destroy, but it cannot force a decisive result if the enemy is willing to take the punishment. Airpower cannot capture territory or drive out a determined, well-protected enemy. Airpower can act as an element of attrition against the enemy's physical and psychological means to resist; it cannot bring conflicts to decisive termination without the use of weapons of mass destruction. Airpower is a vital part of a team effort, not a singular means to win wars. One aspect of human conflict has remained unchanged since the dawn of warfare: the paramount importance of land power as an essential element of any security strategy and the consequent requirement to control populations, territory, and events.

The Next War

War erupted in Northeast Asia unexpectedly and with great violence. Surprised and badly damaged allied and U.S. forces responded to the aggression. United States forces were rushed to the area. All available fighter aircraft were flown in to bolster the defense. Army and marine units were rapidly brought to alert status and scheduled for deployment. Unlike Operation Desert Storm, everyone feared that this new Asian war would be a long and bloody conflict. To complicate matters, the evil spirit of nuclear escalation hung over the participants and threatened to kill millions if the war was not contained.

To add to this conflagration, a simultaneous crisis erupted in the Middle East. A country with friendly relations with the United States was threatened by its larger neighbor. Border incidents occurred, and the larger country demanded that its small neighbor surrender large tracts of oil-rich territory. The friendly country defied its enemy, deployed its small military, and urgently requested help from the United States. The small nation nervously promised to delay the attacker long enough for the arrival of U.S. forces.

With war occurring in Northeast Asia, the United States had little force left to fight a second war in the Middle East. Swift action was demanded to stop the aggressor's scheme and stop the war before America's vital interests were threatened. The enemy had a large force equipped with tanks, armored personnel carriers, and artillery. Ground forces were required to show America's determination and

Prelude

bolster its ally. Faced with this grim situation, the United States president made the decision to rapidly deploy available U.S. ground, air, and sea forces.

A joint task force was formed to command the expeditionary forces. Taking advantage of the lessons from Operation Desert Storm, the United States had wisely pre-positioned a small amount of equipment in the region. The problem was that there was only enough equipment for a beefed-up brigade of tanks and infantry fighting vehicles and a battery of self-propelled artillery. Personnel for this force were quickly flown into the country on civilian airlines. To provide more combat power, the brigade was reinforced with a brigade of light infantry. Plans were made to reinforce this brigade with additional tank and artillery units by sea, but these would take several weeks to arrive.

While the politicians were debating, the enemy attacked across the border. Allied losses in the initial battles were heavy. As always, time was critical. The arrival of a little force now would have more effect than a lot of force too late. If America's ally was to keep fighting, the cavalry would have to arrive soon, just as it did in an old John Ford movie. Some advisers to the president believed that the aggressor would not be willing to engage U.S. forces and all that was needed was to draw another line in the sand. The main defense had to be placed north of the capital, on the best defensible ground, to keep the ally fighting and to gain time for the deployment of heavier U.S. forces.

The U.S. joint task force commander, therefore, issued orders for U.S. forces to assist allied units to block the invader from taking the capital city. The enemy had hundreds of tanks and plenty of artillery, but these were still miles away, strung out in long columns. Blunting the nose of the advance would gain time to draw the pre-positioned equipment and attrit the enemy with the limited quantity of available airpower. For the time being, the Americans and their ally would have to fight outnumbered.

Confusion and chaos reigned in the allied capital. A mass exodus of refugees, streaming away from the fighting, hindered the allied defense. The enemy knew that time was against him. The aggressor wanted to take the capital, bargain for territory, and make a deal before American forces could dramatically change the situation. The aggressor's threats and bold use of force were having a serious political effect. Several nations in the region denied their port and airfield facilities to deploying U.S. forces.

The enemy, sensing the fear and confusion, presented a cease-fire proposal to the United Nations. This cease-fire demanded that American forces leave the Middle East and allow Arab nations to decide their own border issues. Several of America's Middle East allies vehemently objected, recognizing the peace offer as a play to solidify territorial conquest. Others feared the Threat and argued for appeasement. Anxious ambassadors of several countries adjoining the region, dreading the financial loss of another major war, were quick to consider the cease-fire proposal.

The acceptance of a cease-fire by the United Nations would allow the attacker's aggression to be vindicated. The United States was determined to not let this happen. In combat, however, the cost of showing up with forces inadequate to achieve quick and decisive victory is measured in blood. This is the situation that 2d Lt. Bruce Davis now finds himself in.

A light infantry brigade, reinforced by a single armored task force, was given the mission to defend the critical sector that blocked the major axis of the aggressor's line of attack. The light infantry was ordered to dig in and be prepared to fight an uneven battle against an enemy with superior numbers.

The stark truth of this situation is now crystal clear to the riflemen of Second Lieutenant Davis's 1st Platoon. It is a lesson that many Americans seem to have forgotten. It is not just high-tech arms but superior force of will that wins wars. T. R. Fehrenbach, who wrote about another American war, put it this way: "You may fly over a land forever; you may bomb it, atomize it, pulverize it and wipe it clean of life—but if you desire to defend it, protect it and keep it for civilization, you must do this on the ground, the way the Roman legions did, by putting your young men into the mud."

Second Lieutenant Davis and his platoon of riflemen are the ones who have now been put into the mud or, in this case, the sand. You will lead them and make the command decisions.

Section 1

"How the hell are we expected to carry all this stuff?" Specialist Gerber growled, straining under the weight of his large framed pack and the twenty-three-pound machine gun strapped around his shoulders.

No one answered the young man's question. It really didn't require an answer. That was just the way things were in the infantry. Complaining wouldn't change anything.

Sweat rolled down from under 2d Lt. Bruce Davis's helmet as he tramped on. The gold cloth insignia of rank that adorned his sand-camouflaged Kevlar helmet was covered with dust and was almost unrecognizable. The long column of soldiers, bent over with the weight of their loads, continued tramping to the west. Each man struggled to keep up the pace.

Davis walked at the front of the column, closely followed by a young soldier carrying an oversized pack with a long antenna protruding out of it. A steep, rocky ridge on their left paralleled their route to the west. Except for this ridge, the lieutenant could see only rocky brown sand, black pebbles, and small outcrops of flinty rock.

The desert had warmed to a sweltering ninety degrees Fahrenheit since the sun had crested the horizon at 0515 that morning. The heat seemed to explode from the desert floor, making every action, every movement, a supreme struggle.

Weighed down like pack mules, the soldiers worked their way to the western edge of the valley. The tools of modern war are heavy. Each rifleman carried or wore his weapon, helmet, combat harness, and a bulging rucksack. The rucksack contained rifle and machine-gun ammunition, four grenades, rations, one gallon of water, an entrenching tool, a camouflage rain poncho, spare socks, gloves, and extra clothing. In addition, some carried AT4 antitank rockets, M60 machine guns, Claymore mines, and radios. All this had to be transported on their backs.

Yes, they were tired, Davis thought. He and his men had been rushed about for five days. The platoon had assembled and packed their equipment, expressed hurried and tearful good-byes to loved ones, and boarded aircraft. They were sped across the world in cramped, overloaded civilian airliners into an unknown situation in a foreign land. Once they arrived in the area of operations, they had been trucked across miles of bleak, dusty desert. Arriving at their truck drop-off point, the weary infantrymen walked the last five kilometers to their defensive sector.

I hope, Davis confessed to himself, I hope I'm ready. Maybe the rumors are right. It was absurd to think that the enemy would take on the United States. Maybe they'll call a cease-fire in the next couple of days. Maybe the enemy will stop fighting and negotiate as soon as he sees American troops. Maybe the politicians will get it right this time.

Davis trudged on, the dust curling up from the desert floor, covering the column in a low-hanging cloud. The ridge to the left suddenly tapered off and exposed the entrance to a narrow valley.

Sergeant First Class Kevin Piper, the indomitable platoon sergeant and second in command of 1st Platoon, pointed to the southwest and turned the column into the valley without saying a word. Piper was an impressive figure. He was hard as nails and had a reputation for acting first and asking permission later. He stood six feet one inch and had broad shoulders and arms of solid muscle. The men followed Piper's directions unhesitatingly, without question.

The narrow valley they were entering seemed suddenly strange. The vastness of the open desert was now hemmed in and stifled by the two high ridges that ran from east to west. The men marched along the trail that paralleled the northern ridge of the valley. After several more minutes of traveling west they descended down a narrow, winding trail that led out of the valley and arrived at a small hill overlooking a freshly dug antitank ditch.

"OK, we're here," bellowed the confident voice of the platoon sergeant. "Take five while I check out the position."

Drained from their exertions, the men dropped their packs and fell to the ground. The long days of travel and the march from the truck drop-off point had sapped their energy. These grunts needed no encouragement to "take five." The thirty-eight men of 1st Platoon sprawled out in the sun on the top of the hill, opened canteens, and leaned against their rucksacks, happy to be out from under their heavy loads. Precious liquid rolled down parched throats. Three soldiers, members of the platoon headquarters sections, lounged near the lieutenant.

"Jesus, we sure are far enough away from the company," announced Private First Class Cowper, the lieutenant's radioman.

Piper disregarded the comment and walked the crest of the ridge, looking over the ground.

"Do you want me to report in to company HQ?" Davis's radioman asked.

"Not yet," Davis replied slowly as he watched Piper walk off.

Davis dropped his pack on the ground and then sat down next to it, using the large rucksack to support his back. Cowper did the same. Some of the men began opening MREs. There hadn't been time for breakfast on their long march.

"We sure have traveled a long way to get to this shit-hole corner of the world," Cowper said to the lean, tall sergeant sitting next to him.

"Yep, I couldn't have said it better myself," replied Sergeant Mark, the platoon's forward artillery observer. "The map lists this place as Al Sirree—Wadi Al Sirree."

"Well, it sure ain't Kansas," Specialist Hutchinson, Sergeant Mark's radio operator, said with a grin. The men laughed.

Davis sat next to his pack, listening to the exchange, then quietly unfolded his 1:50,000-scale map from his desert battle-dress pants cargo pocket. He studied the map for a moment, then grabbed his handheld global positioning system device, or GPS, from the side pocket of his rucksack. Pushing a button on the GPS, he went through the process of verifying the grid coordinates of his location. After a few minutes, the handheld satellite sensor accurately relayed the location in six-digit military map grid coordinates.

Davis checked his map, thinking that it appeared to be more a work of art than a guide of the area's geography. The twenty-meter contour interval provided too much deviation to clearly visualize the critical military aspects of the terrain. The map did show, however, that the valley offered the enemy a very narrow approach against the battalion's left flank. Obviously, someone had to guard the flank and block the enemy from attacking through Wadi Al Sirree. First Platoon, Bravo Company, had the honors.

Section 1

Wadi Al Sirree measured twelve hundred meters at its widest point; it was about four kilometers long. The valley had high walls to the north and south. On Davis's map the Arabic names for the terrain features were translated in small English letters. The English meaning of the Arabic name for the valley translated roughly as Hidden Valley.

Davis hoped that if an attack came, the valley would remain hidden to the enemy. He wasn't eager to face an enemy mechanized attack, even if his opponent was not touted as a first-class adversary. The thought of his lone platoon left on its own to fend off a serious enemy armored assault was something he hoped he wouldn't have to experience.

Why Wadi Al Sirree? Davis thought as he surveyed the ground. Soldiers rarely have the luxury of knowing the big picture, and I certainly don't know what is going on above company level. My duty is to go where they tell me, lead my soldiers as best I can, and fight where they tell me to fight. I guess in the end, the question "why here?" doesn't really matter. How we plan to fight—now that's a different matter. That's what I get paid to figure out.

Davis stood up and walked to the top of the small hill that dominated the entrance to Wadi Al Sirree. He carried his M16 rifle, map, and GPS. The position overlooked a freshly dug tank ditch. The wide, deep ditch blocked the approaches to the valley. Next to the ditch was a large pile of antitank mines, concertina wire, and metal pickets. Davis's company commander had told him that an allied engineer unit had dug the ditch in preparation for the arrival of the Americans.

After a few minutes Sergeant Piper returned and sauntered up to the platoon leader.

"This is the position that was designated in the warning order, sir. We'll dig in here," Sergeant Piper said. Then with a loud shout he screamed for the squad leaders: "Jordan, Mizogouchi, Tyler—over here."

Davis remained silent. Piper turned and walked toward the oncoming squad leaders, ignoring further discussion with the young officer. Davis stood alone. Alternating glances between the map and the real terrain, he studied the battle area and waited for the right moment to say something to Piper.

The squad leaders huddled around Piper, each kneeling on one knee, their M16s in their right hand, rifle butts against the ground. The three sergeants were in their mid- to late twenties. Staff Sergeant Jordan was a tall, lean, black noncommissioned officer and the most experienced squad leader in the platoon. His handsome looks were soured by lack of sleep. Staff Sergeant Mizogouchi, a second-generation Californian with Japanese ancestry, stood five feet five and had the physique of a lightweight boxer. Sergeant Tyler, a thin, bespectacled man with a worried face, stood behind the other two sergeants.

Piper was right, Davis thought, annoyed by his isolation from the group. The blue "goose egg" that his commander had quickly drawn on his plastic-coated map covered the entire western approach to the valley. This is what the company commander had told them to defend.

Davis looked at the bald hill he was standing on. The ridge lay at the western edge of the opening to Wadi Al Sirree, like the top line of an inverted T. Movement into the valley from the west was permitted by four narrow trails. Each trail could support the movement of only one vehicle at a time. Anyone who wanted to move into Wadi Al Sirree from the west would have to come over the tank ditch and up these trails. The small ridge that Davis was sitting on overlooked the tank ditch and commanded the entrance to each trail.

Davis pondered whether he could accomplish his mission from here. If an enemy forced the ditch and came up the trails into Wadi Al Sirree, he could race for the eastern exit of the valley and hit the battalion's flank. Davis's platoon was the only force guarding that flank.

"I want everyone to start digging in," Piper ordered, his back to Lieutenant Davis. "First Squad has the north, 2d Squad the center, and 3d Squad the south. Mizogouchi, I want you to inventory the engineer dump that someone was so kind to leave for us."

"You got it, Sarge," Mizogouchi replied.

"I want each position dug to standard," Piper said, spitting a wad of black tobacco juice on the desert sand. "No bullshit positions like the ones y'all dug on our last FTX. Your lives may depend on these holes, so dig 'em deep. Any questions?"

The noncommissioned officers glanced at each other and paused. Mizogouchi looked at Davis as if to say something, but Piper cut him off with a glare.

Section 1

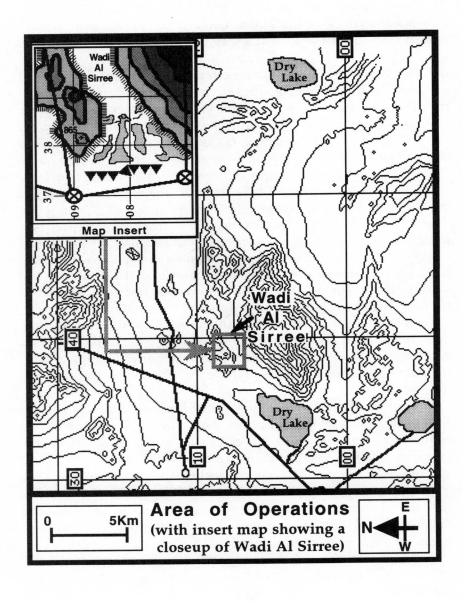

Area of Operations
(with insert map showing a
closeup of Wadi Al Sirree)

14

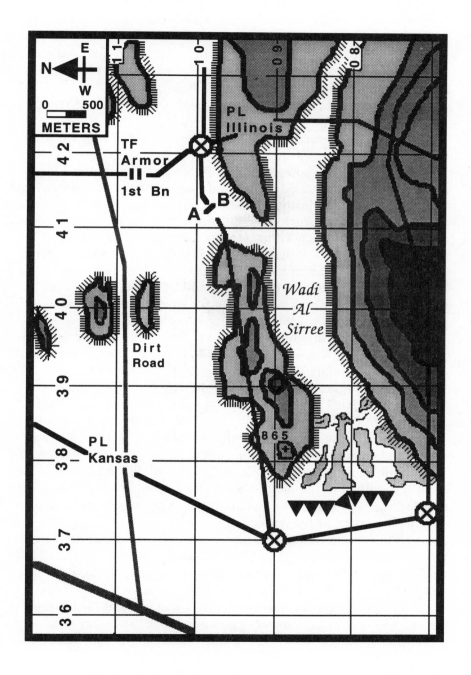

Section 1

"Let's get to work," Piper ordered, concluding the short meeting.

The squad leaders scurried off to designate the location of each position in their squads. Then the soldiers unpacked their tools and began to scrape at the ground. Silently Piper unfolded his entrenching tool and bent the adjustable handle to form a pick.

A couple of black buzzards circled high in the air over Wadi Al Sirree.

"Cowper," Piper yelled, "call the old man and tell him we've arrived in position."

"Roger!" Cowper shouted back, and then busily unhooked his radio hand mike from the side of his rucksack and began broadcasting.

Davis put down his map and reached for the binoculars attached to the right side of his rucksack. From the top of the hill he could clearly see eight to ten kilometers to the west. The ground to the northwest sloped down, then rose to a jagged ridge eight kilometers away on the western horizon. There were three narrow passes in the far ridgeline; each offered exits for armored forces. Between his position and this ridge was nothing but empty desert. If an enemy approached from the west, he would have to cross this open space.

Davis turned his attention to his right flank. The ground immediately to the north was steep—impossible for vehicles to cross and difficult for dismounted soldiers to climb. The south wall of the valley was even higher and more difficult. The north and south walls forced all vehicles to move east-west. The only way into Wadi Al Sirree was through the four trails at the western mouth of the valley. The valley then ran east, four kilometers behind the 1st Platoon position, and ended at another choke point.

The hill occupied by the platoon had good fields of fire to the front. From the hill the platoon's weapons could cover all the trails that led into the valley. The platoon's primary weapons were also well within range of the tank ditch.

Davis looked down and studied the map carefully, tracing the thin brown contour lines with his finger, looking for places that he felt needed further study and reconnaissance. He looked up from the map and stared at the tank ditch.

"Economy of force be damned," Davis said out loud, not caring if anyone was listening. "How am I going to block the enemy with only a platoon? Hell, we could put the entire company in this valley and

16

still have space to spare. Why did they put the tank ditch on the western entrance of the valley?"

"What's that, sir?" Cowper asked.

"Nothing, Private," Davis answered, staring to the west. "Just thinking out loud."

The men struggled with their shovels against the rocky soil. A few talked as they dug, but most were grimly silent. Sergeant Piper was digging in a position about thirty meters to the left of Davis's rucksack. Cowper had also started digging. The entire platoon struck at the dirt like frustrated moles.

Davis slung his binoculars around his neck and walked over to where Sergeant Piper was digging. The sergeant was struggling against the rocky desert soil, swinging his entrenching tool in repeated attempts to crack the desert's hard surface. The dust billowed up at him, hiding the results of his effort. Not to be beaten, he struck again with all his force at the sun-bleached ground. The power of the strike scattered dust and small pieces of rock, but the ground failed to budge.

"It'll take hours to dig in using E tools," Davis sighed, removing his helmet and taking a green rag from his pants pocket to wipe the sweat from his brow.

"It's all we got right now. I've asked the first sergeant to bring us some picks and long-handled shovels," Piper replied tersely, stopping his work. "Top promised me he'd get us some. He's never let me down before."

Davis held his reply and looked past Piper as if he wasn't there. Things just aren't working out, he thought. I'm not leading this platoon, Piper is. He's been without a platoon leader for more than a year. He's used to being in charge. Now that things are getting tense, he doesn't want to take the time to break in a brand-new lieutenant. At the Academy, they always told us to listen to your NCOs. It makes sense to take advantage of experience, and Piper is competent, one of the best. But he is also extremely hardheaded. Somehow I've got to get Piper to support me. I'm willing to listen, but I'm responsible for this platoon. Do I have enough time to gain Piper's trust and confidence?

"Do you think we can stop the enemy at the ditch?" Davis addressed Piper seriously. "Our position doesn't seem right. We need to talk this over."

17

The older man dropped his entrenching tool and took two paces forward, placing himself directly in front of his platoon leader. Piper towered over the smaller officer. In spite of his domineering presence, Davis didn't flinch. The other soldiers, busy with their own holes, continued working.

"L. T.," Piper announced, emphasizing each letter slowly, as if it were a badge of shame, "you've only been here a few days. You don't know anything about this platoon or how to lead it. Tomorrow, if the enemy decides to attack, we had better be dug in."

Davis, sweat stained and dusty, stood tall and straight. He tried to contain his mounting anger, but his eyes gave him away. He was getting used to these lectures, and they had to end.

"Our warning order from company HQ told us to prepare to block the enemy from moving through this valley. They put that friggin' tank ditch there for a reason," Sergeant First Class Piper continued, pointing his muscled arm in the direction of the enemy. "I intend to be ready! We got our orders, Lieutenant. We don't get paid to debate them."

Davis dropped his gaze at Piper and looked over the area to the west. "Is this really where we want to fight?" Davis pressed. "Is this where we can stop him?"

"I don't see a better way. That fucking tank ditch is the key," Piper answered. "If we dig in and cover it with fire, we can kill the bastards as they struggle to cross it. It's as simple as that."

Davis hesitated. He again surveyed the western horizon with his binoculars.

Indecisive orders: In war one should never wait to get the best possible plan. On account of the scarcity of reliable information, the best plan is unobtainable. The most important thing is to have one plan and to adhere strictly to it, so far as possible . . . There is some truth in the old rule that, in war, the simplest plan is the best.

Gen. Waldemar Erfurth

For several seconds, there was an uneasy silence between the two men.

"Look, Piper, I agree that this is the location in the warning order. But the company commander hasn't completed his plan yet. The warning order told us what to do, not how to do it. The battle position the old man drew on my map is big enough for a battalion, let alone a platoon."

"I know Captain Bludgell, Lieutenant, a lot better than you do. The old man will tell us to defend here. He'll want us to take advantage of that obstacle."

"No one ordered us to dig in to cover the goddamned tank ditch," Davis argued, looking at his watch. It was 0900. The day was speeding by and there was so much to do. Getting more irritated with each passing second, he paused and took a deep breath before continuing. "I agree with you that we have to dig in. God knows, we don't have time to waste. But I'm not sure this is where we want to place the platoon."

Piper stroked his chin, already thick with stubble from fast-growing whiskers. Defiantly he kicked a baseball-sized rock down the dusty hill.

"Listen, Lieutenant, I've been doing this for a lot longer than you have. I'm not going to sit around and hope we get some other mission or a gaggle of engineers to do our work for us. Life in the infantry is tough. We have to make do with what we have. If the ragheads decide to come at us, and their artillery slams into us before we dig in properly, it'll be all over. We'll be dead meat. If it's too hard for you, I'll get Cowper to dig your hole."

Davis stared at his NCO, stung by his platoon sergeant's sarcasm. The last remark was not only insubordinate, it was typical of the resentment that appeared to be building up inside Piper. This confrontation had been growing ever since Davis had arrived to take charge of 1st Platoon.

Davis's lips tightened into a thin line. His gray eyes zeroed in on the older man standing in front of him. So far, I've avoided a fight, he thought. Piper is a combat veteran and has led the platoon for over a year. I'm new at this and I've never been in combat. But I'm not totally unprepared. I've trained and studied hard for four years in preparation for this duty. I graduated from West Point, attended the Infantry Officer Basic Course and the U.S. Army Airborne and Ranger schools. That should count for something.

But Piper isn't letting me lead. Since I arrived in the platoon he's treated me like a distant cousin, barely acknowledging my presence. What irritates me the most, Davis thought, is that Piper doesn't even bother to ask my opinion concerning what to do; he merely gives orders to the platoon. He acts like I don't exist. What am I supposed to do? Am I wrong to disagree with my platoon sergeant? Something has to be done.

> However competent an officer may be, and however thorough his earlier training, he is always a risky investment until he pays off in combat.
>
> Gen. Omar Bradley

Davis winced. The short hairs on the back of his neck bristled as he readied for the confrontation. He knew that the situation wouldn't get any better. It was time to set things straight. The decision had to be made as to who would lead 1st Platoon.

"So what do you recommend, Lieutenant?" Sergeant Piper continued, making the "you" sound like a curse word.

> The first thing a young officer must do when he joins the Army is to fight a battle, and that battle is for the hearts of his men. If he wins the battle and subsequent similar ones, his men will follow him anywhere; if he loses it, he will never do any good.
>
> Field Marshal Bernard L. Montgomery

"Sir, the old man wants you on the radio, pronto," Private First Class Cowper interrupted.

No one moved. Davis and Piper stood a few feet apart, staring at each other.

"Sir, it sounds important," Cowper insisted.

Saved by the bell, the collision between platoon leader and platoon sergeant was postponed for a few moments. Davis walked over to Cowper and grabbed the handset of the radio.

"Bravo Six, this is Bravo One-Six, over," Davis said into the transmitter, trying to sound as if he was in charge. He gazed at Piper with determination.

The seasoned NCO stared back, his face the picture of defiance.

"Bravo One-Six, this is Bravo Six. Orders Group to assemble at Charlie Papa in one hour. Be on time. Over."

"Bravo Six, this is One-Six. Roger. Over," Davis replied.

"I say again, be here in one hour. Out."

Davis thrust the handset at Cowper, whose lips twitched into a veiled smile.

"Looks like we better get moving, Lieutenant, if we want to make it in time," Cowper said. "Old man sounds like he's pissed."

Davis wanted to reply that the old man always sounded like he was pissed, but he curbed the urge. The radio message required that he go to the company command post to receive an operations order, which would tell him what to do. The company CP, or Charlie Papa in the phonetic slang of radio procedure, was about three kilometers to the east.

"Well, at least now we'll get the final word. It's about time we were told what's going on," Piper exclaimed, still glaring at Davis.

Davis picked up his nylon battle harness, put his arms through the openings, and grabbed the M16 rifle that was leaning against his rucksack.

"We'll finish this conversation later," Davis said, looking sternly at his platoon sergeant. "You stay here with the platoon. I'll take Sergeant Mark and his RTO with me. You can keep Cowper with you, just in case I need to call you."

"Whatever you say, Lieutenant," Piper replied sarcastically, appearing not to care. "Do you want us to stop digging?"

"No," Davis said as he motioned for Sergeant Mark, the platoon forward observer (FO), to follow him. "Continue with the work until we can decide on our plan. I'll be back as fast as I can."

Piper picked up his shovel, not bothering to salute or acknowledge the departure of his platoon leader. Stepping back to his work, Piper attacked the dirt with renewed vigor.

If you need to increase your understanding of military weapons, read Appendix A now, then go to Section 2.

If you need to increase your understanding of military terms, read the Glossary now, then go to Section 2.

If you are ready to continue, go to Section 2 immediately.

Section 2

The sun rose higher in the clear blue desert sky, glaring down on the three desert-camouflaged soldiers. Lieutenant Davis, Sgt. Bob Mark, and Specialist William Hutchinson trudged out toward the company command post. They walked slowly along the dusty road that ran along the north wall of Wadi Al Sirree. The lieutenant led, followed by Hutchinson and Mark in file. Buzzards circled ominously overhead, as if foretelling the doom of anyone who would be crazy enough to fight for this godforsaken valley.

"Do you think those buzzards know something we don't, Lieutenant?" Mark asked half jokingly as they hurried down the dirt track that led to Captain Bludgell's CP.

"They give me the creeps," Hutchinson interjected, shielding his eyes with his hand as he gazed skyward. "Yesterday, when our trucks stopped to refuel, I woke up and found one of those damn birds right next to my rucksack. You know what he was doing? He was picking at the pockets of my pack with his beak."

"Hell, Hutch!" Mark exclaimed in his country twang. "That there bird was just hungry. He probably thought you had an open MRE in your pack!" Hutchinson shook his head in disbelief. Sergeant Mark laughed at his own remark.

Davis considered the conversation as he walked in silence. The buzzards in this desert seemed unnaturally brave. They didn't seem to fear humans very much. After all, it was their home, not man's.

The big black birds scoured the desert clean of all refuse. More than once in the past few days Davis had seen buzzards eating discarded portions of MREs or picking at the remains of a dead camel.

Soon they might have human remains to feast on.

Davis picked up the pace, shivering from the thought that had just crossed his mind. With his rifle in one hand and the binoculars that were slung around his neck in the other, he led the way to the company CP, reliving the thoughts of the past few weeks.

Davis found it hard to believe that only ten days ago he had been at Fort Benning, Georgia, finishing his course of instruction at the Infantry Officer Basic Course. Back in "the world," most Americans were oblivious to the gathering storm in the Middle East.

Davis thought about his company commander, Capt. Joel Bludgell, who seemed to be a perpetually unhappy man. Bludgell constantly complained that all the important missions went to Alpha Company or Charlie Company. He felt that Bravo Company was the redheaded stepchild of 1st Battalion. Bludgell blamed the battalion for every woe, from trash details to aircraft-unloading operations.

Davis arrived at the company command post and entered an improvised lean-to, created from barbed-wire pickets and camouflage rain ponchos. The shade provided by this arrangement offered some limited relief from the steady rays of the desert sun.

"First Platoon reporting, sir," Davis said, standing tall as he saluted.

"Where's Sergeant Piper?" asked the captain. Bludgell didn't bother to look up at his platoon leader or return his salute. He was writing furiously on a notepad to finish his combat instructions for the company.

"I left him with the platoon to continue preparing our positions, sir," Davis responded.

"Next time bring him here for orders issue," Bludgell snarled, still not looking up. "Until you get your feet on the ground, I want you to be his shadow. I don't have time to teach baby lieutenants the art of war right now."

I feel about as welcome as a prostitute at a church social, Davis thought. The air inside the lean-to is hot enough without Bludgell's blistering comments.

"Grab a patch of sand and take a seat, Lieutenant. I'll issue the order in a few minutes. Take careful notes and brief Piper when you get back."

Section 2

Davis remembered Gen. George S. Patton's words: "Never tell people how to do things. Tell them what to do and they will surprise you with their ingenuity." Apparently, this concept was lost on Captain Bludgell.

Davis nodded coldly and sat down, cross-legged, cradling his M16 rifle in his arms. He nodded an embarrassed hello to his fellow officers and platoon leaders who were already assembled under the lean-to.

Hutchinson and Sergeant Mark followed their lieutenant into the shade. They sat down right behind Davis. Their desert battle-dress uniforms were blotched with white perspiration marks caused by the morning's exertion. Happy to be out of the direct sun, they grabbed their canteens and began to drink.

Davis recognized most of the men seated under the lean-to. Sergeant First Class Rossetti, to his right, was the leader of 2d Platoon. A short, bright-eyed sergeant with thick, dark hair, Rossetti was a competent soldier with a friendly personality and a disarming nature. He was extremely proud of his platoon—the only one in Bravo Company that didn't have an officer as a platoon leader.

Davis half wished that he had been assigned to lead 2d Platoon instead of 3d. He didn't know Rossetti very well but assumed that, compared to Piper, he would be a joy to work with.

Lieutenant Daryl Wilcox, the 3d Platoon leader, sat next to Rossetti. Wilcox was one of the largest men Davis had ever met. He stood six feet seven and had arms like logs and a body like a heavyweight wrestler.

Next to Wilcox, dwarfed by comparison, was the executive officer, 1st Lt. Jeff Sandburg. A wire-thin officer, Sandburg stood only five feet seven inches. He probably weighed no more than 120 pounds dripping wet. Davis had known Sandburg for only a few days, but he had already learned to appreciate Sandburg's intelligence and sense of humor. Of all the officers in the company, Sandburg seemed to be the most capable of the lot. Davis liked him.

Hutchinson and Sergeant Mark, the forward observer, sat quietly behind their lieutenant. Davis was the only officer to bring his FO to the orders issue. An artillery staff sergeant whom Davis didn't know sat next to Captain Bludgell.

The company commander sat on a couple of 7.62mm ammunition boxes; his 1:50,000-scale map lay at his feet. Finally he stopped writing and looked up at the men assembled to receive his orders.

The stillness of the desert engulfed Davis as he waited to hear the words that would send him and his men into combat. The air was electric with a gut-wrenching feeling.

Davis reached for one of his canteens. It was half full. Slowly, one gulp at a time, he drained the canteen. The water was warm and bitter, but keeping hydrated in the desert was essential.

Captain Bludgell had the lean, athletic build of a long-distance runner. He was tall, standing six feet two and weighing about 160 pounds. His crisp features and shaved head gave him a fierce demeanor. But he had worried eyes, and he appeared to Davis to be the kind of man who was constantly worried that someone was standing over his shoulder, watching him.

"OK, let's get this order over with." Bludgell thumbed though the thick pages of the battalion operations order. "Situation. The enemy is expected to attack in two days. Probably his division reconnaissance will be active in our sector tonight and his regimental reconnaissance will be out trying to scout our positions tomorrow night. He will likely attack us just before sunrise on the day after tomorrow."

Bludgell paused to let this information sink in. The officers and NCOs in the lean-to shifted nervously in their positions. The mood was deadly serious. A thick tension hung in the air.

Davis's face tightened. This is it. Combat. We really are going to fight, he thought.

"Battalion says that the enemy strength will be a mechanized regiment, possibly reinforced with extra tanks and a couple of dismounted infantry companies. We have been ordered to stop him long enough for the rest of the U.S. heavy brigade to draw its equipment.

"The battalion believes that the enemy will attack along Axis Viper. They expect the enemy to use the dirt road that runs east-west in our battalion's sector.

"Our friendly situation is pretty simple: we have to hold the line for the next two days until more forces can arrive. An armored brigade's worth of personnel has been flown in-country and is currently drawing its equipment from pre-positioned equipment storage yards. This means that we have to hold on for a day or so. In a couple of days a brigade from 1st Infantry Division will be rushing to join us. They are planning to occupy an assembly area to the southeast on the day after tomorrow. "

Section 2

I wish the Big Red One was here right now, Davis mused. The 1st Infantry Division's nickname, earned in the First World War, was the Big Red One. In that war young American infantrymen were quickly dispatched to Europe to bolster tired Allies and turn the tide against the aggressor. Now, eighty or so years in the future, they are doing the same thing in a different part of the world. Davis couldn't help but wonder if things ever changed. One heavy task force had already drawn its equipment and joined their light infantry brigade. Their battalion had been given one M1A1 tank company to support its defense.

"Bravo Company has pulled the supporting effort again. Our job is to guard the battalion's left flank and block . . ." Bludgell paused as he looked for the name of the valley on the map . . . "Wadi Al Sirree. Battalion doesn't believe that the enemy will be stupid enough to attack this way. They're betting that the enemy will try to push through us quickly by taking the high-speed avenue of approach."

"So we have to sit this one out again while Alpha and Charlie Companies do the real fighting?" Wilcox said with a sneer, moving his big hand over his shaved head to wipe off beads of perspiration. "Captain, my men are ready to fight. Hell, the war will be over before we know it. We didn't come here to watch the bastards in Alpha and Charlie get all the credit."

Sergeant Rossetti fidgeted in his seat. This was an old argument, one that Rossetti gave every impression of wanting to avoid.

"Listen, Wilcox," Bludgell answered, looking at him as if he were made of wood. "We all know how eager you are to win a Combat Infantry Badge."

The officers and NCOs chuckled nervously.

Bludgell's mood changed swiftly. His face got red and his features tightened. The captain pointed to his chest. "I've got mine and I don't need any advice from a shavetail who's never seen combat. It's not your job to worry about the missions we get or about what A Company is doing. Your job is to worry about your platoon," the captain said, raising his voice. "I'll do the masterminding in this outfit. Is that clear?"

Wilcox sat stiffly, bristling from the remark. He was smart enough to know when to be silent, and he had suffered through Bludgell's stinging sermons before. Wilcox had served under Bludgell for the

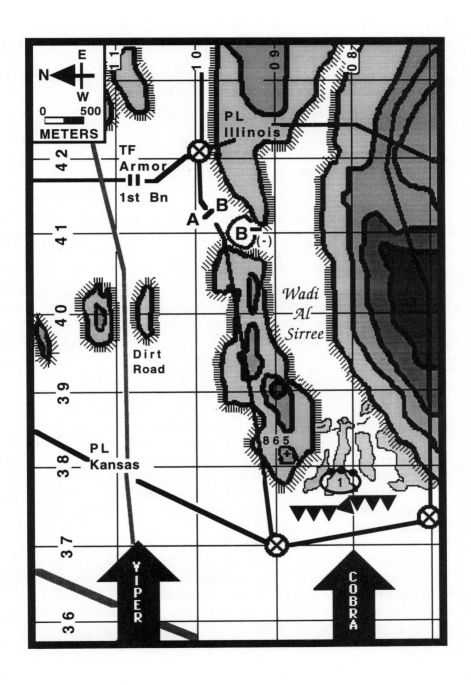

past ten months and had learned the score. He stared back at his commander, tight-lipped and determined, but quiet.

Bludgell was firmly in charge, like a king on a throne. His tone made it clear that no one would be allowed to question his judgment.

Flies swarmed around inside the lean-to, pestering the men as they sat in the shade. The tent was totally quiet except for the buzzing of the flies and the steady voice of the commander.

The CO isn't doing much to relieve the tension, Davis thought. Hell, everybody is scared. Why add to the stress? Does he think we follow him just because he's a captain?

It is a military convention that infallibility is the privilege of seniority.

B. H. Liddell Hart

"Our brigade will use artillery, close air support, and a few attack helicopters to conduct a deep operation against the enemy before he closes on our positions," Bludgell continued, pointing to his map with a metal rifle-cleaning rod. "Hopefully they'll leave us something to shoot at."

Wilcox grunted and leaned forward to look at the captain's map, like a panther ready to pounce on his prey.

"Mission: Bravo Company defends in sector not later than 1800, 22 April, to block enemy forces from penetrating Phase Line Illinois. Be prepared to counterattack enemy forces that may attack east along Axis Viper."

Davis looked at the map in front of Bludgell's feet. He mentally traced the lines that depicted the company operations graphics.

"Commander's intent: the object of the defense is to attrit the enemy units attacking along Axis Viper and force him, with our direct antitank fires, to move to the north. The reason for this is that the brigade plans to destroy the enemy along Phase Line Illinois with Task Force 1-34 Armor. If the enemy attacks along Viper, he will enter the battalion's primary engagement area. Our fires should force him to the northeast into Task Force 1-34 Armor's defensive sector. This will require that the majority of our Javelin medium antitank weapons be sited against an enemy attack along Axis Viper. We can accomplish this by conducting an economy of force effort in Wadi Al Sirree."

Everyone seems cocky, Davis mused. Is this first-fight bluster or true confidence? Will this "exercise in the desert" be a repeat of Desert Storm? But confidence alone won't stop enemy tanks. The odds are against us, even if the enemy isn't the best army in the world. After a certain point, quantity gains a quality of its own.

"Execution: to drive the enemy off the southern edge of Axis Viper and force him to the north, we will deploy two platoons, 2d and 3d, to a BP near the northeast mouth of Wadi Al Sirree. This is Battle Position Bravo, as shown on my overlay."

Davis and the other officers and NCOs searched the commander's map. Each soldier identified the boundaries and positions that would become the setting for Bravo Company's first taste of combat.

"We expect to hit the enemy with Javelins as they drive along Axis Viper, " Bludgell said.

Davis quickly drew the company graphics on his plasticized map while the company commander was talking.

"I will concentrate the main effort of the company in the northwest, against Viper," the commander continued. "Whatever comes down Viper will be ours to engage. This way, Wilcox, you'll have your chance to get into the fight."

Wilcox grinned. "No problem. Do I get the Javelin teams?"

"Negative," Bludgell said curtly. "I'll keep them with me and control their fires personally. When the enemy moves into the range of our Javelin fires, we'll shoot him in the flanks as he runs by. Then we'll engage any supporting infantry he may have following his armor.

"Davis, your platoon will block any movement through the valley. You don't have much to worry about along Axis Cobra. The valley is too constricted for vehicle movement and the antitank ditch will convince them that the approach through the wadi is too risky. I've persuaded the battalion commander that a platoon can block the western approach to Wadi Al Sirree. The old man agreed. I don't care how you plan your defense as long as nothing gets through."

Thank God, Davis mused. At least Bludgell hasn't told me exactly where to fight. I must find the decisive point in my sector and take advantage of it.

Section 2

There is in every battlefield a decisive point, the possession of which, more than of any other, helps secure victory, by enabling its holder to make proper application of the principles of war . . .

Antoine Henri Baron de Jomini

The company commander paused for a minute and then directed his full attention to Lieutenant Davis.

"Lieutenant, just to play it safe, your platoon will get an antiarmor team, with two Javelins, for your use. The tank ditch that was constructed at the western mouth of Wadi Al Sirree was put in by some engineers two days ago. An oil company had built an underground oil pipe ditch there, and our allies merely improved on their original work. I expect you to use the antitank mines and the concertina wire that was dumped somewhere near the ditch."

Davis looked at his map. The area of responsibility he had been issued would put him all alone against a major enemy avenue of approach. He swallowed hard, attempting to clear his throat. "That's an awfully big area to give a platoon."

Bludgell ignored the dimensions of the battlefield. "I didn't realize you were such an experienced tactician, Lieutenant. I know you haven't been in the company long, but in Bravo Company lieutenants are expected to follow orders. Maybe you didn't hear me when I said that battalion believes that the enemy will attack along Axis Viper. Only a fool or an idiot would try to attack through a narrow defile like Wadi Al Sirree."

The captain paused again, pointing with a rifle cleaning rod at the northwest entrance to Wadi Al Sirree, then nodded to the artillery sergeant at his side. "Fire support," he announced.

The sergeant nodded back and then handed a piece of paper to each platoon leader. "Gentlemen, for those of you I haven't met before, let me introduce myself. I'm Staff Sergeant Froude, the company FSO."

Sergeant Froude seemed nervous. He fidgeted with a collapsible metal pointer and tapped erratically on the map at Captain Bludgell's feet.

"After the brigade's deep operation, we can expect to get artillery fires. The battalion has one battalion of 105mm howitzers in direct support of our rifle battalion, and there is a battalion of 155mm howitzers in general support of the brigade. The company will also have its own 60mm company mortars and can call for the 81mm mortar platoon from battalion. I'll control the fires of the two 60mm company mortars and coordinate your battalion mortar and artillery support. I've marked the targets on the commander's map and listed the targets in our sector for you on this target list. You can plot them on your own maps."

The FSO paused to let this information register. His face was a mask of concentration and worry. "If we're really lucky, we may also get some close air support. The brigade has several sorties of F/A-18s and A-10s. If you have a good target—a column of tanks, for instance—call me on the company command net and I'll do my best to alert battalion to get air support. Any questions?"

No one said a word. The sergeant returned to his original position and sat down on an empty 7.62mm ammunition can.

This could get tough, Davis thought. The odds don't look very good, even with the tank ditch supporting 1st Platoon's blocking mission. He looked at the map intently. His attention focused on the large *B* in the center of a BP symbol, which represented the location of BP Bravo. Bludgell expected to fight from Battle Position Bravo and leave 1st Platoon to cover his flank. First Platoon was definitely a sideshow in this operation. Further argument appeared useless. Bludgell wasn't about to change his mind now.

The captain was consumed with his own plan. Two battalions of artillery weren't enough to stop an enemy regiment. The 105mm howitzers were useful against dismounted troops and might do some damage against BMPs, but they certainly wouldn't stop tanks. Even the big 155mm guns had to use dual purpose improved conventional munitions, or DPICM, to damage a tank. DPICM was a very effective artillery shell that exploded over its targets and showered the target area with dozens of little bomblets. During Operation Desert Storm the Iraqis had called DPICM steel rain. But because Davis was defending against a secondary avenue of approach, 1st Platoon would be the last priority artillery support.

31

> No operation plan extends with any certainty beyond the first encounter with the main body of the enemy.
> Field Marshal Helmuth Graf von Moltke

"Second Platoon, on the western side of BP Bravo, has priority of fires," Bludgell added. "First Platoon will get any fires I can spare. Davis, get with Piper and have him help you plan artillery targets to support your defense."

Davis's anger grew with each reference to his lack of ability. It took all of his self-control to stop from exploding. "Sir, I know I'm new here, but our artillery will be effective only against a dismounted enemy attack. With what we have, 105mm and mortars, we won't be able to stop the enemy's armor," Davis replied with careful precision.

"We don't have very much artillery, and what we get will go to the main effort," Bludgell responded. "If you have a high payoff target, we can switch the priority. Get with Piper and he'll show you how it's done."

"What about engineer support?" Davis persisted.

"I don't have any to give. You have that monster tank ditch to block the wadi. All the engineer support I get will go to the main effort," Bludgell continued. "The priority for all combat support assets is BP Bravo."

Davis nodded. He suddenly felt very tired. First Platoon is totally on its own, he thought. I doubt I'll get any help from Bludgell.

Everyone is underestimating the enemy, Davis thought. Maybe this is just a natural reaction after the army's experience in Desert Storm. Am I exaggerating the danger and simply overreacting to my first taste of combat? At least I'll have a free hand with my defense.

"Service support: logistics, supply, and medical as per SOP. We received one hundred M21 antitank mines, fifty M16 antipersonnel mines, and fifty rolls of barbed wire in a class IV supply package about an hour ago. The mines are located in our engineer equipment dump near the northeast mouth of the valley. You will have to place your own minefields. All minefields must be approved by me before they are placed."

Davis plotted the position of the engineer equipment dump on his map.

"A water trailer is located here at the CP and will be replenished each morning. Make sure your men drink plenty of water," Bludgell continued.

Davis studied the map, searching for the decisive point of a battlefield where he could use his weapons to their fullest capacity. Javelin antitank missiles could hit a moving tank at a thousand meters, AT4 antitank rockets at only three hundred meters. The AT4s could stop armored cars and infantry fighting vehicles like the BMP, but they were almost useless against tanks. Only Javelins and antitank mines could stop enemy tanks.

"Command and signal: frequencies are per SOI. Standard call signs in effect. I'll be with 2d Platoon. The XO will be with 3d Platoon. Order of succession of chain of command is XO, 2d Platoon leader, 3d Platoon leader, 1st Platoon leader. Time is now 1115. I want each of you to copy the graphics depicted on my map. What are your questions?"

"Sir, I need more firepower," Davis pleaded. "You've given me two Javelins. With four missiles per Javelin gunner, and only ten AT4s, I don't have much to fight with. I need about fifteen AT4s. And I could use some more Javelin missiles and some more antitank mines."

"Anything else on your shopping list?" Lieutenant Sandburg, the company executive officer, asked with a sly grin.

Davis paused. "Yes, I could use some illumination flares."

"Flares? What do you need those for?" Bludgell questioned. "Why not use your thermals?"

"The Javelins have thermal sights, but I only have night-vision goggles and a few M938 night-vision sights to fire my AT4s, machine guns, and M16s," Davis replied confidently. "Parachute flares might come in handy if the enemy tries to infiltrate my positions at night."

"I'll see what I can do," Sandburg said quickly, before the company commander could respond. "You can pick up as many mines as you can carry. The AT4s are getting difficult to come by. The handheld illumination flares should be no problem. I'll do my best to get them for you before tomorrow morning."

"Don't get yourself killed trying to arm a mine that you don't know how to use," Bludgell interjected, pointing a finger at Davis.

"If you pick up mines from the engineer dump, make sure you follow the arming instructions to the letter. Better get Piper to help you."

"Yes, sir," Davis said, no longer fazed by the continuous injunctions to check with his platoon sergeant. "I've tried digging into this rock with entrenching tools. It just doesn't work. I need picks, shovels, sandbags, and material for overhead cover."

"Sandburg?" Bludgell questioned, realizing that he had forgotten a vital part of their defensive preparations.

"Yes, sir," Sandburg answered swiftly. "Battalion promises me that we will get more class IV materials, including sandbags, timber, and some corrugated metal plate for overhead cover. I also asked for the extra tools. The class IV material will be transported by civilian trucks, which are scheduled to arrive early this afternoon. They'll dump the barrier material at BP Bravo. I'll need a ten-man detail from each platoon to help unload the trucks and move the material to your defensive positions."

"When do you want the detail?" Davis asked.

"Have them here, standing by, in three hours," Sandburg replied, a faint smile playing across his face.

"Wilco," Davis said, nodding to his RTO to call back to Sergeant Piper and inform him of the task. "I could use some help moving the barrier material and mines."

"I'll give you all the support I can," Sandburg said. "I have two HMMWVs, with trailers, on loan until tomorrow noon. We'll have to make good use of them. I'll try to get to you early tomorrow morning."

"Good. Any more questions?" Bludgell asked.

"Yes," Sergeant Rossetti said, pointing to the map. "What if the enemy doesn't come down Axis Viper but punches through on Cobra? Are we going to orient our fighting positions north or south?"

"You don't get it, do you? The enemy isn't stupid. He won't come down the wadi with the tank ditch and Piper's men watching him," Bludgell replied angrily, appearing incensed that the sergeant would question his tactical judgment in front of his platoon leaders. "Don't forget who we're fighting here. These guys aren't much competition. The tank ditch by itself denies the entire avenue to the enemy. I'll leave my map here with the XO for you to copy. Now let's get to work. Dismissed."

The men stood up, saluted, and slowly departed for their units. Captain Bludgell left the command post with Sergeant Froude to inspect BP Bravo. Davis stayed for a few minutes to copy the commander's operations graphics onto his map, then he left the lean-to.

"So, Bruce, are you ready?" Sandburg asked with a smile as Davis exited the makeshift tent.

"Jeff, I'm out all on my own, defending a position four klicks away from the rest of the company, and I hardly know my platoon. How can I complain?" Davis said with a laugh.

"Don't worry. Bludgell is a bit intense, but he's probably right. He knows where to mass the company effort and he's going for the best chance to bag some bad guys before they all surrender. He put you there to keep you safe. Just trust that platoon sergeant of yours and he'll take care of you."

"Piper—he's another problem," Davis said, lowering his gaze. "We don't see eye to eye yet."

"Look, Bruce, everybody is uptight and tired. For Christ's sake, we all realize that we may be in combat in a few hours. Just give Piper a chance. He's one of the best. He fought in Desert Storm as a squad leader in the 101st Airborne Division. Listen to him. He knows what he's doing. If you handle him the right way, he won't let you down."

If you need a better understanding of infantry weapons and tactics, read Appendixes A–B and glossary. Then go to Section 3.

If you need a better understanding of map symbols, see page Then go to Section 3.

If you are ready to continue, go to Section 3.

Section 3

Davis, back with his platoon at the western mouth of Wadi Al Sirree, studied his map. There were several ways he could defend his sector. His mission, he reminded himself, was to block enemy forces from attacking through Wadi Al Sirree. In spite of the fact that Bludgell didn't expect the enemy to attack through Wadi Al Sirree, Davis knew that his mission was critical to the company's success.

> Block—Deny the enemy access to a given area or prevent enemy advance in a given direction. It may be for a specified time. Units may have to retain terrain and accept decisive engagement.
> FM 101-5-1, *Operational Terms and Symbols,* 1985

Davis quickly saw that there were three ways to defend the valley: forward of the trails, behind the trails, or in the trails. He quickly scribbled three sketches to mentally war-game his options.

A forward defense was the simplest option. If the enemy tried to attack through Wadi Al Sirree, he would have to fight through Davis's men first. It would require the preparation of a platoon battle position east of the tank ditch to deny the enemy access into the trails. He would have to improve their present fighting positions and antitank ditch with mines and wire, thus blocking the enemy's advance into the valley. This option would maximize simplicity, mass, and unity of command. Sometimes the simplest plan was the best one.

Davis's second option was a reverse-slope defense at the eastern edge of the four trails that led into the valley. This course of action called for the entire platoon to reposition to the east, abandoning the hill that overlooked the tank ditch. A reverse-slope defense would deny the platoon clear observation of the enemy as he approached the valley, but it would provide better protection from enemy direct and indirect fires. The concept was to allow the enemy to breach the tank ditch and mines, place obstacles to force the enemy to move along the narrow northern trails, and then destroy the enemy at close

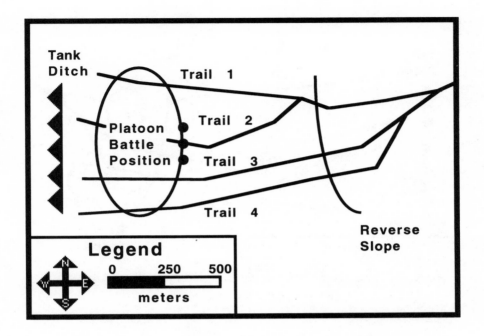

range as he entered the valley. This course of action maximized security and economy of force.

The third option was to block the enemy in each of the four trails that led into Wadi Al Sirree. Davis knew that he had more short-range weapons than long-range weapons. He could divide the platoon into antiarmor ambush teams and assign each team a trail that led into the valley. The platoon could engage the attacker's lead vehicles in selected short-range combat areas along each trail. By fighting a close-range battle in the trails that led into the valley, the platoon could pick off the enemy one at a time. The enemy wouldn't see the defenders until it was too late. This option would maximize surprise and offensive action.

Was there a fourth option? Davis weighed the possibilities.

> You will usually find that the enemy has three courses of action open to him, and of these he will adopt a fourth.
>   Field Marshal Helmuth Graf von Moltke

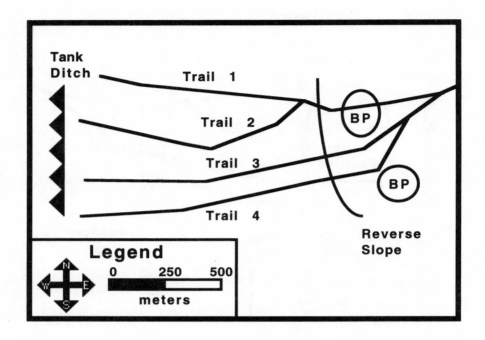

Hell, I can second-guess myself all day, he thought. I need to get cracking. Better to decide now and put a good plan to work rather than waste time trying to decide on the perfect plan.

Davis walked over to Sergeant Piper, who was finishing the work on his two-man foxhole—now three feet deep. The rest of the platoon was dug in at about the same depth. The soldiers were piling up black basalt rocks in front of their positions to form firing parapets.

"Our company commander has positioned everyone but us in BP Bravo. I've drawn our company's graphics on my map," Davis said, kneeling down to talk to his platoon sergeant. "The brigade has the 2d and 3d Rifle Battalions defending the valley to our north. In addition they have a heavy tank task force, acting as a brigade reserve, to stop the enemy if he breaks through our infantry. In a couple of days they expect the 1st Brigade of the 1st Infantry Division to arrive to support us."

Davis stooped down and unfolded his map. The big black lines on his map case depicted the platoon's area of responsibility. "I've been

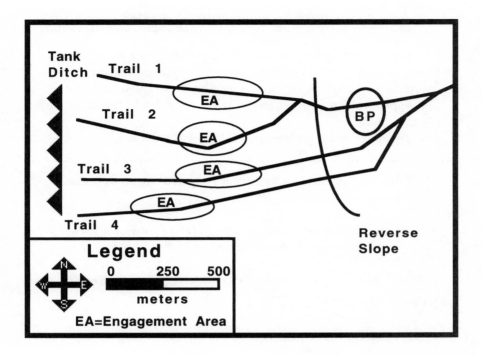

studying our setup here and I think we need to talk. We may have to move our positions."

The decisive point of a battlefield is determined . . . by the character of the position, the bearing of different localities upon the strategic object in view, and, finally, by the arrangement of the contending forces.

Antoine Henri Baron de Jomini

"You've got to be kidding, Lieutenant," Piper complained, loud enough for the entire platoon to hear. He threw his shovel to the ground. It struck the desert floor and sent a billow of fine dust into the air.

The first basic concept in tactics is to achieve a decision.
It is time for Davis to decide.

> Thus decisive action remains the first prerequisite for success in war. Everybody, from the highest commander to the youngest soldiers, must be conscious of the fact that inactivity and lost opportunities weigh heavier than do errors in the choice of means.
> *Truppenfuhrung,* German Field Service Regulations, 1933

If Davis decides to conduct a forward-slope defense, go to Section 4.

If Davis decides to move the platoon and conduct a reverse-slope defense, go to Section 5.

If Davis decides to defend along each trail, go to Section 6.

Section 4

"That's enough, Sergeant!" Davis exclaimed, walking up in front of the older man. "We can't waste any more time."

Piper stood and grabbed his entrenching tool with his right hand. The sergeant stood perfectly still, glaring back at his commanding officer.

The sun burned hot, and a slight breeze blew dust into the faces of the soldiers as they struggled to break into the earth with picks and shovels. Davis and Piper stood like boxers in a ring, only a few inches apart, glaring at each other.

"After all the work we've done here, I think we would be stupid to abandon this position, sir," Piper blurted out defiantly.

"Look, Piper," Davis said in hushed tones, not wanting the entire platoon in on the fracas, "we've got to learn to work together, or we're going to get the hell shot out of us for sure. I'm willing to listen."

Private First Class Cowper stopped digging to watch the argument. The rest of the platoon, sensing the tension, slowly turned their gaze toward their two leaders.

Davis knelt down and pointed to the map on the ground.

"Look, Sergeant, I know you were leading this platoon while I was still a cadet at West Point," Davis commented dryly as he searched for the right words. "But I'm not sure that we—"

Piper cut him off with a mean scowl and a wave of his hand. "Shit, Lieutenant, we're not talking about fighting the old Soviet 8th Guards Tank Army. These guys aren't eight feet tall. Hell, they ain't even four feet tall. I've fought these ragheads before and they don't like to fight. They won't attack a strong position and they'll never get over this tank ditch. It's too deep for tanks or BMPs to cross. If they come, we'll slaughter them with antitank, machine-gun, and rifle fire as they try to cross the ditch."

"I don't know . . ." Davis said, looking toward the excellent tank country that made up the enemy's approach into Wadi Al Sirree.

"You're right that we don't have time to argue, Lieutenant. We should be digging in our positions and laying mines."

The desert was quiet. The soldiers put down their shovels and watched the confrontation between their platoon leader and platoon sergeant.

Damn it! Davis raged inwardly. I just arrived in the unit. My company commander is about as friendly as my plebe calculus instructor, and my platoon sergeant is convinced that I couldn't lead a platoon to the latrine! In a few hours we could be fighting for our lives. I have to make the right decision. But what should I do?

Davis could hear his own breathing. His stomach churned in knots and his heart was beating fast. He turned away from the platoon sergeant and gazed to the west. Maybe we could defend here if we got enough mines and wire to make it impossible for them to break through, he thought. Maybe . . .

"If we stay here, we're going to need more mines and wire to stop them at the ditch," Davis suggested hesitatingly.

Section 4

"Now you're talking, Lieutenant," Piper said with a grin. "If we reinforce our positions to protect us from their artillery, and if we can place more mines and wire on both sides of the antitank ditch, we could hold off an army from here."

Piper kicked the ground with his sand-colored boot, sending a clod of hard desert dirt into his foxhole.

"Believe me," he said confidently, "you just leave it to me. This place will be as tight as a stone castle when we're through with it."

"How many mines do you think it will take?" Davis asked.

"We'll need about one or two hundred. We'll have to work all night," Piper replied without emotion.

"OK, Piper," Davis replied quietly, looking down. He took off his helmet, sat down next to his half-dug hole, and took an olive-drab cloth bandanna from his pants cargo pocket. Slowly he opened his canteen, soaked the rag with water, and wiped his face. Refreshed, he suddenly knew that he was right to compromise with his sergeant. "We'll do it. We'll dig in here. But only if it's a team effort. We start working together now or no deal."

Piper smiled and extended his hand. "You got it, Lieutenant. Trust me. Leadership involves compromise. I know what I'm doing."

Davis took the sergeant's hand and grinned.

The soldiers on the hill watched the two men shake hands and went back to their digging. The infantrymen were too preoccupied with their own troubles to care about their green lieutenant.

"Shit," Piper said, beaming, as he shook the lieutenant's hand. "This will be over in a couple of days and we'll all be headed home."

"Sure. It's all been happening so fast," Davis said with a bleak smile. "I've just arrived. The lives of our men depend on what we decide. I know I still have a lot to learn."

"Lieutenant, you're gonna be fine. We'll get through this OK if you listen to me."

Davis stood motionless, relieved that the decision had been made. He felt as if a great burden had been lifted from his shoulders.

"Look, I don't claim to have all the answers. I just know that we can stop the enemy here. The success or failure of our defense will depend upon the use of our weapons, the ground, and our preparations. We have to consider the range of our weapons, dead space, the mixture of flat trajectory and high-angle fires, antiarmor and antipersonnel fires, and barriers and mines. If we do these things correctly, we can accomplish our mission and keep our people alive."

"Right," Davis answered in a tone between triumph and embarrassment. "I know one thing for sure. We'll do a better job now that we're working as a team."

"I couldn't agree more," Piper said with a wry grin. "Here's what I recommend. I'll supervise the sighting of the weapons, get everyone making range cards, and inspect the fighting positions. You can make up a plan to lay more minefields to reinforce the tank ditch. I'll have a detail ready to lay mines in three hours."

Davis nodded his head in agreement. "How are we going to do this?" he asked.

Piper looked to the west, scanning the terrain for avenues of attack. "I know how these guys fight. If we show them a strong hand—I mean really block the openings to Wadi Al Sirree with obstacles—they'll avoid us and go some other way. If they're stupid enough to attack us along Axis Cobra, we can kill them at the tank ditch. If they come our way, they've got to come across the ditch."

"Right. We'll have to lay mines at both ends of the ditch," Davis said in a determined, serious voice, "to deny movement through the ground where the ditch ends. We could even put some mines inside the ditch, in case they get into it."

"Yeah," Piper replied, his cunning smile broadening. His expression was that of a hunter, preparing to capture his prey. "We'll set concertina wire and mines where the ditch ends. That will tempt the enemy to avoid the wire and entice him to try to breach the tank ditch."

"Let's hope that doesn't happen," Davis said.

"Don't worry. It shouldn't. You said yourself that the old man doesn't think they'll come this way. My guess is that they'll send a small probing attack. Probably no more than a platoon or so. When they come, we'll be waiting for them. They'll never get past the friggin' ditch."

"I wish we had some .50-caliber machine guns," Davis added.

"Hell, Lieutenant, I'd give away an R and R in Bahrain with two belly dancers for the taste of a fifty."

Davis and Piper burst out laughing, happy that they were finally working together. "The FO and I will complete a target list to support the defense. I'll prepare the platoon operations order," Davis announced after a moment.

"I'll have Mizogouchi get a detail together to carry our barrier material and mines into position," Piper said. "It looks like we'll be better off working through the night and sleeping in the day."

"Yes," Davis answered, somewhat overwhelmed by the magnitude of the task ahead of him. "I guess we should."

Davis reached for the canteen on his left hip, found it empty, and unbuttoned the flap on the cover of his right canteen. Barely a quarter of the contents were left. He unscrewed the plastic top and drank the last drop of warm, precious liquid. He made a mental note to check into the water situation when he got back to the platoon.

> He whose ranks are united in purpose will be victorious.
>
> Sun Tzu

Davis had fought the first important battle of his young career. Now, he mused, had he won or lost?

Go to Section 7.

Section 5

Davis stood in front of his platoon sergeant.

"I've had it with you, Piper," Davis grunted, walking up to the older man and standing toe to toe with the sergeant. "We either work as a team or we're gonna get the hell shot out of us."

Piper glared back, not moving. He held his entrenching tool menacingly in his right hand.

"So what do you have in mind, Lieutenant? I'd really like to know, since I've been breaking my back for the last hour trying to punch a hole in this rock-hard hill of ours," Piper growled in a cold, steely, determined voice.

Private First Class Cowper stopped digging to watch the fight. One by one the other soldiers halted their work and turned their attention toward the two leaders.

"Piper, get your rifle and come with me," Davis ordered. The lieutenant grabbed his M16 and slowly walked down the hill. He sauntered off toward the tank ditch without looking back to see if Piper was following.

"You want me to—" Cowper asked.

"Shut up, Cowper," Piper silenced him. "Monitor the radio. I'll be back in a few minutes."

Piper walked off at quick time, trailing after the lieutenant. The platoon remained on the small hill east of the tank ditch, watching their leaders depart. Davis continued a steady stride, carrying his rifle in the crook of his left arm. Piper followed four steps behind the lieutenant.

Davis arrived at the ditch first. He quickly scanned the area, inspecting the work. The ditch was long and well dug. It was approximately 1.8 meters deep, with the spoil from the digging placed in a mound on the friendly, or eastern, side of the ditch. The ditch extended from one hundred meters short of the northern wall of the valley to about three hundred meters short of the southern wall. An attacking armored force would be faced with either breaching the ditch or taking the narrow passages around it.

As Piper neared the tank ditch, Davis heard the metallic click of a magazine being snapped into the sergeant's M16A2 rifle.

Davis turned to face his platoon sergeant.

"Look at our positions, Sergeant," Davis said in a calm and steady voice, pointing back to the soldiers digging into the small rise east of the tank ditch. "This is the view that the enemy will have of us when he gets here. Is that where you want to be when an enemy tank is sitting here?"

Piper hadn't taken the time to look at his position from the enemy's perspective. The shallow holes that the platoon was digging on the rise seemed awfully open and very obvious. The dark dirt and the black rocks piled in front of the holes clearly identified each fighting position. It was instantly apparent that the platoon would be fully within the range of the enemy's supporting fires.

Piper, however, was a proud man. He wasn't ready to give up without an argument.

"They're never going to get over this tank ditch," Piper announced, irritated by the inexorable thrust of Davis's argument. "It's too deep for tanks or BMPs to cross."

"Bull! If mountains and rivers can be overcome, anything built by man can be overcome," Davis argued emphatically. "Especially this puny tank ditch! I'm not willing to put all my trust in one hole in the ground."

"Maybe the bastards will attack us dismounted."

"Be reasonable, Piper," Davis replied sternly. "If the enemy conducts a dismounted attack, what good is the tank ditch?"

Piper didn't answer. He just stared back at the hill where 1st Platoon was assembled.

"Our mission is to block the enemy from using this valley," Davis continued persuasively. "We don't have to defend the tank ditch to do that. But we may be able to use it to trap the enemy."

"Trap?" Piper repeated, expressing disbelief and curiosity.

"If we fight from that hill, Sergeant, we fight a frontal defense against an enemy with superior firepower. We will be as obvious as a neon sign on a dark night. He'll smash us with his tank cannon and heavy machine guns like a flyswatter smashing a bug. It won't matter how well we deploy our weapon systems. He can shoot at us from two thousand meters, well before we could open up on him. Is that what you want?"

Piper kicked the ground with his sand-colored desert boot.

"It's time we come to an agreement," Davis insisted. "The XO tells me that you're the best platoon sergeant in the battalion. I know he's right. I think if we work together we can make the best platoon in the battalion."

A grin came over Piper's face. He looked back at Davis, who stuck out his hand.

"Shit, Lieutenant, all you had to do was ask," Piper said beaming, as he took the lieutenant's hand and shook it vigorously.

"Sergeant, a platoon fighting against itself won't stand up against the enemy, no matter how strong its defenses."

The soldiers on the hill, watching the two men below them shaking hands, began to whistle and applaud. They acted like children who had just seen their parents fight and then watched them make up.

"I guess we've been acting like a couple of jerks," Davis said, pointing to the platoon on the hill.

"Yep, maybe so. You know, it's always like this. Every strong leader has to come to terms with his second in command at some point," Piper responded. "I'm just glad we did it before the battle."

Piper looked to the west, scanning the terrain for avenues of attack.

"Damn it, Lieutenant, I never had this problem during Desert Storm. Basically, all we did then was attack and take a lot of prisoners, but I see what you're getting at and I think you're right."

"Well, I've been looking at the map," Davis said enthusiastically. "I think you'll agree that we'd get chopped up if we tried to take the enemy's tanks and BMPs head on. We need to create a situation where we can use our small force to hit him at close range. His greatest advantage is his long-range fires. What if we were able to arrange our positions so that he couldn't shoot at us until it was too late?"

"Sounds good. I'm with you so far."

"We have to minimize the advantage of their long-range direct fires," Davis said, deliberating. "The only way I can see to do that is to mask our positions behind the hill, on the reverse slope, where the trails empty out into the valley. If we do that, we'll gain security and we might be able to shift the odds in our favor."

"We could destroy the tanks and BMPs one by one, as they come into the mouth of the valley," Piper added. "But we give up the tank ditch."

"Yes," Davis said confidently, "but the ditch could only slow an enemy attack, it couldn't stop an attack. If the ditch slows him, we can use artillery fire to disrupt his movement across the ditch. With artillery fire falling on him, he may rush into our engagement areas buttoned up and unaware."

"Good idea. The enemy may also see our present positions on top of the hill and, if we fix them up right, he might think they're occupied."

"Exactly! We could use the positions we've been digging to deceive him." Davis could see that he had convinced Piper. "Those positions could absorb some of his artillery. On the reverse slope, we can hide from his direct fire and ambush him as he comes out of the narrow passes."

"OK, Lieutenant. Where do you want our primary positions?"

Davis pulled the acetate map from the cargo pocket of his pants and laid the map on the ground. He knelt down, orienting the map to the north, and motioned for Piper to bend down and join him.

"Here's what I think we should do," Davis started, pointing at the tank ditch with his finger. "We can use the reverse slope of the western mouth of Wadi Al Sirree to trap the enemy. We can't be strong everywhere. We have to drive him into a trap where we can use our close-range weapons against him. If we set up our defenses correctly, we can trap him at the openings of the northern trails into Wadi Al Sirree."

Davis pointed to the map and designated the area where he expected to trap the advancing enemy armored vehicles. Piper nodded in agreement.

"First, we create dummy positions on the hill, as you have suggested," Davis continued. "That'll make it look like we're defending forward. Then we'll complete the work on our reverse-slope positions. Tomorrow night we'll move into these reverse-slope positions. We'll divide the platoon in half, covering the trails that open into the valley. You'll take charge of half the platoon in the south, and I'll command the other half in the north."

"We should place several minefields on the eastern ends of the trails that open into Wadi Al Sirree," Piper added, pointing to the map. "We need to do everything we can to get flank shots with our AT4s."

"Yes. We can place wire and mines on the southern edge of the tank ditch," Davis said, pausing, "and make our defense in the south look like a main effort. This may help turn the enemy to the north, where I want to trap him. I'll position the Javelins to target enemy vehicles using Trails 1 and 2, the narrowest of the trails. With only two Javelins, we can't afford to split them up."

"I like the way you think," Piper answered with a smile. "We need to mass our best antitank weapons where they'll do the most damage."

"Concentration and security are the keys to this defense," Davis continued. "To move fast, the enemy will try to exploit gaps in our defense. He'll be looking for holes. As the enemy approaches our defenses, he'll see obstacles to the south, a tank ditch in the center, and fighting positions that overlook the ditch. I'm betting that his natural tendency will be to go north and avoid our strengths. This may force him to take the northern trails that lead into the wadi. At the reverse slope the two northern trails are the most constricted and are the easiest to block. As he gets into the narrow area along the north wall, we'll use mines, Javelins, and AT4s to stop him. If he tries to force his way through the south, you'll hit him with AT4s."

"Let's hope that doesn't happen," Piper said.

"Right. If he attacks south and forces his way through our obstacles, I'll reposition to hit him with my Javelin teams as he tries to get by you. In that case, you stand fast and I'll strike him from behind. What do you think?"

"It sounds like we got a plan, Lieutenant," Piper said, grinning. "But what if it doesn't work?"

Davis paused, eyeing his platoon sergeant closely. "What do you mean?"

"Don't get me wrong, I like it. But we should have a fallback area. What if we can't stop him?"

"What's your recommendation?"

"Designate a rally point along the south wall, to our east. If everything falls apart we can assemble there."

"Good thinking," Davis said, happy that the team was now working together. "You select the rally points. The FO and I will complete the plan. Get a detail together to get our barrier material and mines in position. Start in the south. It looks like we'll be better off working through the night and sleeping in shifts during the day."

"Yes, sir," Piper answered. Then, with parade ground precision, he saluted and marched briskly off to the hill.

Davis returned the salute and turned around to look west, trying to visualize the enemy attack. He reached for one of his canteens, found it empty, and then reached for the other. He could tell from its weight that it was only a quarter full. He unscrewed the plastic top and drank every last drop. He made a mental note to check into the water situation when he got back to the platoon.

> There are circumstances in war when many cannot attack few, and others when the weak can master the strong. One able to manipulate such circumstances will be victorious.
>
> Sun Tzu

The first battle had been won. Now, Davis mused, how was he going to win the second?

Go to Section 42.

Section 6

"That's enough, Piper!" Davis said, exasperated. Grim-faced, he walked over to his sergeant, stiffening with each step. "This shit has to stop. We've got to learn to work together or we're going to get the hell shot out of us for sure."

Piper glared back, standing as straight as a lance. He picked up his entrenching tool and pointed. "So your idea of getting our shit together is to abandon this position after all the work we put into preparing it!"

Private First Class Cowper stopped digging his hole and laid down his small shovel. He sat back, next to his radio, to observe the fight. The rest of the platoon, in turn, slowly stopped working and prepared to watch the fireworks.

"Platoon Sergeant, get your rifle and come with me," Davis ordered, realizing the scene that he was causing. The lieutenant grabbed his M16 and headed west, down the hill, toward the tank ditch.

"You want me to—" Cowper asked.

"Shut up, Cowper," Piper barked, silencing the radioman in midsentence. "Just monitor the radio. I'll be back in a few minutes."

Cowper leaned back against his shallow hole, grinning slightly, unfazed by the sergeant's harsh words. The rest of the soldiers remained on the hill and resumed working on their positions. Davis took off at a steady stride, quickly moving down the hill toward the tank ditch. He carried his rifle in both arms, barrel forward. Piper walked four steps behind him.

Davis arrived at the ditch, climbed down into it, and came up the other side. Here he stopped and scanned the area, inspecting the work. The ditch was well dug. It was approximately 1.8 meters deep, with the sand from the digging placed in a mound on the friendly, or eastern, side of the ditch. The ditch extended from one hundred meters short of the northern wall of the valley to about three hundred meters short of the southern wall. The engineers had done a good job.

As Davis turned to the west, he scanned the enemy's avenues of approach, then looked east. Sergeant Piper, who had followed Davis into the ditch, climbed out of the ditch and joined his platoon leader.

"Look at our positions, Sergeant," Davis said in a steady voice, pointing to the soldiers digging into the small rise east of the tank ditch. "This is the view that the enemy will have of our position when he gets here. Is that where you think we can defeat an armored force?"

Piper looked at the position from this new view. He hadn't taken the time to look at it from the enemy's perspective. The shallow holes that the platoon was digging on the hill seemed awfully open and very obvious. The darker sand, piled in front of each position, and the light green sandbags clearly identified each fighting position. It was obvious to the newest recruit that the position would be within the full range of the enemy's direct fires.

Piper, however, was not ready to give in. He had been leading the platoon when the lieutenant was still a wet-nosed cadet on the Hudson.

"They're never going to get over this tank ditch," Piper responded in a cold and steely, almost mechanical, voice. "It's too deep for tanks or BMPs to cross. Once they see it they'll head north."

"Are you sure? Is this ditch so deep that we can count on it with our lives?" Davis questioned. His voice rose as he replied, and he pointed at the ditch. "This puny tank ditch? The Iraqi antitank ditch that blocked our forces in Operation Desert Storm was much more sophisticated than this and it didn't stop us for long. I'm not willing to put all my trust, and risk the lives of my men, in one hole in the ground."

"Maybe the bastards will attack us dismounted."

"Piper, think about this," Davis answered sternly. "If the enemy conducts a dismounted attack, what good are the positions we designed to defend the ditch? The ditch won't stop dismounted infantry. It didn't stop us just now. Our mission is to block the enemy. We don't have to defend the tank ditch to do that. But we may be able to use it to trap the enemy."

"But—" Piper protested.

"If we sit on that hill, the enemy will see us from far away. We'll have to fight a frontal fight against an enemy with superior firepower. Is that what you want?" Davis insisted.

Piper kicked the ground with his sand-colored boot. He looked to the west, then looked up at his platoon leader with a grim look of determination. Somewhere out there, to the west, was an enemy getting ready to attack.

"Damn it, Lieutenant, I don't know. I never had this problem during Desert Storm," Piper replied. "Things were different then. We had the force to do anything. Now, we're sitting in this godforsaken valley waiting for them to attack us!"

"We don't have time to argue about that now. We have to get ready. Every minute we delay weakens our preparations."

"You're right, Lieutenant," the sergeant said. "It's all been happening so fast. You just arrived. My life and the lives of our men will depend on your decisions. I'm not even sure you know anything about leading a platoon."

"Believe me, I understand. But you've got to work with me. Together we can keep our people alive and accomplish the mission. I need your experience."

Piper stood motionless, listening to his lieutenant.

"I know your reputation. You're a professional and a combat veteran. You know I need your help," Davis said, choosing each word as carefully as if he were moving pieces on a chessboard. "I don't claim to have all the answers. I only ask that you work with me and give me your full support. Our men deserve as much."

Piper stared off to the east, looking back at the hill. A few moments passed. Neither man said a word.

"There's no doubt about that. Those guys should have a team that works together," Piper replied, finally breaking the silence. "A platoon leader and platoon sergeant who can't get along make a bad situation. One of them usually has to go."

"OK, let's give it a try," Davis answered with a wide grin. He stuck out his hand. Piper shook it and returned the grin.

"Shit, Lieutenant, we should have had this discussion a couple of days ago," Piper said, beaming, shaking the lieutenant's hand vigorously.

The men on the hill, watching Piper and Davis shake hands, began to whistle and applaud. It seemed that the team was finally coming together.

"I guess we have been acting like a couple of jerks," Davis said, pointing to the platoon on the hill.

"Maybe so. You know, I've seen this before. Strong leaders have to come to terms with each other at some point," Piper responded. "I'm just glad we did it before the battle."

Davis turned to the west, searching the terrain for clues of the enemy's avenue of attack. The ground was open. Great fields of fire, he thought. Perfect tank country.

"How are we going to do this?" Piper asked.

"I've been thinking about that. After studying the map I believe the area is too large for us to position the platoon in just one or two places overlooking the ditch. The enemy will simply drive around us. If we fight from that hill, he'll plaster us with fire and breach the tank ditch while we're being suppressed by his machine guns and artillery."

"So what can we do?" Piper asked.

"We can catch him in single-file columns in antiarmor ambushes along each of the four trails," Davis answered confidently. "First we place our obstacles to narrow the enemy's avenues of approach, then we prepare a number of positions with interlocking fields of fire along each trail. As the enemy attacks into the trails, he's presented with a number of enemies all at once, firing at him from multiple directions."

"Do we have enough men to do that?" Piper asked.

"I think so," Davis replied, pointing to the east. "If we defend in each trail that leads into the valley, we can minimize their strength in numbers and long-range firepower. When they come up the trails, they'll have to come in single file."

"We won't be able to shoot at him as he crosses the tank ditch," Piper observed.

Forces deployed in depth must confront the enemy with effective antiarmor fires from multiple locations as he tries to maneuver.... The focus of this technique is the enemy force. Mines and other obstacles, infantry positions, and patrols are used to close gaps that cannot be covered by fire due to terrain masking.

FM 7-20, *The Infantry Battalion,* April 6, 1992

"Yes, but it might give us an opportunity to deceive him. He'll expect us to defend the tank ditch. Those positions we're digging could act as a decoy."

"I get it," Piper said, grinning. "He'll see our positions on top of the hill east of the tank ditch and think they're occupied."

"Yes," Davis acknowledged, convinced that he had swayed Piper. "Those dummy positions could absorb some of his artillery. We can use his delay in crossing the tank ditch and his confusion about the dummy positions to call for mortar and artillery fires on him. Then when he forces the ditch and enters the trails, we'll destroy his lead vehicles."

"It's bold, but it could work. It'll be a close-range fight. If we defend each trail, we can kill him one at a time, bottle up the trails, and block the valley."

The two men paused for a moment and looked to the west.

"You know we won't have a chance to withdraw," Piper said calmly, with a determination born from experience. "Once we commit to this defense, we are decisively engaged."

"True. But we could be decisively engaged no matter how we defend. If the enemy comes down Cobra, we have a better chance if we can kill him in the trails, in a close-range infantry fight, before he deploys from column to line formation."

54

"I agree," Piper replied. "OK, Lieutenant, how do you want to organize this?"

The platoon leader, now firmly in charge, pulled his map from the cargo pocket of his desert-camouflaged trousers and laid the map on the ground. He knelt down, orienting the map to the north, then gestured for Piper to bend down and look at the plan.

"This is what I think we should do," Davis started, pointing at the narrow trails that led into the valley. "First, we occupy the positions we've been digging on the hill at night. That'll make it look like we're defending the hill in force. During the early morning, right before daylight, we'll move back to the trails and occupy ambush positions along each one."

Piper watched carefully as the platoon leader drew positions on his map with an alcohol marking pen.

"We'll number the trails one through four from north to south. Trails 1 and 2 will be defended by 1st Squad, Trail 3 by 2d Squad. Trail 4 will be blocked by 3d Squad. I'll retain the two M60 machine guns and the two Javelins with me as a reserve in Position Yankee. If they start to get through any one of the trails, I'll move the reserve to a position to block their advance."

"We'll have to lay extra mines in the south," Piper said in a determined, serious voice. "That ground is less restricted, and the enemy might be able to force through there."

"Yeah. We can set more concertina wire obstacles in the south. Mines and wire should help drive him north. If he gets into the narrow passes, we'll use mines, squad machine guns, and AT4s to stop him."

"Do you really think this is the best way?" Sergeant Piper asked.

There is no approved solution to any tactical situation.
Gen. George S. Patton, Jr.

"We have a better chance at the passes than anywhere else," Davis insisted. "If we hit his lead vehicles in the trails, he'll never get by his own wrecks. What do you think?"

"It sounds like we got a plan, Lieutenant," Piper said, grinning.

Davis had won the first important battle of his young career.

"Great. Let's go," Davis said, happy that the team was now working together. "The FO and I will complete the plan. You'd better assemble a detail and work on our obstacles."

Go to Section 8.

Section 7

When his fighting position was finally complete, Davis put down his shovel. He and Cowper had used steel picks to loosen the ground and entrenching tools to scoop out the dirt. They had piled sand in front of their position and stacked black basalt rocks to create a strong firing parapet. Working all day, they had burrowed four feet into the rocky hill overlooking the tank ditch.

Suddenly the supersonic blast of a Threat aircraft split the air above Davis's head. He dove for the ground. A second ear-shattering shriek occurred as Davis was nose down in the dust of the desert floor.

Startled by the boom, the young lieutenant gathered his courage and looked up. A U.S. Navy F/A-18 was chasing an enemy aircraft. The enemy bird, now just a dot in the eastern sky, pulled straight up to circle back toward his own lines. Suddenly the small black dot burst into a bright orange fireball. The disintegrating aircraft hurtled earthward in a twisting mass of smoke and debris.

Davis's men cheered. There had been no warning of the enemy aircraft's approach. If it had been on a strike run against them, they would have been caught with their pants down.

"See what I mean, Lieutenant? The air force has just about got this here war won already!" announced Piper.

The sun had passed its zenith. Davis motioned for his squad leaders to re-form around him.

"That was probably a navy aircraft, and they won't be in our foxholes to defend this valley if we're attacked," Davis replied laconically before changing the subject to the work at hand. "Let's get back to our operations order."

Sergeant Piper and the squad leaders dusted themselves off, then moved back to Lieutenant Davis and formed a semicircle around him. The lieutenant's map lay at his feet in front of the assembled leaders.

"The point of our defense is to block the enemy from crossing the tank ditch. It's that simple," Piper said as he pointed to the lieutenant's map, which was displayed on the ground in front of them.

> In war so much is always unknown that it frequently happens that the simple to the complex is the rule of war, therefore the simpler, more direct and clearer the beginning the less likely is action to get out of hand.
>
> Maj. Gen. J. F. C. Fuller

"Correct," the platoon leader replied, scratching the plan of defense into the desert sand. "It's all a matter of how we place our weapons. First Squad will cover the north."

Sergeant Jordan, the leader of 1st Squad, nodded.

"Second Squad will cover the center. Third Squad will cover the south. Each squad will have eight AT4s and its squad weapons to cover its assigned areas. I'll have both M60 machine guns and two Javelins in the center. From the center we can range the entire tank ditch. As soon as an enemy comes into our best engagement range, about fifteen hundred meters from our battle position, we'll clobber him with Javelin fire. At the same time, Sergeant Mark will be calling for artillery fires."

"Right," Davis said. "I'll be in the center, with Sergeant Mark, in 2d Squad's position. Sergeant Mark will call for fires for me. I'll use my radio to communicate with you and Captain Bludgell. Piper will be with 3d Squad."

"We'll plaster the enemy with Javelins and whatever AT4s are left as he crosses the tank ditch," Piper commented directly to the squad leaders. "We have six Javelin rounds per command launch unit. When these are gone we'll have to rely on machine guns and small arms. If the enemy does breach the ditch, he'll have to cross one at a time—perfect targets for our antitank weapons."

"Remember," Piper added, "no one withdraws without orders. You're safer to stay in position and fight from where you are. The enemy tank gunners will key on our movement. Once you're out of your holes, you won't have a chance against their armor."

The platoon sergeant, FO, squad leaders, and machine gunners listened carefully, trying to make sure they understood their exact roles. They knew their lives depended on acting correctly the first time. If the enemy attacked, they might not get a second chance.

"What if they break through the minefields?" Sergeant Jordan asked. "I have eight AT4s to stop them. After eight shots, I'm out of tank-killing ammunition."

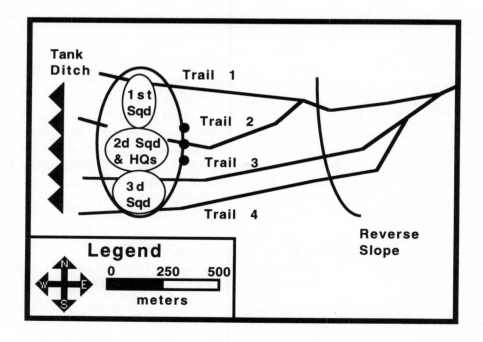

"I don't think they'll fight that tough. Once we kill a few of them, they'll probably turn north to avoid our fires. But if you run out of AT4s, I want you to fire small arms and machine guns at the armored vehicles to keep them buttoned up," Piper concluded. "Right, Lieutenant?"

"Yes, of course," Davis answered, trying to envision the enemy withdrawing as Piper had suggested. "The bottom line is that we have to stop the enemy from crossing the ditch, as Piper has said. I think the antitank mines will make a big difference in our ability to block their attack. We'll have to work most of the night to place enough mines to make this happen."

Sergeant Tyler sighed. "Sir, my men are beat. Working all night won't boost their morale."

"I don't see any other way," Davis said, looking at Piper. "We have to lay more mines. We need to put a minefield, M1, on the north side of the tank ditch. We'll plug the gap on our southern flank with another minefield, which we'll number M3. Last of all, we'll lay M2, to stop him in our engagement area in the center."

"We could set up a couple of triple-strand wire barriers in front of M1 and M3," Jordan added, "reinforcing the minefields. That could convince the bastards that the tank ditch is the path of least resistance."

"Which will put him right in our killing zone," Sergeant Mizogouchi, the leader of 3d Squad, answered with a grin. "My guys are tired, but we'll take care of putting up wire at M3 tonight. It'll take us a while, but we'll have it done by morning."

"Look, I know how little sleep you've had," Davis said sympathetically. "But we've got to make the most of our time. We'll have pretty good illumination for several hours tonight, almost a full moon. We can minimize heat casualties by working at night."

Piper looked nervously at his platoon leader. Two men had fallen ill from heat cramps. The water supply had run low as the temperature rose. No one knew when the two soldiers, both from 2d Squad, would return from the battalion aid station. Davis needed every man he could muster.

"How's 2d Squad doing, Tyler?" Davis asked the 2d Squad leader.

"Both of the men who were medevacked today should be back in two days. Everyone else is fine," Tyler answered, adjusting his

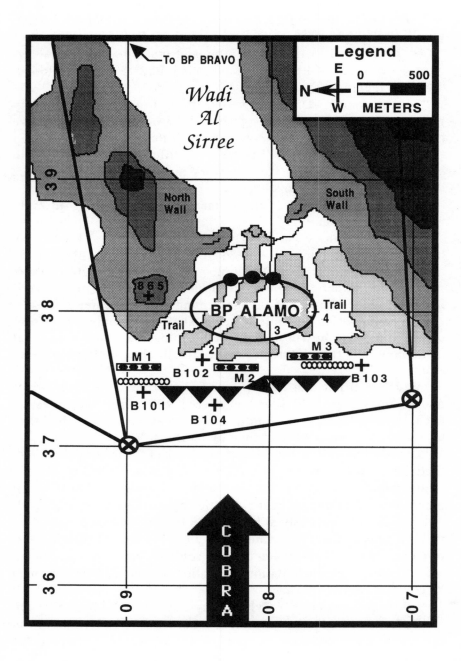

glasses. "I'm lining them up every two hours and forcing them to drink half a canteen of water."

"Good. How's our water supply?" Davis inquired, turning to Piper.

"Lieutenant Sandburg dropped off ten five-gallon cans just thirty minutes ago. He also brought fifteen AT4s, some extra 5.56mm ammunition, twenty white illumination flares, six green and six red star clusters, and ten rolls of concertina wire," Piper reported.

"That'll help," Davis replied with a smile. "So our total is twenty-four AT4s and eight Javelin missiles."

"Twenty-four rounds doesn't sound like a lot to stop them," Mizogouchi replied matter-of-factly.

"That's why the mines are so crucial," Davis rejoined, pausing for a few seconds, searching for something else to say. "We should fire the AT4s in volleys, two at a time at the same target. We'll get better results that way, especially against tanks. Excluding the effects of our minefields, we could destroy fifteen or sixteen enemy armored vehicles. That should be enough to stop them."

The men fidgeted nervously. The thought of imminent combat was on everyone's mind. Fifteen or sixteen armored vehicles was an awesome array to destroy.

"Wilco," Piper replied, ending the meeting. "Make sure there's plenty of small-arms ammunition in each fighting position. I want each man to have four extra magazines, in addition to the seven we brought with us."

The squad leaders nodded.

"All right," Piper said. "Let's get cracking."

Davis stood silent as the squad leaders returned to their men. Piper scanned the northern ridgeline of the valley and pointed to the crest of Hill 865.

"What do you say we climb the north wall and get a good view of the approaches that lead into the valley?" Piper asked.

"I don't know," Davis said with hesitation. "What about our positions? We still have a lot of work to accomplish."

"Your first lesson, sir, is to learn how to delegate tasks. You can't do everything yourself," Piper answered, talking like a father does to his son. "The squad leaders can build this position, and we can tell Cowper and Sergeant Mark to finish your fighting hole."

Davis looked at the tank ditch and then back at the hill where his men were digging. The hill was a beehive of activity as soldiers swung their picks into the hard, rocky soil.

"Let's call it our leader's recon. We'll climb up to the top of Hill 865 and plan our battle while the squad leaders keep everyone working," Piper remarked with a smile. "Well, what do you say, Lieutenant?"

If Davis decides to join Sergeant Piper at a leader's reconnaissance on Hill 865, go to Section 10.

If Davis decides not to join Sergeant Piper, go to Section 11.

Section 8

There was very little talking. The men struggled, sweating in the hot sun, forcing the rocky desert hill to make room for their positions.

Private First Class Cowper put down his E tool and grabbed a pick. He loosened the ground with the pick while Hutchinson used the entrenching tool to scoop out the loose dirt. Working for several hours, the two young soldiers burrowed four feet into the rocky hill overlooking the tank ditch. Then together they packed down the dirt in front of their position and stacked a wall of black basalt rocks. This created an effective firing parapet.

The platoon command post was finished. Cowper smiled and leaned back against the side of the hole to smoke a cigarette. Hutchinson opened a small green packet of rations and began to munch on some beef stew. Cowper's radio sat outside the hole, neglected by its operator.

The rest of the platoon toiled to prepare their positions. A few feet away from Cowper, Lieutenant Davis, Sergeant Piper, and the squad leaders were huddled over a map.

"These positions are only for tonight?" Sergeant Jordan quizzed.

"Roger. We're going to defend each trail."

Suddenly the supersonic blast of an aircraft shock wave split the air. Davis dove for the ground. Shovels and picks flew while men scrambled into their half-prepared holes. Everyone who couldn't make it to his hole fell prone.

Two aircraft, one chasing another, hurtled over their heads. A second ear-shattering sonic boom resounded as Davis was nose down in the dust of the desert floor.

Davis looked up. A U.S. Navy F/A-18 was chasing an enemy aircraft. The enemy bird pulled straight up to circle back toward his own lines. That was his mistake. The U.S. pilot anticipated his move and fired an air-to-air missile. The missile shrieked through the air, accelerating as it flew, tracking the enemy's movements perfectly. The enemy aircraft fired his afterburners, but the missile proved too fast for him. The race was over. The missile ignited the enemy aircraft in a bright orange fireball. The tangled, burning wreckage of the aircraft hurtled to the earth. It was an extraordinary sight, played out on the stage of the blue heavens, in full view of the men of the platoon. Davis's men cheered.

"See what I mean, Lieutenant? The air force has just about got this war won already," Piper announced.

Davis rose to his feet and nodded. He picked up his notebook and continued issuing his operations order.

There had been no warning of the enemy aircraft's approach, Davis realized. If that son of a bitch had been on a strike run against us, we could have been slaughtered.

A battle sometimes decides everything; and sometimes the most trifling thing decides the fate of battle.

Napoleon

"Cowper!" Davis shouted, "stay glued to that radio. If the company announced an early warning for those aircraft and you didn't catch it, I'll have you digging ditches all day!"

"Roger, sir!" Cowper replied, embarrassed, realizing he had let the platoon down.

Davis reflected that it was Cowper's job as RTO to keep the platoon leader in constant communications with company headquarters. If friendly radars had known of the approaching enemy aircraft, the warning "Red air, moving east from NK3007" would have been announced over the company radio frequency. Why is everything so hard?

The sun passed its zenith as Lieutenant Davis finished issuing his operations order to the squad leaders.

"The point of our defense is to maximize surprise and offensive action to stop the enemy in the trails. We'll place most of our obstacles in the south to help drive him north into the narrowest trails. Once the enemy arrives at the tank ditch, he'll either try to cross it or go north. As soon as he gets near the ditch, we'll call for artillery on him. As he enters the trails, I expect you to destroy the lead vehicle in each trail," Davis continued, pointing at the map. "Once the lead vehicles are destroyed, the enemy will have trouble getting around them. To block the trails, we must surprise the lead vehicle and destroy them with the first shot."

> Of all keys to success in war "unexpectedness" is the most important. By it a commander, whether of an army or a platoon, can often unlock the gates which are impregnable to sheer force.
>
> B. H. Liddell Hart

"First Squad will cover the narrowest trails, numbered 1 and 2," Davis ordered, sketching out the deployment in the sand with his bayonet. "Sergeant Piper will set ambush positions along Trail 1 to engage the enemy in the Trail 1 engagement area. Sergeant Jordan will set up ambush positons along Trail 2 to engage the enemy in the Trail 2 engagement area."

Piper stared at the sand diagram. Sergeant Jordan looked at Davis and nodded.

"Second Squad will cover Trail 3," Davis continued. "Third Squad will cover Trail 4. Each squad will have eight AT4s and their squad weapons, and mines to block the enemy vehicles that enter the engagement areas along each trail. If we stop their lead vehicles, we

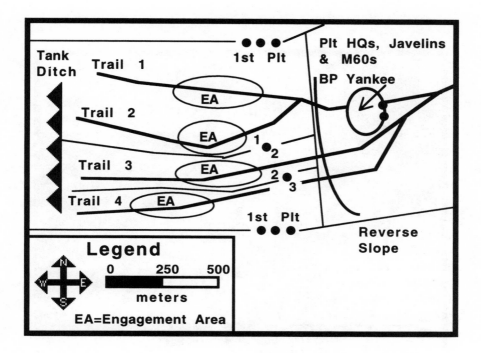

will bottle up the trails and force them to stop and dismount their infantry. This will gain time for us to withdraw to BP Yankee."

"Right," Piper said. "If they dismount infantry our artillery will have an easy target. Stopping their lead vehicles could convince them to reconsider their attack through Wadi Al Sirree."

"I'll have two M60 machine guns and two Javelins at BP Yankee to stop them if they get by you. Trails 1 and 2 join at the reverse slope. This is where our main effort will be," Davis explained. "No one will withdraw without my order. I'll order each of you to pull back to Position Yankee after we block the trails."

"I'll be at Yankee with the lieutenant," Sergeant Mark interjected. "My radio will be on the fire direction center's frequency. Call your fires in to Lieutenant Davis and I'll relay them on the artillery net."

"I'll use my radio to communicate with each of you," Davis continued. "Now and then I'll have to switch frequencies to call Captain Bludgell."

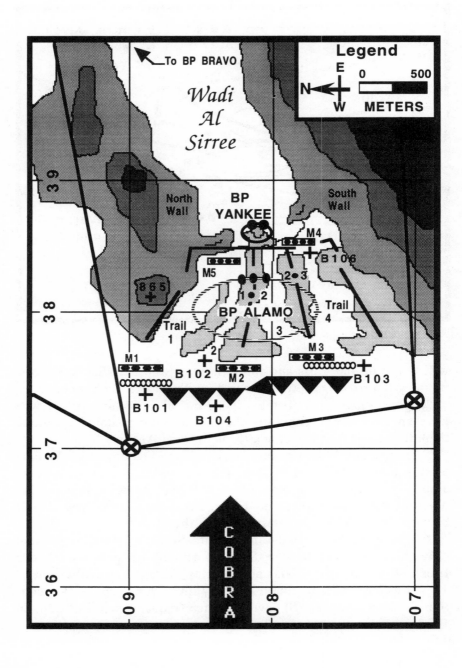

"We have to stop the enemy in the trails," Piper emphasized. "Each squad leader will have to figure out the best positions to fight from. If we can stop the enemy in each engagement area, we can win."

The squad leaders and machine gunners listened carefully as the lieutenant finished his operations order. Each man knew that his life depended on the skill with which he executed the orders.

"If everything goes the way I plan, the enemy will attack along the north wall, along Trail 1 or 2. This is the narrowest approach. Trail 1 or 2 leads him into our heaviest antitank fires, in engagement areas just west of Position Yankee. This is where I want to trap him," Davis continued.

"But sir, if you put all the Javelins in the north, he may come from the south. Shouldn't we put one in the south?" Sergeant Tyler asked.

"Negative," Davis replied. "We only have two Javelins. Mass is essential. Two are barely enough. One would be nearly worthless."

Sergeant Tyler nodded his acceptance. The other squad leaders indicated their agreement with similar gestures.

"Sergeant Piper, have I forgotten anything?" asked Davis.

"Yes, sir. We've already laid a point minefield, M3, in front of Trail 4. Tonight M2 will be put in, then M1. Mark them carefully and you can arm the mines in the morning. We'll start M4 tomorrow morning. We'll put up M5 last."

Several men sighed. They were tired. Now they faced another night without rest.

Little minds try to defend everything at once, but sensible people look at the main point only; they parry the worst blows and stand a little hurt if thereby they avoid a greater one. If you try to hold everything, you hold nothing.

Frederick the Great

"What if they break through Trail 2, and I can't reach you on the radio?" Sergeant Jordan asked. "I only have eight AT4s to stop them. After eight shots, I'm out of tank-killing ammunition. What do I do then?"

"I'll be waiting at BP Yankee," Davis said. "Besides, if you get eight hits, no one's coming through that trail. Once you run out of antitank ammunition and can't reach me, take up the best positions you can and use small-arms and machine-gun fire. This will keep their armored vehicles buttoned up. Tankers can't see much when they have to close all the hatches. Keep shooting at them and stay put and fight until I call for you to join me on BP Yankee."

The men were silent. This mission demanded that each squad support the other without being able to view the entire battlefield. It was like fighting in four alleys all at the same time. It could work, but it required good shooting and determined defenders.

"I promise you no one will be left behind," Davis said earnestly.

"We need to put up more wire in front of Minefield M3. A couple of strong triple-strand barriers, reinforcing the minefield, will help turn the enemy toward the north," Piper added.

"I'll take care of it tonight," answered Sergeant Mizogouchi, the leader of 3d Squad. "My men are beat, but we'll have it done by morning."

"Look, I know how tired you all are," Davis said. "We've got to make the most of the time we have. We'll have a full moon for several hours tonight. That'll make the work a little easier. Besides, we have to maximize our work at night."

> One who has few must prepare against the enemy; one who has many makes the enemy prepare against him.
>
> Sun Tzu

Piper looked at his platoon leader. Two men had fallen ill from heat cramps this afternoon. The water had run low as the temperature rose. Davis needed every man he could muster.

"How's 2d Squad doing, Tyler?" Davis asked.

"Both of the men who were medevacked today should be back in two days. Everyone else is fine. I'm lining them up every two hours and forcing them to down half a canteen of water."

"Good. We can't afford any more losses to the heat. How's our water situation?" Davis asked, turning to Piper.

"Lieutenant Sandburg dropped off ten five-gallon cans just thirty minutes ago. He also brought fifteen AT4s, thirty corrugated steel sheets, twenty white illumination flares, and six green and six red star clusters," Piper reported.

"Excellent," Davis replied. "That puts our total at twenty-four AT4s and eight Javelin missiles."

"We could stop thirty-two armored vehicles if everybody hits right the first time," Piper said.

"I'll be happy if we just stop two or three in each of the passes," Davis said. "Besides, I want you to fire the AT4s in volleys, two at a time at the same target. We'll get better results that way, especially against tanks. So our best tally by antitank fires, excluding mines and artillery, would be more like fifteen or sixteen."

The men fidgeted nervously. The thought of imminent combat was on everyone's mind.

"How about establishing an OP on top of Hill 865?" Tyler asked.

Davis considered the question. He had only a few men as it was and each squad would be defending a separate trail. A platoon could be expected to do only so much. Could he afford to split up his small force even more?

If Davis decides to concentrate his forces, go to Section 25.

If Davis decides to establish an observation post on Hill 865, go to Section 47.

Section 9

"Let's go," Davis said as he adjusted his web gear and grabbed his M16 from inside the fighting position. "We'll get a better view of the battlefield from higher ground."

"Jordan, you're in charge," Piper ordered. "We'll be back in thirty minutes. Leave a fire team to guard these positions and move the rest of the men to the south edge of the tank ditch. Pound in those barbed-wire pickets we got from the company first sergeant. We'll lay the wire as soon as I get back."

Jordan nodded. "Yeah, Sarge. I'll make it happen."

Davis walked to the northwest, down the hill to a narrow, steep trail that led up the north wall to Hill 865. Sergeant First Class Piper, his M16 held at the ready, followed close behind. The men panted as they climbed. The heat was stifling. They stopped halfway up, on a small ledge, to catch their breath.

"Why'd you join the army, Lieutenant?" Piper asked as they stood on the ledge.

"Why? What kind of question is that, Sergeant?"

"Just curious," Piper answered. "You come from a military family?"

"Yes, I do. The Davises have always been soldiers or marines. It's in our blood. I have a brother in the Marine Corps and another in the army. It's what we do. The Davises are warriors."

"Not me. I joined to earn a college education. Once I got in, I found out I liked it. Haven't gotten around to finishing college yet."

The two men resumed their climb, walking for several hundred meters in silence. As the sun rose higher in the sky, the temperature reached one hundred degrees Fahrenheit. Struggling against the heat and the ascent, the two soldiers slowly moved up the hill.

Suddenly Davis stopped and raised his hand to Piper, signaling him to get down. Crouching behind a big rock, Davis raised his binoculars to search the ground in front of them.

"I could have sworn I saw something moving," Davis said in a whisper. "I can't see anything now."

"Where?"

"Over there, on top of that rise," Davis replied, pointing. The two men waited nervously for several minutes. Davis continued to scan the area with his binoculars.

"It was probably an animal," Piper finally announced. "We haven't had any indications that the enemy is in our area."

"You're probably right, but let's keep alert," Davis said as he switched off the safety on his M16 rifle.

Roll the dice.

If you roll 2–4, go to Section 16.

If you roll 5–9, go to Section 17.

If you roll 10–12, go to Section 28.

Section 10

"That's where we need to go," Piper said, pointing at the high ground to the north. "It'll take us about forty minutes."

"OK," Davis said as he adjusted his web gear and grabbed his M16 from inside the fighting position. "I could use the walk."

"Jordan," Piper yelled. "You're in charge. Get a detail to lay those mines. When we get back I'll expect you to have most of them laid out. Don't try to bury them, just lay them on the surface."

Jordan nodded in agreement. "Yeah, Sarge. I'll make it happen."

Davis walked around the northern end of the tank ditch and headed east, with Sergeant First Class Piper, his M16 at the ready, following close behind. The men panted as they struggled up the hill. The heat was stifling.

"Why'd you join the army, Lieutenant?" Piper asked as they trudged forward.

"Why? What kind of question is that, Sergeant?"

"Just curious. You come from a military family?" Piper continued.

"Yes, I do. The Davises have always been soldiers, or marines. It's in our blood. I have a brother in the marines and another in the army. It's what we do."

"Not me. I joined to earn a college education. Once I got in, I found out I liked it. Haven't had a chance to finish college yet. Maybe I'll finish school once this is all over."

The two men climbed for several hundred meters in silence. Davis led; Piper followed close behind. They found a narrow, winding trail and slowly trekked up it. As the sun rose higher in the sky, the temperature reached one hundred degrees Fahrenheit. A huge black crow flew overhead, interrupting the quiet of the desert with its portentous cawing.

Suddenly Davis stopped and raised his hand, signaling for Piper to take cover. Crouching behind a big rock, Davis raised his binoculars to search the ground ahead.

"I could have sworn I saw something moving," Davis said in a whisper. "Where?"

"Over there, on top of that rise," Davis said, pointing. "I don't see anything now."

The two men waited for several minutes. Davis continued to scan the area with his binoculars.

"It was probably a crow," Piper replied. "We haven't had any reports that the enemy is in our area."

"Maybe so, but let's keep alert," Davis said as he switched off the safety on his M16 rifle.

Roll the dice.

If you roll 2–4, go to Section 16.

If you roll 5–12, go to Section 17.

Section 11

"Negative. We don't need to. I can see fine from here," Davis said, trying to take charge of the situation. He unfolded his map and beckoned for the platoon sergeant to bend down as he pointed out key terrain features on the map. "Besides, I need the time to complete the artillery plan with Sergeant Mark."

Piper, his mouth full of chewing tobacco, spat a thin, dark brown string into the dust. "OK," he said. "I'll get the men to work on the minefields."

The platoon continued working. Davis and Sergeant Mark finished their artillery plan. Minefields M1 and M2 were completed on the flanks of the tank ditch. Wire was strung along the west side of the ditch to keep the enemy infantry and sappers out of the obstacle. Piper sighted the machine guns and Javelins of the headquarters section. The rest of the platoon continued to dig and improve their fighting positions. Piper kept the platoon working throughout the day, squeezing every minute of preparation out of the available time.

Night arrived in slow, colorful stages. First the sun glowed orange-red as it sank over the horizon. Then the shimmering heat of the day was suddenly cooled by a comfortable breeze. The western horizon became gorgeous hues of orange, red, and yellow. For a moment, Davis forgot about the task at hand. He sat in awe and marveled at the beauty of the celestial spectacle playing out before him. Then his thoughts turned to preparations for the battle that lay ahead.

The BP was almost complete except for the requirement for overhead cover on the top of each fighting position. Davis hoped that the company XO, First Lieutenant Sandburg, would come through with the building materials he had promised at the company operations order meeting.

Davis contemplated his combat power. He had a total of thirty-eight men, including two Javelin gunners with their ammunition bearers, two M60 machine gunners and their ammunition bearers, and his two-man forward observer team. That left twenty-eight other men to fire AT4 antitank rockets, squad automatic weapons, and M16 rifles. That was all he had. He hoped that it would be enough.

The moon shone brightly, making the hard work of laying wire and placing antitank mines a little easier. The desert was an eerie scene in the bright moonlight, a world of half-lit shadows. After a while, Davis discovered that he could operate in the dim light almost as well as in the day. More importantly, it was much cooler.

Around midnight, the noise of artillery became more discernible. Sporadic cannon fire pounded the ground far to the west.

Davis observed the quiet desert night with his night-vision-goggles. The company radio net was filled with routine reports, interrupted by a few intelligence updates from battalion that were passed over the command net by the company XO.

Sometime after midnight Davis settled into his position, hoping for a few minutes' rest. He had pushed himself and his men hard in the hot desert sun. More than anything, he looked forward to a few hours' sleep. With Cowper pulling guard, he leaned back in his fighting position and quickly dozed off.

"Sir, it's Sergeant Mizogouchi on the radio," Cowper said in a zombielike voice as he shook his lieutenant.

Davis twitched, surprised out of his sleep. Slowly he gained his senses and grabbed the radio handset from Cowper.

"One-Six, this is One-Three. Over," Mizogouchi called on a squad radio to the platoon leader.

"This is One-Six. Send it. Over," Davis replied.

"I hear an engine. I can't see a vehicle, but I hear it," Mizogouchi reported.

"Roger. It could be a friendly allied armored car. They're supposed to be in front of us to the west. Keep observing and call me as soon as you can determine a location."

"Roger, One-Six."

Tense, quiet minutes ticked by into hours. Everyone strained to observe the phantom enemy that Mizogouchi had reported. No one saw or heard anything, and no other action was reported.

If that was an enemy reconnaissance vehicle, Davis reflected, he certainly was careful not to blunder into our positions. Could he know where our positions are? Do they have someone watching us? How else could he have avoided being seen? Hell, what am I saying? It was probably Mizogouchi's imagination.

Davis checked his watch and waited, searching to the west for any indication of the enemy. The night passed slowly. He had always been told that the hardest part of any battle was the waiting. Now he realized that it wasn't so much the waiting as it was the thinking. Your mind plays out all your fears when you're sitting in a foxhole, thousands of miles from home, peering out at the dark. Nerves quickly get on edge as you expect to be in mortal combat at any second.

Am I sure that my men can stop the enemy from infiltrating our positions? Davis thought. Can I block the enemy in Wadi Al Sirree if he decides to attack down Axis Cobra? Have I put up enough mines and wire?

A thousand questions circulated in his head. He looked at his watch. It was now 0340. He lay down with the receiver pressed to his ear.

*   *   *

"Wake up, Lieutenant," Sergeant Piper said as he nudged his platoon leader.

"Huh? What the hell?" Davis mumbled, groggy from lack of sleep. He was sitting in his two-man fighting position with a poncho liner pulled over his body.

"Sir, it's already 0630. Time to inspect our positions," Piper replied, dropping a brown MRE ration into his platoon leader's foxhole. "You must have nodded off right before stand-to."

"Shit! Sergeant, why didn't you get me up?" Davis protested feebly.

"Don't worry, sir. I reported to the commander on time. Everything is going fine. You worked your butt off last night. You needed a couple of extra hours' sleep. We'll all need it tomorrow if the enemy attacks."

Davis rubbed his tired eyes and then reached for the MRE that the sergeant had thrown at his feet. Now that it was daylight he would have to double-check each position.

"What about Mizogouchi's report of an enemy vehicle last night?" asked Davis.

"We didn't have any other reports all night," Piper reported. "Lieutenant, he never saw anything, he just thought he heard something. Noise carries far in the desert at night. It was probably a case of the first battle nerves."

Davis opened his MRE and surveyed the contents. "Corned beef hash again," he complained.

"You never had it so good!" Piper said with a devilish grin. "By the way, while you were sleeping the battalion destroyed a BRDM in the north. It got all the way into the tank battalion sector before it was knocked out."

"Damn. That's pretty good reconnaissance. How did they get by our entire battalion?" Davis said, finally gaining full consciousness.

"Don't know. Maybe we weren't looking for the obvious. Maybe they came straight down the road," Piper mused. "The latest intel from battalion is that the enemy overran an allied reconnaissance company that was screening to the west about forty klicks from here. Things may get pretty exciting very soon."

"So, did our allies fight or did they just turn tail?" Davis asked.

"They fought," Piper replied, spitting a wad of chewing tobacco juice on the dust. "The XO came by while you were sleeping and dropped off thirty corrugated steel sheets, twenty antitank mines, about six hundred sandbags, ten additional AT4s, and thirty-five gallons of water."

"I'll never say another bad thing about company headquarters," Davis said with a smile.

"Guess what else the XO told me."

Davis shrugged his shoulders. "We're all going on R and R in Bahrain in the next two hours?"

"Shit, Lieutenant, get real," Piper said with a smirk. "Bludgell named our position here BP Alamo."

"Alamo?" Davis said, looking up at the sergeant as he swallowed a spoonful of cold corned beef hash. "Is that supposed to be funny?"

This time Piper shrugged. "You know the CO. He's from Texas. Don't ask me how his mind works."

Davis looked over at Sergeant Mark and the two RTOs. They were sprawled on the ground, their poncho liners covering them, sound asleep. Cowper slept on his side, with his precious radio near his chest.

"The men are beat, sir," Piper protested, anticipating Davis's need to act. "Tired soldiers won't fight well."

Davis knew that the soldiers were tired. Conservation of their strength was critical.

"I recommend we let everyone catch a little sleep. We're ahead of schedule. The war can wait." The muffled rumble of distant explosions could be heard way off to the west.

"Hey, Sergeant, I'm tired, too."

"Sir, if you don't give these men a few hours' rest, there may not be anyone awake to defend this position tonight."

Davis looked at his watch. The cumulative effect of hard work, heat, and fear had worn the men ragged. Davis knew that his men needed rest. Maybe Piper was right.

Davis has to decide!

If Davis decides to let the men rest, go to Section 12.

If Davis decides to continue working, go to Section 13.

Section 12

"OK, we'll sack out for three hours," Davis decided. "Post security and wake everyone up at 1030."

"Yes, sir," Piper said. Fatigue edged his voice as he continued. "As soon as we get up, we'll finish our holes and put up the overhead cover."

The tired soldiers rigged ponchos over their fighting positions to provide shade from the rising sun. Knowing that their buddies were standing guard, they fell asleep. Sergeant Piper and a few men pulled perimeter security.

Davis pulled out the remainder of his MRE from the brown plastic package. MREs weren't the epitome of fine dining, Davis thought, but they beat going hungry. He looked over BP Alamo as he munched on the barely edible breakfast. Most of the soldiers were already sleeping. The BP was quiet as a graveyard.

After three hours had elapsed, Piper walked over to Davis's position, carrying a map in his left hand.

"Let's conduct a leader's recon," Piper said enthusiastically. "I'll put Sergeant Jordan in charge here. I think we could get a great view of our sector from Hill 865."

If Davis decides not to conduct a leader's reconnaissance to Hill 865, and stays at the battle position, go to Section 53.

If Davis decides to conduct a leader's reconnaissance to Hill 865, go to Section 96.

Section 13

Davis shook his head. "Not yet. We have plenty of mines left to lay. They won't stop tanks unless we set and arm them."

"Yes, sir," Piper agreed. "I guess this heat is getting to me. I'll tell the squad leaders that they can start their rest plans after all the minefields are laid. That'll keep 'em going."

"Good idea," the lieutenant replied with a grin. "You can tell 'em that I'll be checking each fighting position this afternoon. The Javelin and machine-gun positions better be perfect."

Piper smiled a weary smile and then shouted for the squad leaders, who slowly trudged over to him. Like a padre in church, Piper delivered a sermon that was direct and full of fire and brimstone. After a few minutes Piper dismissed his loyal congregation, and the squad leaders, energized by the platoon sergeant's exhortations, scurried off to accomplish their tasks.

The desert sun bore down on them, making each job difficult. The sweat-stained men moved about the position like zombies. Piper was everywhere, checking, cajoling, and inspecting. He verified the overhead cover by making two men jump on the roof of every fighting position. If the cover didn't hold the weight of two men, it wouldn't be much protection against enemy artillery.

Sergeant Piper walked carefully over to Davis's fighting position. Davis was sitting outside his hole, watching the last stages of the sunset.

"The squads have completed their positions," Piper announced. "We have a few more mines to lay, but all in all, we're ready."

"I've been thinking about tomorrow," Davis said, looking up at his platoon sergeant. Piper kneeled down on one knee.

"Shoot, Lieutenant, what's on your mind?"

"Are we sure that we can stop the enemy from infiltrating into our sector?" Davis questioned. "Can we block him in this valley if he decides to attack down Axis Cobra? Have we put up enough mines and wire?"

78

"Don't get the jitters now, sir," Piper said with a broad smile. "All we have to do is stop them at the tank ditch. We'll be fine. Trust me."

> An obstacle loses 50 per cent of its value if you stand back from it, allowing the enemy to reconnoiter the approaches and subsequently to cross without interference.
> Field Marshal Sir Bernard L. Montgomery

"Sure, you're right," Davis said, nodding his head.

"We're almost ready," Piper insisted. "This is turning into a textbook position. We've laid out our weapons to cover the dead space and every approach into the valley. It took a lot of work, but we've dug nineteen two-soldier fighting positions, each position with a corrugated steel roof, reinforced with rocks and four layers of sandbags. We have open firing ports dug into the flanks of every bunker for antitank weapons to fire to the front and the oblique."

"On top of that we laid more mines and barbed wire than I can count," Davis added. "I don't know what's bugging me. I guess I'm just a little nervous."

"We all are, sir. Don't worry, you'll do fine, just fine. Well, I better troop the line and make some last-minute checks with the squad leaders. I'll order them to execute a sleep plan and rotate the men's duties between sleeping, working, and security. We still have jobs to do."

Piper walked off into the dark. Davis settled into his fighting position. Cowper sat patiently nearby, ready to offer his lieutenant the radio handset at the first sign of trouble.

The night hours passed slowly, uneventfully. The company radio net was filled with routine reports, interrupted by a few intelligence updates that were passed over the company command net by the company XO.

Hell, I wish I'd thought of digging some crawl trenches between our positions, Davis reflected. Then again, in this rocky soil such a task would have taken us forever.

During the night, the sky far to the west, behind the jagged ridge, was lit up by the bright flash of explosions and the eerie glow of artillery flares. Davis was tense with anticipation but relieved to know that the flashes to the west were still far away.

Section 13

"One-Four, this is One-Six," Davis whispered into the transmitter of his radio. "Do you see anything?"

"Negative. Don't worry, One-Six, I don't think they'll attack at night," Piper replied with the quiet confidence of a veteran soldier. "They'll probably sign a cease-fire agreement tomorrow, anyway."

Maybe Piper's right, Davis thought. Hell, once they find out they're up against the United States, they'll probably head for home.

The night wore on without incident. The reports sent over the radio remained routine. Davis lay down with the receiver of Cowper's radio pressed to his ear.

"One-Six, this is One-Three. Over," an excited Sergeant Mizogouchi announced over his squad radio to the platoon leader.

"This is One-Six. Send it. Over," Davis replied.

"I hear helicopters. They sound pretty far away," Mizogouchi reported.

"Can you tell where they are? Do you see them? Over."

"Not sure. The sound is off to the southwest. Over."

Davis paused before answering. Damn, I wish he could have seen those helicopters, Davis thought. Where did they go? Was it a troop-carrying helicopter or a scout? Ours or theirs? Hell, they're probably friendly and nobody told us they were in the area. Mizogouchi is just jumpy. He's hearing things again, like last night.

"The sound's gone now," Mizogouchi added.

"Call me if you sight anything. Out," Davis ordered.

The hours passed. At 0300 the rumble of distant artillery foretold that the time of battle was drawing near. Suddenly Davis heard the distinct crack of grenades and machine guns to the east.

"Cowper, get company headquarters on the radio."

Cowper tried in vain for several minutes to call Captain Bludgell. "Sir, I can't get anyone on the radio. I think we're being jammed."

Why can't I reach the company commander? Davis contemplated the consequences of this event. Could the enemy be attacking in our rear? Had they conducted an air assault? If so, why did they leave me alone?

The night sky faded into a light shade of gray. The sound of battle in the east rose to a crescendo. The sky near BP Bravo was illuminated by tracers and explosions.

The tension mounted. The noise of artillery started again. The sounds of big guns and rockets pounding the ground could be heard now to the west. The steady drumbeat of artillery shells grew ominously nearer with each passing minute.

It doesn't look like the enemy was eager to sign a cease-fire, Davis thought. Every indication is that combat is imminent. I can sense that the men are nervous. Fear is in the air. You can't see it or smell it, but it's there, as real as if it were made of flesh and blood.

Billows of black smoke could be seen on the western horizon. Davis put down his night-vision goggles and trained his binoculars in the direction that he expected the enemy armor to advance. The ground to the west of BP Alamo sloped downward for four kilometers, then gradually rose for an additional four kilometers to a jagged ridge on the western horizon. Between BP Alamo and this ridge was nothing but empty desert. As the enemy approached from the west, he would have to cross this open space against the brigade's deep fires. Unfortunately, Davis knew how weak those deep fires were: only one battalion of 155mm artillery and a few sorties from navy F/A-18s and air force A-10s. The carrier-based F/A-18s had a short loiter time because of the distance of the battlefield from the aircraft carrier that they called home. The A-10s, on the other hand, could stay longer because they were from an allied air base forty kilometers to the south. The A-10s, potent tank killers, had the disadvantage of being old, big, and slow. With the improvements in air defense systems in the past years, the A-10's survivability was always a matter of pilot skill and luck.

Maybe the enemy won't attack through my valley, Davis thought.

A flight of F/A-18s screamed overhead, flying low over Wadi Al Sirree. The aircraft headed west to attack the advancing enemy columns.

"Sir, I've been eavesdropping on the artillery net," Sergeant Mark reported. "All the long-range stuff is engaging the enemy. We'll be in battle with the main force soon."

The sound of outgoing 155mm artillery shells punctuated Mark's words. The rounds arced high overhead and exploded to the west, detonating with a rumble that shook the ground in Wadi Al Sirree. A pair of F/A-18s roared across the sky to the north, dropping cluster bombs on the advancing enemy armor.

Section 13

I hope the brigade punches the hell out of them, Davis thought. We need every chance we can to even these odds.

> In offensive and defensive tactical actions, commanders fight the enemy throughout the depth of his disposition with fires and with attacks on his flanks and rear. They attack committed and uncommitted forces and synchronize the attack of enemy artillery in depth with close operations. Such in-depth operations degrade the enemy's freedom of action, reduce his flexibility and endurance, and upset his plans and coordination.
>
> FM 100-5, *Operations*, 1993

The sound of multiple explosions resonated from the area beyond the jagged ridge to the west.

"That's our stuff," Davis shouted to his men. "Get ready. The enemy will be on us in about twenty minutes."

Davis focused his binoculars on the exits of the jagged ridge, eight kilometers to the west. The passes were filled with dust and smoke. Suddenly, dark objects began racing out of each pass. Then scores of vehicles, moving in high-speed columns, quickly exited the narrow defiles and raced east across the broken desert terrain.

"There they are," Davis declared, pointing to the distant ridge. Sergeant Mark gave his lieutenant a worried look, then put the radio receiver back to his ear and continued eavesdropping on the artillery radio frequency.

The rumble of explosions increased. The detonations sounded like the strike of a huge hammer, pounding the earth to the northwest. Davis watched with silent satisfaction as one of the lead enemy columns was blanketed with the impact of cluster bombs and 155mm artillery shells. A number of vehicles in this column were struck by bomblets and burst into flame. More vehicles, however, bypassed the wreckage and continued on their determined path to the east.

American planes darted above the advancing enemy formations. A volley of antiaircraft missiles greeted the attacking aircraft. A fiery explosion registered the midair destruction of one of the F/A-18s. Several other aircraft, having already dropped their ordnance, ignited their afterburners and roared back to the east, attempting to outrun the enemy's effective missile defenses.

The sound of outgoing artillery shells suddenly died. The battlefield grew ominously quiet. Our deep operation is over, Davis thought. Now it's the enemy's turn.

"That's it, sir," Mark announced, confirming Davis's suspicions. "The F/A-18s are heading home. We may get some A-10s later. We'll get fires only if we can target a large formation of armored vehicles."

Every man faced to the west, watching the enemy columns get closer. The sound of bursting artillery, pounding a steady path from west to east, interrupted this short interlude of quiet. The explosions moved with precision in an inexorable wall of exploding steel toward the American positions.

Balls of orange flame erupted in the openings to the trails on the western edge of Wadi Al Sirree. The earth shook under the thunder of the enemy's 152mm guns. The bursting artillery shells showered the American positions with rocks and dirt.

"Shit, here it is. Incoming!" Cowper screamed as he dove for the bottom of his fighting position.

A storm of fire exploded over BP Alamo. The shelling rose in intensity to a deafening roar as the earth exploded in fire and smoke. With a flash of crimson, one round after another roared in on the defenders. Engulfed in fire and flying steel, BP Alamo became a burning charnel house.

Davis looked to the west over the parapet of his fighting postions. The shelling was too precise, he thought. It was as if the enemy had an observer targeting each fighting position.

Roll the dice.

If you roll 2–5, go to Section 15.

If you roll 6–9, go to Section 62.

If you roll 10–12, go to Section 48.

Section 14

Cowper jumped under the roof of his fighting position. Davis quickly followed him into the protection of their small bunker.

Seconds later a hail of shells landed all around BP Alamo. In quick succession a volley of eighteen shells smashed into the hill overlooking the tank ditch. The noise was tremendous.

The barrage consumed Davis's senses. Like an angry storm, the enemy artillery attempted to pound the Americans into the ground. Davis hugged the bottom of his hole, helpless to stop the power of the enemy fire. He held his arms over his head as rocks and flying metal tore at the top of his fighting position.

The shock wave caused by the artillery crushed in around Davis, causing his nose to bleed. He didn't know what to do but he had to do something. He had to see what was happening. Quickly he raised his head to the firing aperture. The detonations had created large black holes in the rocky hill. He watched in horror as positions to his left and right took direct hits from the enemy's deadly accurate artillery shells.

Suddenly a round landed close to Davis's position and forced him back to the bottom of his foxhole.

Roll the dice.

If you roll 2–5, go to Section 29.

If you roll 6–9, go to Section 48.

If you roll 10–12, go to Section 58.

Section 15

Through the thick smoke Davis could see two columns of enemy armor racing toward Wadi Al Sirree from the west. A battalion-sized unit of enemy tanks and armored infantry fighting vehicles was heading directly for him. The enemy was about eight hundred meters away and closing fast.

Davis ducked down and hugged the bottom of his fighting position. The enemy artillery fire continued to pulverize BP Alamo. Flying metal filled the air, whizzing past at high speed in a terrible trajectory of death.

The enemy fire is extremely accurate. Too accurate! Davis thought. Either they have an observer nearby or they're using laser-guided artillery shells.

"Sir, I finally got through to battalion mortars," Cowper yelled. "They're pulling back. The company has been shot to hell. They have enemy infantry all over the place. We're on our own."

"Enemy infantry?" Davis questioned. A puzzled look streaked across his tired face. "The bastards must have conducted an air assault in our rear! Why in the hell have they left us alone?"

The enemy artillery fire slackened. The dazed survivors of BP Alamo raised their heads to see the battlefield.

"Medic, medic!" someone screamed.

"Fetterman is dead. So is Gerber," another voice shouted.

"Everybody check your weapons," Piper bellowed. "The enemy will be here soon."

"Get those Javelins ready," Davis stood up and shouted to the Javelin gunners in the positions to the left and right. "Don't fire until the enemy gets to the minefield!"

Two explosions detonated two hundred meters to their front. "Take cover. Incoming!" Cowper screamed.

A single artillery round exploded directly on top of a position on the north edge of BP Alamo. The high-explosive shell disintegrated the position in a blast of fire and smoke. Davis fell over from the force of the blast. His ears were ringing so badly he could barely hear Private Cowper.

"Shit! They're going to take us out one at a time with artillery," Cowper cried, shaking with fear. "We've got to get out of here!"

Roll the dice.

If you roll 2–4, go to Section 32.

If you roll 5 or 6, go to Section 39.

If you roll 7–12, go to Section 55.

Section 16

The two men hiked up Hill 865.

Davis moved steadily, carrying his M16 facing forward, his canteens sloshing at his sides. The sound of distant artillery, almost like the rumble of a thunderstorm off on the horizon, emanated from the west.

"It sounds like somebody is catching hell up front," commented Davis.

Piper nodded phlegmatically. "I'm sure our allies will be running our way soon. I never worked with these guys before, but from what I saw of Desert Storm, they won't hold out long."

"Maybe so," Davis replied, praying silently that Piper was wrong. "At least our air force will have a chance to soften up the enemy before they hit us."

"Don't count on it," Piper said with a shrug. "In the infantry you've got to take care of yourself. We can't count on any help other than our own company and battalion."

As if to dispute Piper's comments, the far-off hum of helicopter rotors filled the air to the east. Two low-flying choppers, moving several kilometers off to the men's right, chopped through the air, heading west.

"Well, it looks like somebody decided to help. Those babies will sure give 'em hell," Davis announced, pointing to the U.S. Army Apache and OH-68 Warrior helicopter team. Piper didn't answer. Both men watched as the helicopters flew over the western ridgeline and out of view.

The two men finally arrived at the top of Hill 865. Davis climbed onto a large boulder to get a better view. He brought his binoculars to his eyes.

Three shots shattered the tranquillity. Bullets ripped into Davis's left arm, knocking him off the boulder. He dropped his binoculars and M16 and hit the ground with a hard thud.

What is happening? I have to move, Davis thought. He felt a burning sensation in his arm. He was confused. Mustering his strength, he forced himself to stand.

"Get down, Lieutenant! Take cover!" Piper yelled. The sergeant jumped up and fired a few rounds in the direction of their attacker. Davis stood in front of the boulder, dazed by his wound and the impact of the fall. Piper climbed up a few steps to drag him out of the field of fire.

The enemy rifles barked again.

Davis felt the impact of the rounds as they entered his chest. He tumbled backward, doubling over.

Piper crawled close, grabbed Davis's boot, and pulled the downed officer behind a large, jagged rock outcropping. The sergeant then spun around on his belly and leveled his M16 rifle in the direction of the enemy fire. He blasted off a full magazine of ammunition.

Time hung in the air, still, frozen. Davis looked up at the clear blue sky. He felt his heart beating fast. He was having trouble breathing. Each gasp for air was a painful struggle. It had all happened so quickly, he thought.

"Don't move, Lieutenant," Piper warned. "We must have stumbled onto an enemy observation post. I'll get you out of here."

"No, I'm—"

"Hang on, Lieutenant!" Piper urged as he changed magazines in his M16. "Don't give up."

Davis couldn't reply. He was choking for air. His mouth tasted of blood and dust, and he felt terribly cold. A thousand questions boiled in his mind. Why couldn't he move or turn his head? Slowly the sounds of battle drifted over him. The muffled blast of a grenade, the slow, deliberate fire from Sergeant Piper's M16, and the short, sharp burst from the enemy sniper rifle were the last things he heard. Suddenly the world went black.

After a few spasmodic gasps, Davis stopped breathing and died.

Go to Section 37.

Section 17

Davis trod steadily, carrying his M16 facing forward. The two Americans hiked up Hill 865.

The sound of distant artillery, an ominous rumble of impending action, echoed from the west. "It sounds like somebody is catching hell up front," Davis said quietly.

Piper nodded impassively. "I'm sure our friends will be running our way soon. I never worked with our ally before, but from what I saw from Desert Storm, they won't hold out long."

"Maybe so," Davis replied, hoping that Piper was wrong. "I'll bet a week's pay that our planes plaster the enemy before he even gets close to us."

"You're on," Piper said with a grin. "I never count on guys I don't know. In the infantry you've got to take care of yourself. If we get help, it'll be from our own company and battalion."

The two men finally arrived at the top of Hill 865. Davis climbed over to a group of boulders that nature had piled haphazardly on the top of the hill. Piper sat next to Davis behind a large rock and took several gulps of warm water from his green plastic canteen.

Davis raised his binoculars and scanned the valley below him. Hill 865 was part of a large ridge that blocked Wadi Al Sirree from view. From 865 he saw a large, open expanse of desert. The view was spectacular. From the northern slope of Hill 865 the ground gently sloped to the north and ended in another steep ridge about twenty kilometers away. A single dirt road, only two kilometers to the north, ran from east to west. This was avenue of approach Viper. Below him, to the north and northeast, Davis saw U.S. forces preparing defensive positions to block the Axis Viper approach.

"We look awfully alone out here in this big open place. Perfect tank country," Davis mentioned. "At least Wadi Al Sirree is more confined. It offers us some constricted avenues of approach to ambush an attacker."

"Yeah, it's just a beautiful place," Piper joked as he crawled next to his officer and took in the view. "It's hard to believe that they're paying us to visit such exciting vacation spots."

Davis continued to search the area with his binoculars. To his left front, toward the west, he saw a single-lane tarmac road that led to the steep ridge on the northern horizon. The ground gradually sloped up to the northwest until it reached another jagged ridgeline on the western horizon. Except for the two roads and a few smaller hills of rock, everything was wide open. The area was like a huge football stadium, about thirty to forty kilometers of open playing field in the center, surrounded by steep walls on the north and western approaches. Davis's platoon was defending the extreme south-central flank of this stadium.

The far-off chop of helicopter rotors filled the air to the northeast. Davis saw two black dots skimming low off the desert floor heading west. He ducked down behind the rocks, exposing himself only enough to view the helicopters. The sound grew louder.

"They look like a Warrior and an Apache attack helicopter team to me. Seems like we're getting some help after all. Sergeant, I believe you owe me some money," Davis declared with a sly smile.

The helicopters passed beneath them in the valley to the north, moving west at high speed. A small OH-68 Warrior led. Another helicopter, a bigger, heavily armed Apache AH-64 attack helicopter, followed three hundred meters behind. The helicopters soon disappeared into the jagged ridge on the western horizon.

"Wait a minute, Lieutenant. I thought you said air force," Piper quibbled. I don't remember you saying anything about any army helicopters." Both men looked at each other and chuckled.

The crisp sound of an AK-47 rifle interrupted the conversation.

Davis instinctively ducked. A bullet struck the rocks only inches in front of him. He quickly hit the ground and fired a burst of M16 fire in the direction of the enemy.

"I'm hit!" Piper yelled as he dropped his M16 and fell down, stunned by the impact of the round in his chest. Piper lay sprawled in the open, five meters away from Davis.

Another round struck near Davis, scattering dust and rock fragments inches from his head. He rolled to his left, behind a big rock, gaining protection from the enemy sniper. Lying on his back he looked toward Piper. "Piper, how bad are you hit?"

Silence. Davis heard only the sound of the wind blowing across the rock-studded hill.

"Piper!" Davis screamed.

"Bad. I'm hit bad," Piper wheezed. "I'm bleeding. Feels like I'm losing a lot of blood. I need some help, Lieutenant."

Damn it! Davis thought. I'm up here all by myself without a radio and no way to get support. I can go for the sniper or help Piper. Which will it be?

Davis has to decide!

If Davis decides to help Piper, go to Section 51.

If Davis decides to get the sniper first, go to Section 52.

Section 18

The platoon settled into their night positions along Battle Position Alamo. Davis scanned the area to the west for one last time before the sun went down. The ground to the northwest of BP Alamo sloped downward for four kilometers, then gradually rose for an additional four kilometers to a jagged ridge on the western horizon. Between BP Alamo and this ridgeline was nothing but empty desert. As the enemy approached from the west, he would have to cross this open space.

Second Squad established OP North on Hill 865. Davis stayed in constant radio communications with the OP and Bravo Company headquarters.

With the aid of individual rifle night sights, the OP could detect light sources far into the distance. His four-power M937 individual night sight was excellent for close-range scanning but inadequate for long-range observation. Unless the enemy sat out in the distance with a flashlight, there was little that the OP on Hill 865 could accurately observe until daybreak. Once day dawned, he could use his seven-power binoculars and his handheld GPS to send accurate spot reports to his platoon leader.

As the night wore on, the company radio net was filled with routine reports, with an occasional intelligence update report from the battalion, relayed over the company command net by the company XO. Around midnight, the sky far behind the jagged ridge to the west was lit up by the bright flash of explosions and the eerie glow of artillery flares. Several artillery shells pounded the ground to the west.

"One-Four, this is One-Six," Davis whispered into the transmitter of his radio. "Do you see anything?"

"Negative. Don't worry, One-Six. I don't think they'll try a night attack," Piper replied with the confidence of a veteran soldier.

You're scaring yourself for nothing, Davis thought. Piper's right. They won't attack tonight. Davis settled into his position with the receiver of his radio pressed to his ear, hoping for a few minutes' rest.

"One-Six, this is One-Three. Over," an excited Sergeant Mizogou-chi announced over his squad radio to the platoon leader.

"This is One-Six. Send it. Over," Davis replied.

"I see an armored vehicle just west of the tank ditch."

Davis sat up, filled with electricity. He fumbled for his PVS-7 night-vision goggles and turned them on. With the goggles against his eyes, he scanned the area to the southwest. A group of three men, near a Russian-made armored car, were crouching near the wire. It was the enemy.

"I got the bastards in my sights," Piper whispered over the radio.

Before Davis could answer, the silent night sky was shattered by a ripping explosion. An AT4 from the far south side of BP Alamo fired at the armored car. The antitank rocket hit short of the enemy vehicle, exploding against the rocks in a bright orange-yellow fire-ball of light and sparks.

The platoon opened up with machine guns and rifles all along the front of the battle position. Grenades popped from M203s and hurtled toward the tank ditch, falling short of the armored car. The startled enemy soldiers quickly jumped aboard their vehicle. The armored car rapidly fled to the west, unscathed.

"Cease fire! Cease fire!" Piper bellowed at the top of his lungs.

A couple of M16 rifles continued to fire in the direction of the burning embers of the AT4 round.

"God damn it. Stop shooting!" Davis yelled.

As if to dispute the platoon leader's order, someone fired a white parachute flare high into the air over the tank ditch.

"Now what? Who in the hell is shooting flares?" Davis shouted over the radio, exasperated at his platoon's lack of fire discipline. He could hear Sergeant Piper yelling in the background to stop firing. "Cowper, change frequencies to the company net," ordered Davis.

Cowper, fascinated by the descent of the parachute flare, reacted slowly to the lieutenant's request. As the flare hit the ground west of the tank ditch, Cowper checked the frequency and changed to the company command net.

The firing slowly died off. An eerie calm descended on BP Alamo.

Piper arrived at the lieutenant's fighting position and reported, his words mixed with embarrassment and dismay.

"No casualties, sir. Someone got excited and fired without permission, then all hell broke loose as everyone opened up. The men are jumpy and tired. We scared the enemy away, but I don't think we got any of them. If we could have held our fire, we might have bagged that BRDM with a Javelin."

"Bravo Six-Six, this is Bravo One-Six," Davis reported over the radio to his commander, nodding to Piper that he understood what had happened.

"Bravo One-Six, this is Six-Six. What's going on over there? Have you got enemy contact?"

"Affirmative. A BRDM tried to sneak through, over the tank ditch. We scared him off to the west. No casualties and no enemy kills. Over," Davis reported.

"Roger," Bludgell responded, sounding agitated. "Don't waste your ammunition unless you have clearly identified targets. I don't want you killing any of our friendly forces who may be out there."

"Roger, Six-Six. It was definitely enemy. Over," Davis answered, embarrassed at having botched his first contact.

"If it was enemy, it was probably a reconnaissance patrol. Stay alert. Out."

"Stay alert and calm," Davis mimicked cynically. "What the hell does he think we're doing?"

"I'll find out who our trigger-happy AT4 gunner was and kick his ass. Then I'll pass the word. Nobody fires unless ordered to," Piper replied.

Davis nodded. God, I'm tired, he thought.

Go to Section 20.

Section 19

Davis again thought of something Napoleon had once said: "Once you have made up your mind, stick to it; there is no longer any if or but—"

"I'm not changing a damn thing," Davis swore quietly to himself.

"What's that, sir?" Cowper asked in a hushed whisper.

"Nothing," Davis replied. "I'm not about to run around in the dark like a chicken without a head trying to find Piper. He knows the plan and I trust him to do the right thing. We'll give Piper some more time. He's heard the artillery and is probably headed our way. Give me the handset."

Cowper handed the transmitter to Davis.

"OP South, this is One-Six. Keep a keen eye on our southern flank. I'm worried that the enemy may try to infiltrate our sector along Trail 4."

"Roger, One-Six. Don't worry. I have a clear view of Trails 3 and 4. It's all quiet now. If anything comes up Trail 4, I'll see it."

"Roger, OP South," Davis answered. "Keep me informed. Out."

Davis waited pensively for word from Piper. Cowper stayed glued to the receiver in vain. Bright flashes and the muffled noise of distant explosions emanated from the north.

Suddenly Cowper perked up and gave the handset to Davis. "Sir, it's Piper."

"One-Six, this is One-Four," the familiar voice of Sergeant Piper echoed over the radio net. "Had some radio problems—just got them fixed. We're moving slowly, being careful to avoid getting lost and blundering into a minefield. I'll arrive in about ten minutes."

"Roger, One-Four, take your time. Everything is OK here. Out," Davis replied, happy to hear that Piper would arrive soon.

"I'm going to try to get some rest," Davis announced confidently to Cowper as he gave him back the radio handset. "Stay alert. Wake me the moment Piper arrives."

"Roger, sir," Cowper answered.

Davis curled up under his thin plastic rain poncho and yearned for the most precious commodity on the battlefield—sleep. After a few moments he dozed off.

"Wake up, Lieutenant," Sergeant Piper said as he nudged his platoon leader.

"Huh? What the hell?" Davis replied, groggy and sore from sleeping in the cramped confines of his position. His legs and neck ached. Hadn't he just closed his eyes a few minutes before? Faint streaks of dawn proved that this conclusion was wrong. The early-morning desert air was blessedly cool.

"Sir, it's 0515. Time to inspect our positions," Piper replied, passing a brown MRE ration into his platoon leader's foxhole. "You must have nodded off right before stand-to."

"Shit! Cowper, why didn't you get me up?" Davis protested feebly, looking at his RTO. The sky was slowly turning a light blue-gray hue.

Cowper, at the other end of the two-man position, merely shrugged.

"Don't worry, Lieutenant. Everything's fine," Piper said with a wide grin. "I told Cowper to let you rest. You needed it. I can't have my platoon leader turning into a zombie on me, now can I?"

Davis rubbed his tired eyes, then reached for the MRE. He was embarrassed to have missed the platoon's stand-to time. Now that it was daylight he would have to get up and talk to his men, reassure them that they were ready, and double-check each fighting position.

"I had everyone up at stand-to at 0500," Piper continued. "And don't worry, I reported to the commander exactly on time."

"Did the OPs report any more enemy contact?"

"Negative, sir. The artillery fire you called must have scared them away," Piper said with a grin. "That was a damn good move, Lieutenant. I always wanted a lieutenant who could call for fire."

"Thanks," Davis replied, smiling, rubbing the sleep from his eyes, "but Sergeant Mark deserves the credit."

"Yeah, well, I'll bet you a month's pay that what we fired at last night was an enemy reconnaissance patrol, aiming to check us out. I doubt that they saw any of the positions we'll occupy tomorrow. Our reverse-slope positions are very well concealed."

"How about our patrol?"

"They're still out. I sent Mizogouchi to the trails with four men. He just reported to me that the northern pass is clear and that the XO is on his way down Trail 1 to meet us. No signs of the enemy. No dead or wounded were discovered where the artillery fell," Piper said. "Battalion, however, destroyed a BMP and a couple of BRDMs last night."

"Uh-huh," Davis said thoughtfully. "That's what those explosions were."

"Right," said Piper. "It looks like Alpha Company destroyed a BRDM. Could have been one of the vehicles Tyler saw."

"Alpha Company, huh?" Davis asked, wiping the sleep from his eyes. "Maybe Bludgell is right. Maybe they'll bypass us and go straight down the road, just as he expected."

"That wouldn't break my heart any," Piper replied with a grin. "I'm going to start setting Minefield M4 in thirty minutes. After that I'm going to let as many men sleep as I can spare. They'll be exhausted by dark if they don't. I'll keep the observation posts manned, to provide us early warning."

"Good job, Sergeant," Davis answered, happy to have Piper on his side. Davis ripped open a brown cereal bar package from his MRE, took a bite, then looked up at Piper. "I'll walk the terrain from the western side of our positions this morning to get the enemy's perspective. I want to see what they'll observe when they enter our engagement areas."

"If you plan to get out of sight from BP Alamo," Piper answered, "you'd better take Cowper and a few others with you for protection. I don't want to lose you now that I know you can earn your pay."

Davis smiled again. The team was forming well, he thought.

"Hey, sir," Cowper declared, pointing to the northeast, "company's arrived."

An HMMWV, with an overloaded trailer slowly bouncing behind it, jolted to a halt on the low ground just northeast of Davis's position. The open-top truck carried two men—the driver and a passenger. The back of the HMMWV was piled high with boxes and rolls of wire.

Dust billowed as the truck stopped. An early-morning breeze carried the cloud up to Davis, covering him, Piper, and Cowper in fine-powdered sand.

The company XO, First Lieutenant Sandburg, slowly climbed out of the HMMWV and ambled up the hill. "Looks like I got here just in time for breakfast," Sandburg said with a grin.

"Jeff, in spite of the dust you just stirred up, I'm happy to see you," Davis said, standing up and extending his hand to the officer. "Care for an MRE?"

Sandburg laughed. "No thanks. Good morning, Sergeant Piper. How's life treating you?"

"Oh, things are just dandy," said Piper, spitting a wad of tobacco juice on the ground. "I've found a home in the army."

The three men chuckled.

"By the way, good job on bagging that enemy OP yesterday," said Sandburg. "You guys denied a very critical observation post to the enemy. God only knows how things would have turned out if that damn OP was up there calling in artillery on you when the enemy attacked."

"Yeah, Tyler's squad did it," Davis replied proudly. "We were surprised to see that they had artillery laser designators."

"So was battalion," Sandburg expounded somberly. "It looks like the bad guys are using their best troops and equipment to spearhead this offensive."

"I agree," Piper added. "The guys manning that OP didn't leave us anything on their map and even zeroized their radio frequency before we zapped them. Remarkable discipline for an army from this part of the world."

"So we're really in for a fight, aren't we?" Davis replied earnestly.

"It appears so," Sandburg answered. "The rumors of a cease-fire here are just that—rumors."

"Lieutenant Sandburg," Sergeant Piper asked impatiently, "what's the latest intel from battalion about the situation in our area?"

"Things are looking pretty serious. This won't be like Desert Shield. The enemy isn't going to give us six months to prepare. Looks like we rested on our laurels too long. His new air defense weapons are already taking a toll on our aircraft. Battalion also says that they have plenty of artillery."

"Any ground action yet, Jeff?" Davis interjected.

"The enemy overran an allied reconnaissance company that was screening to our west. The battle took place about forty kilometers from here," Sandburg announced seriously. "The enemy is heading toward us, as you are well aware from last night's infiltration attempt. Things should get exciting very soon."

"So, did our allies fight or did they just turn tail?" Piper asked, placing a fresh wad of chewing tobacco in his mouth.

"They fought, Sergeant, and died."

Piper spat a wad of tobacco juice on the dust near Sandburg's feet. "Well, sir. Let the bastards come. We'll be ready. You can count on 1st Platoon."

"I'll pass that on to the CO," Sandburg replied, noting the sergeant's determination. "But I didn't come here just to depress you both. I need to drop off these supplies. My borrowed wheels are already overdue."

Davis smiled. Sandburg was a good man.

"In the back you'll find thirty corrugated steel sheets, ten antitank mines, about six hundred sandbags, ten more AT4s, and thirty-five gallons of water," Sandburg announced, pointing to his HMMWV. "There's an additional thirty M21 antitank mines in the trailer."

"Jeff, I'll never say another bad thing about company headquarters," Davis promised with a laugh.

"Sir, you want me to get some of the guys to unload everything?" Piper asked.

"Negative," Davis replied. "These positions won't be occupied when the enemy attacks. We're going to move to reverse-slope positions at the opening of the valley, back to the east. Jeff, I'd like you to take these supplies up to my reverse-slope positions. We'll unload your hummer there. I'll give you two men to take you where we want it."

Sandburg nodded.

"Carlson!" Sergeant Piper's voice boomed. "You and Ward get off your asses and unload three water cans from the XO's hummer. Then go with the XO to BP Yankee. Once you get there, unload all the mines and building materials." Two soldiers shot out of their holes and ran over to Lieutenant Sandburg's HMMWV. Sandburg turned to go.

"Well, I've got work to do. You two take care."

Piper saluted. The short lieutenant returned the salute and tramped back down the hill. Carlson and Ward climbed into the backseats of the HMMWV. Sandburg slowly climbed in and drove off to the east. The lieutenant and his sergeant watched the company XO drive away.

"Get the men to work on finishing their positions," Davis ordered.

"Wilco, we'll finish before nightfall," Piper replied as he took off his helmet and brushed the sweat from his closely shaved head. "Don't worry, we'll be ready."

Davis looked over at Sergeant Mark and Specialist Hutchinson, the forward observer's RTO. The two artillerymen sat in their positions, eating breakfast and brewing a cup of coffee. The smell of their coffee filled the air.

"The men are beat, sir," Piper protested, deflecting Davis's need to act. "Maybe we should take a break. Tired soldiers won't fight well."

If Davis decides to keep working, go to Section 85.

If Davis decides to let the men rest, go to Section 87.

Section 20

The sun rose. There had been no further contact with the enemy during the night.

Maybe there won't be a battle, Davis thought.

"Lieutenant," Sergeant Piper said as he marched over to the platoon leader's foxhole, "it's time we got everybody working again."

It was already 0600. The night had passed with a monotonous tenseness. Davis hadn't slept much. The fatigue was beginning to take its toll. His body ached from head to foot. His eyes burned from the strain of hours of peering through night-vision goggles.

Section 20

"Have some breakfast, Lieutenant," Piper proclaimed, throwing an MRE into his hole. "This is the last of our supplies. I'll have to ask the XO to get us another couple of boxes."

Davis rubbed his tired eyes, then reached for the MRE that the sergeant had thrown at his feet. During the night Davis had told Piper to grab some sleep while he lay awake listening for infiltrators. Davis struggled to get out of his fighting position.

"Relax," Piper said. "Everything's going fine. The patrols reported in from their search areas. No contact. No sign of anyone west of the tank ditch. We must have scared away the enemy before he could drop off anyone else."

"Battalion destroyed a BMP and one BRDM last night in the north," Davis reported. "It looks like Alpha Company destroyed one BRDM with AT4s. I heard the report on the company net last night after you hit the sack."

"Alpha Company got first kill, huh?" Piper commented, crouching down to squat by the side of Davis's position.

"Maybe Bludgell is right," Davis added, opening his brown MRE bag and dumping the contents at his feet. The small aluminum foil packages lay unappetizingly in a mound at the bottom of his fighting position. He reached for the familiar shape of a cereal breakfast bar. "Maybe they're going to come straight down the road, just as he expected."

"Sir, that wouldn't break my heart any," Piper disclosed with a tobacco-stained grin. "I'm going to start setting Minefield M4 in thirty minutes."

"Good," Davis answered as he ripped open the brown cereal bar package and devoured its contents.

"Hey, sir," Cowper announced, pointing to the east, "we got company."

An HMMWV, with an overloaded trailer bouncing behind it, jolted to a halt in the low ground just east of Davis's position. The open-top truck carried two men—the driver and a passenger. The back of the HMMWV was piled high with boxes and rolls of wire.

Dust billowed into a fine white cloud of powder as the truck stopped, covering Davis and Piper.

Lieutenant Sandburg slowly climbed out of the HMMWV and ambled up the hill. "Looks like I got here just in time for breakfast," Sandburg proclaimed as he came within earshot of Davis.

"Jeff, in spite of that dust shower you just gave me, I'm happy to see you," Davis said, extending his hand to the officer.

Sandburg laughed. He nodded a polite greeting to Sergeant Piper and grabbed Davis's hand, yanking him out of his fighting position.

"Any casualties from the firing last night?" the XO demanded.

"Negative," Davis answered, embarrassed over that incident. "We thought we saw something near the tank ditch. The men are pretty jumpy."

"Sure. Just try to save your ammo, will you? I can't be making too many more trips out here. My borrowed wheels are already overdue!"

Davis smiled. "You're a good man, Sandburg."

"I brought you some presents. I overloaded my hummer so bad I didn't think I'd make it. In the back you'll find thirty corrugated steel sheets, twenty antitank mines, about six hundred sandbags, ten additional AT4s and thirty-five gallons of water. There's ten more M21 antitank mines in the trailer."

"Jeff, I'll never say another bad thing about company headquarters," Davis promised with a chuckle.

"I'll get some of the guys to unload everything," Cowper said.

Several soldiers from Davis's platoon gathered around the HMMWV and began unloading the trailer.

"Looks like you had a busy night," Sandburg announced as he surveyed the platoon's position. "You'll need to get overhead cover on each of your fighting positions as soon as possible."

Davis nodded. "We don't intend to fight from these positions. I plan to defend in each of the four trails of the western entrance of Wadi Al Sirree. We'll move to our actual ambush positions along each trail early tomorrow morning. If they try to come this way, we'll block them in these narrow trails," Davis explained, pointing to the west.

"Bold plan," Sandburg replied enthusiastically. "By the way, good job on bagging that enemy OP yesterday."

"Yes, sir, we were lucky he didn't get us first," Piper responded.

"I should have sent out patrols to clear the high ground before I started to prepare my defense," Davis added, assuming responsibility for the near disaster. "Lesson learned."

"Don't be so hard on yourself," Sandburg said with a smile. "You knocked out a very critical enemy observation post and blocked his reconnaissance from getting through last night. I'd say you're earning your pay."

"We should have waited until that BRDM got closer before engaging," Davis confessed. "So what's the big picture?"

"Things look pretty serious. This won't be like Desert Shield. The enemy isn't going to give us six months to prepare. He's already on the move."

"I agree, sir. Those guys on Hill 865 weren't amateurs," Piper proclaimed, shooting a stream of tobacco juice on the desert floor. "Anybody fighting yet?"

"Yes. The enemy overran our ally's reconnaissance troop that was screening about forty kilometers from here. They got pretty badly mauled before they pulled back. Now the only guys to the west are the enemy."

"Well, sir," said Piper, "let the bastards come. We'll be ready."

"I'll pass that on to the CO," Sandburg responded. "By the way, the commander labeled your position here Battle Position Alamo."

"Alamo?" Davis questioned, scribbling the name onto his map. "Is that supposed to be funny?"

"As I recall, the good guys didn't win there," Piper chimed in, a quizzical look on his face.

"Bludgell's from Texas. You know how he is. I guess he thinks that this will be in the history books someday. Don't let it get to you," Sandburg commented with a sly smile.

"If we tried to stop them from the Alamo, we'd all end up like Davy Crockett," Davis replied dryly.

Sandburg laughed. "You're probably right. You've got a good plan. Don't change it now. The old man is convinced that this is a sideshow anyway. He's too busy preparing BP Bravo to worry about you."

"Thank God for small miracles," Davis retorted.

"Carlson! What the hell are you guys waiting for?" Sergeant Piper's voice boomed as he changed his attention to the newly arrived supplies. "You and Ward get off your dead asses and help the others unload this stuff."

Two soldiers shot out of their holes and joined a group of seven other riflemen who were busy unloading Lieutenant Sandburg's HMMWV.

"Excuse me, sirs, I've got to see that those dumb asses don't blow themselves up unloading the mines," Piper said as he saluted and sauntered toward the XO's HMMWV.

"Looks like Piper's in true form," Sandburg said with a laugh, as soon as Piper was out of earshot. "You're lucky to have him."

"Yes. He's steady. He knows what to do. Yesterday, we finally became a team," Davis replied, looking down the hill at the men scurrying around the HMMWV.

"Combat does that," Sandburg declared quickly, then realized that he sounded like he was preaching and quickly changed the subject. "Battalion says that the bad guys have plenty of artillery."

"Here's my fire plan. Please pass it on to the boss," Davis requested. "We'll be ready."

"I know you will," Sandburg reassured him. "Good luck. We expect action tomorrow morning. Battalion still predicts that you won't be bothered. We're convinced that the enemy will attack along Viper."

"I hope you're right," Davis said. "Do you think we can stop him?"

"Nobody knows if he'll fight. He certainly has the potential. He's obviously willing to beat up on our ally. It remains to be seen whether he'll tangle with us."

Piper waved to Davis and Sandburg from the bottom of the rise, signaling that the trailer and HMMWV were now unloaded. The platoon sergeant started walking back up the hill.

"Well, we won't find out by debating it here," Sandburg concluded. "I've got work to do. Good luck, my friend. We'll talk again when this is all over." The short lieutenant smiled, shook Davis's hand, and ambled back down the hill, returning Piper's salute as they passed each other en route. Davis watched the XO drive away.

"Get the men to work finishing their ambush positions," Davis said to Piper. "I want all the mines armed before nightfall."

"Wilco. We need to get our overhead cover straight before then also," Piper replied as he took off his helmet and brushed the sweat from his closely shaved head. "After that I'm going to let as many men sleep as I can spare," Piper proclaimed with a large wad of chewing tobacco in his mouth.

Davis scanned his position and shook his head. "Not yet. Those mines we just unloaded won't do us any good if we just leave them there in a pile. We have to keep everybody working. I want to double-check each position."

"Christ, sir. The men are beat. They can't be climbing up those hills all day and working all night. Maybe we should let everybody rest for a few hours."

Davis knew the men were tired. Hell, he was exhausted too. But the enemy was on his way and would certainly hit them tonight or early tomorrow morning. The muffled rumble of distant explosions could already be heard off to the west.

Davis has to decide!

If Davis decides to let the men rest, go to Section 22.

If Davis decides to keep the men working, go to Section 33.

Section 21

The night crept by, second by agonizingly slow second.

The company radio net was ominously quiet, filled with routine reports and an occasional intelligence update from battalion that was passed over the command net by the company XO. In spite of every attempt to stay awake, Davis nodded off.

Around midnight, Davis awoke with a nervous jerk. He opened his canteen and splashed some water on his face. Looking to the western horizon, he saw the distant flash of explosions and the eerie glow of artillery flares. God, I'm tired, he thought as he struggled to keep alert. He sat against the side of his fighting position with the receiver of Cowper's radio pressed to his ear.

"One-Six, this is OP North. Over," an excited voice announced on a squad radio to the platoon leader.

"This is One-Six. Send it. Over," Davis replied, trying his best to sound alert. The steady, far-off beating sound of helicopter rotors rose from the southwest.

"Helicopters, flying just above the ground, headed our way. Fast!"

Davis didn't reply. He shook Cowper to make sure his RTO was awake.

The sound of swirling rotor blades filled the air. The full moon highlighted several Russian-made transport helicopters as they flew low along the south wall of Wadi Al Sirree, heading east. A lift of four helicopters sped past the 1st Platoon's positions before anyone could react. They appeared to be heading toward Captain Bludgell's BP Bravo.

"Cowper, change the radio freq," Davis ordered, "company net!"

Cowper quickly struggled with the radio, then handed his platoon leader the mike.

"Bravo Six, this is One-Six. Enemy helicopters headed east toward you. We counted four choppers. We hear another group approaching. I'll take the second group under fire."

"Roger, One-Six," Bludgell replied over the company command net. "For Sod's sake, try to stop them. I'll find out if the other group has already landed. You stay in position and continue the mission."

Cowper watched in awe as the second group of helicopters came into range.

"Cowper, now, platoon net," Davis ordered curtly.

Cowper changed the frequency to let Davis talk to his squad leaders.

"This is One-Six. I want all small arms fired in front of the helicopters as soon as they're in range. I'll initiate fires. Watch my tracer," Davis ordered into the hand mike.

"Roger, One-Six," the familiar voice of Sergeant Piper replied.

Davis looked to his left. "Are the machine guns ready?"

"Ready, just bring on the targets," reported Specialist Gerber, the senior machine gunner. One soldier stood erect and held the bipod legs of the M60 machine gun, supporting the gun for its antiaircraft role. Gerber stood behind him and cradled the machine gun in his shoulder, waiting to fire.

Davis put down the hand mike. The enemy was using every trick in the book, he thought. They were trying to land a company behind his positions. The next group of helicopters approaching the valley was probably a second lift. The enemy obviously wanted Wadi Al Sirree.

"Here they come!" an excited voice shouted. Davis watched the horizon with his night vision goggles. He pointed toward the southern flank of the valley. "Fire!" At the same instant, Davis fired a full thirty-round magazine from his M16 in front of the fast-flying helicopters.

Gerber opened up with a stream of 7.62mm bullets. Every rifle and machine gun in the platoon fired on the advancing helicopters. Tracers flew through the night sky, making sparks as they hit the rocks on the side of the south wall to the flank of the platoon's positions.

The enemy aircraft scattered, breaking formation and flying lower to the ground to escape the incoming arc of tracers. The lead aircraft veered violently up and right, gaining altitude to avoid the steep southern wall of Wadi Al Sirree.

The platoon continued firing at the fleeing helicopters. Three of the enemy birds swerved south, then flew due east, high against the southern wall of the valley, out of range of the platoon's small arms. No one could say whether the platoon's fire had hit any of the enemy aircraft.

"Damn it! Didn't even get close!" Davis yelled.

Our positions on Battle Position Alamo are designed to stop an enemy from the west, not from the east, Davis realized. The enemy has landed in my rear. Should I move to our ambush positions now?

The sound of mortar fire began to the southeast.

"That must be Bludgell trying to hit the enemy LZ," Piper yelled over his radio. "We better reposition a squad for rear security."

Davis considered the possibilities. BP Yankee, his reserve location for the defense of the trails, offered a good position for firing to the east. He hadn't planned on that, but surprise is the nature of war.

Do I move now or risk waiting until just before daylight?

Davis has to decide whether to move to his ambush positions and reorient Position Yankee to stop an assault from the east, or keep everyone in position.

A force within striking distance of an enemy must be suitably disposed with regard to its battle positions, being ready at all times to fight quickly if surprised.
Field Marshal Bernard L. Montgomery

If Davis decides to move to ambush positions along each trail, go to Section 23.

If Davis decides to keep everyone in place at BP Alamo, go to Section 88.

Section 22

Davis looked at his watch. The men were exhausted. It had been a tough week. The cumulative effect of the hard work and the fear had worn the men ragged.

"Sir, if you don't give these men a few hours' rest, there may not be anyone awake to defend this position tonight."

Maybe Piper was right, Davis brooded.

"OK. We'll sack out for three hours. Post security. Wake everyone else up at 1030."

"Yes, sir," Piper said, fatigue edging his voice as he continued. "As soon as we get up, we'll finish our holes and put up the overhead cover."

The tired soldiers pulled ponchos over their fighting positions to provide shade from the rising sun. Secure in the knowledge that their buddies were standing guard, they quickly fell asleep. Sergeant Piper stayed alert with the security force.

Battle Position Alamo lay as quiet as a graveyard.

At 1030 Piper got everyone up. The soldiers stretched pained muscles and cramped joints as they struggled out of their diminutive fighting positions. A two-man fighting position makes a poor bedroom. Reluctantly but obediently, the infantrymen left their fighting positions to lay wire, place and arm antitank mines, and fill sandbags.

They worked all day. The effort was backbreaking. The sweat-stained men moved about the position like zombies. The desert sun bore down on them, making each task difficult.

Piper was everywhere, checking and inspecting. He verified the overhead cover by making two men jump on the roof of every fighting position. If the position didn't hold the weight of two men, it wouldn't be much protection against enemy artillery.

The ambush positions along each trail were ready. BP Yankee was dug in soft sand and had to be reinforced by sandbags and rocks. It had taken a tremendous effort, but the platoon was dug in with overhead cover in good keyhole shots along each trail. Each two-soldier fighting position was three to four feet deep. The corrugated steel roofs were reinforced by rocks and four layers of sandbags. Each position provided its occupants protection to the front and overhead while still allowing fire to the front and the oblique.

Hell, I wish I'd thought of establishing some rally points to exfiltrate to in case of an emergency, Davis thought. Well, it's too late now,

Maybe the enemy won't attack this way, Davis hoped. The evening sky faded into a light shade of gray. The tension mounted as the sun went down. All the dread ever known seemed to be waiting somewhere out there to attack them.

Go to Section 21.

Section 23

"Piper! Squad leaders! Assemble on my position, now!" Davis screamed as he grabbed the radio hand mike from Cowper.

"OP North, this is One-Six," Davis declared slowly into the microphone of his radio transmitter. "Listen carefully. Did any of those helicopters land near Position Yankee?"

"Negative, One-Six," the excited soldier announced. "They all landed farther to the east. Somewhere south of BP Bravo is my guess."

"Affirmative, OP North," replied Davis. "Stay where you are and keep an eye on the air assault forces and the western trails. Report to me as soon as you see anything."

What is the enemy doing? Davis wondered. He must be trying to conduct a night infiltration with dismounted infantry to seize Wadi Al Sirree in advance of their armor.

Piper and the squad leaders scrambled over to Davis's fighting position. One by one they arrived to listen to Davis's instructions.

"We've got enemy in our rear, probably attacking the company right now. If we're lucky, they won't come our way," Davis said grimly. "Now it's beginning to make sense. The enemy has launched an air assault to hold the north end of Wadi Al Sirree, the exit. That's why he landed to take BP Bravo. His next move may be to launch a dismounted attack to secure the western entrance."

"Right," Piper agreed. "If his air assault forces are trying to hit us from the east, you can bet that they'll back them up with a dismounted attack from the west as well. They'll try to take us from both directions."

"That's a good possibility," Davis replied. "OP North is watching both ways. I'll use artillery to hit them as soon as they're identified. Mark, do you have contact with any fire support right now?"

"Yes, sir, I got through to the 105mm battery," Mark reported.

"All right, this is it. You all know the plan. Move to your ambush positions along each trail. I'll set up Position Yankee looking both ways. You stop them from the front. I'll back you up and block any attempt by their infantry to take us from the east. If you see a dismounted attack developing, call me ASAP, and I'll call for fires through Sergeant Mark. Any questions?"

Everyone was pensively quiet. The soldiers knew that a life and death struggle was about to begin. Only their breathing broke the silence.

"OK, let's go. Good luck. Call me when you're in your positions."

Each squad leader shouted orders, and the squads quickly left Battle Position Alamo for their individual ambush positions.

Davis assembled his group. Counting himself, he had thirteen men altogether: his RTO, the FO, the FO's RTO, two Javelin teams, two M60 machine-gun teams, and Specialist Eisler, the platoon medic. Davis led his group due east along the ridge that headed back to BP Yankee. The ridge offered the safest route to avoid the lethal tank and antipersonnel mines that the Americans had placed along every possible mounted avenue of approach into Wadi Al Sirree.

In thirty minutes Davis's tired team reached Yankee. Davis sent Gerber and his ammo bearer, Private First Class Fetterman, forward to check out the position and ensure it was safe to occupy. After a few tense minutes the staunch machine gunner returned to Davis's small group.

"It's clear, sir," Gerber announced quietly. "No sign of the enemy. I left Fetterman there to secure the position."

Mark, Gerber, Spellman, Montoya, and Chambers huddled next to their lieutenant.

"Gerber, you and Spellman set up your machine guns facing east, toward Battle Position Bravo," Davis whispered. "If you see anyone moving from the east, fire. Chambers and Montoya, I want you to set up as planned. You've got to destroy any vehicles that come up Trail 1 or 2."

Davis's team quickly occupied BP Yankee, splitting the sectors of fire as ordered. One by one Cowper received reports from each squad as they occupied their ambush positions along each trail. Mark, Hutchinson, Cowper, and Davis occupied a four-man position on a small rise overlooking Trails 1 and 2 on the western edge of Yankee.

Davis waited. The sounds of fighting from the east diminished. The bright full moon slowly arced across the sky, turning the night into a world of half-lit shadows. Gerber and Spellman rapidly dug new firing positions, facing east.

"One-Six, this is OP North. I've spotted enemy infantry moving in column south of the tank ditch. Looks like twenty to thirty. They're heading toward Trail 4."

"Roger, OP North," Davis answered calmly. "One-Three, did you monitor?"

"Affirmative, One-Six," Mizogouchi replied. "We can't see them yet, but we're looking. Our Claymores are ready."

"Don't fire on them until you have to. Let me try for artillery first," Davis ordered. "OP North, where are they now? Give me a good fix."

A few seconds passed as OP North determined the enemy's map coordinates.

"One-Six, this is OP North. They're moving pretty fast. They must not know Mizogouchi is there. Looks like they'll be at target Bravo One-Zero-Three near the south wall in two minutes."

"Roger, OP North. I'll call for fires. You adjust. One-Three, keep your heads down," Davis calmly ordered over his radio. He nodded to Sergeant Mark, who was already talking on the radio with the artillery fire direction center.

"One-Six, they've stopped to get organized before pushing into the pass. They're right on top of One-Zero-Three. For God's sake, hurry up, One-Six."

"Mark, we need it now," Davis declared.

"Roger, 105mm VT in effect," Mark said into the hand mike, disregarding the lieutenant. Completing his call to the guns, Mark turned to Davis. "It's on the way, sir."

"Stand by, OP North, rounds on the way," Davis ordered over his radio, excitement in his voice. "One-Three, we're firing Bravo One-Zero-Three now."

"Shot," Mark screamed.

"Shot!" Davis relayed.

"Roger, One-Six," Mizogouchi whispered on the other end of the radio, "we see the enemy now. I can't believe it. They've formed a perimeter exactly at Bravo One-Zero-Three."

Suddenly the southwest entrance to Wadi Al Sirree was lit by bright flashes. The scream of U.S. artillery filled the air. Bright orange and yellow bursts of VT, variable-time-fused 105mm shells, fell among the attacking enemy infantry.

"One-Six, this is OP North. You're right on target. Keep pouring it on. Repeat."

Mark stayed glued to his transmitter, relaying the firing information as fast as he received it. Davis heard the unmistakable sound of VT ammunition exploding in the trails. The U.S. shells detonated eighteen feet above the ground, sending a deadly array of white hot metal fragments down on the enemy infiltrators.

"I'm repeating fires now," Sergeant Mark announced jubilantly. "Then I'll walk the fires from our last grid to the west. Looks like we'll get 105mm HE and illumination falling one hundred meters west of Bravo One-Zero-Three in a few minutes."

Davis nodded, noting the deadly efficiency in Sergeant Mark's voice.

"One-Six, this is OP North. Repeat," the OP declared, observing the latest volley of artillery shells now falling at Bravo One-Zero-Three. "You're hitting them! Repeat."

The shelling continued for ten minutes—which seemed like hours—and then there was silence. The silence was suddenly more terrifying than the noise of the artillery.

Did we get them all? Davis worried. Has the enemy gotten through?

"One-Six, this is One-Three," Sergeant Mizogouchi reported from Trail 4. "There's no movement at all at Bravo One-Zero-Three. We can hear them crying and moaning out there. If anybody survived, he's wounded or run off. No one is moving east along Trail 4."

"Roger, One-Three," Davis replied, relieved to know that a major threat to his defense had been thwarted. "Good job, OP North. Over."

"Roger, One-Six. Things seem to be heating up near BP Bravo."

Davis could hear the sound of small-arms fire, the thump of grenades, and the crash of muffled explosions from the east, emanating from Battle Position Bravo.

"Sir, I got through to the company. It's the old man's RTO," Cowper reported as he handed the mike to Lieutenant Davis.

"Bravo One-Six, this is Bravo Six-Six Alpha," Captain Bludgell's RTO announced over Cowper's receiver.

"This is One-Six. What's the situation? Over."

"We're under attack. The CO's been hit, and we lost the mortars. Sergeant Rossetti is in charge. I can't find the XO."

"Can you hold?" Davis asked. He could hear the sound of machine-gun fire in the background of the Six-Six Alpha's transmission.

"The shit here is really bad. I don't know if we can hold. Can you help us?"

The radio suddenly went silent.

"Six-Six Alpha, this is One-Six. Over," Davis repeated, trying to reestablish contact. "Six-Six Alpha, this is One-Six. Over."

"Sir, I've lost contact too," Sergeant Mark said. "I've tried all our frequencies. The only stations I can reach are in the platoon."

"Cowper, check out the radio," Davis ordered. "Check the antenna."

"I've already done that, sir. It's OK," Mark said.

"Sir, I can't get anyone on the company net," Cowper added with annoyance. "I think they're being jammed. The ridgelines protect us from enemy jamming, but the rest of the battalion isn't as lucky. We must have only enough power to talk to the close stations."

"Keep trying," Davis responded. "I may need some more artillery soon. Get through somehow. Mortars, 105mm, anything."

"Wilco, sir," Mark replied, buoyed with confidence from his recent success. "I'll find a way."

Should I go to help the company or continue with my mission? pondered Davis. If I leave here, am I disobeying orders or am I saving the company?

Davis has to decide!

**If Davis decides to move to the east to help the company,
go to Section 102.**

**If Davis decides to stay and continue the mission,
go to Section 99.**

Section 24

The artillery swept over them like a violent storm. The shells changed from the ear-shattering detonations of high explosive to the relative bang of the strike of smoke rounds. Huge geysers of smoke blanketed the positions around the western approach to the valley.

Then, just as suddenly as a summer storm, the artillery stopped. It moved off to the high ground along the south wall of Wadi Al Sirree.

"Everybody get ready," Davis screamed. "What are our casualties?"

The surviving defenders of Yankee faced toward Davis and gave him a thumbs-up. Davis surveyed the hands, mentally taking count.

Specialist Gerber crawled over to Spellman's M60 position. "Spellman and Herr are dead, sir. The M60 is smashed."

"Sir, it's OP North," Cowper declared, giving the radio handset to Davis.

"One-Six, I see another column of enemy tanks and BMPs heading to the east. They're just coming out of the trails now. I can't tell if it will follow the lead column. There's too much smoke and dust now. Request permission to pull back!" OP North begged.

Hell, pulling back made no sense now, Davis thought. The enemy is behind me already!

"Negative, OP North," Davis ordered, the emotion showing in his voice. "The bastards have their infantry behind us. I must know if you see them coming our way. Stay in position."

Smoke covered the position. Davis could barely make out the silhouette of each fighting position.

"OK, they're using smoke for a reason. Javelin gunners, use your thermals."

"Sir, we got company!" Gerber screamed as he swung his machine gun and fired a long burst of 7.62mm bullets to the east.

The sound of Gerber's M60 machine gun turned everyone's attention to the east.

Roll the dice.

If you roll 2–7, go to Section 101.

If you roll 8–12, go to Section 100.

Section 25

"We need to concentrate our force," Piper interjected. "If we're attacked, how would they get back down to us? What if we put them up there and then we have to pull out?"

"I agree," Jordan announced. "Our defense will require every man we have. We don't want a single rifleman wasted."

"Well," Davis replied slowly. "I certainly can't leave two men up there all alone. A platoon can only do so much."

"That's correct, sir," Mizogouchi added. "Besides, Hill 865 is pretty steep. Our guys would never get back down to us in time."

"OK," Davis assented. "I'd feel better with an OP out, but you're probably right. We do have good observation from here."

The soldiers went back to work, and the time passed quickly as the platoon completed a long list of important tasks. Positions were improved, target reference points were marked, range cards were prepared, mines and wire were laid. They started building up cover over each fighting position with a thick layer of sandbags and rocks covering each roof. Men worked feverishly laying barbed wire and laying and arming tank mines. The platoon was still digging in and filling sandbags when the sun set.

Davis agonized over his plan. He thought through each step of the battle, playing it in his mind's eye and trying to anticipate the enemy's actions. He wished he had a few hundred more mines but realized how tired his men were. Even if he had more mines, he could never lay them in time.

I hope we don't have a fight tonight, Davis thought. We need some rest. We've worked hard all day in the blistering sun, eaten cold rations for two days, and had precious little sleep. Does everyone go into combat this tired?

The sun slowly dipped toward the horizon. Night arrived and the shimmering heat of day was suddenly cooled by a comfortable breeze. As the sky grew dark, Piper ordered Sergeant Mizogouchi to post security on BP Alamo while the rest of the platoon placed more mines and finished their fighting positions.

The hard work of laying wire and placing antitank mines was made a little easier by the bright moonlight. The dark desert offered an eerie scene of moonlit shadows. In spite of the advantages of working in a cooler environment, the men were still exhausted. More than anything, the tired soldiers looked forward to a few hours' rest.

Davis knew that sleep was a luxury he could not afford just yet. He checked the positions and conferred with Sergeant Piper. Only after supervising the placement of Minefields M1 and M2 did he move back with Cowper, Sergeant Mark, and Hutchinson to their nighttime positions on BP Alamo.

The night grew cold. The drop in temperature was only ten to fifteen degrees, but it felt like winter to the men who had been sweating all day in the oppressive heat. The cold night made Davis shiver.

Am I shivering from the drop in temperature or from the thought that the enemy might be out there, trying to get through the mines and wire to kill us? Davis mused as he reached into his pocket to pull out a piece of candy that he had saved from his dinner ration. Tomorrow we must put in more mines and wire, no matter how tired we are.

Roll the dice.

If you roll 2–6, go to Section 86.

If you roll 7–12, go to Section 97.

Section 26

A grenade rolled in front of Davis's position. Without hesitating, the lieutenant reached for the deadly explosive, grabbed it with his right hand, and pitched it back toward his attackers with all his might.

The grenade exploded in midair, several feet from the lieutenant's position. The shock of the explosion threw Davis and Cowper against the ground.

"You OK?" Davis asked, slightly stunned by the blast.

"I think so. Good move, Lieutenant," Cowper replied as he quickly rolled to his left and started firing again at the attacking enemy.

Davis rolled back to his position, just in time. An enemy soldier was running straight for Davis, blazing away with his AK-74.

The lieutenant coolly pointed his M16 at the attacker and fired, knocking him to the ground. The enemy soldier fell to his knees and looked up at Davis, surprised and confused. Davis fired again and the man fell facedown into the dust.

Cowper fired his M203. The 40mm grenade detonated in the middle of an attacking enemy squad. When the smoke cleared, the enemy soldiers lay sprawled on the ground, a grotesque testimony to the power of the 40mm fragmentation grenade.

Gerber's machine gun opened up again on the stunned enemy. Pinned down by the fire, the attackers sought shelter in a shallow wadi. Gerber's tracers sliced through the darkness like a laser beam in the night, cutting down the figures who dared to dart for the protection of the south wall of Wadi Al Sirree. Gerber then changed his aim point and raked the enemy infantry hiding in the ditch. His steady bursts of 7.62mm bullets hit one enemy soldier after another. After several more seconds the enemy riflemen were silenced.

The enemy attack had been stopped. The Americans held their fire.

Wounded men, crawling for dead space from the searching machine-gun bullets, moaned in mortal pain from the shallow wadi.

"La tear mee. Arjook. Sa ednee," an enemy soldier cried in Arabic. "Ana jaree."

"Surrender!" Davis ordered, standing and holding up his arm to warn his men not to shoot.

A man stood up from the ditch and fired a submachine gun at Davis, spraying the dirt in front of him.

Cowper immediately fired a 40mm grenade. The explosion ripped through the crowded enemy sanctuary. Without orders, Davis's men opened fire. They fired furiously, savagely, at the dark shapes hugging the ground. They didn't stop until their magazines were empty.

"Cease fire!" Davis yelled. A few M16s fired several more shots. The blood lust and fear were strong. "Cease fire!"

There was no sign of life from the clump of enemy soldiers in the wadi.

"I wonder what *la tear mee* means," Cowper exclaimed, loud enough for Davis to hear.

No one answered him. The battlefield was quiet. Davis rubbed his tired eyes. Daylight was quickly approaching.

I've got to contact Bludgell and tell him what has happened, Davis thought. The enemy will be upon us soon.

Davis looked at his watch. It was 0458.

"Cowper, try to get the CO on the line," Davis ordered.

Cowper attempted to reach the company commander. Failing to make contact, he checked the radio. He disconnected the antenna and the connections and felt the radio for punctures. Taking the hand mike, he made several attempts to reach company headquarters.

"No dice, sir. I can't get anyone at company," Cowper complained. "I've tried all our frequencies. I can talk to Piper and the OPs but no one else. I think we're being jammed. We only have enough power to talk to the close stations."

"Keep trying! We've got to get through."

The night sky was fading into a light shade of gray. As the dawn grew close, the tension mounted. The area to the west, beyond the next set of hills, rumbled with the sound of distant artillery. Everyone knew that the time of battle was drawing near. Davis could sense that the men were nervous. Fear was in the air. You couldn't see it or smell it, but it was there, as real as if it were made of flesh and blood.

Davis said a silent prayer. God, my ears are ringing! Please don't let the enemy attack. Maybe the enemy won't attack through my valley, Davis thought.

The sky grew lighter with the flashes of artillery fire on the horizon. OP North reported that he had switched from night-vision goggles to binoculars.

"Sir, I've got OP North on the line," Cowper announced, handing Davis the receiver-transmitter.

"One-Six, I see them in the passes. Here they come!" the OP reported. "Oh my God, there's so many of them!"

"Damn it," Davis yelled. "Give me a proper spot report. Where do you see them?"

"A column of vehicles . . . forty to fifty of them, coming out of the pass at Grid NK353154."

The report was punctuated by the distant bark of cannon fire and the roar of jet aircraft. Scores of 155mm artillery shells screamed through the air, arcing high overhead, filling the early morning with the sound of death. The rounds exploded to the west, falling on the targets reported by OP North, detonating with a rumble that shook the ground in Wadi Al Sirree.

The brigade must be executing their deep operation, Davis thought. They're trying to attrit the enemy before the Threat closes within direct fire range. The brigade's artillery, navy F/A-18s, and air force A-10 attack aircraft pounded the advancing enemy armored columns. From the sounds of the explosions, the brigade's fight was having some success.

"One-Six, this is OP North." He sounded in more control of himself this time. "They're taking a beating. I see three . . . no . . . make that five burning vehicles. Our planes are giving them hell.

"They're still coming, One-Six. The lead of the column appears to be heading southeast. At least twenty vehicles. The rest of the column, probably one hundred plus, is headed east." OP North paused for a few minutes, as if he was confirming what he saw. "I say again. One column appears to be attacking along Cobra. Over."

"Roger, OP North. I understand," Davis said, trying to sound calm. "Continue to report once you confirm they're in the trails. Then call in the targets as we've planned. Over."

"Wilco, One-Six."

Section 26

Davis's worst fears appeared to be coming true. The enemy was sending a portion of his armor to force its way into Wadi Al Sirree.

"Sergeant Mark, relay the report that we just got from OP North," Davis declared to his FO, pointing to the map. "Maybe we can hit him with air support when the tanks are in the trails."

"Right . . . uh . . . I'm working on it, sir," Mark responded hesitantly. "Right now all the CAS is going in for the deep operation."

As if on cue, a flight of F/A-18 attack aircraft screamed overhead.

American planes darted above the advancing enemy formations. The aircraft flew low to the ground to avoid the enemy's lethal air defenses. In spite of this, a volley of antiaircraft missiles greeted the attacking aircraft. A fiery explosion registered the midair destruction of one of the F/A-18s. Several other aircraft, having already dropped their ordnance, ignited their afterburners and roared back to the east attempting to outrun the enemy's effective missile defenses.

The friendly artillery fire against the advancing enemy weakened, then suddenly died away. The battlefield grew quiet. Our deep operation is over, Davis thought. Now it's the enemy's turn.

"That's it, sir," Mark announced, the radio receiver still pressed against his ear. "The F/A-18s are heading home. We may get some A-10s later. We can call for fire whenever we have a platoon or more of armored vehicles to shoot at."

Tense seconds ticked by. Every man faced to the west, watching the enemy columns get closer. The sound of bursting artillery, pounding a steady path from west to east, interrupted this short interlude of quiet. The ground trembled as the explosions of the enemy shells hammered their way toward the friendly positions.

The enemy artillery increased in intensity until Wadi Al Sirree erupted in a flash of fire, rocks, and flying steel that pelted the sides and tops of the fighting position. The turmoil drove the soldiers to seek cover. From the bottom of his fighting position, Davis waited for the shelling to subside.

"I must see what's happening," Davis exclaimed. He rose from the bottom of the fighting position and peeked out of the bunker's aperture.

Davis watched in horror as he observed one of the foxholes on Position Yankee take a direct hit from a Threat 152mm artillery shell. The heavy artillery sliced through the position like a boulder smashing a house of cards. Specialist Spellman and Private First Class Herr, manning one of the M60 machine guns, had been blown to hell.

The shower of high-explosive artillery shells slowly shifted to the walls of the valley as huge geysers of white phosphorus filled the area with smoke.

Davis pressed the hand mike to his ear. OP North was screaming on the radio. "I see another column heading to the east, just coming out of the passes now. I can't tell if it will follow the lead column. There's too much smoke and dust now. Request permission to pull back!" OP North begged. Davis depressed the hand mike. He had to decide.

If Davis decides to order OP North to withdraw, go to Section 34.

If Davis decides to leave OP North in position, go to Section 35.

Section 27

The night had passed with a monotonous tenseness. Davis hadn't slept at all. It was already 0700. The fatigue was beginning to take its toll. His body ached from head to foot. His eyes burned from the strain of peering through the green world of the night-vision goggles.

"Have some breakfast, Lieutenant," Piper said, throwing an MRE into Davis's foxhole. "This is the last of our supplies. I'll have to ask the XO to get us another couple of boxes."

Davis rubbed his tired eyes, then reached for the MRE. During the night Davis had told Piper to grab some sleep while he lay awake listening for infiltrators.

121

"We were probably shooting at critters last night," Piper announced. "There's no sign of anyone near the tank ditch. Maybe it was just our imaginations."

"Maybe we're just not looking hard enough. It looks like Alpha Company destroyed a BRDM last night," Davis reported. "I heard it on the company net after you hit the sack."

"Alpha Company, huh?" Piper commented, squatting by the side of Davis's position. "Lucky them."

"The enemy will probably come straight down the road, just as Captain Bludgell expected," Davis added, opening his brown MRE bag and dumping the contents at his feet. The small aluminum foil packages lay unappetizingly in a mound at the bottom of his fighting position. He reached for the familiar rectangular shape of a cereal breakfast bar.

"Sir, that wouldn't break my heart any," Piper disclosed with a grin. "I'm going to start setting Minefield M4 in thirty minutes."

"Good," Davis answered as he ripped open the package and devoured its contents.

"Hey, sir," Cowper proclaimed, pointing to the east. "We got company."

An HMMWV with an overloaded trailer bouncing behind it jolted to a halt in the low ground just east of Davis's position. The open-top truck carried two men—the driver and one passenger. The back of the HMMWV was piled high with boxes and rolls of wire.

Dust from the movement of the vehicle carried on as the truck stopped, covering Davis and Cowper in a powdery cloud.

The company XO had arrived with supplies and the word that the enemy had overrun the coalition's reconnaissance company that was screening forty kilometers to the west. Sandburg reported that Captain Bludgell had labeled Davis's position the Alamo.

Davis explained to the XO how he planned to fight the battle. His men would man the positions at the Alamo at night; then, just before dawn, they would move to ambush positions. The platoon command post, the Javelins, and the M60 machine guns would move to BP Yankee as a reserve.

The XO asked if Davis had placed an observation post on the high ground along the south or north wall of the wadi. Davis replied that this wasn't necessary because he could see the tank ditch fine from the Alamo. Lieutenant Sandburg was concerned about the level of preparation. He observed that only a few of the positions at BP Yankee had adequate overhead cover. He was also concerned about the large pile of mines near the tank ditch that had not yet been laid. Lieutenant Sandburg left, taking a copy of Davis's defense plans with him to deliver to Captain Bludgell.

Davis felt uneasy. Sandburg had pointed out several weaknesses in the platoon's defense. Time to correct them was slipping by.

Urged on by Davis, the platoon continued working. Sergeant Piper reduced security to two men and ordered everyone to work on the defenses in an attempt to make up the lost time. Even so, the overhead cover on the fighting positions at Yankee was not completed by nightfall.

"We should have worked the men straight through, rather than resting," Davis muttered. "We're not ready."

"Damn it, sir. You can't work twenty-four hours a day. Soldiers have to rest. These men won't be able to fight if they're exhausted," Piper protested. "We can only do so much. Besides, we're more than a match for those ragheads."

"But we need to make up for lost time, just in case they fight better than you think," Davis insisted. "Keep working on the minefields."

Piper nodded and left to brief the squad leaders.

Davis watched the sun sink over the western horizon from his position on Alamo. The company radio net was quiet, filled with routine reports and an occasional intelligence update from battalion that was passed over the command net by the company XO.

Just before midnight, the sky to the west was lit up by the bright flash of explosions and the eerie glow of artillery flares. Davis alerted the platoon. Tired eyes peered out of small openings in their fighting positions. Everyone strained to see an attacker coming at them in the night, but no enemy was observed.

The squad leaders positioned along BP Alamo continued to send negative reports. God, I'm tired! Davis thought, dreaming of a soft bed and clean white sheets. How long had it been since he slept in a bed? Only nine days ago? He sat with his back against the dirt wall of his fighting position with the receiver of his radio pressed to his ear. Next to him Cowper was snoring quietly.

Suddenly, a steady far-off beating sound, growing closer by the minute, indicated the enemy's approach. "Helicopters. I hear helicopters,"

Davis whispered, nudging Cowper to get up. He scanned the horizon with his night-vision goggles.

"Everyone! Wake up. Enemy helicopters. At nine o'clock, moving east!" Piper shouted. The full moon highlighted the Russian-made transport helicopters as they flew low along the south wall. Four helicopters sped past before anyone could react. They appeared to be heading toward Captain Bludgell's Battle Position Bravo.

"Cowper, change the radio freq," Davis ordered. "Company net!"

Cowper quickly struggled with the radio, then handed his platoon leader the mike.

"Bravo Six, this is One-Six. Enemy helicopters headed east toward you. We counted four choppers. We hear another group approaching. I'll try to take them under fire."

"Roger, One-Six," Bludgell replied over the company command net. "For God's sake, try to stop them. I'll find out if the other group has already landed. You stay in position and continue the mission."

Cowper watched in awe as the second group of helicopters came into range.

"Cowper, now, platoon net," Davis ordered.

Another flight of helicopters followed the first. A few riflemen fired their weapons at the fleeting targets with no apparent effect.

Davis hadn't had enough warning time to organize his fires against the incoming enemy.

What will I tell Bludgell now? Davis thought. The enemy's using every trick in the book, landing infantry behind our positions. Now he's trying to reinforce the air assault with a second lift of troops. He obviously wants Wadi Al Sirree.

The sound of rifle fire and the detonation of grenades echoed in from the east.

"Bravo Six-Six, this is One-Six. Over," Davis pleaded.

"One-Six, this is Bravo Six-Six Alpha. We're under attack. We'll get back to you. Out."

The sounds of battle near Battle Position Bravo grew louder. The noise from machine guns and rocket-propelled grenades entered the deadly concert.

Davis waited anxiously for Bravo Six-Six Alpha to call back. The call never came. Precious minutes passed. Sergeant Mark crawled over to Davis's position.

"I don't like this, sir," Sergeant Mark commented, his voice tinged with fear. "I can't get anyone on the company mortar net."

"Yeah, I agree," Davis replied. "Cowper, call Sergeant Piper on the radio and tell him to get here pronto."

Sergeant Piper ran over to the platoon leader's position. "What do you want to do, Lieutenant?"

"I don't know. I wish I knew where the enemy landed or if he's headed our way. What do you recommend?"

"This doesn't look good at all," Piper acknowledged. "Can you reach anyone on the radio?"

"Negative. The company has gone off the air," Davis answered.

"The bastards are attacking the company, and we can't do a thing to help," Piper responded. "We'd better occupy our daytime defense and put out some security to our rear."

"What if he's sent a unit to attack us from the rear?" Sergeant Mark questioned.

Davis paused and considered the possibilities. I should have set an OP to observe the length of Wadi Al Sirree, he thought. It's too late for that now. I don't have anyone to spare. Position Yankee offers the best position to fire to the east and still keep my platoon close enough together to execute my original plan. The question is, do I move now or risk waiting until just before daylight?

Surprise makes it possible to take the enemy unawares, to cause panic in the ranks, to paralyze his will to resist, to drastically reduce his fighting efficiency.
Gen. V. G. Reznichenko (primary author of *Taktica*, the capstone fighting manual of the Soviet, and later Russian, armed forces)

"Squad leaders, assemble on my position, now," Davis shouted, no longer worried about noise discipline. The squad leaders scrambled over to Davis's fighting position and joined Davis, Piper, and Sergeant Mark.

"Enemy helicopters landed in our rear. BP Bravo is under attack. The only reason the enemy would do that is to clear this valley in preparation for an early-morning attack by his armored forces," Davis declared grimly. "That makes us pretty important."

"How's that, sir?" Mark asked.

"We can't do anything to help the company, but we can do our best to stop the enemy from taking this valley," Davis declared with determination. "The way I see it, the enemy may own the eastern opening of Wadi Al Sirree, but we still hold the western edge. I want you to move to your positions now. I'll set up BP Yankee looking both ways. How long will it take you to brief everyone and get your equipment ready?"

"We can all be ready to move in fifteen minutes," Piper answered.

Everyone remained silent. Only the men's heavy breathing indicated that they were there at all.

"OK. Let's go. Move out in fifteen minutes. Call me when you're in position."

Each squad leader shouted orders, and the squads quickly left Battle Position Alamo for their positions.

Davis assembled his group and guided them due east along the ridge that led back to BP Yankee. The ridge offered the safest route to avoid the lethal antitank and antipersonnel mines that Davis's men had placed along every possible mounted avenue of approach into Wadi Al Sirree.

Forty-five minutes after Davis issued his orders, his tired team reached the outskirts of their position. Gerber cautiously moved forward to check out Yankee. He squirmed up a small rise while the rest of the team crouched below.

"Gif, tak adem!" someone on the eastern side of the crest shouted.

"Enemy!" Gerber screamed as he opened up with his M60 machine gun.

Gerber's machine gun lit up the night sky. He expended a full belt of thirty rounds at the enemy in a matter of seconds. Davis and the rest of his team hit the dirt.

Tracers arced overhead as a furious volley hit Gerber. The tracers sliced through the young machine gunner. Gerber's weapon stopped firing and the American rolled down the hill.

"Let's go, get up to that rise. Now!" Davis ordered.

The men rushed forward, meeting their foes at the crest. Davis reached the crest of the ridge and plopped to the ground. He saw enemy infantry running everywhere. They must have reached Yankee only a few minutes before us, Davis thought.

Cowper reached the position next to his lieutenant and was immediately cut down by a stream of fire from an AK-74 rifle.

Davis fired his M16 at the enemy rifleman who had killed Cowper. The enemy soldier took all five slugs. The shock from the rounds knocked the attacker off his feet. Enemy machine-gun fire raked the crest of the rise. One American after another was struck.

Davis rose to take aim and was hit in the shoulder and chest. Spinning backward, he fell off the crest, spiraling head over feet.

"No. I must get up," Davis said as he died, his lifeblood oozing onto the desert floor.

Davis is dead. His platoon has failed in its mission. The enemy holds the entrance to Wadi Al Sirree and may launch attacks into the American flank at will.

One of the major reasons that Davis lost was that he failed to secure his position before he established his defense. In the defense, platoons and squads use both active and passive measures to enhance security. Platoons also add to their security by actions taken to deny enemy reconnaissance elements accurate information on friendly positions. This includes the destruction of enemy reconnaissance elements and the use of deception.

Active measures include the use of observation posts and patrols and the establishment of specific levels of alert within the platoon. Passive measures include camouflage, control of movement, noise and light discipline, and the use of ground sensors, night-vision devices, and night-vision sights.

Davis failed to establish observation posts and send out patrols. The enemy was able to learn about his positions and deploy a heliborne force to seize the key terrain in the western mouth of Wadi Al Sirree. Without observation posts, Davis had no early warning of the enemy's movement. Because he didn't patrol the high ground along the north and south walls, Davis failed to detect the enemy's deep reconnaissance team.

Go to Section 3 and try again!

Section 28

The two soldiers were almost to the crest of Hill 865. The rumble of distant artillery emanated from the west. It sounded like the low, dull roar of a far-off Kansas thunderstorm.

"It sounds like somebody is catching hell up front," Davis announced.

Piper nodded phlegmatically. "I'm sure our allies will be running our way soon. I never worked with these guys in action before, but from what I saw in Desert Storm, our Arab friends don't fight very well."

"Maybe so," Davis replied, praying silently that Piper was wrong. "But they're up front nonetheless. Hopefully our air force will have a chance to soften them up before they hit us."

"Don't count on it," Piper shrugged. "Here we don't have anywhere near the air forces we had in Desert Storm, and we conducted almost a month of air attrition before we launched the ground attack. Besides, in the infantry you've got to take care of yourself. We can't count on any help, other than our own company and battalion."

As if to dispute Piper's comments, the faint hum of helicopter rotors filled the air to the east. Two helicopters sped past them in the valley to the north, moving west at high speed. A small OH-68 Warrior led. Another helicopter, a bigger, heavily armed Apache AH-64 attack helicopter, followed three hundred meters behind. The helicopters soon disappeared behind the jagged ridge on the western horizon.

"Well, it looks like somebody has decided to help," Davis said, looking back at Piper. "Those babies will sure give 'em hell."

Piper didn't answer. They continued walking up a narrow path that led to the top of Hill 865. Davis carried his M16 facing forward, ready for action. Piper remained ten paces behind and watched the helicopters clear the ridge at the western horizon.

Soon their hike ended at the top of the hill. Davis climbed onto a large rock to get a better view. Just as he brought the binoculars to his eyes, he saw the sun glint from an object up ahead. He instinctively dove for cover.

A bullet ricocheted off the rocks only inches in front of him. Davis ducked and quickly returned fire with his M16.

"Where are they?" Piper asked from behind a pile of rocks, firing several quick bursts in the general direction of the fire.

"I'm not sure. There's some kind of position up here!" Davis screamed indignantly. He couldn't see the enemy, but he knew that he had to be close—less than a hundred meters away. Davis fired off four rounds and rolled on the hard, rocky ground to another firing position.

"I'm coming to you," Piper shouted, then he jumped up and fired a few rounds in the direction of their attacker.

The crack of an AK-74 assault rifle filled the air.

Piper ducked down behind the same large rock that Davis was hiding behind. The air whistled with the sound of incoming rifle fire. A few rounds hit the rock, showering the two Americans with dirt and dust.

"Thank God he can't shoot worth a piss!" Davis yelled.

"I think he's just over there, next to those jagged rocks," Piper said calmly. "We must have surprised him. He's probably an OP from one of their division reconnaissance teams."

Damn it! Davis thought. I've allowed myself to get separated from my platoon, and I didn't even bring my RTO.

The officers and men who permit themselves to be surprised deserve to die, and the commanding general will spare no effort to secure them their deserts.

Gen. D. H. Hill, C. S. A.

The enemy fired again.

"Sounds like there's more than one," Piper observed.

"Look, we've got to get them. Maybe we should try to take them prisoner," Davis suggested.

"That's pretty funny, Lieutenant. The way I see it, they're the ones who have pinned us down. Besides, with only the two of us, they've got a pretty good chance of taking us prisoner!"

Davis rolled to his right and fired several rounds in the enemy's direction. The bolt on his M16A2 rifle held to the rear as he fired the last round from his thirty-round magazine. He rolled back behind the cover of a rock and pushed the magazine button on the receiver's right side, dropping the magazine on the ground. Quickly he exchanged the empty magazine for a fully loaded one and slid the bolt forward.

"Well, you're right. We can't sit here all day. Any suggestions?" Piper demanded angrily, changing his half-empty magazine for a fully loaded one.

"You throw a couple of grenades in their direction. Then fire like hell to cover me. I'll rush forward to that rock," Davis said, pointing to a boulder twenty meters to their front. "Maybe that'll flush 'em out. If they move, I'll get them."

Piper lay on his back behind a pile of loose rocks, waiting to roll to the left and fire at his attackers. The rocks next to him shattered from the impact of the enemy's bullets. Dust and stone chips splattered the veteran sergeant.

"I've had enough of this shit," Piper replied with a vengeance. "Let's do it."

Piper then pulled out two M67 fragmentation grenades from the loops of his ammo pouch. He pulled loose the wires of the pins and prepared to throw. He then pulled the pin of one of the grenades and nodded to his lieutenant.

Davis rolled to his right and fired a full magazine of M16 ammunition in the direction of the attackers. Piper threw the first grenade, then another. The grenades exploded and sent dirt and rocks flying into the air. Davis rushed forward at a high crawl, his rifle in front of him perpendicular to his body, while Piper plastered the enemy position with M16 fire.

Davis's heart raced as he crawled forward. Just as Piper expended his last round, Davis rolled into position onto his back.

Davis was now in grenade range of the enemy position. During the rush he had gotten a good fix on the enemy sniper. The enemy had piled up stones and covered the top of the position with plywood, sandbags, and rocks. Davis grabbed a grenade from the side of his ammo pouch, pulled the pin, and hurled it at the enemy position.

The grenade exploded just in front of the enemy position. Rocks and dirt flew everywhere, adding to the shrapnel effect.

"Now Piper, let's get them!" Davis screamed as he rolled to a prone position and fired. One man, staggering from the blast of the grenade, got up to run.

Davis aimed his rifle and dropped the enemy soldier before Piper could fire. Piper rose to a kneeling position and fired three shots from his M16 toward the enemy.

"Good shot, Lieutenant," Piper acclaimed in a vicious, bloodthirsty tone. The sergeant appeared to be white hot with anger over his close brush with death. "Cover me while I check them out."

Davis held his rifle tight against his right cheek, his aim darting back and forth across the area where the enemy soldier lay. He was totally focused. He felt that the entire world could hear his heart beating. Davis stayed glued to his weapon, aiming in the direction of the enemy and covering Sergeant Piper.

Piper crawled forward. There was a long period of quiet as Piper inched toward the enemy position. Suddenly the peace was interrupted as Piper jumped up and fired several quick shots.

"It's OK, Lieutenant," Piper yelled. "Come on up." Davis lowered his rifle and strode over to Piper.

"There were two of them," Piper announced. "This one was destroying his radio and maps when I got him. You got the other, right through the back of the neck."

"Search them. Let's grab what we can that has intelligence value and head back to the platoon."

The dead enemy radio operator lay on his back. Two large red holes punctured his chest. A pool of blood gathered in the dust beneath him, soaking into the dry dust.

"Yes, sir," Piper responded as he searched the enemy radio operator's pockets and pack. "There doesn't seem to be much here. The map's not marked. These guys aren't even wearing unit patches."

Davis stared at the dead man. His victim couldn't have been more than twenty years old.

"All right," Davis commented, his voice noticeably cool and controlled. "The enemy probably knows where we are. At least he only observed our night positions in front of the tank ditch. That could work in our favor. Now let's get back to the platoon and get ready for him."

Go to Section 18.

Section 29

The ground three hundred meters in front of Davis rocked with explosions. There was little he could do except press his body against the hard ground and pray for the artillery to end.

Cowper cringed low in the two-man hole next to his platoon leader. The RTO strained to hear the radio, pressing the receiver hard against his ear. Davis struggled to see. From the slit of his bunker he could observe the enemy at the tank ditch.

I must get some artillery on them, he thought.

"Cowper! Try to get Sergeant Mark," Davis ordered, his voice colored with urgency.

Enemy artillery shells slammed into BP Alamo. Dirt was falling all over them. Dust filled the air, entering Davis's mouth and lungs, making it difficult to breathe.

"No luck, sir. He's not answering!" Cowper yelled frantically, choking from the swirl of dirt caused by the artillery.

Davis grabbed the hand mike from Cowper.

"Charlie Five-Five, this is One-Six," Davis shouted, trying to reach his forward observer. "Five-Five, this is One-Six. Over."

There was no response.

"Damn it!" Davis shouted. "I'm going to Sergeant Mark's hole."

A terrific explosion rocked the ground just meters in front of Davis's foxhole.

"Are you OK?" Cowper shouted in between the roar of exploding shells.

"Yes," Davis yelled. "Wait here. I'll be back!"

Cowper looked at his platoon leader with disbelief.

Roll the dice.

If you roll 2 or 3, go to Section 40.

If you roll 4–7, go to Section 48.

If you roll 8–12, go to Section 62.

Section 30

"I'll send an M60 to Position Zulu," Davis answered. "If the enemy infantry attacks from the east, the M60s will engage them and give us time to reorient our defense."

"Understood, One-Six," Piper answered stoically. "That's the best we can do right now."

"Roger. Call me if you have contact. One-Six, out."

The sound of mortar and machine-gun fire echoed from the east, attracting Davis's attention. He gave the radio handset back to Cowper and yelled for Gerber to move to his position for instructions. Gerber, followed by his ammunition bearer, Private First Class Fetterman, arrived at Davis's position and knelt next to their lieutenant.

"Specialist Gerber, I want you and Fetterman to move to Position Zulu and stop any enemy infantry who try to take us from the east. You know how to get to Position Zulu. Do you think you can find it in the dark?"

The noise of the battle near BP Bravo increased in volume.

"No problem, sir," Gerber replied confidently. "Fetterman and I will take as much ammo as we can carry and head that way now. We'll follow the north wall until we find the holes we dug there. It'll take us about ten minutes to get into position."

Davis considered a moment before answering. "Good. Get there quickly. I don't have a radio to spare, so you're on your own. I'm

133

counting on you to protect our rear in case those helicopter troops head our way. Pick a position where you can hit them in the flank if they come toward us from the east. If anything goes wrong, remember our rally point at the south wall."

Gerber nodded and walked back to his gun. He talked with Fetterman for a few moments, then put on his rucksack and picked up his M60 machine gun. Private First Class Fetterman carried a rucksack with five cans of M60 ammunition. The two men marched off into the dark.

The sounds of fighting from the east diminished. The bright full moon moved slowly across the sky, casting shadows on the rocky ground.

"One-Six, this is OP North. I've got infantry heading up into Trail 4."

It was all beginning to make sense now, Davis realized. The enemy had launched an air assault to seize the north end of Wadi Al Sirree, the exit. Now he was conducting a night infiltration attack to secure the western entrance of the valley. The enemy might have tried to air assault right on BP Yankee if our surprise fire hadn't scared him.

"One-Six, this is OP South. I see enemy infantry moving one hundred meters southeast of Bravo One-Zero-Three. They're coming along the south wall toward Trail 4."

"Roger, OP South. I'll call for fires. You adjust," Davis ordered over his radio.

Davis nodded to Sergeant Mark, who was already on the radio with the artillery fire direction center. He had been trying in vain to reach the mortars. Frustrated by the attempt, he switched frequencies.

"Sir, I can't reach anyone at company, but I've got the 105mm FDC on the line," Mark reported, his voice infused with worry.

"Yes, damn it! Anything."

"105mm VT . . ." Mark requested, calling for variable-time-fused 105mm howitzer ammunition. "On the way, sir."

"Stand by, OP South," Davis ordered over his radio.

"One-Six, they've stopped to get organized before pushing up the trail. Hurry up, One-Six."

"Shot!" Mark screamed.

"Roger, One-Six," a voice whispered on the other end of the radio. "We see them now. Hurry up."

The southwest entrance to the valley was lit by bright flashes as three artillery shells detonated, marking the strike of the rounds.

"One-Six, this is OP South. You're close. Direction two-six-zero degrees. Add one-zero-zero. Enemy infantry in the open. Fire VT for effect."

Sergeant Mark spoke frantically into his radio handset to make the corrections to land the artillery on target. A few seconds passed and new bursts of light exploded to the southwest.

"You're right on target," OP South reported. "Pour it on. Repeat!"

The scream of incoming artillery filled the air. Bright orange and yellow bursts of VT shells fell among the unsuspecting enemy infantry.

Mark stayed glued to his transmitter. The well-trained artillery sergeant relayed the firing information as fast as he received it. The unmistakable sound of 105mm variable-time-fused shells exploding in the trails was the sweetest melody he had heard all night. The U.S. shells detonated eighteen feet above the ground, sending a deadly array of white hot metal fragments down on the infantry below.

"One-Six, this is OP South. Good effects. Keep it coming!" The shelling lasted for ten minutes. One deadly burst followed another. Then there was silence.

Did we get them all? Davis wondered. He waited for OP South to report. The silence was suddenly terrifying.

"One-Six, this is OP South. There's nobody moving in the impact area. Scratch thirty or so enemy infantry."

Go to Section 54.

Section 31

Davis's team moved quickly back to Position Yankee, taking the ridge to avoid friendly mines. In thirty minutes they reached a rise near BP Yankee.

"Gerber, take Fetterman and go forward and check that BP Yankee is clear," Davis ordered in a hushed voice. "Spellman, set up your machine gun to cover him. Everyone else, cover Gerber's move."

The platoon lay on line, fifty meters west of Position Yankee. Gerber inched his way forward.

"It's all clear, sir," Gerber yelled from the other side of the rise. "No sight of the enemy. Come on in."

Davis motioned for everyone to move forward. The soldiers quickly picked up their gear and moved silently into their old positions.

"Gerber, you and Spellman set up your machine guns facing east, toward Battle Position Bravo. We may get some visitors from that direction," Davis ordered. "Javelin gunners, set up to engage targets that try to exit Trails 1 and 2."

The team quickly prepared for battle, checked their weapons, and laid out extra ammunition. While they were setting up, Cowper received a status report from each squad. Sergeant Mizogouchi had lost two KIAs in the fighting in Trail 4. Both had been killed by enemy small-arms fire.

Two men killed! Davis thought. What could I have done better? How many more will die today?

The sounds of fighting from the east diminished, then stopped altogether. In spite of repeated attempts, Cowper could not reach anyone on the company or battalion radio frequencies.

"One-Six, this is OP North. I see infantry heading toward you from the east. Grid follows."

Davis held his breath. It now made sense. The enemy had launched an air assault to hold the north end of Wadi Al Sirree, the exit. He was now launching a dismounted attack to secure the entrance.

"One-Six, this is OP North. I see enemy infantry moving west at NK391078. They're behind you. Must be from the air assault. They're moving along the south wall."

"Roger, OP North. I'll call for fires. You adjust," Davis calmly ordered over his radio. Davis nodded to Sergeant Mark, who was already on his own radio trying to call for fire. Mark tried in vain to reach the mortars. Frustrated by the attempt, he switched frequencies.

"Sir, I can't reach anyone at company or battalion!" Mark reported nervously.

"Try the 105mm FDC," Davis ordered. "Stand by, OP North, we're trying to get the artillery now."

Mark worked furiously at the radio. "Lima Seven-One, this is Charlie Five-Five. Over."

"Mark, any luck?" Davis pressed.

"Yes, sir, I've got 'em on the line," Mark answered quickly. "I'm getting them to take the mission."

"Fire it! As fast as you can," Davis answered.

"Infantry company in the open. Grid NK389078. Request VT. Fire for effect," Mark proclaimed, the hand mike close to his ear. "On the way, sir!"

"Stand by, OP North," Davis ordered over his radio.

"One-Six, they've stopped to get organized before moving to take Yankee. Hurry up, One-Six."

"Shot!" Mark screamed.

"I see them now," Gerber whispered.

"Hold your fire, everyone," Davis announced calmly. "Wait for the artillery."

In a sudden flash, the ground east of Position Yankee was lit by bright explosions. The screech of incoming artillery flew through the air. Bright orange and yellow bursts of VT, detonating eighteen feet above the ground, showered the enemy with white hot metal shards.

"One-Six, this is OP North. You're right on target. Keep pouring it on. Repeat."

Mark stayed glued to his transmitter, relaying the firing information as fast as he received it. Davis saw the terrible effects of the 105mm variable-time-fused shells exploding, tearing away at the attacking enemy. Still the enemy kept coming, rushing forward whenever the artillery fire slackened.

"Fire!" Davis yelled.

Two M60 machine guns blazed away at the enemy infantry. Round after round spit into the southeast portion of Wadi Al Sirree, catching the enemy infantry in a terrible dilemma of death between bullet and shell.

"I'm adjusting fires now," Sergeant Mark shouted. "We'll get 105mm HE and illumination falling in a few minutes. Danger close. Take cover."

The enemy infantry waited for a lull in the artillery, then with a loud shout rose up and charged toward Position Yankee.

"Here they come!" Cowper screamed as he fired an M203 grenade at the enemy. His 40mm grenade plopped into a group of attacking enemy soldiers, knocking two attackers to the ground.

"Everyone get down!" Davis tried to scream above the firing. "Danger close."

Artillery shells exploded everywhere. Davis hugged the dirt as the ground trembled and the sound of flying steel filled the air. The shelling lasted only five minutes, then an eerie silence pervaded the smoldering desert east of Position Yankee. Davis scanned the area with his night-vision goggles. Nothing moved. The effects of the artillery fire had been devastating. We've stopped their infantry cold, Davis thought.

The night sky was fading into a light shade of gray. As the dawn grew close, the tension mounted. The area to the west, beyond the next set of hills, rumbled with the sound of distant artillery. The sky grew lighter with the flashes of artillery fire on the horizon. OP North radioed that he had switched from night-vision goggles to binoculars to observe toward the west. Everyone knew that the time of battle was drawing near.

Davis crawled to the top of the rise on Position Yankee. He could see the top of the ridge on the western horizon. He put down his night-vision goggles and scanned with his binoculars. Davis couldn't see the ground between him and the ridge from his current position, but he had learned it by heart in the past day. The ground to the northwest of BP Alamo sloped downward for four kilometers, then gradually rose for an additional four kilometers to the jagged ridge he was now viewing on the western horizon. Between BP Alamo and this ridge was nothing but empty desert. As the enemy approached from the west, he would have to cross this open space against the brigade's deep fires.

Unfortunately, Davis knew how weak those deep fires were—only one battalion of 155mm artillery and a few sorties from navy F/A-18s and air force A-10s. The carrier-based F/A-18s had a short loiter time because of the distance of the battlefield from the aircraft carrier that they called home. The A-10s, on the other hand, could stay longer because they were from an allied air base forty kilometers to the south. The A-10s, potent tank killers, had the disadvantage of being old, big, and slow. With the improvements in air defense systems in the past years, the A-10's survivability was always a matter of pilot skill and luck.

Maybe the enemy won't attack through my valley, Davis thought.

A flight of F/A-18s screamed overhead, flying low over Wadi Al Sirree. The aircraft headed west to attack the advancing enemy columns.

"Sir, I've been eavesdropping on the artillery net," Sergeant Mark reported. "All the long-range stuff is engaging the enemy. We'll be in battle with the main force soon."

The sound of outgoing 155mm artillery shells punctuated Mark's words. The rounds arced high overhead and exploded to the west, detonating with a rumble that shook the ground in Wadi Al Sirree. A pair of F/A-18s roared across the sky to the north, dropping cluster bombs on the advancing enemy armor.

I hope the brigade punches the hell out of them, Davis thought. We need every chance we can to even these odds.

Deep operations are those directed against enemy forces and functions beyond the close battle. They are conducted at all levels with fire, maneuver, and leadership. Deep operations affect the enemy through either attack or threat of attack. They expand the battlefield in space and time to the full extent of friendly capability. Effective deep operations facilitate overall mission success and enhance protection of the force.

FM 100-5, *Operations,* 1993

Section 31

The sound of multiple explosions resonated from the area beyond the jagged ridge to the northwest.

"That's our stuff," Davis shouted to his men. "Get ready. The enemy will be on us in about twenty minutes."

Davis focused his binoculars on the exits of the jagged ridge, eight kilometers to the northeast. The passes were filled with dust and smoke. Suddenly, dark objects began racing out of each defile. Scores of vehicles, moving in high-speed columns, quickly exited the narrow openings in the far-off ridge and raced east across the broken desert terrain.

"Sir, I've got OP North on the line," Cowper said, handing Davis the receiver-transmitter.

"One-Six, here they come!" the OP reported.

"OP North, what about his armor?" Davis asked calmly. "Where is he going?"

"Roger, One-Six. I see a column of vehicles, about a hundred of them, exiting the pass at Grid NK353154."

The rumble of explosions increased. The detonations sounded like the strike of a huge hammer, pounding the earth to the northwest. Davis listened with silent satisfaction to the impact of cluster bombs and 155mm artillery shells.

"One-Six, this is OP North. They're taking a beating. I see three . . . no . . . make that five burning vehicles. Our guys are giving them hell."

From the sounds of the explosions, OP North was right. The brigade's deep fight was having some success.

"They're still coming, One-Six. The lead of the column appears to be heading southeast. At least twenty vehicles. The rest of the column, probably one hundred plus, is headed east." OP North paused for a few minutes, as if he was confirming what he saw. "I say again. One column appears to be attacking along Cobra. Over."

"Roger, OP North. Good report," Davis replied, sounding calm and confident in spite of this information. "Continue to report once you confirm that they're near the tank ditch, then call in the targets. Over."

"Wilco, One-Six."

They're sending a separate detachment of tanks and BMPs to attack through Wadi Al Sirree, Davis thought.

"Sergeant Mark, if I ever need air support, it will be when the enemy reaches the tank ditch," Davis informed his FO, pointing to the map. "Relay the report we just got from OP North. Maybe it'll be juicy enough to get us some support."

"Right . . . uh . . . I'm working on it, sir," Mark responded. "It looks like all the CAS is going in for the deep operation."

Suddenly a flight of F/A-18 attack aircraft rumbled overhead, proving Mark's words. The aircraft flew low to the ground to avoid the enemy's lethal air defenses.

American planes darted above the advancing enemy formations. A volley of antiaircraft missiles greeted the attacking planes. A fiery explosion registered the midair destruction of one of the F/A-18s. Several other aircraft, having already dropped their ordnance, ignited their afterburners and roared back to the east, attempting to outrun the enemy's effective missile defenses.

The sound of outgoing artillery shells suddenly died away. The battlefield grew ominously quiet. Our deep operation is over, Davis thought. Now it's the enemy's turn.

"That's it, sir," Mark announced, the radio receiver still pressed against his ear. "The F/A-18s are heading home. We may get some A-10s later. We can call for fire whenever we have a formation of armored vehicles to shoot at."

The sound of bursting artillery, pounding a steady path from west to east, interrupted this short interlude of quiet. The ground trembled as the explosions of the enemy shells marched their way toward the friendly positions.

The explosions grew louder. The earth shook under the thunder of the enemy's 130mm and 152mm guns. Balls of orange flame erupted in the openings to the trails. The bursting artillery shells fell in volleys that marched east like a wave, exploding one after another, over the trails and into the valley itself. Smoke shells fell intermixed with high-explosive shells. Huge geysers of white phosphorus filled Wadi Al Sirree with dense white smoke. After several minutes the explosions shifted farther east, but the smoke lingered like a thick fog.

"I see another column heading to the east, just coming out of the passes now. I can't tell if it will follow the lead column. There's too much smoke and dust now. Request permission to pull back!" OP North begged.

If Davis decides to order OP North to withdraw, go to Section 34.

If Davis decides to leave OP North in position, go to Section 35.

Section 32

The enemy armored vehicles deployed into battle line and began spraying the American positions with machine-gun fire.

"Sir, I jumped frequencies and got through to the company headquarters. They're pulling back. Captain Bludgell is dead. Bravo Company is headed east. They're in really bad shape. Lots of dead and wounded. The enemy is all over the place. Maybe we should pull out."

Davis ignored his RTO.

"Fire at the lead tank," Davis shouted to Specialist Chambers, in the position to the left.

Chambers nodded. The antitank gunner was kneeling in the open firing trench next to his covered position, with the Javelin on his shoulder. He sent a worried glance back to Lieutenant Davis.

Davis coolly stood up, out of his fighting position, so that the men to his flanks could see him. He shouted again, "Get ready!"

When the smoke cleared away, it was the man with the sword, or the crossbow, or the rifle, who settled the final issue on the field.

Gen. George C. Marshall

Now it's up to me and my infantrymen, Davis thought.

"Top engagement mode," Davis shouted in a cracked voice, indicating how the javelins were to be set to attack their targets. "Fire as soon as they hit the minefield."

The survivors to his right and left gave the lieutenant a thumbs-up signal to indicate that they were ready.

An enemy tank burst into flames nine hundred meters in front of Davis's position. Other enemy vehicles deployed, discharging smoke from their grenade launchers and engine smoke generators. The wind, blowing from the west, rolled the smoke into Wadi Al Sirree.

They found the minefields, Davis thought with morbid satisfaction. It won't take long now before we educate them about our antitank missile positions. Come on, you bastards, we're ready for you.

The smoke grew thicker, obscuring the tank ditch. Explosions from M21 antitank mines interrupted the haze with brilliant flashes as they were detonated by advancing enemy vehicles. Davis could see vague shapes moving in the artificial fog. Suddenly a tank crashed through the smoke at high speed, firing its machine guns as it raced forward.

"Fire!" Davis shouted.

Specialist Chambers's Javelin missile fired, sending exhaust smoke, flame, and debris to the rear of his position. The missile darted up and accelerated toward the moving enemy tank.

The Javelin impacted on the top of the turret with a loud boom, halting the tank's forward movement a few seconds after impact. The missile warhead tore through the thin top armor of the tank and ignited the ammunition inside the turret. In a tremendous flash, the turret exploded and leaped six feet into the air, then crashed back down on the burning hull.

"HOOAHH!" Chambers yelled.

A BMP raced past the dead tank. The other Javelin gunner fired. The missile sped to this new target and exploded directly above the small, one-man turret. The vehicle came to a screeching halt and burst into flames. The conflagration devoured all the life that had once been inside.

Another BMP raced forward, firing its cannon at the defenders. In a shower of sparks and flame a powerful M21 antitank mine ripped through the BMP's soft underbelly. The force of ten and a half pounds of explosive detonated under the advancing armored vehicle, immediately transforming it into a smoldering hunk of burning metal.

Undaunted, a third BMP moved toward the hill. Disregarding the fate of its comrades, the vehicle stopped and fired its 30mm cannon at Davis's men.

Another Javelin missile fired. The round shot from the launch tube and raced through the air, striking the stationary BMP in the front of the turret. The conically shaped turret exploded, ripped clean off its chassis, and soared into the air in a burst of white hot sparks.

The squeaking clatter of tank tracks indicated that more enemy armor was on the way.

"It's time to get out of here!" Sergeant Mark yelled. "We're not going to get any more help!"

Davis had to decide. Withdraw, or stay and fight?

If Davis orders everyone to withdraw, go to Section 45.

If Davis decides to stay, go to Section 61.

Section 33

"No," Davis announced decisively. "We'll rest later. Right now we'll prepare. If we aren't ready by tomorrow, we can rest for all of eternity."

The sun set at 1850, bringing cool relief to the desert. Davis kept the platoon working throughout the day, squeezing every minute of preparation out of the available time. He ordered the squads to work on their ambush positions in each trail. While the platoon was working, the headquarters section manned BP Alamo against the possibility of a night infiltration across the tank ditch.

> This is the normal reaction of fighting men as quickly as the danger appears to vanish, unless they are under very strong control. They tighten up when the immediate pressure rises; they relax as the immediate pressure lifts. Of themselves, they will not remain vigilant, even though they be battle-wise. The degree of vigilance depends altogether on the measures taken by their leaders. Unfortunately, the majority of junior leaders have this same tendency.
>
> Gen. S. L. A. Marshall

Position Yankee was complete before dark. Minefields M1, M2, M3, and M4 were also complete. Davis directed his headquarters section and the two attached Javelin teams to occupy BP Alamo at 50 percent alert. One man in each position slept while the other stood watch. In this fashion, almost everyone could get a few hours of precious rest.

Davis observed the quiet desert night with his night-vision goggles. He smiled as he thought about the name *Alamo*. Maybe Captain Bludgell had a sense of humor after all. Davis contemplated his firepower: two Javelins with eight rounds, thirty-four AT4s, and two M60 machine guns. Near his position were thirteen men who would leave with him for Position Yankee. That was all he had as a reserve. He hoped it would be enough.

It was two in the morning when he heard the sound of helicopter rotors. The full moon silhouetted the Russian-made transport helicopters as they flew along the high wall of the hill south of Davis's position. The helicopters sped past 1st Platoon's positions before anyone could react. They headed toward Captain Bludgell's BP Bravo. Davis heard more helicopters heading toward BP Alamo.

"Cowper, give me the handset," Davis ordered. "Company net."

"Bravo Six, this is Bravo One-Six. Four helicopters have passed east, over my position, through the valley. I can't see their landing zone. We hear another group approaching. I'll take them under fire."

"Roger, One-Six," Bludgell replied over the company command net. "For God's sake, try to stop them. I'll deal with the group that's already landed. You stay in position and continue the mission."

Cowper watched in awe as the helicopters came into range.

"Cowper, now. Platoon net," Davis ordered. Cowper changed the frequency to let Davis talk to his squad leaders.

"This is One-Six. I want all small arms fired in front of the helicopters as soon as the bastards are in range," Davis swore into the hand mike.

Davis looked out toward the west. "Are the machine guns ready?"

"Ready, just bring on the targets," reported Specialist Gerber, the senior machine gunner.

The enemy is using every trick in the book, Davis thought. They have landed a company behind my position and are now trying to reinforce them with a second lift. The enemy obviously wants Wadi Al Sirree.

"Here they come!" a voice shouted.

Every rifle and machine gun in the headquarters section opened fire on the advancing helicopters. Tracers flew through the night sky and made sparks as they hit the rocks on the side of the mountain. The enemy aircraft scattered, breaking formation and flying lower to the ground to avoid the incoming arc of tracers.

One helicopter, hugging too low to the ground to avoid the small-arms fire, hit the side of the mountain. The fireball lit up the night sky. The wreckage of twisted metal and burning flesh slid down the side of the mountain like an angry lava flow.

The men of the headquarters section cheered and continued firing at the fleeing helicopters. No one could say if their small-arms fire had any direct effect on the remaining three aircraft.

The sound of mortar fire thudded to the east.

"That must be Captain Bludgell trying to hit the enemy landing zone," Piper yelled over his radio. "We better put out some security to our rear."

Davis considered the possibilities. If he moved an entire squad to the rear, he wouldn't be able to defend forward. A rifle platoon can do only so much. If he sent a couple of men armed only with M16s, they could provide early warning but not much else. Or he could orient his two M60 machine guns toward Position Yankee to cover the platoon's rear. That would weaken his defense of the forward areas, but he expected an armored attack down the trails. The Javelins could handle the trails. He wished he could add a couple of riflemen, but there were no more men to spare.

"OK," Davis answered. "I'll move back to Yankee now and cover the rear from there. If the enemy comes that way, we'll be ready for him."

"Roger," Piper answered stoically. "Tell me when you've occupied Yankee. Good luck."

Davis organized his team on Position Alamo and headed east along the ridge that led to Position Yankee. In twenty-five minutes they were in Yankee.

The sound of mortar and machine-gun fire echoed from the east.

"Specialist Gerber, Specialist Spellman, over here!" Davis yelled to the M60 machine gunners. The soldiers ran over to their platoon leader. "Place both machine guns to the east. Fire at anything that moves. The enemy has landed an air assault force near BP Bravo and they may try to get at us from the east."

"No problem, sir," Gerber replied enthusiastically. "Spellman and I got you covered."

Spellman nodded, indicating that he understood the mission.

"Good. Dig in fast and stay alert. I'm counting on you to protect our rear in case those helicopter troops head our way."

Gerber nodded and picked up his M60 machine gun. Gerber and Private First Class Fetterman—Davis's ammunition bearer and assistant gunner—carried their entrenching tools and six cans of M60 ammunition to a position fifty meters to the rear of Davis's position. The two men oriented their deadly weapon to the east and quickly began digging in. Spellman and his assistant dug in twenty paces south of Gerber's gun.

Davis now had only two Javelins, six AT4s, one M203, and three M16s facing the trails that led into Wadi Al Sirree.

The sounds of fighting from the east diminished. The bright full moon slowly moved across the sky, turning the night into a world of half-lit shadows. Tension mounted. Everything grew quiet.

The battlefield is cold. It is the lonesomest place which men may share together.

To the infantry soldier new to combat, its most unnerving

characteristic is not that it invites him to a death he does not seek. To the extent necessary, a normal man may steel himself against the chance of death.

The hardest thing about the field is that it is empty. No people stir about. There are little or no signs of action. Over all there is a great quiet which seems more ominous than the occasional tempest of fire.

It is the emptiness which chills a man's blood and makes the apple harden in his throat. It is the emptiness which grips him as with a paralysis. The small dangers which he had faced in his earlier life had always paid their dividend of excitement. Now there is a great danger, but there is no excitement about it.

Gen. S. L. A. Marshall

"One-Six, this is OP North. I've got infantry heading up into Trail 4."

Davis held his breath. A night infiltration followed by an early dawn attack by armor was the worst possible scenario. It now made sense. The enemy had launched an air assault to hold the north end of Wadi Al Sirree, the exit. He was now launching a dismounted attack to secure the entrance. In the morning the enemy would launch his main attack down Wadi Al Sirree if the infantry attack succeeded. Could Davis stop him?

"Trail 4, get ready for enemy infantry attack," Davis ordered over his radio. "I'll call fires forward of target Bravo One-Zero-Three. Over."

Davis nodded to Sergeant Mark, who was already on the radio with the artillery fire direction center.

"Roger, One-Six," a voice whispered on the other end of the radio. "We see them now."

Davis heard the unmistakable sound of Claymore mines going off to the southwest. Machine-gun fire and the high-pitched crack of assault rifles filled the air. The battle for the trails had begun.

"I'm calling for fires now," Sergeant Mark exclaimed. "Looks like we'll get 105mm HE falling two hundred meters east of Bravo One-Zero-Three in a few minutes."

"Hurry up, damn it!" Davis swore, annoyed at the delay. Grabbing the hand mike from Cowper, Davis tried to get in touch with Squad 2. "Trail 3, can you assist Trail 4?"

148

"Negative. If we move now, they'll flank us!" Squad 2 reported over the sound of rifle fire.

"The bastards are attacking Trail 4. Fire for effect, Bravo One-Zero-Three," Davis shouted to Sergeant Mark.

Mark attempted to call for fire. The tension mounted as the noise of firing in the trails rose.

"Mark, where's the artillery?" Davis questioned. "We can't wait anymore. What's the delay?"

"Sir, I can't get anyone to respond," Mark answered, exasperated.

Davis has to decide. Squad 3 needs help. If they don't get artillery support soon, they could be overrun and Davis's defense will be turned. His force at Yankee is the only reserve. If he goes forward with the reserve, he commits his force, and he will be attacking an enemy infantry force in the dark that outnumbers him. Can he take that risk? On the other hand, if he stays, he could reorient to block Trails 1 and 2 from Yankee and use the advantages of occupying prepared defensive positions to accomplish his mission.

Does he go forward, or stay put and wait for the artillery?

If Davis decides to stay at Position Yankee, go to Section 36.

If Davis chooses to move his reserve to counterattack the enemy near Trail 4, go to Section 50.

Section 34

"Roger, OP North," Davis ordered calmly. "Move now. Get out while you still can."

"Affirmative, One-Six."

The sound of the radio was quickly replaced by the screech of artillery.

"Incoming!" a scared voice shouted.

Section 34

The ground in front of Davis erupted in fire and flame with the detonation of 130mm and 152mm artillery rounds. A steady rain of searing metal and exploding shells pinned the infantrymen to the bottom of their fighting positions. The pounding was terrific.

Cowper crouched low in his position, next to his platoon leader, true to his duty of monitoring the radio. The RTO strained to hear the radio, pressing the receiver hard against his ear.

Dirt was falling all over them. Dust filled the air, entering Davis's mouth and lungs, making it difficult to breathe. He grabbed the hand mike from Cowper.

"Six-Six, this is One-Six," Davis shouted, trying to reach his company commander. "Six-Six, this is One-Six. Over."

There was no response.

"Damn it!" Davis shouted. "Cowper, keep trying."

The noise was tremendous. The ground shook from the power of the shells. Rocks and flying metal pelted the sides and tops of the fighting position.

The infantrymen fell to the bottom of their holes, seeking refuge from the flying, lethal shards of steel. The barrage intensified. Davis forced his body back up to the aperture of his bunker and struggled to see the battlefield.

Roll the dice.

If you roll 2–4, go to Section 58.

If you roll 5–12, go to Section 62.

Section 35

"Negative, OP North," Davis ordered calmly. "Stay in position. You are more good to us there than down here. I need your eyes. Continue to report."

"Roger, One-Six."

The sound of the radio was again replaced by the scream of several incoming shells. Cowper cowered low in the hole, next to his platoon leader. The fire was not as intense as before, but everyone hugged the ground in anticipation of the worst. The RTO strained to hear the radio, pressing the receiver hard against his ear. Most of the enemy shells fell up ahead, on the front slope of Battle Position Alamo. The searing metal from the exploding shells tore BP Alamo to bits. Position Yankee was hit by an erratic volley of 130mm shells.

"Sir! It's OP North," Cowper shouted in between explosions. "The enemy column's at target reference point Bravo One-Zero-One!"

Dust filled the air. Davis crouched lower in his hole. He grabbed the hand mike from Cowper. It is with artillery that war is made, Davis thought, remembering the words of Napoleon.

The impact of each artillery round made Davis shudder. Slowly the fire slackened, shifting farther east.

"Thank God," Davis declared, his voice muffled by the roar of the exploding shells. "Everyone OK?" Sergeant Mark and Specialist Hutchinson nodded.

"Did you hear the report of enemy tanks at Bravo One-Zero-One?" Davis shouted.

"No!" Mark yelled. "Hutchinson, give me the radio."

Davis looked back to the east toward Bravo.

"I can't reach the 105s anymore!" Mark screamed.

"Forget them," Davis ordered. "Change frequencies and call for 155mm. We won't stop tanks with popguns."

With Mark still listening to the radio hand mike receiver, Hutchinson pulled the radio closer to read the frequency window. The RTO read the 155mm artillery battalion frequency from the plastic wrist coder on his left forearm and quickly changed frequencies.

"I've got them, sir!" Mark exclaimed jubilantly. "Victor Seven-Six, this is Charlie Five-Five. Fire for effect, target Bravo One-Zero-One. Over."

"Give it to them, west of Trail 1," Davis said, designating the northern trail of the western approach to Wadi Al Sirree.

Soon, Mark had the artillery falling at Bravo One-Zero-One.

"Lieutenant, keep it up. OP North says you're right on," Cowper yelled, his Kevlar helmet tilted on his head and the hand mike pressed hard against his ear. Davis's ears were ringing from the noise of the artillery shells, but he heard Cowper's shouts and grinned.

"That's the style, Mark. Keep pouring it on!" Davis yelled.

Sergeant Mark huddled against the back of the fighting position. He took the hand mike from Cowper and held one radio mike to one ear listening to OP North and one radio mike to the other, calling for fire from the artillery battalion FDC. His long radio antenna extended out from the protection of the earth, wood, and sandbagged bunker. The sergeant screamed into the handset, adjusting the fire.

The sound of U.S. 155mm artillery filled the air as U.S. shells smashed into Bravo One-Zero-One. Mark quickly shifted fires onto the enemy, based on OP North's accurate sightings.

"DPICM in effect," Mark shouted, then he gave Davis the platoon net handset. The dirty-faced FO was grinning from his success at controlling the artillery. "It's OP North."

On the field of fire it is the touch of human nature which gives men courage and enables them to make proper use of their weapons. One file, patting another on the back, may turn a mouse into a lion; an unexpected GI can of chocolate, brought forward in a decisive moment, may rally a stricken battalion. By the same token, it is the loss of this touch which freezes men and impairs all action.

Gen. S. L. A. Marshall

"The artillery knocked out three BMPs and a tank at Bravo One-Zero-One. The pass is not blocked. I say again, Trail 1 is still open, but we've given them a bloody nose. Over."

"Roger, OP North, how many are there?" Davis questioned.

"About forty vehicles," Sergeant Tyler reported. "Looks like they may try to come through at Bravo One-Zero-Four."

"Roger," Davis replied calmly, nodding to Sergeant Mark. "We'll fire at Bravo One-Zero-Four."

The American artillery continued pounding the area filled with congested enemy vehicles just west of the tank ditch.

"We're kicking the shit out of them at Bravo One-Zero-Four. Keep firing," OP North shouted through Davis's radio receiver.

But the enemy kept coming, racing forward, disregarding the artillery fire unless stopped by a direct hit. Davis could see black smoke rising high in the sky from the impact of the rounds. He heard the sound of enemy machine guns and the blast of tank main gun fire.

"They're blasting the dummy positions on the Alamo to shreds," OP North reported. "They must think that's where our artillery observers are. I'm glad you're not there."

"I'm glad too," Davis commented, nodding to Mark.

Mark was too busy to respond. He stayed glued to the artillery net. A huge explosion roared from somewhere to the west of the tank ditch. Thick black smoke billowed to the sky. Another enemy tank had apparently hit a well-placed antitank mine.

"Sir, we're going to lose our fires," Mark confessed nervously. "The artillery has to move."

"Shit, not now," Davis shouted in disbelief. "How about the 105s or the mortars?"

"No response. I can't get them on the radio. They must have been taken out by the enemy barrage."

"Call the artillery and tell them I have a company-sized target at Bravo One-Zero-Four." Davis grabbed Sergeant Mark by the arm and looked at him with murderous, determined eyes. "Make them fire for us! Tell them anything. They can't leave us now!"

Mark turned to his transmitter with determination. He shouted obscenities on the radio, conveying the lieutenant's anger into the hand mike.

Another large explosion occurred, out of sight from Davis's position. Davis looked at the smoke and saw pieces of a tank turret flying into the air to the west of the hill. A series of secondary explosions sent green and red tracers shooting madly into the sky.

"Sir, OP North!" Cowper yelled, handing the lieutenant the mike again.

"One-Six, they came around to the north end of the tank ditch and entered Minefield Mike 1. The mines are kicking their ass. Two tanks and one BMP were destroyed in Mike 1."

"Which way are they coming now?" Davis asked.

"Not sure. They seem confused. A couple of BMPs have dropped off some infantry. Looks like they're putting men in the tank ditch. They're trying to break down the tank ditch with shovels and picks."

"Roger, OP North. Keep calling it in. We're trying to get mortars."

The sky to the west was lit with the explosions of American artillery, which crashed into the long lines of crowded enemy vehicles. Smoke billowed to the heavens from the west.

"You're hitting them. Keep firing!" OP North screamed with morbid glee.

"That's it, sir," Mark yelled. "That's the last volley. The 155s have to move now. We're on our own." The sound of friendly cannon fire, whistling overhead, was replaced by the sound of tank and machine-gun fire.

"They're driving over their own vehicles. They're crossing the tank ditch now," OP North reported. "They're still trying to force their way through Trails 1 and 2. "

"Roger. One-Four, did you monitor? They've got BMPs and tanks crossing the ditch now. Stand by. They'll be on you soon."

"We need more artillery," OP North cried over the radio. "If we don't stop them, they'll be coming up Trails 1 and 2 in a few minutes."

Davis didn't have the courage to tell him that the cannons were moving and that he could not reach the mortars. He felt his stomach tighten. *How many of us will live to see the night?*

Davis's Javelin gunners, Chambers and Montoya, waited in tense anticipation of the first enemy armored vehicle to poke its nose over the hill.

Clouds of white smoke suddenly billowed skyward from the area near the northern end of the tank ditch. Davis could see the white smoke from his position on Yankee.

The enemy must be using his vehicle smoke systems and smoke pots to conceal their advance. Damn it! I wish we had some artillery right now! Davis thought.

Enemy mortars began to strike the American positions to support their breach of the tank ditch.

"Incoming!"

Roll the dice.

If you roll 2 or 3, go to Section 58.

If you roll 4–12, go to Section 67.

Section 36

"Listen up," Davis announced to the small group of men that lay in their positions near him. "Things look tough. The enemy has attacked us with dismounted infantry. Probably a company or two. We're going to fight from this position soon. The enemy is breaking through. Get ready."

Davis heard the last of the Claymore mines going off. Squad automatic weapons and the bark of AK-74 assault rifles fought an angry duel in the west.

"Specialist Gerber, there isn't much time. You and Spellman check your machine guns," Davis said, his voice punctuated by the sharp sound of fighting in the trails.

"I still can't reach anyone," Mark confessed.

"Roger. Keep up the fire," said Davis, annoyed at his inability to get artillery support. "Cowper, can you reach Mizogouchi?"

"No luck yet, sir."

"Keep trying," Davis ordered with a voice as crisp as gunfire. "Chambers, Montoya, secure the Javelins and use your rifles. This will be an infantry fight."

The soldiers prepared their weapons and huddled in their fighting positions, peering into the moonlit landscape.

Grenades and RPGs detonated in the vicinity of Trails 3 and 4. The enemy is trying to take us out one at a time, Davis thought.

"OP North reports that he has lost sight of the enemy," Cowper announced.

"Damn it," Davis cursed. "Get Piper on the radio."

"One-Six, this is One-Four," replied Piper. "I've repositioned my team to look south. There's no enemy along Trail 1 or 2. I can't contact our positions at Trail 3 or 4. Do you want me to pull back?"

"This is One-Six. Negative. Stay in position. I'll keep up the artillery and hope we'e hitting them. Out."

Bright explosions interrupted the darkness. The sound of rifle and machine-gun fire and the dull thud and crash of M203-launched 40mm grenades brought the noise of the battle in Trails 3 and 4 to a crescendo. Then an ominous quiet returned to the battlefield.

"Cowper, keep trying to get Mizogouchi!" Davis shouted. "I have to know what's going on!"

Cowper tried repeatedly to reach Squads 2 and 3 but to no avail. Davis got more nervous with each passing second.

"Mark, we've got to get some support," said Davis. "You have to get through to the guns."

"I'm trying, sir. Nothing so far. I've tried all the frequencies," Mark replied, despondent. "Maybe we should pull out and try to make it to BP Bravo. Maybe we could get help there."

Davis was going to respond when suddenly he heard something moving to the southwest.

"There! At nine o'clock!" Chambers whispered as he aimed his M16 toward the advancing silhouettes.

"Steady, hold your fire," Davis ordered. "No one fires until I give the word. Mark, try again. We need artillery ASAP!"

"I'm working on it, sir," Mark answered quietly.

Davis's men lay in their positions, watching the enemy move cautiously along Trail 3. They advanced in groups of threes and fours.

The lead element paused every few meters to scan the terrain for defenders. The enemy's point man was only twenty meters away.

"Now! Fire!" Davis screamed.

Machine guns and rifles opened up. A steady stream of red tracer bullets ripped toward the exit of Trail 3. The enemy infantry hunkered down, avoiding the fire from Davis's lone machine gun.

Suddenly the gun jammed. Gerber pulled open the cover and frantically tried to clear the stoppage.

A whistle blew. Forty to fifty enemy infantry rushed forward to take BP Yankee.

"Mark, where's my artillery fire?" Davis screamed.

While the enemy infantry charged forward, BP Yankee was plastered with fire from the southern flank. The enemy had worked their way around the position and set up a light machine gun to catch Yankee in enfilade.

Bullets ripped through the position.

"They got Hutchinson. They killed him!" Mark screamed in panic, throwing down his radio handset and falling to the ground to avoid enemy fire. Davis fired his M16 at a moving shadow to his front. The shadow fell.

Tracers lit up the position, bouncing and ricocheting in all directions. Gerber's machine gun opened up again, the staunch gunner having cleared his weapon. Few soldiers returned fire except the M60 gunner and the lieutenant. The enemy was right on top of them.

"Come on, damn it. Fire!" Davis screamed. "Mark, you son of a bitch, use your rifle!"

> It is beyond question that the most serious and repeated breakdowns on the field of combat are caused by failure of the controls over human nature. In minor tactics the almost invariable cause of local defeat is fundamentally the shrinkage of fire. In the greater number of instances this shrinkage is the result of men failing to carry out tasks which are well within their power.
>
> Gen. S. L. A. Marshall

Cowper fired his rifle, then fell backward in the fighting position. Davis looked down inside the dark hole, grabbed Cowper, and stuck his hand into a mass of pulp where Cowper's face had been. Enraged, Davis aimed his weapon and blasted the remaining rounds from his thirty-round magazine.

An explosion erupted from the M60 position. The machine gun stopped firing. Smoke and the smell of cordite filled the air. Shadows were moving now inside Position Yankee.

Davis lowered his weapon and dropped two enemy infiltrators attempting to get behind Position Yankee.

"Mark, are you OK?" Davis screamed. "Report! Who's left?"

Two attackers rushed Davis's position from the front. Davis hit one. The man fell backward, dropping his grenade. The other hit the ground and sailed his potato masher grenade right in front of the lieutenant's position.

Roll the dice.

If you roll 2–4, go to Section 58.

If you roll 5–12, go to Section 56.

Section 37

It was great pity, so it was,
This villainous saltpetre should be digg'd
Out of the bowels of the harmless earth,
Which many a good tall fellow had destroy'd
So cowardly; and but for these vile guns,
He would himself have been a soldier.

Shakespeare

Davis failed in his mission. He made two big mistakes. He didn't anticipate the enemy's actions and he disregarded the principle of security.

The ability of the combat leader to anticipate is a critical military skill. Every combat commander must anticipate the enemy's actions and reactions and must be able to foresee how operations may develop. Combat leaders must know how the enemy fights and know the capabilities of their own unit. Predictions about the enemy and even one's own troops can never be relied on with certainty, but it is nevertheless essential to anticipate what is possible and likely and prepare for those possibilities.

Davis failed to anticipate the requirements of the mission and think through to the finish what his small command needed to do to accomplish the mission. He failed to put himself in the enemy's shoes and attempt to predict how the enemy would fight to take Wadi Al Sirree. But as Gen. S. L. A. Marshall has written, this is easier said than done:

> Again for the small unit commander, there is need to seek the true meaning of the counsel given . . . "Anticipation is 60 percent of the art of command. . . ." It is very easy to say "Anticipate!" and very hard to do it. This is especially true of the commander who is about to take his troops against the enemy. The layman imagines vaguely that the job is well-nigh done when, after due consideration of the ground, the commander decides by what general paths his men are to move against the enemy. Yet this is the lesser portion of his responsibility.

The second lesson to be learned involves security. The concept of security is so important that it is considered one of the nine principles of war in U.S. military doctrine. The principle of security states that you should never permit the enemy to acquire an unexpected advantage. Knowledge and understanding of the enemy are key ingredients of this principle. Security protects the force and is an important means to increase friendly combat power. Security enhances freedom of action by reducing friendly vulnerability to hostile acts, influence, or surprise. Security results from the measures taken by a command to protect itself from surprise, observation, detection, interference, espionage, sabotage, or annoyance. Risk is an inherent condition of war; the application of the principle of security does not suggest overcautious behavior or the avoidance of calculated risk.

Davis failed to provide for security, particularly his own security. He disregarded the principle of security by going forward into unknown territory without adequate forces. He should have sent out squad-sized combat patrols immediately after assuming the defensive sector. The combat patrols' mission is to clear the sector of any observation posts that might have been inserted by the enemy's reconnaissance units.

A skilled opponent will insert, or leave behind, reconnaissance teams to provide information on his opponent's defenses. Usually, for a regimental-sized Threat force, this involves half a dozen observation posts (OPs). Each OP will consist of two to four soldiers, armed with high-power radios and observation devices. These OPs will occupy key terrain or good vantage points to report on the defender's activities and to identify weaknesses in the defense. The mission of these OPs is to report, not to fight. If you bump into them, however, they will defend themselves. That's what happened to Davis and Piper.

History is full of examples of leaders who have gone forward to reconnoiter without taking adequate security. Some are lucky and nothing happens. Others, like Stonewall Jackson in the American Civil War, or the heroic Maj. Gen. William Frishe Dean of the Korean War, learned this lesson the hard way. General Jackson was mistakenly killed by his own troops when he returned from a reconnaissance forward of friendly lines at the Battle of Chancellorsville. Major General Dean was captured by the North Koreans in 1950 while he was conducting a reconnaissance during the ferocious fighting for Taejon.

In both cases the loss of the leader caused confusion and hesitation. History proves that the immediate effect of a commander or platoon leader's death is a loss of initiative while the unit establishes command on the battlefield. In short, leaderless units tend to remain stationary in the defense and lose momentum in the attack. Modern midintensity conflict brings increased speed and tempo to operations on the AirLand battlefield. Instead of having hours or days to replace dead leaders, units must be able to do so in minutes or seconds.

Commanders and their subordinates must constantly look for ways to increase their security. Squad-sized combat patrols are the means to accomplish this for the infantry platoon.

**Go to Section 3
and
try again.**

Section 38

Davis remembered the words of Napoleon: "War is waged only with vigor, decision, and unshaken will; one must not grope or hesitate."

The lieutenant shook his head. "We have to do it. If we don't put out OPs in a location where they can see and provide us early warning, we won't stand a chance. We take more risk without them."

"You're right, Lieutenant," Piper added. "We'll need all the early warning we can get."

Davis turned toward Sergeant Tyler.

"You have the mission. The OPs are critical. Get up there, dig in, and camouflage your positions. Don't fire unless you're stepped on."

Sergeant Tyler nodded.

"If the enemy is sighted, call us on the radio. If you can't get through, fire a white flare. Once you have confirmed that the enemy is in the trails, follow the white flare with a star cluster. If the enemy is coming along the north side into Position Yankee, fire a green star cluster. If he's coming in the south, toward X-Ray, shoot a red star cluster."

"Green in the north, red in the south," Tyler repeated.

"Roger," Davis confirmed.

"I'll call for artillery and mortar fires on the trails based on those signals," Mark chimed in.

The squad leaders nodded.

Observation posts must be sited for maximum view of the surrounding area, for clear radio communications, and for defensibility.

FM 7-20, *The Infantry Battalion,* 1992

"Before we get too involved in our preparations, I want to patrol the high ground on our flanks," Davis explained, completely in charge of the situation. He unfolded his map and beckoned for the platoon sergeant to bend down to see as he pointed out key terrain on the map.

"Jordan's squad will check out the high ground on the south wall, Tyler's squad the north wall. Mizogouchi, get your men to work putting in Minefield M1. Mark and I will use the time to complete the artillery plan."

Each squad leader nodded. Piper grinned.

"One more thing, Lieutenant," Piper chimed in. "I've checked out a good rally point. There's some old oil pipe trenches dug into the side of the hill at NK390078. We can jump into those if things go to shit. No one can see us in there unless they walk right up on us."

"Good work." Davis's voice was soft and low. He spoke carefully as each of his squad leaders scribbled notes in their pocket notebooks. "We'll call that Rally Point 1. We'll establish a second rally point at the opening of the pass that runs to the southwest. The grid for Rally Point 2 is NK430080.

"The plan rests on the OPs," Davis declared in a voice edged with steel. "Our observation posts must warn us when the enemy heads our way. If everything goes bad, our contingency plan is to rally at one of these locations."

The squad leaders circled the locations of the rally points on their plastic-covered maps.

"I want a report from each squad leader on how much water and how many MREs you have in each squad," Piper commented. "Then I'll take the Javelin and M60 machine gunners to work on Position Yankee."

"OK." Davis nodded his agreement as he stood up to signal the end of the orders briefing. "If there are no further questions, I think we're ready to get started."

"All right," Piper said, obviously happy with the way things were working in the platoon. "You heard the man. Let's get cracking."

The group broke up, each squad leader returning to his men to brief them. In twenty minutes the patrols departed. Sergeant Mizogouchi took his squad to the northeast side of the tank ditch and began laying Minefield M1. Piper took the Javelin and machine-gun teams to dig positions on BP Yankee. After leaving Specialist Chambers in charge of constructing BP Yankee, Piper returned to supervise the placement of the minefields and the completion of the work on BP Alamo.

Davis and Sergeant Mark completed the artillery plan in a few hours. Davis discussed the fire plan with Sergeant Piper and made a few adjustments based on the veteran soldier's recommendations. Suddenly the sound of firing on the north wall interrupted their work.

"Sir, it's Sergeant Tyler on the radio for you," Cowper announced. "He's got contact."

Davis rushed to Cowper and brought the radio handset to his ear. Piper strolled to Davis's side, patiently waiting for information about the platoon's first contact.

"One-Six, this is One-Two," Tyler reported jubilantly. "I've had a firefight with two enemy soldiers in an observation post on top of Hill 865. We killed them both. We tried to capture them, but no dice. No friendly casualties. We captured an AM radio, a laser artillery designator, and a map. There are no marks on the map."

"Good work, One-Two," Davis answered, relieved that the platoon's first contact with the enemy had gone so well. "Send their gear and anything else you think will help the intel guys back to my location. I'll report it to higher."

Davis reported the incident to Captain Bludgell. The knowledge that the enemy had laser artillery designators was particularly frightening. Such laser designators were used to aim precision-guided munitions (PGMs) onto targets with pinpoint accuracy. It was surprising to find out that the enemy had this level of technology, but with the plethora of sophisticated military equipment for sale on the world market, it had only been a matter of time until these tools became commonplace.

Section 38

Sergeant Tyler radioed in that he had established OP North at 1530. Sergeant Jordan at OP South reported "set" a few minutes later. The patrols returned and their acting squad leaders organized their men to continue the backbreaking work of preparing their defensive positions and establishing minefields. Night arrived, fighting back the day with a magnificent display of color. The sun glowed orange-red as it sank over the horizon, which turned gorgeous hues of orange, red, and yellow. Then a comfortable breeze slowly dissipated the shimmering heat of the day. For a moment, Davis sat in awe and marveled at the beauty of the celestial spectacle playing out before him as the sky turned a final shade of dark cyan.

Davis's thoughts wandered from the beautiful skyline to the cruel realities of the coming battle. The enemy was out there; the two soldiers whom Tyler's men killed proved it. Tomorrow he and his men would be in combat.

Piper placed two security posts on the forward-slope positions at BP Alamo and then left to supervise the completion of Yankee and X-Ray. Davis stayed near BP Alamo, assisting in Mizogouchi's efforts to lay the minefields. The moon shone brightly, making the hard work of laying wire and placing antitank mines a little easier. The desert in the bright moonlight was an eerie scene, a world of half-lit shadows. Davis received hourly reports from Piper and the squad leaders on the progress of the work. The men are exhausted, Davis thought. The anxieties of combat have added to the stress. More than anything, the men want to sleep. In spite of this they seemed confident. I've pushed them hard, but they've seen the purpose behind what we must do. Will we be ready in time? Will I be up to it when the moment comes?

As the night work continued, Davis discovered that he could operate in the half-light almost as well as in the day. More importantly, it was much cooler. During the early hours of the night, Davis's men worked on the fighting positions at BP Alamo. Piper reported that BP Yankee was almost complete and that his men had begun work on X-Ray and Zulu.

The squad leaders kept everyone working. They enforced their own sleep plans, according to Piper's guidance, to provide some rest for the weary soldiers. No more than two men per squad were allowed to sleep at the same time. Everyone else worked hard to get ready for battle. Each squad rotated duties between sleeping, working, and security.

Davis wondered whether he was making the right decisions.

It is quite normal for the commander who is experiencing battle for the first time, no matter what his rank or length of training, to devote most of his time to worrying about the welfare and conduct of his men instead of continuing to ply himself with the questions: "Am I at my right place? Am I doing the right things?" This is a perfectly human trait. Indeed, it would be commendable if it were not excessively costly. For it can be said without qualification that the commander who so concerns himself will not have time to organize a coordinated attack and supervise its proper execution. Most young commanders learn this by being bruised their first time in battle or else they never learn it and continue to waste men's lives. But the ounce of prevention is worth a pound of cure. It needs to be impressed on the young officer's mind throughout his training that this will be his normal urge, once he engages the enemy and that he must be prepared to resist it stoutly if he is to command soundly.

Gen. S. L. A. Marshall

Davis thought for a moment about his tired, small band of soldiers, far from home and country. He remembered a quote he had once read from Clausewitz: "If no one had the right to give his views on military operations except when he is frozen, or faint from heat and thirst, or depressed from privation and fatigue, objective and accurate views would be even rarer than they are." Davis realized that, in the field, decision making was a difficult and fatiguing task.

He smiled. There was no time for second guessing himself now. Too much remained to be done. After checking the placement of the minefields, he moved back with Cowper to join Sergeant Mark and Specialist Hutchinson, who were standing watch on BP Alamo. Everything appeared to be on track. Davis radioed Piper, who was still working at Position X-Ray, that he was going to try to grab a few hours of sleep. Davis settled into his fighting position in the center of BP Alamo and after a few seconds, he quickly slithered into unconsciousness.

"Sir, it's OP North on the radio," Cowper announced in a zombie-like voice.

Davis shook himself awake. The excited voice on the radio served as a shot of caffeine, jolting him to consciousness. Cowper thrust the hand mike into his palm. "It's Sergeant Tyler."

"One-Six, this is OP North. Over," an excited Sergeant Tyler announced.

"This is One-Six. Send it. Over," Davis replied in a quick breath.

"I hear an engine. I can't see anything, but I hear it," Tyler reported.

"Roger, OP North, continue to observe," Davis replied professionally. He was amazed at how calm he was. "Call me as soon as you can determine a location."

"Wilco, One-Six."

I have only a few men here, Davis thought. Everyone else is with Sergeant Piper working on BP Yankee and X-Ray. What is the enemy doing? The more darkness hinders sight, the more you must replace actual vision by skill and care, he thought. The enemy must be trying to infiltrate scouts into our positions to find out where we are.

Davis called Piper to get the rest of the platoon back to the defensive position on the hill. "One-Four, this is One-Six. I want you to stop working on X-Ray and get back to BP Alamo. We've got an enemy vehicle approaching from the west. They may be trying to infiltrate our positions. I say again, get back to BP Alamo," Davis ordered.

"Say again," Piper replied, his voice garbled in an intermittent radio transmission. "It will . . . gather everyone . . . get there . . ."

"Damn these squad radios," Davis swore. Cowper stood by helpless while Davis tried several more times to reach Piper. Each time the results were worse, until he could not hear Piper at all. Minutes seemed like hours as Davis contemplated an attack by the enemy against his small force. Davis's palms grew sweaty in anticipation. He pressed the receiver tightly against his ear.

"One-Six, this is OP North. I see them. Two enemy armored cars at Grid NK371087. They've stopped right below me!"

"Mark, get some artillery on that, ASAP!" Davis screamed to his forward observer in the adjacent fighting position.

"I monitored. Stand by. I'm working on it now," Mark answered as he processed the call for fire on his radio.

"Stand by, OP North, arty on the way," Davis answered.

The minutes took forever.

I've always heard that the hardest part of any battle is the waiting, thought Davis. Now I realize that it isn't so much the waiting as it is the thinking. At night, in the quiet, your mind plays out your fears. Self-confidence tends to wane when you're sitting in a foxhole, peering out at the dark, expecting any minute to be in mortal combat.

"There's three of them now! Three armored cars!" Tyler reported, the emotion making his voice crack. "They're dismounting troops."

Davis heard the sound of artillery pieces firing from the east.

"Shot! Artillery on the way, Lieutenant!" Mark shouted.

The whine of three outgoing artillery shells filled the night sky. Suddenly the ground three kilometers west of Hill 865 glowed with the sparks of explosions. The earth rumbled with the impact of the 155mm rounds.

"You're over, One-Six. Drop two hundred," OP North corrected.

"Mark, drop two hundred!" Davis yelled. "Fire for effect."

"Roger!" Mark answered as he quickly relayed the firing corrections to the guns.

More artillery arced through the dark sky.

The target area was awash in brilliant light. Davis could see the impact of the rounds. The flash from the explosions flickered like the light from a huge flashbulb.

"You're right on target. They're running away," OP North announced.

Davis grinned. The observation posts had paid off.

Three more outgoing rounds whined overhead and splashed into the area near the entrance to the north pass.

"They're running away," Sergeant Tyler reported. "I've lost them. They must have gone to the north. I can't tell if we got any."

"OP North, do you see any infantry?" Davis asked.

"Negative, but my night sights are only so good," OP North replied.

"Keep alert. I'm worried about a dismounted infantry infiltration. Call me if you see anything. One-Six, out."

Davis waited a few seconds, then called the company CP, informing Captain Bludgell of the action and the direction of enemy movement. Davis tried again to reach Piper on the radio. Repeated attempts had met with failure. Davis got more worried by the minute. Piper still had more than half of the platoon and was totally out of contact. Davis watched the western horizon, scanning periodically with his PVS-7 night-vision goggles.

It's taking Piper too long, thought Davis. What if the enemy is trying to infiltrate our positions? What if that BRDM is only part of an enemy force trying to get into Wadi Al Sirree? Maybe Piper is in trouble. Maybe the enemy has infiltrated already and Piper has been captured. A thousand questions circulated in Davis's head. He looked at his watch.

The sounds of muffled explosions from far to the west echoed through the valley. The moon, which had illuminated the desert so well earlier, was now sinking over the horizon. It was very dark.

If the enemy tries a dismounted infiltration of our positions now, he might be able to get by us without our knowing. Maybe I should go get Piper myself.

Davis must decide!

If Davis decides to wait for Piper, go to Section 19.

**If Davis decides to move back to find Piper,
go to Section 92.**

Section 39

The enemy column reached the tank ditch. Special dozer tanks led the way, easily pushing through the barbed wire and filling the tank ditch with dirt.

Davis could barely discern the outlines of the dark enemy vehicles in the thick white smoke. The BMPs and tanks set up a firing line west of the ditch and opened up on BP Alamo with concentrated main gun and machine-gun fire.

The platoon's return fire was minuscule. The soldiers of 1st Platoon who had not been killed by enemy artillery fire were pinned at the bottom of their fighting positions by flying shrapnel and direct fires.

I must do something! Davis thought. He raised his head to observe the tank ditch.

A tank was working its way into the ditch. It struggled there for several moments, then climbed out on the east side. Picking up speed, it crashed through a pillow of smoke, firing its machine guns as it raced by.

A Javelin missile was fired, sending exhaust smoke, flame, and debris to the rear of the position. The missile darted up and down as it accelerated toward the fast-moving target.

The Javelin missile hit the tank in the top of the turret. The high-explosive antitank warhead tore through the soul of the tank, bringing the enemy vehicle to a horrific grinding halt. Thick, oily black smoke billowed skyward from the openings of the fractured turret. Another tank moved forward, passing the burning hulk to the right. The second tank lumbered toward BP Alamo and turned its turret toward Davis.

"Hit the dirt!" Davis screamed.

Roll the dice.

If you roll 2–4, go to Section 41.

If you roll 5–12, go to Section 58.

Section 40

"Here we go again. Incoming!" Cowper yelled. "Take cover."

The ground in front of Davis erupted with exploding shells and searing metal, throwing him back to the bottom of his hole. Davis rose up to survey the damage. Sergeant Mark's hole, thirty meters from Davis's position, had taken a direct hit and was nothing more than a smoldering black void. Davis could see no sign of his forward observer or Hutchinson.

Cowper cowered low in the hole, next to his platoon leader. The RTO strained to hear the radio, pressing the receiver hard against his ear. Dirt was falling all over them. Dust filled the air, entering Davis's mouth and nose, filling his lungs. It was almost impossible to breathe.

Davis crouched back into his hole. He grabbed the hand mike from Cowper. The sound of artillery, pounding a steady path from west to east, filled the air. The ground trembled. Enemy artillery whistled overhead.

"Cowper," Davis exclaimed. "Change frequencies. Find the 155mm artillery battalion's frequency. Get them on the line for me, ASAP."

Cowper pulled the radio closer to read the frequency window. He read the 155mm artillery battalion frequency from the plastic wrist coder on his left forearm.

"Set, sir," Cowper yelled over the bursting shells. "Victor Seven-Six, this is Bravo One-Six Alpha."

Davis surveyed the scene. Enemy tanks and BMPs were scattered in front of the tank ditch, squirming and struggling to find a way across the obstacle. A huge explosion near the tank ditch sent parts of a tank high into the air. Thick black smoke billowed to the sky. Another enemy tank had become a victim of a well-placed antitank mine.

"Sir, I've got them," Cowper screamed with joy.

Machine-gun bullets raked the top of Davis's position, throwing dirt and rocks into the hole. Both men ducked lower. Davis grabbed the receiver.

"This is Bravo One-Six. The enemy is attacking along Cobra. I've got at least twenty vehicles west of the tank ditch now!"

"Identify yourself," came the answer over the radio receiver.

"Damn it!" Davis pulled up Cowper's arm to observe the wrist coder on his left forearm. He read the self-authentication tables. "I self-authenticate Alpha Kilo November. Now, damn it! Fire for effect, target Bravo One-Zero-Four, four tanks. Over."

Soon, Davis had the artillery falling at Bravo One-Zero-Four.

"Lieutenant, keep it up. You're right on target," Cowper yelled as he observed the engagement area.

Davis sat in the bottom of the hole, his Kevlar helmet tilted on his head and the hand mike pressed hard against his ear. His ears were ringing from the noise of the artillery shells, but he heard Cowper's shouts and grinned.

The sound of U.S. 155mm artillery filled the air as the shells smashed into Bravo One-Zero-Four. Davis quickly shifted fires onto other enemy targets.

"Cowper, take the hand mike." Cowper traded places with his lieutenant. The American artillery continued pounding the enemy.

"We're hitting them. Keep firing," Davis yelled to Cowper. The lieutenant bravely observed the fires from the opening in his position. He could see black smoke rising high in the sky from the impact of the rounds.

"DPICM in effect," he shouted.

The artillery tore apart several vehicles, but the remainder of the attackers kept moving, forcing their way through the ditch. A firing line of enemy tanks engaged BP Alamo with continuous fire. Enemy machine-gun tracers and tank cannon blasted the American positions on the hill east of the tank ditch.

Bullets bounced off the rocks and tore the sandbags of Davis's fighting position to shreds. Davis ducked, too slowly. A bullet struck him in the head. His body jerked back violently and fell in a heap at the bottom of the fighting position. He emitted no words, no sounds. A 12.7mm round from a tank-mounted machine gun had pierced his Kevlar helmet and ended his life.

Go to Section 46.

Section 41

The 125mm round from the enemy tank struck the Javelin gunner's position. When the smoke cleared, Specialist Chambers and his assistant gunner were gone.

A BMP raced past the tank and charged up the northern trail of Wadi Al Sirree. Other BMPs fired machine guns and 30mm cannons at the survivors of BP Alamo.

"Shit, they're getting past us!" Davis screamed.

The platoon returned fire at the advancing armored vehicles without effect. Two more BMPs struggled out of the tank ditch. The lead BMP hit an antitank mine. The mine sent a stream of molten metal up into the belly of the BMP. Exploding from inside out, the BMP disintegrated in a burst of fire and black smoke.

Most of Davis's men were down. Many had head wounds. Davis could hear the screams of the wounded in between the roar of enemy tank cannon and the blast of enemy machine guns.

"Sir, we have to make a run for it!" Sergeant Mark yelled. "Let's get the hell out of here!"

Davis looked at Cowper. Cowper's radio hand mike was ready.

Davis has to decide!

If Davis orders everyone to stay, go to Section 43.

If Davis orders a withdrawal, go to Section 45.

Section 42

The temperature rose as the sun passed its zenith. Piper gathered the squad leaders around him to receive the lieutenant's operations order. Davis marched back up the hill and huddled with his subordinate leaders. Together, Davis and Piper pointed out the reverse-slope positions that would allow maximum use of the platoon's antitank weapons against an enemy attack along Axis Cobra.

The platoon sat in a semicircle around Davis. Sergeant Tyler sat to his left, Piper to his right, then Jordan and Mizogouchi.

"Situation." Davis started the operations order using the format that had been drilled into him at the Academy. "The enemy will probably attack us just before sunrise on the day after tomorrow. We can expect that he will send out reconnaissance tonight and tomorrow night."

He next explained the platoon's mission, then how he expected his men to execute the mission. He pointed to his map, spread out in front of his squad leaders, to highlight the key terrain and the locations of friendly units. He went into considerable detail discussing the priority of tasks necessary to accomplish the defense.

"Tonight, we'll occupy the positions on top of the small rise overlooking the tank ditch. We'll call this position BP Alamo."

The men chuckled. "I guess that makes you Davy Crockett, sir," Jordan said with a laugh.

"Right," said Piper with a smile, "and I'm Jim Bowie."

"If we stay in those positions when the enemy's main attack comes, we could end up the same way as Crockett and Bowie did," Davis added soberly.

The men nodded. This was not a game. This was the real thing. Jordan sat stoic, unmoving. Tyler fidgeted nervously and refocused his attention on the map spread out before him. Mizogouchi retrieved a cigar from his pocket, lit it, and took a long draw.

"Tomorrow night we'll move to BP Yankee and X-Ray," Davis explained. "We'll conduct a reverse-slope defense designed to destroy the enemy as he exits the eastern edge of the trails into the valley."

Section 42

Suddenly a supersonic blast split the air high above their heads. Davis dove for the ground, hitting the sand hard. The squad leaders automatically scattered for cover. A second ear-shattering boom followed the first as Davis was nose down in the dust of the desert floor.

The cringing lieutenant looked up. A U.S. Navy F/A-18 was chasing an enemy aircraft. The enemy jet, flying straight to the east, suddenly engaged his afterburner. The enemy pilot pulled his bird straight up, trying to circle back toward his own lines. That was his final mistake.

The U.S. pilot apparently anticipated his prey's move. From a mile away the F/A-18 fired an air-to-air missile at the fleeing enemy aircraft. The missile shrieked through the air, accelerating as it flew, matching the enemy's evasive moves with its own changes in direction. In a last-ditch attempt to break the lock-on, the enemy aircraft dove violently to the north. The missile proved faster and the race was over. The high-explosive heat-seeking missile flew right into the enemy aircraft's jet engine and exploded. The aircraft disintegrated in a bright orange fireball and the tangled wreckage hurtled earthward. There was no chance for the enemy pilot to eject.

Davis's men cheered. "Kicked his ass!" one of the soldiers shouted in boyish triumph.

> Find the enemy and shoot him down; anything else is nonsense.
> Capt. Baron Manfred von Richthofen

Davis stood up and brushed the dust off his desert-camouflaged uniform.

"Damn it, Lieutenant," Piper swore with a grin. "I'm getting too old for this kind of work."

Davis nodded, rubbing his jaw. The enemy aircraft had surprised everyone. No one thought the enemy would be bold enough to challenge U.S. aircraft. The bad guys were acting pretty cocky.

"See what I mean, Lieutenant? The fly guys have just about got this war won already," Tyler announced.

"Already won?" Davis questioned. "If he's so defeated, how come he has the balls to send reconnaissance aircraft against us?"

There was no warning of the enemy aircraft's approach, Davis thought. If he had been on a strike run against us, we could have been slaughtered.

A battle sometimes decides everything; and sometimes the most trifling thing decides the fate of battle.

Napoleon

"Cowper, get on the company net and report that aircraft," Davis commented calmly, looking at the radio sitting idly outside the platoon command post position. "Ask them where our early warning was."

"Roger, sir!" Cowper replied earnestly, sensing how important his role as RTO was to the survival of the platoon.

"OK, Lieutenant. Let me back-brief you on how our defense is going to be conducted," Piper said as he looked at the lieutenant's map. "I'll occupy Position X-Ray. I'll have 1st Squad and most of 2d Squad. I'll also have ten AT4 antitank rockets at X-Ray and orient toward the west. We'll mine the trails and the exits of the trails. As soon as an enemy vehicle comes over the top of the hill, we'll hit him."

"Yes. Our success will depend upon our ability to see what the enemy is doing." Davis paused a few seconds while he drew a quick diagram of the plan in the sand. "We'll number the trails from north to south, one through four.

"Tyler, your mission is to establish and man two observation posts. Establish one on the north wall, on Hill 865. We'll call that one OP North. Establish the second OP on the south wall, high enough to see both the east and west sides of Wadi Al Sirree. Attach your SAW gunners and the rest of your squad to Sergeant Piper."

"Sir, two of my men are at the battalion aid station," Tyler responded. "I'd like to keep my squad together."

"Five men is plenty to man two OPs," Piper interjected. "You should have Private First Class Henry back tomorrow. Top told me he's doing fine."

"I understand your concerns, but I'm giving you the OP mission because it's critical to our success," Davis declared, complimenting

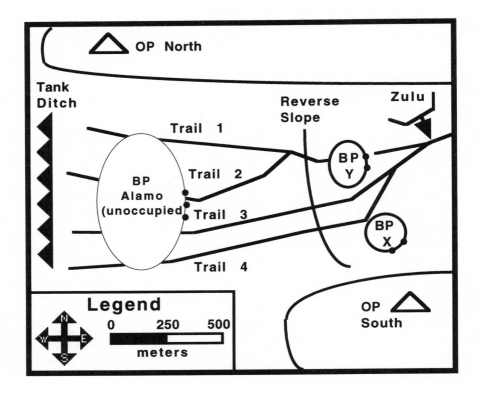

Tyler. "Both observation posts will have to use their squad radios to send us spot reports and call for fire. It's vital that the OPs stay alert and report accurately. I trust you with this important mission. You must be in position before dark tonight."

Sergeant Tyler nodded obediently, smiling at the confidence the lieutenant was demonstrating in him.

"I'll be at BP Yankee with Sergeant Mark," Davis continued. "The OPs will send spot reports to me, and I'll tell Mark where to fire. I'll use my radio to communicate with Sergeant Piper and the OPs."

"You can count on my men, sir," Tyler added.

"There's no doubt of that," Davis answered. The lieutenant pointed to the sketch of BP Yankee on the sand in front of them. The three squad leaders listened intently. "On Yankee I'll have two Javelins with four missiles each, fourteen AT4s, two M60 machine guns, and 3d Squad. As the enemy comes east of the tank ditch and over or around the hill to the north, we'll hit him with artillery and block his path with mines. As he breaks through the mines and begins to exit the narrow trails, we'll strike him with Javelin and AT4 fire from Yankee and X-Ray."

Davis switched to the map and pointed to the exit of the four trails. Trail 1, in the north, joined Trail 2 at the eastern mouth of Wadi Al Sirree. BP Yankee would be in easy range of these trails. Trails 3 and 4, to the south, which also exited close together on the eastern edge of the Wadi Al Sirree opening, were in range of Position X-Ray.

"We'll have the advantage of mass and surprise," Davis continued. "The enemy will have to attack up the trails one or two vehicles at a time while we wait, unobserved, on the reverse slope. He won't see us until we are already firing at him. This will minimize the long-range fire advantage of his tanks and BMPs."

The platoon sergeant, FO, squad leaders, and machine gunners scribbled notes in their pocket notebooks as the lieutenant finished his operations order.

"Does everybody understand?" Davis asked. "Stand-to is at 0500. We'll send patrols out to sweep the area at 0600. We'll conduct a rehearsal tomorrow at 1000."

The soldiers nodded.

"Remember, we want to trap the enemy along the north wall, where the trail is narrow and where we'll have our heaviest antitank fires," Davis continued. "We'll lay some mines in each trail, but we'll mass our mines where the trails empty into Wadi Al Sirree. This way we'll be able to cover our minefields with direct fire from our reverse-slope positions."

The men breathed a collective sigh. They were tired. The work that had been accomplished so far had been exhausting. The thought of being up all night did not encourage them.

Fatigue makes cowards of us all.

Gen. George S. Patton, Jr.

"OK, Lieutenant," Piper said, spitting tobacco juice on the ground. "We'll start laying mines just east of the tank ditch—M1 in the

Section 42

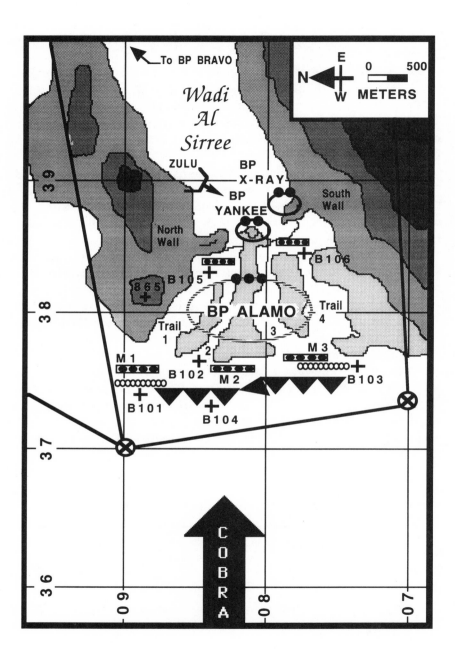

178

north, M2 in the center, and M3 in the south. Then we'll mine the trails working north from Trail 4 to Trail 1. We'll reinforce the south by blocking the southern trails with barbed-wire obstacles."

Ignoring the men's expressions of fatigue, Davis added, "To complete our obstacle plan, we'll put in Minefields M4 and M5 to stop the enemy as he crests the hill and comes into our engagement area."

"Sir," Tyler replied, looking at the other squad leaders for support. "That's a lot of work for one platoon. I think we could all use some rest."

"You're right, but we can't afford to rest yet. At least not all of us at the same time," Davis expounded with a slight smile, placing his hand on Tyler's shoulder. "Sergeant Piper will develop a sleep plan—only two men resting in each squad at one time. The rest will have to keep working. We have to lay the minefields now, while we have the time. Mark the minefields and clearly identify footpaths through them."

"Right," Piper acknowledged. "But what if the enemy attacks in the south and breaks through the minefield? I only have ten AT4s to stop him. After ten shots, I'm out of ammunition."

"We can't be strong everywhere. That's why we must force the enemy north by placing the heaviest obstacles in the south," Davis said, pointing to the map. "If he does break through, fire small arms and machine guns to keep him buttoned up. I'll either fire my Javelins from BP Yankee or reposition them to Zulu to support you."

"I'll send Gerber and a few men to dig holes on Zulu. We'll also need to lay some wire in front of Minefields M3 and M4," Piper added. "A couple of strong triple-strand barriers, reinforcing the minefields, will help turn the enemy your way."

"I'll take care of the wire tonight," replied Sergeant Jordan, the leader of 1st Squad. "It will take us a while, but we should have it done by morning."

"Look, I know how tired you all are," Davis proclaimed sympathetically. "We can't afford to waste a minute. At least we'll have pretty good illumination tonight, with a full moon most of the time. That'll make the work a little easier. Besides, it's cooler working at night. We can't afford any more heat casualties."

Piper looked at his platoon leader. Two men had fallen ill from heat cramps this afternoon, both from Sergeant Tyler's 2d Squad.

Section 42

The water had run out as the temperature rose. Davis knew that every man was needed.

"How's our water situation?" Davis asked.

"We've used five of the ten five-gallon water cans that Lieutenant Sandburg dropped off. The men have already filled their canteens," Piper reported. "We have all the ammunition and food we need. The company XO also dropped off twenty white illumination flares, six green star clusters, and six red clusters."

"Good," Davis replied. "I want both OPs manned tonight. Make sure they have plenty of flares and that they have night-vision sights. I want them to carry enough water to last for twenty-four hours."

"We're short on PVS-7 batteries, barbed-wire gloves, and picket pounders. We should have enough batteries for our night-vision devices for tonight," Piper added. "We'll need to be resupplied tomorrow."

Davis swallowed hard, a pained expression on his face. Did everything always have to be so hard?

"Don't worry," Piper insisted, "I've already called the company first sergeant. We'll get everything we need later today."

"Sir," Sergeant Tyler interrupted, "I'm not sure it's such a good idea to leave two or three men all by themselves up there in the dark. We're pretty spread out as it is. Don't you think it would be wiser to concentrate the platoon at night in a perimeter defense? We'll be sitting ducks up there if the enemy finds us. How will I get back to you if you're attacked?"

Is Sergeant Tyler right? thought Davis. Am I spreading my platoon too thin?

All eyes turned to Davis. It was his decision.

If Davis decides to concentrate his forces and not send Tyler away to establish OPs, go to Section 25.

If Davis decides to establish the observation posts tonight, go to Section 38.

Section 43

If we run now, we die. If we stay, we die. Is there no way out?

"Damn it! We don't stand a chance if we run," Davis shouted. "Stand fast. We're fighting here. Keep up the fire!"

Davis fired his M16 toward an enemy tank attempting to push through the tank ditch.

"Damn it! Keep firing!" Few of the Americans heard their platoon leader's voice over the din of battle.

A BMP raced forward, firing wildly as it sped to the east. Tracers struck the advancing enemy armored vehicle without effect. An M60 machine gun, two positions down from Davis's hole, engaged the BMP. The distraction caused by the 7.62mm rounds gave another soldier just enough time to fire his AT4 and send the BMP to hell. A second BMP followed, bypassing his smoldering leader, and was blown apart by an antitank mine.

Undaunted, more BMPs followed. Davis's machine guns rattled and scraped the sides of the passing vehicles; however, the steady stream of armor-piercing incendiary bullets merely bounced off the hard flanks of the advancing enemy armor. Showered with sparks from the strike of Davis's guns, the BMPs drove on. A few BMPs were stopped by AT4s. More vehicles were missed than were hit.

The platoon was almost out of antitank missiles.

A tank crested the tank ditch and raced toward the defenders, slewing its turret to the right and left and firing its machine guns as it raced by. Two BMPs followed closely behind. The vehicles zig-zagged wildly as they sped through the smoke trying to avoid mines and burning vehicles.

"They're getting past us!" Davis screamed.

The trailing BMP surged forward, detonated a mine, and exploded. It crumbled to pieces in a burst of black smoke and flame.

Tracers filled the air. Several of Davis's men were down. Many had head wounds. The screams of the wounded could be heard in between the roar of exploding vehicles. One of the Javelins was knocked out of action, its gunner sprawled on the desert floor in a puddle of bright red blood.

Bullets ripped at the sandbags of Davis's fighting position. Cowper, his M203 pointed up out of the hole, pummeled the advancing enemy with grenade fire.

Another BMP suddenly exploded in a burst of orange flame and black smoke as a Javelin round hit its target. Twisted metal flew through the air. The turret came off the BMP and landed upside down on the hull.

From inside their bunkers, a few of Davis's men fired their M16s at the enemy vehicles in defiance. Their spirit was short lived.

An enemy detachment moved to battle formation west of the tank ditch and continued the attack. Moving on-line, they poured a continuous volley of devastating machine-gun, 30mm cannon, and 125mm tank gun fire into the American position. One after another the defensive positions were blown apart. The Americans stopped firing.

Davis was down to a handful of men. He couldn't reach anyone on the radio. From his position, it was hard to see if anyone was alive. The entire area of Wadi Al Sirree was filled with smoke from vehicle exhaust, smoke generators, blazing vehicles, and burning smoke pots. The engagement area in front of his position was completely obscured. Davis surveyed the scene, scanning the smoke for enemy movement.

"Sir, look out!" Cowper shouted.

Two enemy tanks rocked to a halt behind a burning BMP, two hundred meters in front of BP Alamo, and leveled their guns at Davis's men.

Roll the dice.

If you roll 2–8, go to Section 58.

If you roll 9–12, go to Section 93.

Section 44

After several moments Davis threw four smoke grenades to cover their move.

The enemy armor kept advancing, firing as it came forward.

"Let's go. Everyone out!" Davis ordered, shouting as loud as he could.

Davis and Cowper crawled from their bunker and ran up the hill in short, quick rushes. Machine-gun bullets whizzed all around them. Sergeant Mark, the only survivor from his fighting position, jumped up and tried to follow Davis. A 30mm cannon round exploded to his left. The searing projectile cut him in half.

Cowper was also hit in the back and fell over. Davis dove for cover. An enemy machine gun plastered the area where Cowper lay dying. Davis ducked behind the body of his RTO and checked the soldier for a pulse. Cowper was dead.

Bullets from several enemy weapons sliced into the dirt in front of Davis, striking Cowper's body. At the same time one of the SAW gunners from 2d Squad rushed rearward to Davis's right, attempting to run away from the fire. The soldier moved three feet from his position before he was hit by an enemy machine-gun burst. The tearing bullets knocked him off his feet and threw his lifeless body to the ground as if he were a broken doll. No one else was moving. The only Americans Davis could see were already dead.

The trail of green tracer machine-gun bullets marched toward Davis in small geysers of spurting sand. He raised his head to look for a way out. He never felt the round that struck him.

Go to Section 3 and try again.

Section 45

The battered infantrymen fired at the enemy entering the engagement area. Tanks and BMPs halted to plaster the position with cannon and machine-gun fire. The volume of the enemy's direct fire was over-whelming. Suddenly, no one was firing at the attackers.

"OK, Cowper, tell everyone to make a break for it," Davis said, his voice tinged with urgency.

"All stations, this is One-Six Alpha," Cowper transmitted. "Leave now. Get out while you still can. Take any wounded with you."

The sound of the radio was quickly replaced by the blast of BMP cannon fire. The ground in front of Davis detonated in smoke and flame as the 30mm shells exploded. Davis ducked to the bottom of his hole as the enemy fire ripped apart the roof of his position.

Cowper crouched low, next to his platoon leader. The RTO strained to hear the radio, pressing the receiver hard against his ear.

"Sir, no response!" Cowper shouted in between artillery explosions.

Davis was consumed with fear and anger. The platoon is being pulverized by enemy fire, he reflected despondently. I've got to do something! Dejected, he waited for a few seconds for the fire to slacken, then struggled up to the aperture of his position to see the battlefield.

Roll the dice.

If you roll 2 or 3, go to Section 44.

If you roll 4–7, go to Section 55.

If you roll 8–12, go to Section 58.

Section 46

The object of fighting is to kill without getting killed. Don't disperse your force; you can't punch with an open hand; clench your fist; keep your command together.

Fight when holding, advancing or retiring; always fight or be ready to fight.

Aim at surprise; see without being seen. If you meet a man in a dark room, you jump; you should always try to make your enemy jump, either by day or by night. A jumping man can't hit.

Never remain halted without a look-out. Sentries must be posted, no matter what troops are supposed to be in front of you.

Guard your flanks and keep touch with the neighboring units. Try to get at the enemy's flanks.

Send information back to your immediate commander. Negative information is as important as positive. State time and place of your message. You cannot expect assistance from your superiors unless you tell them where you are and how you are situated.

Hold what you have got and what you gain. Never withdraw from a position until ordered to do so.

WHEN IN DOUBT, FIGHT IT OUT.

Maj. Gen. J. F. C. Fuller

Platoons and squads normally defend as part of a larger force to disrupt, disorganize, delay, or block an attacking enemy. The defense is usually chosen when there is insufficient strength to attack. A defense is a coordinated effort by a force to prevent an attacker from achieving his objective. The purpose of the defense must be to seize the initiative, turn the battle against the enemy, and create conditions for offensive operations. The challenge of the defender is to gain the initiative and keep the enemy reacting and unable to execute his own plan.

Wadi Al Sirree is a defile—a narrow passage. The defense of a defile can be executed either in front of, within, or behind it. Each option holds advantages and disadvantages for the defender.

The selection of any of these options depends on the nature of the enemy. Orson Scott Card in his book *Ender's Game* explained the importance of understanding the enemy: "There is no teacher but the enemy. No one but the enemy will ever tell you what the enemy is going to do. No one but the enemy will ever teach you how to destroy and conquer. Only the enemy shows you where you are weak. Only the enemy tells you where he is strong. And the only rules of the game are what you can do to him and what you can stop him from doing."

Defensive tactics and techniques have evolved along with combined-arms warfare over the past forty years. With this development, eight fundamentals have become the key to defensive success at the platoon and company levels. Keep them in mind when you plan future defensive missions.

- **Depth.** Position your forces in depth and place obstacles in depth. Depth gives you a way to absorb the attacker's initial blow and time to figure out what he is up to. It gives you the ability to develop the situation and the time and space to maneuver and concentrate your combat power where it is needed. In this case Davis chose to conduct a frontal, forward-slope defense of Wadi Al Sirree. His defense was linear and his obstacles, what few he could place, were almost linear as well.
- **Dispersion.** Spread apart your critical assets so that you can mass their fires without massing the weapons. In this case Davis massed his M60 machine guns and Javelins in the center of his defense, making them easy targets for the enemy's direct fire weapons.
- **Security.** Take away the enemy's reconnaissance and you are on the road to victory. Deny him the ability to see your preparations and you add to your ability to win. There are many ways to protect your platoon from surprise attack. Some ways are passive (dispersion, camouflage, noise and light discipline, hide or defilade positions, etc.); others are active. The most critical active security measures are to conduct patrols against enemy observation posts and to establish your own observation posts.
- **Terrain Sense.** Study the terrain, whenever possible by walking it, riding over it, or observing it from a vantage point. Reconnoiter from both your view and the enemy's. Know what the terrain will

allow you and your enemy to do. See where it slows him down or forces him into tight column formations. Find the best covered and concealed positions that dominate likely enemy avenues of approach. Note terrain that allows the enemy to concentrate maneuver forces. See where you have enough space and fields of fire to concentrate your available firepower. Note positions from which you can counterattack in depth into the flanks of an enemy force. See where you can position your forces to survive the enemy's initial heavy concentrations of artillery fires. Note the best terrain for positioning observation posts well forward of your defensive positions to observe likely avenues of approach. See where obstacles can be placed and tied in with natural obstacles to create effective barriers to enemy movement.

- **Stop the Enemy's Rate of Advance.** Threat attacks are based on two principles, speed and mass. A heavily mechanized enemy usually plans to win by sustaining a high rate of advance (two to three minutes per kilometer) and pushing a lot of combat power forward fast. Use existing natural obstacles or place barriers to block forward movement and separate his forces. Concentrate enough indirect and direct firepower to kill him quickly, or at least to kill his lead elements all at once. If you try to pick off his vehicles one by one, he will overrun you before you know it. Compress the enemy's vehicles into a small area, then attack them with all the firepower you have. You don't have to outnumber the entire enemy force. You just have to outnumber them in your constricted, selected engagement areas.

- **Mass Combat Power in the Right Time and Place.** A well-trained mechanized threat will mass his forces where you least expect them and will create at least a three-to-one advantage over you in men and equipment. To beat him, you must develop enough friendly combat power to reduce the odds. This is done in two ways. First, you have to see your enemy while he is still well forward of your defensive positions; this will provide you time to decide what your opponent is up to and where you need to concentrate your forces. Second, you must have units skilled in maneuver that can respond quickly to on-the-spot orders (FRAGOs) and move rapidly to the threatened sector. If you can do that and hit your enemy where he is vulnerable, you can win.

• **Force the Enemy to Fight in Two Directions.** When you engage the attacking force, maneuver your units into positions that force the attacker to turn and fight in two directions. He will always have a flank exposed to somebody; this gives the opposing commander a very tough command and control problem. He cannot concentrate his fires but has to split them. You can, therefore, reduce his combat power by half.

• **Counterattack.** You cannot stay in position, taking whatever your attacker dishes out. Draw him into your engagement areas and counterattack his exposed flank by fire or by fire and movement to finish him off.

You have fought and lost.
Learn from this defeat.
Return to Section 3 and try again.

Section 47

"I want an OP manned tonight," Davis added forcefully. "Have him use a squad radio to stay in touch with me. His call sign will be OP North. I want him high on the north wall. I expect him to identify targets for our mortar and artillery fires."

"Wilco," Piper replied. "Tyler, you have the OP on the north wall, on Hill 865. Make sure each soldier carries plenty of water. I also want them to have an M937 individual night sight, PVS-7 night-vision goggles, and half a dozen flares."

Sergeant Tyler nodded.

"Tyler," Davis declared, pointing to his map, "if the enemy is sighted, the OP calls me on the radio. If he can't get through, tell him to fire a white flare. Once he confirms that the enemy is in the trails, follow the white flares with a star cluster. If the enemy is coming in the north, along Trail 1 or 2, fire a green star cluster. If he is coming in the south, along Trail 3 or 4, shoot a red star cluster."

"White when he sees the enemy. Green if he comes to the north along Trail 1 or 2, red if he comes to the south on Trail 3 or 4," Tyler repeated.

"Correct," Davis confirmed.

"If we can't talk on the radio, I'll call for artillery and mortar fires on the trails based on these signals," Mark chimed in. "It won't be as accurate as talking to the OP, but it will provide us with a backup if commo fails."

"Good idea," Davis replied, nodding to Sergeant Mark. "The OP will warn us where the enemy is. Without the warning, our defense will not work."

The squad leaders nodded. Everyone understood the seriousness of the task.

"All right," Davis said, "any more questions?"

"I think you and I should check out the OP on Hill 865 before it gets dark. From there we'll have a good view of the enemy's approaches," Piper said, pointing to the high ground to the north. When Davis didn't answer right away, Piper asked, "Well, what about it, Lieutenant?"

If Davis decides to conduct a leader's reconnaissance to Hill 865, go to Section 9.

If Davis decides to interrupt his platoon's preparations and send patrols to the high ground on both sides of Wadi Al Sirree, go to Section 49.

If Davis decides to continue preparations and send Sergeant Tyler on a patrol to Hill 865, go to Section 91.

Section 48

The ground trembled with the bursting enemy shells. The artillery fire was extremely accurate, Davis thought. Too accurate. He felt like an ant, getting ready to be stepped on.

"Shit, they must have an observation post that is calling artillery fire in on us!" Davis screamed as a powerful 152mm round destroyed the Javelin position to his right flank. The U.S. positions were being taken out one at a time. Too few enemy shells were landing to indicate a normal artillery barrage.

Could they be using precision-guided artillery shells? Davis wondered.

Davis watched in horror as the second Javelin position was smashed by a pinpoint explosion. Suddenly a flash of fire and steel engulfed Davis's fighting position. The force of the impact of the enemy shell collapsed the overhead cover and buried the lieutenant in sand and rock.

Davis hit hard against the earth. He felt numb all over, then he blacked out.

When he finally opened his eyes, he saw that he was covered with sand and blood. It took a few moments before he realized that he was still with the living. As he began to move his limbs he discovered that his legs were crushed under the weight of the roof's sandbags. He recoiled in horror as he saw that Cowper's bloodied and mangled body had taken most of the impact of the artillery blast.

Flies buzzed everywhere. Davis was numb and sick. His mouth had a coppery red-blood taste. He tried to move rocks and pieces of metal off his legs. He couldn't seem to focus his eyes. He struggled to look at his watch.

There were people walking around him. Someone was shouting. He waved his hands. "Help me!"

In seconds he was surrounded by enemy soldiers. They dragged him up out of the hole and raised him to his feet. Davis struggled to stand but his legs failed him and he fell to the ground. The enemy soldiers shouted at him and kicked him. Davis recoiled from the blows, using his right arm to guard his face.

Suddenly someone, sounding very official, barked commands in a language Davis couldn't understand. The kicking stopped. Hands reached down and jerked him up. Davis screamed in pain.

The next thing he knew he was lying on the back of a truck, bouncing down a rough desert trail. A mean-looking guard, brandishing an AK-74 assault rifle, sat near the tailgate of the truck. The guard's eyes were filled with hatred as he stared at Davis.

Lieutenant Bruce Davis was now a prisoner of war. He had failed in his mission. Every soldier in his platoon was either dead or captured. The enemy had broken through Wadi Al Sirree and driven the Americans to the east.

Go to Section 46.

Section 49

"Negative. No one is going anywhere until we patrol the high ground on our flanks," Davis declared, completely in charge of the situation. The lieutenant unfolded his map and beckoned for the platoon sergeant to bend down to see as he pointed out key terrain.

"Send Jordan's squad to check out the high ground on the south wall," Davis ordered. "Send Tyler's squad to check out the north wall. Get Mizogouchi to work on putting in Minefield M1. Mark and I will use the time to complete the artillery plan."

"Wilco," Piper responded with a grin, happy to see that the lieutenant was making some smart tactical moves. "While you're doing that, I'll get the work started on BP Yankee."

The patrols departed. Sergeant Mizogouchi took his squad to the northeast side of the tank ditch and began laying Minefield M1. Piper put one M60 machine-gun team on security in the positions overlooking the tank ditch. He took the other machine-gun team and the attached Javelin gunners to dig positions on BP Yankee.

Davis and Sergeant Mark had nearly completed their artillery plan when the sound of firing on the north wall interrupted their work.

"Sir, it's Sergeant Tyler on the radio for you," Cowper announced urgently.

"One-Six, this is One-Two," Tyler reported. "We found two enemy soldiers in an observation post on top of Hill 865. We killed them both. We tried to capture them but no dice. No friendly casualties. We captured an AM radio and a map. There's no marks on the map."

"Good work, One-Two. Bring anything you find on the bodies that could give us information about the enemy. I'll report it to higher."

Davis reported the incident to Captain Bludgell.

I have to assume that the enemy OP informed their unit of our positions in front of the tank ditch, Davis thought. Maybe we can use this knowledge to fool them into thinking that we're defending on the forward slope at BP Alamo.

The platoon worked throughout the day. Second Squad established OP North on Hill 865. Minefields M1 and M2 were completed and wire was strung along the east side of the antitank ditch at its south end.

Davis occupied his battle position to the east of the tank ditch with the machine guns and Javelins of the headquarters section. The rest of the platoon moved to their ambush positions to continue digging, improve their overhead cover, and catch a few hours of badly needed rest.

Davis was in constant communication with the OP and company headquarters. The sun set and the platoon continued to work in the moonlight, feverishly building, digging, and placing obstacles in preparation for the enemy's assault.

As the night wore on, the company radio net was filled with routine reports. Cowper attentively monitored the net and informed Davis of the few intelligence updates from battalion that were passed over the command net by the company XO.

Around midnight, the sky to the west was lit by the bright flash of explosions and the eerie glow of artillery flares. The noise of artillery gradually became more pronounced. Obviously a battle was taking place somewhere to the west, Davis thought.

At 0130 Piper and 3d Squad arrived to relieve the headquarters section from their security duty. With Piper in charge, Davis leaned back in his fighting position to catch some badly needed rest. He quickly fell asleep.

"Lieutenant," Piper whispered as he gently shook his platoon leader. "Wake up. We got someone near the tank ditch."

Startled, Davis sat up. "What's the situation?"

"There's a vehicle near the tank ditch. Jordan's on the line for you," Piper said as he handed the lieutenant the mike.

Davis pressed the radio receiver to his ear.

"One-Six, this is One-One. Over," an excited Sergeant Jordan announced over his squad radio to the platoon leader.

"This is One-Six. Send it. Over," Davis replied, energized by the burst of adrenaline the thought of immediate action had created.

"I see an armored vehicle just west of the tank ditch."

Davis fumbled for his night-vision goggles and turned them on. He placed them to his eyes and scanned the area to the southwest.

Davis saw the enemy. A group of three men close to an armored car were crouching near the wire.

"I got him in my Javelin sights," Specialist Chambers half whispered from the position just to the left of Davis's hole.

"Hold on, Chambers. Wait for my orders. They got some men on the ground, and I want everyone to get a shot at them," Davis ordered in a voice as cold as ice.

Cowper handed the lieutenant the radio mike.

"One-One, this is One-Six. Pop an illumination flare over the intruder. I'll nail him with a Javelin. Over."

"Roger, One-Six." Jordan replied. "Give me a few minutes."

Davis waited. He picked up his night-vision goggles and watched.

"Sir, I got a good picture in my thermal sights. I can hit him," Chambers yelled.

"I heard you the first time, Chambers. Wait until the flare is up," Davis proclaimed firmly. "I want to let the machine guns get the chance to take out the infantry." Tense seconds passed. Finally the flare exploded southeast of the tank ditch. It ignited right above and behind the enemy vehicle. The light displayed an armored car with two soldiers standing outside, searching to the west with some kind of binoculars or night-vision devices. As soon as the flare illuminated, the two enemy soldiers scrambled back to their armored car.

"Fire!" Davis screamed. Chambers fired. In less than six seconds the speeding Javelin antitank missile impacted against the top of the armored car in an inferno of flying metal, burning flesh, and orange-yellow light.

The platoon opened up with machine guns and rifles all along the front of the battle position. The enemy soldiers who had managed to miss the burning debris from the exploding vehicle were cut down by a steady stream of red tracers.

Davis reported the destruction of the BRDM to Captain Bludgell.

The night sky receded into early-morning twilight. The area to the front of BP Alamo was as quiet as a church on a Monday morning. Maybe there won't be a battle in my sector, Davis thought. Maybe we scared them away.

"Lieutenant," Sergeant Piper said as he threw an MRE into his platoon leader's foxhole. "Have some breakfast. This is the last of our supplies. I'll have to ask the XO to get us another couple of boxes."

Davis rubbed his tired eyes, then reached for the MRE that the sergeant had thrown at his feet.

"Any word from the patrol?" he asked.

"Jordan reported in a few minutes ago. He checked out the BRDM and sent a fire team along the south wall. No sign of anything except one destroyed BRDM and three dead enemy soldiers just west of the tank ditch. Jordan's men put the bodies in the tank ditch and buried them with sand. No contact on the south wall. OP North can see almost everything on the north wall. No one got up there last night. We may have gotten them all."

"So far, so good," Davis mused. "Battalion destroyed a BMP last night in the north. I heard it on the company net after you hit the sack."

"Hey, sir," Cowper announced, pointing to the east. "We got company."

An HMMWV with an overloaded trailer bouncing behind it jolted to a halt on the low ground just northeast of Davis's position. The open-top truck carried two men—the driver and a passenger. The back of the HMMWV was piled high with boxes and rolls of wire.

Dust billowed as the truck stopped. An early-morning breeze carried the cloud up to Davis, covering him, Piper, and Cowper in finely powdered sand.

The company XO, First Lieutenant Sandburg, slowly climbed out of the HMMWV and ambled up the hill. "Looks like I got here just in time for breakfast," Sandburg said with a grin.

"Jeff, in spite of that dust shower you just gave me, I'm happy to see you," Davis announced, standing up and extending his hand to the officer. "Care for an MRE?"

Sandburg laughed. "No thanks. Good morning, Sergeant Piper. How's life treating you?"

"Oh, things are just dandy," Piper answered, spitting a wad of tobacco juice on the ground. "I've found a home in the army."

The three men chuckled.

"Any casualties from the firing last night?" the XO asked.

"Negative," Davis answered, proud to report his first combat action against the enemy. "It looks like 1st Platoon drew the first blood of the war."

"Yes. And you did one hell of a job. My compliments."

"Yeah, we were lucky," Davis replied.

"Lucky. Shit, sounds to me like just plain good tactics. Your guys did a great job," Sandburg said with a smile. "You knocked out a very critical enemy observation post and destroyed an enemy reconnaissance patrol trying to get through your lines. That sounds to me like you earned your pay."

"Too bad we didn't find out anything from their maps," Piper commented. "They even changed the radio frequency before we zapped them."

"It was Chambers who hit the BRDM. Best damn Javelin gunner in the battalion!" Davis announced proudly.

"I brought you some presents," Sandburg said, pointing to his HMMWV. "I overloaded my hummer so bad I didn't think I'd make it. In the back you'll find twenty antitank mines, about six hundred sandbags, ten more AT4s, and thirty-five gallons of water. There's an additional thirty M21 antitank mines in the trailer."

"Jeff, I'll never say another bad thing about the bastards at company headquarters," Davis confessed with a smile.

"I'll get some of the guys to unload everything," Cowper offered. Several soldiers from Davis's platoon gathered around the HMMWV and began unloading the trailer.

Sandburg surveyed the platoon's position. "You'll need to get some overhead cover on each of your fighting positions as soon as possible."

Piper nodded. "These are just our night positions."

Sandburg gave Piper a brief, curious look.

"We plan to mount our defense by setting an ambush in each of the four trails behind us," Davis declared. "Our best chance to block the entrance to the valley is to knock out enemy vehicles as they try to come up the narrow trails. We'll move to our actual ambush positions along each trail early tomorrow morning."

Davis handed the company executive officer his fire plan for the defense of the trails of Wadi Al Sirree.

"Excellent plan," Sandburg replied after studying it.

"What's the big picture?" Davis asked.

"Things are looking pretty serious. This won't be like Desert Storm. The enemy isn't going to give us six months to prepare. Battalion says he's already on the move."

"No shit, sir," Piper said, grinning. "Those guys on Hill 865 weren't amateurs."

"The enemy overran an allied reconnaissance company that was screening to the west. The battle took place about forty kilometers from here," Sandburg reported in a serious tone. "Things should get exciting very soon."

"So, did our allies fight or just turn tail?" Piper asked.

"They fought, Sergeant. And died."

Piper spat a wad of chewing tobacco juice on the dust near Sandburg's feet. "Well, let the bastards come. We'll be ready."

"I'll pass that on to the CO," Sandburg replied, looking in the direction of the blackened and burned-out BRDM. "By the way, the commander labeled your position here as Battle Position Alamo."

"Alamo?" Davis questioned, scribbling the name onto his map. "Is that supposed to be funny?"

"As I recall, the good guys didn't win there," Piper chimed in, deadly serious.

"Bludgell's from Texas. You know how he is. I reckon he thinks that this will be in the history books someday. Don't let it get to you," Sandburg sympathized with a wry smile.

"We won't be fighting here anyway," Davis replied dryly. "If we tried to stop them from the forward slope of this rise, we'd all end up like Davy Crockett."

Sandburg laughed. "You're probably right. You've got a good plan; don't change it now. BP Alamo includes the trails on his graphics. The old man is convinced that you all are a sideshow anyway. He's too busy preparing BP Bravo and going to meetings at battalion to worry about you."

"Thank God for small miracles," Davis commented with a whimsical grin.

"Well, I've got to get back," Sandburg announced. "Good luck. We expect action tomorrow morning. Battalion still predicts that you won't be bothered. We're convinced that they'll attack along Viper. You should be OK here."

"I hope you're right, Jeff," Davis replied.

The short lieutenant smiled, shook Davis's hand, and trudged back down the hill. Lieutenant Davis and Sergeant Piper watched the company XO drive away.

"Get the men to work on finishing their ambush positions," Davis ordered. "I want all the mines armed before nightfall."

"Wilco, we need to get our overhead cover straight before then also," Piper replied as he took off his helmet and brushed the sweat from his closely shaved head. "After that I think we should let the men get some sleep."

Davis scanned his position and shook his head. "Not yet. Those mines we just unloaded won't do us any good if we leave them there in a pile. We have to keep everybody working. I want to double-check each position."

"Christ, sir. The men hardly slept last night," Piper argued, with tension mounting in his voice. "They did a great job yesterday and last night. There is no immediate threat, so now is the safest time to relax. I think they deserve to rest for a few hours."

I know we're all tired, Davis thought. Tired soldiers make mistakes. Mistakes in combat cost lives. How far can I push them before I step beyond what is possible? The muffled rumble of distant explosions could be heard way off to the west, punctuating the seriousness of the issue.

Piper stood quietly, waiting for his lieutenant to speak.

Davis has to decide!

If Davis decides to let the men rest, go to Section 22.

If Davis decides to keep the men working, go to Section 33.

Section 50

"Hansen, Montoya, Chambers, get your gear and get ready to move," Davis ordered. "Cowper, get Gerber and Spellman."

"What's the plan, sir?" Mark asked.

> If we go forward we die. If we go back we die. It is better to go forward.
>
> Ancient Zulu motto

"We're moving to Trail 4. We've got to counterattack *now!*"

Mark looked at his platoon leader in disbelief. "Sir, I could call for fires better from here."

"We're moving forward, Sergeant," Davis declared, ending the argument, "and I need you with me. Chambers, leave the extra Javelin rounds here. Carry only one round with the launcher." The soldiers prepared to move.

"Check your weapons." The soldiers huddled around their platoon leader.

"OK, here's the situation. Enemy infantry is attacking Trail 4. Our mission is to counterattack and drive them west, back down the trails. We'll move out in a wedge. I'll lead at the point of the wedge. Gerber, your M60 machine-gun team is on my right. One of the Javelin teams with M16s—Chambers—on my left," Davis said, pointing. "Spellman, your team's on my right. Cowper, stay right behind me. Mark, you're right behind Cowper."

Davis waited a few seconds to let this sink in.

"We're going to find the enemy in Trail 4 and try to find a position where we can get on line and attack him with rifle and machine-gun fire. When I tell you to get on line, I want you all to hit the ground and fire until I tell you to stop."

The soldiers looked up at their platoon leader. The sound of rifle and machine-gun fire and the dull thud and crash of 40mm grenades mingled with the sound of exploding Claymore mines. Bright explosions interrupted the darkness in the vicinity of Trail 4.

A kaleidoscope of thoughts, more emotions than logic, rushed through Davis's mind. I'm committing my reserve. Am I doing the right thing? If I don't use my reserve now, I may not get another chance.

When the situation is obscure, attack.

Gen. Heinz Guderian

"Everybody got the plan?" Davis asked in a determined voice. He paused long enough to sense if there was any indecision. No, Davis thought, everyone is scared, but everyone is willing.

"Let's go!" The wedge moved out slowly at first, but Davis soon picked up the pace.

"Cowper, keep trying to get Mizogouchi!" Davis shouted as they marched forward. "Tell 2d Squad to hold their fire."

The small reserve force carefully bypassed the minefields and moved down the ridge toward the firing. Davis knew that there was no time for caution. He had to be bold and quick. For what he had in mind, timing was crucial. The sounds of fighting diminished, and Davis picked up the pace again.

Within minutes the reserve was on a small rise that lay in the northern part of Trail 4. Davis could see firing. Tracers from squad automatic weapons and rifles ricocheted off rocks as Mizogouchi's men attempted to stop the enemy from moving north. Davis motioned for everyone to take up firing positions.

"Mark, I need fires standing by and fired on my command. Do you understand? At my command!"

"Wilco, sir," Mark replied quietly, sounding perplexed. He took the handset from Hutchinson and yelled at the FDC officer to make sure he understood. The desert resounded with the sharp crack of small-arms fire and the dull thuds of exploding grenades.

"There! On the high ground. At one o'clock!" Gerber whispered as he aimed his M60.

"Steady, Gerber. I see them too. Hold your fire. No one fires until I give the word," Davis ordered. "Mark, stand by. I want everything at once. Are the guns laid on and ready?"

"Roger," Mark answered, unsure of what the lieutenant had in mind. "But, sir, shouldn't we—"

Davis raised his hand to silence his forward observer. "I want the artillery fire at my command," he ordered in a hushed voice.

A large group of enemy soldiers slowly worked their way around the northern flank of Trail 4. The enemy assembled slowly, apparently waiting to mass for their attack and overrun Mizogouchi's defending force.

Seconds ticked by. The Americans held their fire. The men lay prone against the edge of the rise, watching the enemy come over the opposite ridge in groups of three and four. The enemy infantry, unaware that the Americans lay in ambush to their flank, were assembling only two hundred meters away.

Suddenly the enemy infantry began to move forward. Forty to fifty men moved east, crouching in the dark, in a move to flank Mizogouchi and his men defending Trail 4.

"Now! Fire!" Davis ordered. "Mark, artillery, now!" A steady stream of red tracer bullets sliced into the unsuspecting enemy. Soldiers slammed to the ground, surprised at the fire that appeared to come out of nowhere. A few tried to shoot back, but confusion reigned and many more fell to the ground, never to rise again.

"Mark, where's the damned artillery?" Davis swore.

"On the way!" Mark screamed, happy to hear the screech of incoming 105mm artillery on his target.

The U.S. artillery exploded directly south of the enemy infantry. "Adjust fire!" Davis yelled. "Drop two hundred."

Mark was already on the radio, adjusting the artillery fire to hit the target. "Sir, that's dangerously close!"

"I'm aware of that; fire it!" Davis shouted. "Call it in."

The M60 machine guns, positioned next to Davis, continued blazing away. They did the devil's work, pinning the enemy to the ground. Round after round tore into the surviving enemy soldiers as they struggled down the side of the hill. A few appeared to lose their nerve and tried to run to the west. Gerber and Spellman cut them down like a scythe on ripened corn.

The artillery adjusted onto the target. Hundreds of tiny metal fragments exploded above the enemy, slaughtering the huddled survivors. After a few moments the artillery stopped. Gerber's machine gun swept the field with fire, searching out anything that moved.

"Cease fire," Davis ordered. "Report."

"Everyone here's OK, sir," Mark declared.

"Cowper, get the squad leaders on the radio and find out how many casualties we have."

Minutes passed as the reports filtered in. The squad leaders all responded as the shock of the battle wore off.

"One-Six, this is One-Four. We lost two men killed in 3d Squad, Fryer and Satre. One man in 2d Squad is wounded in the arm. The medic has him and says he can stay with us until we can arrange evacuation. A few other minor scrapes. No other serious casualties."

"Hell, sir, I guess we killed an entire company of enemy infantry," Mark announced proudly, still lying in a prone position next to his lieutenant. "You sure knew how to call this one."

"Yeah. I'll bet you that Fryer and Satre wouldn't agree with you. Let's move back to Position Yankee."

Roll the dice.

If you roll 2 or 3, go to Section 90.

If you roll 4–12, go to Section 31.

Section 51

"I'm coming, Piper. Hold on!" Davis yelled. He spun around onto his belly, leveled his M16 rifle in the direction of the incoming fire, and blasted off a full thirty-round magazine of ammunition.

Time hung in the air, still, frozen. Davis changed magazines in his rifle, then crawled toward Piper. Davis's heart was beating fast.

The dirt in front of Davis jumped with the strike of the enemy round. Davis rolled twice to his left, fired off a few rounds, then continued crawling.

"Don't move, Piper," Davis shouted, almost out of breath. "We must have stumbled into an enemy observation post. I'll get you out of here."

"No, get the—"

"Hang on, Sergeant!" Davis exclaimed. Piper was only a few feet away.

The short, sharp burst from the enemy sniper rifle was the last thing Davis heard before the enemy bullet entered the back of his neck. He lay facedown in the dirt and died.

Go to Section 37.

Section 52

"Hold on!" Davis yelled. He spun around on his belly, leveled his M16 rifle in the direction of the incoming fire, and blasted off a full thirty-round magazine of ammunition. "I'll get to you as soon as I take this guy out!"

Time hung in the air, still, frozen. Davis changed magazines in his rifle, then crawled to the left, looking for a better shot at his antagonist. He felt his heart beating fast.

The dirt in front of Davis jumped with the strike of the enemy round. Davis rolled to his right, fired a few rounds, and continued crawling.

"Don't move, Piper," Davis shouted as he changed magazines in his M16. "We must have stumbled into an enemy observation post. I'll get you out of here."

Piper didn't respond.

From his new position, Davis was within grenade range of the enemy, who had piled heavy stones to form the walls of their fighting position. The top of the position was covered with plywood, sandbags, and rocks.

Davis unhooked a grenade from the flap of his ammo pouch, pulled the pin, and flung the grenade. It exploded just in front of the enemy position. Rocks and dirt flew everywhere, adding to the shrapnel effect.

One man, staggering from the blast, got up to run. Davis dropped him with a well-aimed shot from his M16. Another enemy soldier stood up and fired his AK-74 at Davis before Davis could respond. Davis was hit in the left shoulder. He dropped his M16. The force of the bullet's impact spun him around and knocked him to the ground. With a surge of strength he crawled behind a rock to hide from the enemy's fire.

His M16 lay in the open, just beyond his reach. His left arm and side were numb. He groped for his rifle but recoiled his hand as a burst from an AK-74 struck inches in front of his fingers.

I'll never get out of here, Davis thought. I can't reach my rifle.

Digging his heels into the dirt, Davis pushed himself closer to the rock protecting him from the enemy.

"Amreekee!" the enemy taunted. "Inta intahate."

Davis pulled another hand grenade from his ammo pouch strap. It was his last grenade. This one would have to count. His left arm was useless. He wedged the grenade under a heavy rock to keep the arming device from igniting, then gently pulled the pin free. Deftly he clasped the grenade with his good arm, holding down the arming spoon as he pulled it from the rock.

Davis waited and listened. An eternity seemed to pass. Suddenly he heard the dull tread of a boot displacing a rock. It sounded close.

It's now or never, Davis thought.

Davis tossed the grenade over his head, toward the sound. The explosion detonated so close that rocks, dirt, and debris scattered over him. As the dust settled, the hill was bathed in an ominous silence.

Davis rolled to his good side. The second enemy soldier lay face up on the ground, a bloody corpse, splattered by Davis's grenade.

It took thirty minutes before Davis's men reached him and another hour before a medevac chopper arrived. In that time Sergeant Piper bled to death. Davis was seriously wounded, but his wound was not mortal and he would survive. Sergeant Jordan, the senior NCO in the platoon, took charge. For Davis the war was over.

Go to Section 37.

Section 53

"Negative. We still have too much to do," Davis announced authoritatively. "Get everyone up and working. We've got to finish the minefields and lay more barbed wire."

Piper looked down and kicked a rock at his feet. "OK. Whatever you say, Lieutenant."

The infantrymen obediently left their fighting positions to lay wire, place and arm antitank mines, and fill sandbags. The soldiers worked, sweat stained and thirsty, in the hot desert sun. In spite of their bests efforts, they didn't have time to lay the concertina wire in three strands, with the standard layer of two rolls on the bottom and one on top. As a compromise they laid single rows of concertina wire on the west side of the tank ditch.

Piper was everywhere, cajoling and inspecting. He verified the overhead cover on every fighting position by making two men jump on top of each roof. If the position didn't hold the weight of two men, it wouldn't be much protection against enemy artillery. As evening fell, the squads rotated duties between sleeping, working, and security.

Davis felt confident. The platoon had worked effectively in the past twenty hours, and he was satisfied with the relationship he had developed with Sergeant Piper. BP Alamo wasn't as ready as he would have liked, but at least the platoon was dug in with overhead cover. Each two-soldier fighting position was three to four feet deep. The corrugated steel roofs were reinforced with rocks and several layers of sandbags. Each position provided its occupants reasonable protection to the front and overhead, while still allowing fire to the front and the oblique.

Hell, I wish I'd had time to put in more mines and wire, Davis swore to himself. I also wish I could have dug some crawl trenches between our positions.

The night was spent in work and worry. The company radio net was filled with routine reports, interrupted only by a few intelligence updates from battalion that were passed over the command net by the company XO.

Maybe they'll attack at midnight tonight. Yes, they'll probably come at midnight, Davis thought.

Around midnight, the sky to the west was lit up by the bright flash of explosions and the eerie glow of artillery flares. The sounds of big guns and rockets pounded the ground far to the west.

"One-Four, this is One-Six," Davis whispered into the transmitter of his radio. "Do you see anything?"

"Negative. Don't worry, One-Six, they won't attack at night," Piper replied with the confidence of a veteran soldier.

You're scaring yourself for nothing, Davis thought. Piper's probably right. Maybe they won't attack tonight. Hell, once they find out they're up against the United States, they'll probably head for home.

At 0330 Davis settled into his position, hoping for a few minutes' rest. God, I'm tired! Davis thought. He leaned against the dirt wall, with the receiver of Cowper's radio pressed to his ear. The bright full moon sank slowly over the western horizon. Now only starlight illuminated the desert night.

"One-Six, this is One-Three. Over," an excited Sergeant Mizogouchi transmitted over his squad radio to the platoon leader.

"This is One-Six. Send it. Over," Davis replied.

"One-Six, I hear helicopters in the distance," Mizogouchi reported.

"Can you tell where they are? Do you see them? Over."

"Not sure. They sounded like they were to my south. The sound's gone now. Over."

Davis crawled out of his fighting position, stood up, and took off his helmet. He listened intently to the hum of the rotors from the southwest. It sounded like a group of helicopters was flying east around the large mountain to the south. Davis jumped back down to the radio and grabbed the handset.

"Can you tell whether they're friendly or enemy?" Davis asked, his voice pressed with urgency. "I've got to know where they're headed."

"Unknown," Mizogouchi replied, sounding embarrassed. "I can't see them."

Damn, I wish we could have seen those helicopters, Davis thought. Where did they go? Were they troop-carrying helicopters or scouts?

Ours or theirs? Hell, they're probably friendly and nobody bothered to tell me.

"Keep looking and call me if you sight anything. Out," Davis ordered. He switched the frequency and relayed the report of helicopters to Captain Bludgell with the caveat that they were probably American.

"Call me back when you can tell me for sure what's happening. I can't react to noises in the dark. Out," Bludgell replied curtly.

Suddenly to the east Davis heard the sound of small-arms fire, the thump of grenades, and the crash of muffled explosions.

"One-Six, this is One-Four. Sounds like there's a battle going on near BP Bravo."

"Roger, One-Four," Davis answered Piper apprehensively. "Stand by. I'll find out what's happening." Davis quickly changed radio frequencies.

"Bravo One-Six, this is Bravo Six-Six Alpha," Captain Bludgell's radioman announced over the radio receiver.

"This is One-Six. What the hell's happening? Over."

"We're under attack by enemy infantry. The CO's been hit and we lost the mortars. Sergeant Rossetti is in charge. I can't find the XO."

"Can you hold?" Davis asked, surprised at this unexpected turn of events. He could hear the sound of machine-gun fire in the background of Six-Six Alpha's transmission.

"The shit here is really bad. The enemy is all over the place. Can you help us?"

The radio suddenly went silent.

"Six-Six Alpha, this is One-Six. Over," Davis repeated, trying to reestablish contact. "Six-Six Alpha, this is One-Six. Over."

"Sir, I've lost contact too," Sergeant Mark complained. "I've tried all our frequencies. The only stations I can reach are in the platoon."

"Cowper, check out the radio," Davis ordered. "Check the antenna."

"I've already done that, sir. It's OK," Mark said.

"Sir, I can't reach anyone on the company net," Cowper said, his voice edged with worry. "They're not transmitting."

The clamor of the battle at BP Bravo echoed through the valley. Slowly the sounds of fighting from the east diminished, then stopped altogether.

Section 53

Davis took the handset from Cowper and quickly changed to the platoon frequency.

"One-Four, this is One-Six," Davis reported calmly over the platoon radio frequency to Piper. "Those helicopters that One-Three heard must have been enemy. They must have circled around the mountain to the south and landed some infantry behind BP Bravo."

"One-Six, what are we going to do now?" Piper asked. "Can you reach company or battalion?"

Davis considered his options. Why can't I reach the company? Could the enemy have destroyed everyone on BP Bravo? If so, why did they leave me alone? What if the enemy destroyed Bludgell and was now turning on me?

"Negative. I've tried several times." Davis paused, recognizing the hard truth of his platoon's situation. "We're on our own. There's nothing we can do for the company now. Just keep an eye out for any enemy who may come our way down the valley from the east. Continue the mission as planned."

The night sky faded into a light shade of gray. The tension mounted as dawn arrived. A steady drumbeat of distant artillery shells grew nearer.

The situation looks grim, Davis thought. The enemy has probably taken BP Bravo. Had enemy air assaults also disrupted the U.S. artillery?

Billows of black smoke could be seen on the western horizon. The lieutenant put down his night-vision goggles and scanned to the west with his binoculars. He trained them in the direction that he expected the enemy armor to advance.

The ground to the northwest of BP Alamo sloped downward for four kilometers, then gradually rose for an additional four kilometers to a jagged ridge on the western horizon. Between BP Alamo and this ridge was nothing but empty desert. As the enemy approached from the west, he would have to cross this open space against the brigade's deep fires. Unfortunately, Davis knew how weak those deep fires were—only one battalion of 155mm artillery and a few sorties from navy F/A-18s and air force A-10s.

Piper ran over to Davis's position. "Things don't sound so good," Piper said, taking a moment to catch his breath. "If the enemy has taken BP Bravo, shouldn't we pull out?"

"Withdraw," Davis said, "and go where?"

A flight of F/A-18s screamed overhead, flying low over Wadi Al Sirree. The aircraft headed west to attack the advancing enemy columns.

"Sir, I've picked up some transmissions on the artillery net," Sergeant Mark reported. "All the long-range stuff is engaging the enemy. We'll be in battle with the main force soon."

The sound of outgoing 155mm artillery shells punctuated Mark's words. The rounds arced high overhead and exploded to the west, detonating with a rumble that shook the ground in Wadi Al Sirree. A pair of F/A-18s roared across the sky to the north, dropping cluster bombs on the advancing enemy armor.

"We're staying," Davis said to Piper, with a finality that ended all discussion. "That's our stuff firing now. The brigade is fighting its deep operation. Maybe our air support can even the odds a bit."

Deep operations are actions against enemy forces not yet in contact with friendly forces. Deep operations prevent the enemy from massing, and they create opportunities for offensive action by the defender. A deep operation enables the defender to separate the attacking echelons; disrupt the attacker's command and control, combat support and combat service support; and slow the arrival times of succeeding echelons. Battalions may participate in deep operations in accordance with brigade or division plans.

FM 7-20, *The Infantry Battalion,* 6 April 1992

"OK, why not?" Piper replied, nodding to Davis. "I guess this is as good a place as any to fight. We're ready."

The sound of multiple explosions resonated from the area beyond the jagged ridge to the northwest.

"That's our stuff," Davis shouted to his men, hoping to bolster their confidence. "Get ready. Enemy armored vehicles will be here in about twenty minutes."

"Well, I better get back to my position," Piper said with a determined grin. "I'll see you when this is all over."

Section 53

"You can count on it," Davis beamed back.

Piper rushed back to his foxhole. Davis focused his binoculars on the exits of the jagged ridge eight kilometers to the northeast. The passes were filled with dust and smoke. Aircraft darted over the ridge, launching their missiles at targets that Davis couldn't see. Suddenly, dark objects began racing out of each pass. Scores of vehicles, moving in high-speed columns, emerged from the passes. The vehicles quickly exited the narrow defiles and raced east across the broken desert terrain.

"There they are," Davis declared, pointing to the distant ridge. Sergeant Mark gave Davis a worried look, then put the receiver back to his ear and continued eavesdropping on the artillery radio frequency.

The rumble of explosions increased. The detonations sounded like the strike of a huge hammer, pounding the earth to the northwest. Davis watched with silent satisfaction as one of the lead enemy columns was blanketed with the impact of cluster bombs and 155mm artillery shells. A number of vehicles in this column lurched to a halt and burst into flames. More vehicles, however, bypassed the wreckage and continued on their determined path to the east.

American planes darted above the advancing enemy formations. A volley of antiaircraft missiles greeted the attacking aircraft, and a fiery explosion registered the midair destruction of one of the F/A-18s. Several other aircraft, having already dropped their ordnance, ignited their afterburners and roared back to the east, attempting to outrun the enemy's effective missile defenses.

The sound of outgoing artillery shells suddenly died away. The battlefield grew ominously quiet. Our deep operation is over, Davis thought. Now it's the enemy's turn.

"That's it, sir," Mark announced, the radio receiver still pressed against his ear. "The F/A-18s are heading home. We may get some A-10s later. We can call for fire whenever we have a formation of armored vehicles to shoot at."

Tense seconds ticked by. Every man faced to the west, watching the approaching enemy columns. The sound of bursting artillery, pounding a steady path from west to east, interrupted this short interlude of quiet. The explosions moved with precision in an inexorable wall of exploding steel toward the American positions.

210

The detonations grew louder. Balls of orange flame erupted in front of the tank ditch. The earth shook under the thunder of the enemy's 152mm guns. The bursting artillery shells showered the American positions with rocks and dirt.

"Shit, here it comes!" Cowper screamed. "Oh my God!"

The earth in front of the tank ditch exploded in fire and smoke.

Roll the dice.

If you roll 2–5, go to Section 14.

If you roll 6–12, go to Section 62.

Section 54

To the east Davis heard the din of distant battle: the sound of small-arms fire, the thump of grenades, and the crash of muffled explosions.

"One-Six, this is One-Four. Sounds like there's one helluva battle going on near BP Bravo."

"Roger, One-Four. Stand by. I'll try to find out the situation," Davis said as he quickly changed radio frequencies.

"Bravo One-Six, this is Bravo Six-Six Alpha," Captain Bludgell's radioman announced over the radio receiver.

"This is One-Six. What the hell's happening? Over."

"We're under attack. The CO's been hit and we lost the mortars. Sergeant Rossetti is in charge. I can't find the XO."

"Can you hold?" Davis asked, surprised at this unexpected turn of events. He could hear the sound of machine-gun fire in the background of Six-Six Alpha's transmission.

"The shit here is really bad. The enemy is everywhere. Can you help us?"

The radio suddenly went silent.

"Six-Six Alpha, this is One-Six. Over," Davis repeated, trying to reestablish contact. "Cowper, check this out."

The RTO fiddled with the radio, checking the connections and trying to make a radio check on the company net.

"Sir, I can't get anyone," Cowper reported. "I've tried all our frequencies. The only stations I can talk to are Piper and the OPs."

"Did you check the antenna?" Davis asked.

"Yes, sir. It's OK," Cowper replied, worried. "I think we're being jammed. We must have only enough push to reach the close stations. I can only talk to the platoon stations."

"Keep trying! We have to reach company or battalion," Davis urged.

As the dawn grew close, the tension mounted. The night sky faded into a light shade of gray. OP North radioed that he was switching from night-vision goggles to binoculars and continuing to observe.

We're all alone, Davis thought. Please don't let them attack. Maybe they won't attack through my valley. The muffled rumble of distant explosions thundered off to the west. The noise grew louder.

Davis knew that the time of battle was drawing near. He contemplated his firepower. On BP Yankee he had a total of nineteen men. This was Davis's main effort. He would have liked to send a full fire team with Gerber, but with only nineteen men he couldn't afford to weaken his defense any further.

A flight of F/A-18s screamed overhead, flying low over Wadi Al Sirree. The aircraft headed west to attack the advancing enemy columns. Explosions flashed on the western horizon.

"Sir, I've picked up some transmissions on the artillery net," Sergeant Mark reported. "The brigade is engaging the enemy. We'll be in battle with the main force soon."

The sound of outgoing 155mm artillery shells punctuated Mark's words. The rounds arced high overhead and exploded to the west, detonating with a rumble that shook the ground in Wadi Al Sirree. A pair of F/A-18s roared across the sky to the north, dropping cluster bombs on the advancing enemy armor.

I hope the brigade punches the hell out of them, Davis thought. We need every chance we can get to even these odds.

> The means available for conducting deep operations may be limited in number and effect, but must be clearly identified and positioned . . . Air delivered weapons . . . and field artillery are the chief weapons of deep operations.
>
> FM 71-100, *Division Operations,* June 1990

The sound of multiple explosions resonated from the area beyond the jagged ridge to the northwest. Tense seconds ticked by.

"That's our stuff," Davis shouted to his men. "Get ready. The enemy will be on us in about twenty minutes." Sergeant Mark gave Davis a worried look, then put the radio receiver back to his ear and continued eavesdropping on the artillery radio frequency.

The low, heavy rolling sound of explosions increased. Cannon and rocket shells hammered the ground to the west like a blacksmith pounding on a forge. Davis listened with silent satisfaction as the enemy columns were hit with CBU-87 cluster bombs and 155mm artillery shells.

"Sir, OP North on the radio," Cowper announced, handing Davis the receiver-transmitter.

"One-Six, here they come!" Sergeant Tyler reported nervously. "There's a hell of a lot of shit heading our way!"

Davis heard the distinctive bark of Specialist Gerber's M60 machine gun off to the east. The enemy's air assault forces must be moving away from Bludgell and toward me, Davis thought. Maybe they intend to clear the valley with infantry from east to west.

"Damn it," Davis swore, "give me a proper spot report. Tell me what you see."

"A column of vehicles . . . hundreds of them, coming out of the pass at grid NK353154." Tyler was silent for a few moments.

"One-Six, this is OP North," Tyler reported after a while, sounding a bit calmer. "They're taking a beating. I see three . . . no . . . make that five burning vehicles. Our planes are giving them hell."

Good, thought Davis. Maybe this will be easy after all. I wish I knew how Gerber was doing. No time now to worry. He's a good man. He'll do his duty.

American planes thundered above, heading for the advancing enemy formations.

213

"One-Six, they're still coming. The lead formation of the column appears to be heading southeast. At least twenty vehicles. The rest of the column, probably one hundred plus, is headed due east." Tyler paused for a few minutes, as if he was confirming what he saw. "I say again. One column appears to be attacking toward us along Axis Cobra. Over."

"Roger, OP North. Good report," Davis replied slowly, measuring every word for its effect on the men who were listening on the radio. "Execute as planned. Report to me as soon as the enemy is in the trails, then call in the targets. Over."

"Wilco, One-Six."

The enemy was heading right for him. Davis's worst fears appeared to be coming true.

A volley of antiaircraft missiles exploded high in the air on the western horizon. A fiery explosion registered the midair destruction of one of the F/A-18s. Several other aircraft, having already dropped their ordnance, ignited their afterburners and roared back to the east, attempting to outrun the enemy's effective missile defenses.

The sound of outgoing artillery shells suddenly died away. The battlefield grew ominously quiet. Our deep operation is over, Davis thought. Now it's the enemy's turn.

"That's it, sir," Mark announced, the radio receiver still pressed against his ear. "The F/A-18s are heading home. We may get some A-10s later. We can call for fire whenever we have a formation of armored vehicles to shoot at."

"Sergeant Mark, I'll need artillery support when the enemy gets in the trails," Davis requested as he pointed out the target area on his map.

"Right . . . uh . . . I'm working on it, sir," Mark responded, hesitating between radio messages. "I've got contact with the 155mm FDC right now."

"One-Six, this is OP North. The planes have stopped attacking the enemy," Tyler reported over the radio, confirming the forward observer's words to Lieutenant Davis. "The lead column that broke away from the main body is still heading toward us."

That's just great, Davis thought. They're sending a small detachment, forward of their main body, to take Wadi Al Sirree and flank the battalion.

The ratt-a-tat-tat of an M60 machine gun sputtered from the platoon's rear. Gerber—he's still at it! Davis thought. Hang on soldier! I've got the horde coming my way.

"I see another column heading east. I can't tell if it will follow the lead column. There's too much smoke and dust now. Request permission to pull back!" Sergeant Tyler at OP North begged.

It was time to make a decision. Davis took the mike from Cowper's hand.

**If Davis orders Sergeant Tyler to withdraw,
go to Section 57.**

**If Davis decides to order Sergeant Tyler to stay, go to
Section 59.**

Section 55

The ground exploded twenty feet in front of Davis.

This is it, Davis thought. I'm not going to make it.

The next shell landed right on top of the young lieutenant. The incoming round exploded. In a flash of fire and steel Davis was thrown through the air.

When Davis finally opened his eyes, he was covered with blood. It took a few moments for him to realize that he was still among the living.

As Davis began to move his limbs, he discovered that his legs were broken. He recoiled in pain. Flies buzzed everywhere. Davis was numb and sick. His mouth had a coppery red-blood taste. He couldn't move his legs. He looked around his position and saw the body of an American soldier several feet to his left. At first he

215

couldn't tell who it was. The body didn't have a head. Then he saw the radio on the corpse's back and realized that it must be Cowper.

Davis couldn't seem to focus his eyes. He saw people walking around him. Someone was shouting.

He waved his right hand. "Help me!"

In seconds he was surrounded by enemy soldiers. They pulled at him, took his watch and wallet, and kicked him when he wouldn't respond to their commands to get up. Davis recoiled from the blows, using his right arm to guard his face.

Suddenly the kicking stopped. He was so numb now he couldn't even feel the pain. Finally, someone sounding very official barked commands in Arabic. Hands reached down and jerked Davis up. He screamed in pain.

The next thing he knew he was lying in the back of a truck, bouncing down a rough desert trail. A mean-looking guard, brandishing an AK-74 assault rifle, sat near the tailgate of the truck. The guard's eyes were filled with hatred as he stared at Davis.

Lieutenant Bruce Davis was now a prisoner of war. He had failed in his mission. Every soldier in his platoon was either dead or captured. The enemy had broken through Wadi Al Sirree and driven the Americans to the east.

Davis had three options for the defense of Wadi Al Sirree: defend forward of the trails, inside the trails, or behind the trails. He selected to defend forward of the trails, from BP Alamo, which overlooked the antitank ditch. This option engaged the enemy at maximum range and required that 1st Platoon destroy the enemy as he crossed the antitank ditch. To increase the strength of this defense, he reinforced the antitank ditch with wire obstacles and minefields.

Defiles limit the area for maneuver and combat; they favor the placing of obstacles and hindrances . . . The defense of a defile can be executed either [1] in front of, or [2] within, or [3] behind the defile. The main battle field is chosen in front of the defile when the defile must be held open for following forces.
Truppenfuhrung, German Field Service Regulations, 1933

The greatest weakness of the BP Alamo position was that the defense was linear and placed the entire platoon within the range of all the attacker's weapons. Field Marshal Erwin Rommel once said, "It is easy to break a line." The disadvantage of a linear defense is that the enemy can mass superior combat power and break the defense at any single point. Fighting a mechanized, armored enemy who possessed superior direct fire capability made the forward-slope battle position defense an impossible task for lightly armed infantrymen.

In addition, Davis failed to conduct a personal reconnaissance of the battlefield from the enemy's point of view. Another quote from the 1933 German Field Service Regulations, *Truppenfuhrung,* illustrates this point: "If conditions permit, the terrain must be reconnoitered also from the hostile point of view."

Davis failed to do this. He did not look at his position from the enemy's perspective. His positions were in plain view of the enemy and were easy prey for a determined observation post capable of calling in artillery fires or a skilled gunner in a tank or BMP. Davis underestimated the enemy's firepower, and this error was fatal.

In the final analysis, victory or defeat depends significantly on the leaders' understanding and application of tactics. Sun Tzu, the great Chinese military philosopher, described the essence of tactics in the following words:

> If I am able to determine the enemy's dispositions while at the same time conceal my own then I can concentrate while he must divide. And if I concentrate while he divides, I can use my entire strength to attack a fraction of his. There, I will be numerically superior. Then, if I am able to use many to strike few at the selected point, those I deal with will be in dire straits.

Davis employed the wrong tactics for this situation. Learn from your mistakes and try again.

Davis failed in his mission.
Go to Section 3 and try again!

Section 56

The explosion sent Davis reeling backward from the shock of the blast. He felt numb all over, then he was encircled in darkness. When he finally opened his eyes, he was covered with debris and blood. As he began to move his limbs he discovered that his legs were crushed under the weight of the roof's sandbags.

He recoiled in horror. Cowper's bloodied and mangled body was lying inches from him.

Davis felt sick. He was thirsty, and his mouth had a coppery red-blood taste. He couldn't seem to focus his eyes or move his legs. He started removing dirt and pieces of metal from his legs. He struggled to look at his watch. It was 1320. He had been out for more than eight hours.

There were people walking around. He began to wave his hands.

Suddenly he was surrounded by enemy soldiers. They pulled him up, slapped him around, and threw him in the back of an open truck filled with dead and dying American soldiers.

Second Lieutenant Bruce Davis was now a prisoner of war.

There is an old Zulu battle motto: "If we go forward we die. If we go back we die. It is better to go forward."

Go back to Section 3 and try again!

Section 57

"Yes, OP North," Davis ordered calmly. "Move now. Get out while you still can."

"Wilco, One-Six."

The sound of the radio was quickly replaced by the screech of artillery.

"Incoming!" somebody shouted. The ground in front of Davis erupted in fire and flame. Davis fell to the bottom of his hole and prayed for the artillery barrage to end.

Cowper cowered low in the hole next to his platoon leader. The RTO strained to hear the radio, pressing the receiver hard against his ear.

"Sir! It's OP South," Cowper shouted in between artillery explosions. "The enemy column is at target Bravo One-Zero-One!"

Dirt was falling all over them. Dust filled the air, entering Davis's mouth and lungs, making it difficult to breathe. He grabbed the hand mike from Cowper.

"Six-Six, this is One-Six," Davis shouted, trying to reach his company commander. "Six-Six, this is One-Six. Over."

There was no response.

"Damn it!" Davis swore. "We've got to get artillery support."

The noise was deafening. The artillery kept falling. Rocks and flying metal pelted the sides and tops of the fighting position. Davis felt nauseous. Forcing himself to concentrate, he struggled to see the battlefield.

Roll the dice.

If you roll 2–6, go to Section 62.

If you roll 7–12, go to Section 67.

Section 58

A horrendous explosion blasted close to Davis's position. In a blinding burst of fire, flying shards of hot steel tore Davis to pieces. He never had a chance to feel the pain before he died.

Go to Section 46.

Section 59

"Negative, OP North," Davis ordered calmly. "Stay in position. You are more good to us there than down here. I need your eyes. Continue to report."

"OK, One-Six, whatever you say."

The sound of the radio was replaced by the scream of enemy artillery. The area near the tank ditch and the openings of the trails into Wadi Al Sirree took a tremendous beating by the enemy's artillery.

"The positions on BP Alamo are being torn apart," OP South reported. Davis smiled slyly, happy that he had not chosen to defend the valley from the forward slope.

"Get ready! We should be receiving incoming artillery shortly," Davis yelled at the top of his lungs to the men in BP Yankee. Mark, Hutchinson, and Cowper ducked down inside their four-man fighting position. "Their artillery will be passing over us soon!"

Cowper sat low in the hole right next to his platoon leader. The RTO strained to hear the radio, pressing the receiver hard against his ear. Davis took one last look and dropped down next to Cowper. The four men waited for the artillery.

"Sir! It's OP North," Cowper shouted in between the rumble of artillery explosions. "The enemy column is at TRP Bravo One-Zero-One!"

Davis crouched lower in his hole. He grabbed the hand mike from Cowper. "Bravo Six, this is One-Six," Davis shouted, trying to reach his company commander. "Bravo Six, this is One-Six. Over."

There was no response.

"Damn it!" Davis shouted. "No one is answering. Cowper, switch to the company jump frequency."

Cowper fumbled with the buttons on the top of the radio.

"Set, sir!"

"Bravo Six, this is One-Six," Davis repeated.

"One-Six, this is Six-Five," the company XO reported, sounding harried and out of control.

Thank God, Davis thought. We've worked through the jamming.

"We've been badly shot up. Most of the company is dead," Sandburg reported in short, broken sentences. "We got hit by the air assault. They took us by surprise. I had to pull out of BP Bravo. What's your situation?"

"Six-Five, I've got at least twenty vehicles attacking along Cobra. I need artillery support."

The sound of artillery, pounding a steady path from west to east, filled the air. The ground trembled.

"One-Six, I can't help you," replied a voice edged in sorrow. "You're on your own for now. We have reports of . . . hold it, I'll try to get back to you."

The XO's transmission was abruptly cut off.

"Bravo Six-Five, this is One-Six."

The receiver remained silent.

The thunder of the artillery grew louder. Balls of orange flame erupted in the western trails of Wadi Al Sirree. The earth rocked under the pounding of the enemy's heavy artillery. The shells walked their way up the valley, pounding a path of destruction to the east, getting closer to Davis's men with each passing second. It is with artillery that war is made, Davis thought, remembering the words of Napoleon.

Section 59

"Look out, here it comes!" Cowper screamed. "Incoming!"

Cowper dove under the protection of his shelter. The earth to the front of BP Yankee exploded in fire and smoke. Davis sat close to Cowper, weathering the storm of fire. Dirt was falling all over them. Dust filled the air, entering Davis's mouth and nose, filling his lungs. It was hard to breathe.

The impact of each round shook BP Yankee like an earthquake. Rocks and flying metal pelted the sides and tops of the fighting position. Each impact pushed Davis against the ground. The rounds fell close, but soon the fire slackened. The artillery slowly shifted to the center of the valley and rolled off to the east.

"Thank God," Davis announced, his voice muffled by the roar of the exploding shells. "Everyone OK?"

Sergeant Mark and Specialist Hutchinson stuck their heads up and nodded.

"Sir, Mizogouchi reports one man wounded. BP X-Ray took a heavy pounding, and Piper was still getting a report," Cowper announced.

Davis rose up and looked to the east. Smoke lingered low to the ground to the east in Wadi Al Sirree. Enemy artillery was now falling north of BP Bravo, whistling overhead on its way to impact other American positions in Davis's battalion. With BP Bravo in enemy hands, the attackers had apparently shifted their artillery to targets outside of Wadi Al Sirree.

"Did you hear the report of enemy tanks at Bravo One-Zero-One?" Davis shouted.

"No!" Mark yelled. "Hutchinson, give me the radio."

Davis looked back to the east toward Bravo.

"I can't reach the company or battalion mortars!" Mark screamed.

"Forget them," Davis ordered. "Change frequencies and call for 155mm. We won't stop them with mortars."

Hutchinson pulled the radio closer to read the frequency window. He read the 155mm artillery battalion frequency from the plastic wrist coder on his left forearm. Sergeant Mark started shouting into the transmitter as soon as Hutchinson finished with the buttons.

"Victor Seven-Six, this is Charlie Five-Five. Fire for effect, target Bravo One-Zero-One. Over."

222

"I've got them, sir!" Mark exclaimed, jubilant.

"Give it to them right here," Davis said, pointing to his map at the location of the northern trail. "Trail 1."

Soon Mark had the artillery falling at target Bravo One-Zero-One.

"Lieutenant, keep it up. OP North says you're right on target," Cowper yelled, his Kevlar helmet tilted on his head and the hand mike pressed hard against his ear. Davis's ears were ringing from the noise of the barrage, but he heard Cowper's shouts and grinned.

"Mark, keep pouring it on! Repeat!" Davis yelled, using the artillery term that indicated to continue firing at the same target.

Sergeant Mark huddled against the back of the fighting position. He held one radio handset to one ear, listening to OP North, and one radio handset to the other ear, calling for fire from the artillery battalion FDC. His long radio antenna extended from the protection of the earth, wood, and sandbag-reinforced bunker. The sergeant yelled into the handset, adjusting the fire.

The sound of U.S. 155mm artillery filled the air as U.S. shells smashed into Bravo One-Zero-One. With OP North guiding his fires, Mark quickly shifted deadly DPICM shells onto the enemy.

"DPICM in effect," Mark screamed into his hand mike.

"Sir, OP North." Cowper handed his lieutenant the radio transmitter.

"OP North. Report," Davis yelled.

"We knocked out three BMPs and a tank at Bravo One-Zero-One. Also, the second trail is blocked. I say again, Trail 2 is blocked. Looks like they're trying to come through at Bravo One-Zero-Four. Over."

"How many are there?" Davis questioned.

"Looks like about twenty-five vehicles," Sergeant Tyler reported.

"Roger," Davis replied calmly. "We're firing Bravo One-Zero-Four now. Tell me when they're at Bravo One-Zero-Two."

The American artillery continued pounding the narrow northern trails.

"We're kicking the shit out of them at Bravo One-Zero-Four. Keep firing," OP North shouted through Davis's radio receiver.

But the enemy kept coming, in spite of the deadly artillery fire. Davis could see black smoke rising high in the sky from the impact of the rounds.

"They're crossing the tank ditch by pushing wrecks into the ditch and driving over their own vehicles," OP North reported. "There are two BMPs and a tank struggling to exit the tank ditch right now."

Enemy machine-gun tracers and tank cannon projectiles blasted the unoccupied BP Alamo. Davis watched as the bullets bounced off the rocks and tracers flew harmlessly overhead, high in the air.

"I'm glad we're not in BP Alamo," Davis confessed, nodding to Mark. Mark was too busy to respond. He stayed glued to the artillery net.

A huge explosion roared to the west of the tank ditch. Thick black smoke swirled to the heavens. Another enemy tank had hit a well-placed antitank mine.

"Sir, we're going to lose our fires," Mark said nervously. "The artillery has to move."

"Shit—not now," Davis shouted. "How about mortars?"

"No response. They must have been taken out by the enemy."

"Call the artillery and tell them I have a company-sized target at Bravo One-Zero-Two." Davis grabbed Sergeant Mark by the arm and looked at him with murderous, determined eyes. "Make them fire for us! Tell them anything. They can't leave us now!"

Mark looked stunned, then shouted into the radio transmitter, conveying the lieutenant's anger into the handset.

Another huge explosion occurred forward of the hill, out of view of Davis's position. Davis saw the smoke and pieces of a tank turret flying into the air to the west of the hill. A series of secondary explosions sent green and red tracers shooting madly into the sky.

"Sir, OP South!" Cowper yelled, giving the lieutenant the handset again.

"One-Six, they came around to the south and entered minefield Mike 3. Two tanks and one BMP destroyed in Mike 2. They won't try that way again. They got the hell blown out of them!"

"Which way are they coming now?" Davis asked.

"Not sure. They seem confused. Somehow they got men in the tank ditch. They're breaking down the tank ditch with shovels and picks. Most of them are in the north. With Trail 2 blocked it looks like they're going to try to force their way up Trail 1."

"Roger, OP South. Keep adjusting the fires. We're trying to get mortars."

Suddenly the sky to the west burst with the explosions of American artillery crashing into the long, crowded lines of enemy armored vehicles. Thick black smoke billowed skyward as a testimony of the artillery's destruction.

"That's it, sir," Mark yelled. "That's their last volley. They have to move the guns now."

"They're breaking through the tank ditch, but the minefields are slowing them down," OP North reported.

"Roger. Break. One-Four, did you monitor? Over. They've got BMPs and tanks coming up Trail 1. Stand by. They'll be on us soon."

"One-Six, this is One-Four, understood. We're ready."

"We need more artillery," Sergeant Tyler, at OP North, cried over the radio. "If we get more artillery now, we can stop 'em."

Davis didn't have the courage to tell everyone over the radio that the cannons were moving and that he could not contact the mortars.

"One-Six, this is One-Four. We've taken three casualties. Friedman is wounded in the leg and Johnston and Moyer are dead. Both killed by artillery."

Davis felt his stomach tighten. His little band of defenders was paying dearly for Wadi Al Sirree, he thought. Two men are dead, and one is wounded. How many will live to see another day?

"They've dismounted a platoon in the tank ditch," OP North reported. "We're not getting any fire now. Where's the artillery?"

The enemy continued to work on the ditch. Smoke billowed from the west. The enemy is using his vehicle smoke systems to hide his breach of the tank ditch and the trails, Davis thought. Damn it! I wish we had some artillery right now!

The platoon waited in their reverse-slope positions—Piper to the south in BP X-Ray with eight men, one wounded, and Davis in BP Yankee with eighteen men, one wounded. Davis's Javelin gunners waited tensely for the first enemy armored vehicle to poke its nose over the hill.

"One-Six, they're crossing the ditch now!" OP North screamed. "Get me some fire and I'll try to target them."

"Roger, OP North, there's no more artillery. Keep reporting. Everyone, get ready."

"Three BMPs and two tanks are headed along the north wall on Trail 1 now," OP North reported.

Enemy artillery began to strike the American positions again, to support the breach of the tank ditch.

"Look out!"

Roll the dice.

If you roll 2, go to Section 58.

If you roll 3 or 4, go to Section 62.

If you roll 5–12, go to Section 94.

Section 60

"Now, Chambers, fire! Get the bastard!"

Specialist Chambers, kneeling with his eye pressed against the missile tracking unit sight, depressed the Javelin trigger. He fired his last missile. The missile burst out of the tube in a loud roar and flew a jumping, erratic path to the stationary enemy tank.

The Javelin missile hit the top of the tank. The warhead burned through the tank and sent a molten stream of energy into its turret. The tank ignited in a surge of smoke and flame as its ammunition exploded.

The tank behind the exploding hulk turned its turret in Davis's direction, apparently eager to avenge the death of the lead vehicle. The enemy tank fired its machine guns in a wide, wild arc as the turret turned. BMPs moved forward under the cover of the tank's fire.

Davis watched as Chambers jumped out of his hole to grab the last remaining Javelin round near the dead gunner to his left. Chambers secured the round and threw himself to the ground. He worked furiously to place the guidance system onto the missile. Machine-gun bullets ripped through the American positions.

A BMP forced its way around the first burning tank and advanced another fifty meters before it was ripped apart by an antitank mine. Undaunted, another BMP tank moved up behind the burning wreck and pushed it through the minefield.

"Fire our last missile at that BMP!" Davis screamed.

Chambers placed the Javelin missile on his shoulder. At the same moment, the BMP fired.

Roll the dice.

If you roll 2 or 3, go to Section 55.

If you roll 4–7, go to Section 65.

If you roll 8–12, go to Section 58.

Section 61

No, the slaughter comes in the pursuit, Davis thought, steeling his soul with determination. If we run now, they have us. If we fight, we can take some of these bastards with us. "Stand fast. We're fighting here. Keep up the fire!" Davis shouted.

The entire platoon fired at the advancing armored vehicles as the enemy entered the platoon engagement area.

A tank pushed a destroyed BMP into the ditch. Other tanks and BMPs churned down the sides of the ditch. Loose sand and rocks crumbled under the weight of the metal monsters. Enemy infantry, braving the fire from Davis's men, flung themselves into the channel to break down the sides with shovels and picks. Several tanks, with special plows mounted in the front, scooped up dirt and brushed it into the obstacle. Soon, several BMPs were working their way out onto the eastern side.

Piper's machine guns roared, knocking down the dismounted attackers as they raised their heads from the tank ditch or raced to dismount from their BMPs. The AT4s destroyed several BMPs as they closed on BP Alamo, confusing the fighting even more with their exploding ammunition. Machine guns rattled and scraped the sides of other BMPs and tanks as they zigzagged through the minefields, searching for a safe route to advance. Tracers and armor-piercing incendiary bullets bounced off the hard flanks of the advancing enemy armor in a shower of sparks.

The American antitank fires slackened as the platoon ran out of antitank weapons. A tank crossed the minefield, crested the hill, and raced toward the center of the valley, slewing its turret to the right and left and firing machine guns as it raced by. Two BMPs followed closely behind, heading up Trails 1 and 2. The vehicles jinked wildly as they raced through the smoke, trying to avoid mines and burning vehicles.

"Shit, they're getting past us!" Davis screamed.

A BMP moved closer to BP Alamo, spraying the position with close-range automatic cannon fire. As the BMP entered the center minefield, it exploded in a shower of sparks. The mine detonated a stream of fire up into the belly of the BMP. Exploding from inside out, the BMP crumbled in a burst of black smoke.

Tracers filled the air. Many of Davis's men were down—wounded or dying. Davis could hear the screams of the wounded in between the roar of exploding vehicles and the clamor of machine guns. Specialist Montoya knocked out two enemy tanks before a third beast blasted the Javelin gunner's fighting position to oblivion.

Bullets ripped at the sandbags of Davis's fighting position. Cowper, his M203 pointed up out of the hole, shot a grenade at an advancing BMP. The grenade hit the moving vehicle but had no effect. The enemy had gained the upper hand in the battle.

Suddenly the roar of jet engines filled the air. A U.S. A-10 ground attack fighter, dropping flares from its tail section, dipped its wings on an attack run against the enemy tanks advancing through Wadi Al Sirree. The A-10 came from the west, taking the enemy from the rear.

Another group of BMPs raced forward, charging across the breached tank ditch. The A-10 attacked them with a fierce shower of 30mm cannon fire. The lead BMP exploded in a burst of orange flame and twisted metal. A few of Davis's men cheered from inside their bunkers. They were finally getting some support. A second A-10, firing its powerful 30mm antitank cannon, destroyed another BMP and a tank.

Antiaircraft missiles, shoulder-launched versions of an improved SA-14, streaked through the air at the retreating A-10s. Hundreds of green machine-gun tracers chased the retreating U.S. aircraft. One aircraft exploded in a brilliant red-yellow fireball. Twisted, burning pieces of metal fell to the ground far behind Davis's position.

Wadi Al Sirree filled with the smoke. The engagement area in front of Davis's position was now crowded with dead soldiers and burning vehicles. For a short time 1st Platoon had effectively blocked the enemy from entering Wadi Al Sirree.

But the enemy was determined. The sound of approaching armored vehicles rose from the west. Another wave of machine-gun fire cut through the dense smoke that obscured the area around the tank ditch. Bullets struck wildly all across the front of BP Alamo.

"Sir, look out!" Cowper shouted, pointing to two enemy tanks near the entrance to Trail 1 that were moving cautiously forward to take BP Alamo in enfilade.

"Chambers! We've got to get those tanks!" Davis screamed to his last remaining Javelin gunner. The lieutenant pointed at the silhouettes of two tanks emerging from the smoke.

Chambers signaled that he understood and prepared his Javelin for firing.

The two enemy tanks halted behind a burning BMP and leveled their guns at Davis's men.

Roll the dice.

If you roll 2 or 3, go to Section 58.

If you roll 4–9, go to Section 60.

If you roll 10–12, go to Section 93.

Section 62

A 152mm artillery shell detonated yards away from Davis's position, showering it with steel, dirt, and rocks. Wadi Al Sirree was consumed by exploding artillery shells.

My God, I can't breathe! Davis thought. We're finished!

Davis's worst fears appeared to be coming true. The enemy was heading right for him. Pieces of deadly metal flew through the air. Geysers of dirt and stone billowed from the desert floor. Dust and smoke were everywhere.

The devastating shock of the exploding shells crushed in around Davis's position. He gasped for breath as each new round seemed to suck the air from his lungs. His ears were ringing. He slowly picked himself up from the bottom of his position and rubbed the dirt from his mouth and nose.

In spite of the flying steel, Davis struggled to see the battlefield. He looked over to Sergeant Mark's fighting position. It was his last futile act.

A 152mm shell landed right on top of Davis's position. The explosion ripped his position apart like a pin puncturing a balloon, instantly killing the lieutenant and everyone near him.

General Douglas MacArthur once said, "That's the way it is in war. You win or lose, live or die—and the difference is just an eyelash."

Sometimes, all the skill in the world cannot overcome the odds.

Go to Section 3 and try again!

Section 63

The artillery tore at the bunkers as if they were made of cardboard. Debris, twisted metal, and shattered timber were scattered about the defensive position by the blasts of the enemy shells.

Davis pressed against the hard ground, looking for sanctuary from the searing metal whizzing overhead. He felt trapped.

He struggled up to the aperture of his bunker to survey the scene. The fighting positions had been devastated. Smoldering black holes had replaced many of the sandbag and dirt bunkers. The enemy shells were landing with unbelievable accuracy. Every shell seemed to hit something, and they kept falling. The noise was overpowering. Rocks and flying metal pelted the sides and tops of his fighting position. The enemy fire increased in intensity and Davis fell back to the bottom of his bunker and prayed.

Roll the dice.

If you roll 2–8, go to Section 62.

If you roll 9–12, go to Section 67.

Section 64

An AT4 antitank rocket, fired from Sergeant Piper's position, exploded against a rock to the left front of the enemy tank. The tank stopped and quickly slewed its turret toward BP X-Ray, scanning the newest threat.

"Fire!" Davis screamed. "Now!"

Chambers fired. The ends of the Javelin missile exploded, shooting the warhead racing toward the enemy tank. Chambers quickly ducked under cover after firing the missile.

The Javelin missile hit the enemy tank in the turret. The tank resonated with the impact like a bell being hit with a heavy hammer. The hatches opened and fire and smoke spewed skyward. The enemy tank crew never made it out. The tank sat lifeless, flickering its soul to the smoke-filled desert air.

The immediate battlefield grew suddenly quiet. To the north Davis heard the distant blasts of tank cannon and the terrible thud of artillery fire.

"One-Six, this is OP North," Sergeant Tyler announced jubilantly. "They've had it! The tanks and BMPs that are left have held up west of the trails. It looks like they're going to send infantry forward to clear you out before they risk any more armor."

Davis breathed a sigh of relief. We've gained some time, but we can't hold back another attack, he thought.

"One-Six, this is OP North. Did you copy?"

Davis waited a few moments to catch his breath. "Roger, OP North. Good job. We're going to try to break contact now, before the infantry closes on us."

"It looks like two BMPs are moving forward to support the infantry," reported OP North.

Davis hesitated. This pause in the battle was his best chance to break contact, he thought. But if we run now, while the enemy rushes us with BMPs, we'll get slaughtered. I'll have to leave a rear guard.

"We'll handle the BMPs and the infantry. Your mission is over. Lay low and wait for nightfall. Meet me at our rally point no later than 2100," Davis said as he searched his map for the rendezvous point. "One-Four and OP South will withdraw now. Do you understand?"

"Affirmative, One-Six. We'll be there before 2100," OP North responded somberly. "Wait for us."

"We'll wait. Stay on the radio and try to keep clear of the trails. The enemy will be all over them. One-Four, did you monitor?"

"Roger, One-Six," Piper replied. "I'll pick up OP South and Gerber on the way. Be careful of those BMPs."

"Wilco. Good luck. I'll meet you at the rally point. Out."

Davis gave Cowper the radio handset. Then he crawled out from his bunker and waved to Mizogouchi to meet him. Mizogouchi ran in short, quick rushes to his platoon leader's position. Sergeant Mark, Mizogouchi, and Davis knelt in the open firing position on the right side of Davis's bunker.

"We only have one AT4 and the two SAWs left, sir," Mizogouchi reported in a breathless gasp. "It's not enough to stop them, and the SAW ammo is almost out."

"OK, listen up. Now is our chance. We have about ten minutes before their infantry gets here. Grab your weapons and the wounded," Davis ordered. "We'll make a break for it. We'll run to the south wall and try to link up with Piper."

Mizogouchi pulled a stained map out of his battle-dress pants cargo pocket and laid it in front of them.

"I'll stay behind with the SAWs to provide covering fire," Davis ordered. "Mizogouchi, you're in charge. Mark, you go with Mizogouchi. Change your radio frequency to mine so I can link up with you when I pull out of here."

Sergeant Mark nodded.

"Get to the south wall as fast as you can. Then head east until you reach the rally point," Davis said, pointing to his map. "Hide there for a few hours. I'll meet you there. If I don't show up in a reasonable amount of time, take off and head southeast. The 1st Brigade of the 1st Infantry Division is supposed to be eight kilometers southeast of us. We have to try to link up with them."

"Wilco," Mizogouchi replied. "You can count on me."

"I know that," Davis answered with a bleak smile as he put his hand on the sergeant's shoulder. "Just don't try any heroics. We've done enough for one day."

"Sir, I don't want to leave you here," Mizogouchi said. "Why don't we . . ."

"There's no time for argument," Davis concluded, ending the discussion. "Give me the last AT4 and your squad radio and then get everyone moving."

"Yes, sir." Mizogouchi nodded, touching his hand to his helmet in a hasty salute, then he rushed back to gather the men. Sergeant Mark checked the radio's frequency and contacted the platoon sergeant.

"Sergeant Mark, contact Piper on the radio," instructed Davis. "Make sure he withdraws and meets you at the rally point. Wait for Sergeant Tyler there too. Don't leave anyone behind.

"Cowper, go with Mizogouchi," Davis said.

Cowper looked at his platoon leader in disbelief.

"That's an order, soldier. Get cracking. You're more good to me with the platoon. I'm counting on you to make contact with friendly forces when we try to link up with the units of the 1st Infantry Division."

Cowper grudgingly obeyed and placed the precious radio on his back. Mizogouchi assembled his men. One soldier had been killed in the fight and four were wounded. Two of the wounded were serious and had to be carried on makeshift litters. Mizogouchi handed his platoon leader the last remaining antitank weapon.

Davis threw four white smoke grenades to cover their exit and ordered the group to move out. Quickly the infantrymen, carrying their wounded and their equipment, withdrew to the southeast.

Davis watched his men leave. The two SAW gunners, Private First Class Ward and Specialist Reardon, flanked Davis in his fighting position. Reardon armed a Claymore mine and set it out to the flank of his position.

The sound of distant firing rumbled off to the north. The burning tanks and BMPs in the platoon engagement area crackled and sizzled, occasionally exploding as fuel or ammunition was touched off by the flames. Then Davis heard the shouts of enemy infantry.

"Here they come, sir," said Specialist Reardon, the SAW gunner to Davis's left. Reardon pulled back the charging handle of his SAW.

Davis observed several enemy riflemen approaching. The enemy squad moved in bounds between the smoking remains of their demolished vehicles. Five soldiers brandishing assault rifles moved cautiously around the right side of the burning enemy tank that Davis's men had just destroyed.

"Fire!"

Before the enemy soldiers could react, Reardon and Ward cut them down with a stream of 5.56mm bullets. Ten more enemy rushed forward.

Davis, kneeling in his bunker, fired his M16 at the enemy riflemen. His well-aimed shot knocked an enemy soldier off his feet. Davis transferred his aim to another soldier. The crack of his rifle dropped the second attacker in front of a smoldering, wrecked tank.

The rest of the enemy soldiers dove for cover. An enemy machine gun opened fire at the Americans from the west. Soon several machine guns were firing, their bullets slicing into Davis's position as the gunners found their target.

Davis ducked down inside his bunker. Ward, hit by an enemy machine-gun burst, was knocked back into the rear of his fighting position. The young fighter died instantly.

Now there are only two of us, Davis thought.

"A BMP is coming down the trail!" Reardon shouted. Davis waited as the BMP raced past the wrecks, its 7.62mm machine gun blazing at Davis, closing the distance for the kill. A stream of machine-gun bullets pelted their position. Both Americans hugged the protective wall of the bunker, avoiding the fire. Davis reached for the last AT4. He prepared the antitank missile for firing and calmly waited for the advancing BMP to get within range.

"When I say go, you fire your Claymore," ordered Davis. "Then open up with your SAW. When the Claymore goes off, I'll hit him with the AT4."

"Right," Reardon declared quickly.

"Now!"

Roll the dice.

If you roll 2–4, go to Section 66.

If you roll 5–12, go to Section 68.

Section 65

Bullets ripped at the dirt in front of Davis's firing position. Tracers filled the air. Several of Davis's men were hit.

The enemy BMP turned toward the center of the company and rolled forward, firing directly at Davis's position. Cowper aimed his M203 at the advancing enemy vehicle. The round landed near the flank of the vehicle, distracting the gunner for one vital second.

The lead BMP suddenly exploded in a burst of orange flame and black smoke as the last Javelin round hit its target. Twisted metal flew through the air. The BMP burst into flames.

Davis's men cheered. Davis surveyed the scene, scanning the horizon for enemy movement.

"Sir, look out!" Cowper shouted.

An enemy tank raced out of the smoke and screeched to a halt behind the burning BMP. The big 125mm gun swung toward Davis's men.

Roll the dice.

If you roll 2–9, go to Section 58.

If you roll 10–12, go to section 55.

Section 66

The BMP moved closer, churning up the sand as it steadily climbed the hill.

The rocket hit the side of the BMP, burning a hole in the crew compartment and exploding the vehicle in a fiery burst of orange flame and black smoke. A second BMP raced through the smoke, quickly jinking to the right to move around the burning BMP. The second BMP fired a long burst from its 7.62mm machine gun.

The SAW gunner fired a continuous burst at the advancing armored vehicle. The effort was futile. The BMP charged forward, fire spewing from its machine-gun port. The SAW gunner fell backward, riddled with bullets.

The enemy vehicle was right in front of Davis. He reached for a grenade. It wouldn't stop a BMP, but he didn't have anything else. He pulled the pin and lobbed the grenade at the onrushing enemy vehicle.

The BMP's machine gun fired just as Davis's grenade exploded against its turret. The shock of the grenade knocked Davis out of his hole, and he fell face down on the dead SAW gunner. Davis's shoulder and chest were burning. He tried to get up. The effort failed and he rolled backward, down under the cover of his bunker.

"I must get up," Davis tried to cry out. The words were muffled in his throat as he died and his lifeblood oozed onto the desert floor.

Frederick the Great, the famous general and leader of eighteenth-century Prussia, once said, "When a general conducts himself with all prudence, he still can suffer ill fortune; for how many things can oppose his labours!"

Davis died, but he fought well. Sometimes even the best warriors are overcome by chance and the friction of war.

Go back to Section 3 and try again.

Section 67

The enemy artillery rolled over them like a furious thunderstorm. Within seconds the deadly explosions were falling far to the east.

"Cowper, try to reach Piper," Davis ordered.

The clamor of explosions gave testimony to the progress of the enemy as they moved along Trail 1.

"Sir, it's OP North. He says he can't see a thing with all the smoke," Cowper announced.

"Good, maybe then the bastards won't see us either," Davis answered.

"Sir, I got through to battalion mortars. They're pulling back. The enemy is all over the place," Sergeant Mark reported grimly, a look of disbelief on his dirty face.

Davis ignored his forward observer. The lieutenant coolly stood up in his foxhole and looked to the two antiarmor gunners in positions on the left and right sides of BP Yankee.

"Get that Javelin ready," Davis shouted to Specialist Chambers, in the next position to the left. Chambers knelt with the Javelin on his shoulder, facing the oncoming enemy vehicle.

Montoya, the other Javelin gunner, gave the lieutenant a thumbs-up to indicate that he was ready to fire. His thermal sight was firmly attached and he was in position, scanning for targets.

"Stand by," Davis shouted in a cracked voice. "Fire as soon as they exit the smoke."

The smoke got thicker and started to roll down into the trails of Wadi Al Sirree. Suddenly a tank crashed through the smoke at high speed, firing its machine guns as it raced by.

Chambers spotted the tank first. "I got it," he yelled. His Javelin missile fired, shooting exhaust smoke, flame, and debris to the rear of BP Yankee. The missile darted up and down as it accelerated toward the fast-moving target.

The missile hit the tank. The two tandem, high-explosive warheads tore through the thin top armor of the turret and ignited the ammunition. The vehicle pitched violently to one side and came to a screeching halt, exploding in a fiery ball of orange and crimson.

A BMP plunged through the smoke and raced past the tank. Montoya fired, sending the BMP to its fate in a shower of sparks and flame. The back door slammed open but the flames had already devoured any life that had once been inside.

A second BMP raced forward, bypassing the burning hulks. The BMP sped past Davis, firing its 30mm cannon.

"Shit, they're getting past us!" Davis screamed as he ducked inside his position to avoid the lethal explosions of the enemy's cannon.

A tremendous explosion stopped this BMP. Fire gushed out of the ground as the vehicle hit a well-concealed antitank mine. The mine sent a stream of fire up into the belly of the tank. The vehicle, exploding from inside out, disintegrated in a burst of black smoke.

More BMPs and tanks followed. Davis's team on BP Yankee continued to fire at the advancing armored vehicles. Machine guns rattled and scraped the sides of the passing tanks and BMPs ineffectually. The AT4s hit a few vehicles; the Javelins, on the other hand, were deadly accurate. A flurry of American AT4 antitank rockets exploded toward the advancing enemy. Two more BMPs were stopped by AT4s.

The enemy was fighting hard, trying to get out of the antitank ambush surrounding them. Threat machine guns and cannon sprayed the American positions. Two of Davis's men were hit by enemy fire. Fetterman lay on his back, clutching his head with both hands and kicking up the ground inside his blood-soaked position. His anguished screams filled the air in between the roar of exploding vehicles and flying lead. After a few seconds, Fetterman stopped kicking and lay still.

Like trapped animals, the attackers struck back hard. Another group of BMPs pushed forward. The lead BMP was suddenly shot from above and exploded in a burst of orange flame and black smoke. Twisted metal flew through the air. The turret came off the BMP and landed upside down on the hull. A U.S. A-10 ground attack fighter roared overhead, dropping flares from its tail section.

Davis's men cheered. They were finally getting some support.

A second A-10 fired its powerful 30mm antitank cannon at the enemy vehicles. A tank became the A-10's next target and was transformed into a smoking hulk by the slow-flying armor killer.

Section 67

The sky suddenly filled with enemy antiaircraft missiles. Several shoulder-launched SA-14 missiles streaked through the air at the retreating A-10s. Hundreds of machine-gun tracers, fired from BMPs and tanks, chased the American aircraft.

One aircraft exploded as it fled east. The plane was caught by an enemy missile and erupted in a brilliant red-yellow fireball. Twisted, burning pieces of metal fell to the ground, far behind Davis's position. The pilot never had a chance to eject. The other aircraft flew low to the ground, escaping to the east.

The lead company of the enemy advance guard continued to move forward. Wadi Al Sirree soon filled with thick white smoke from vehicle smoke generators, blazing vehicles, and burning smoke pots. Bypassing the burning vehicles along Trail 1, an enemy tank cleared the minefield and headed toward BP Bravo.

Chambers fired another Javelin, destroying the fleeing tank. The engagement area was now crowded with burning Threat vehicles. Chambers sent a worried glance back to Lieutenant Davis. "I've got one missile left," Chambers shouted.

Suddenly a tank burst out of the smoke and came to a halt behind some burning BMPs. The tank leveled its gun, searching through the smoke for Davis's men.

Roll the dice.

If you roll 2 or 3, go to Section 58.

If you roll 4–10, go to Section 69.

If you roll 11–12, go to Section 93.

Section 68

The missile smashed against the side of the BMP, burning a hole in the crew compartment and exploding the vehicle in a fiery burst of flame and smoke. A second BMP pushed through the smoke, maneuvered around its burning wingman, and blazed away at Davis.

Davis ducked back into the bunker. Specialist Reardon, one of the SAW gunners, jerked back violently, hit in the shoulder and chest by the angry bullets from the charging BMP. Spinning backwards, he fell down under the cover of his bunker, landing on his back.

The BMP, swinging its turret to the east, bypassed Davis's position and raced to the east.

Davis waited for the BMP to get out of range and then ran over to Reardon. The lieutenant knelt down next to his wounded soldier and held him in his arms.

"Lieutenant, I . . ." Reardon mumbled weakly and then suddenly gasped for breath and died. Davis checked the soldier's pulse. Nothing. Davis paused for a silent moment, drained from the loss of another one of his men. Slowly he passed his hand over Reardon's face, gently closing the dead man's eyelids. He grabbed Reardon's identification tag, snapped it free, and quickly picked up the dead solider's SAW. The weapon had a half-full canister of ammunition attached.

Davis sensed that the lull would not last. He knew that he had to get back to his platoon. Davis crawled a few yards, waited, then ran toward the south wall of Wadi Al Sirree. Smoke from burning vehicles helped conceal his withdrawal.

The sounds of battle rose again from the north, indicating that the main battle was occurring north of Wadi Al Sirree. Running from cover to cover, Davis finally reached the south wall of the wadi. He stumbled along the wall heading east, searching for the rally point.

"Halt!" a voice rang out.

"Davis, is that you?" a voice shouted from a rocky position along the southern wall.

"Piper?" Davis yelled as he ran toward the voice. "Piper! Am I glad to see you!"

Section 68

Piper grabbed the lieutenant and pulled him down into a hasty firing position behind a pile of big basalt rocks. The rest of the survivors of the platoon huddled around Piper. The men from OP North and Gerber were not with Piper.

"We have twenty-four men left, counting you. I don't know about Tyler and his two men. The men from OP South are with us."

"What about Gerber?" Davis was concerned about the M60 gunner he had sent to cover the rear of the platoon's position.

"We haven't seen him. No one's heard his machine gun firing."

Davis winced. Twenty-four men. Counting Gerber, Fetterman, Tyler, and his two men, 1st Platoon had lost fourteen men.

"We have four men wounded. Two are serious and have lost a lot of blood," Piper announced, grim-faced. "What are your orders?"

"I know it's no consolation, but we left a lot more of them lying out there on the battlefield," Davis proclaimed, loud enough for all to hear.

"Shouldn't we try to link up with Bravo Company?" Sergeant Mark asked.

"The company, or what's left of it, isn't anywhere near BP Bravo," Piper interjected. "My guess is that there's nothing east of us but the enemy."

"Well, we can't go south—the mountain is too steep," Davis said as he unfolded his map. He studied the terrain for a few seconds. His finger traced a narrow trail that led southeast to where a part of the 1st Infantry Division lines were supposed to be. "We're heading southeast. We'll fight our way back if necessary, and we'll carry our wounded with us."

"Sir, we don't stand a chance," Sergeant Mark pleaded. "Our wounded need medical treatment. Maybe—maybe we ought to surrender."

"We don't know for sure that the brigade from 1st Infantry is to our southeast," Piper said, looking nervously at Davis. "They could be miles away by now. With only one heavy brigade in-theater, would they risk its destruction?"

"If you won't surrender the unit, maybe I could stay with the wounded and surrender. You could carry on," Mark continued.

A wounded soldier on a makeshift stretcher groaned from the pain of his wounds. The man, Private Carlson, was delirious. His friends stood around him while one man gently raised his head to allow him to sip some warm water from an almost empty canteen.

"We've done our job here, sir," Sergeant Mark said softly. "It's time to think of the wounded."

"Surrender?" Davis questioned. "Americans surrender?"

"Battalion has cut and run, sir," Mark answered. "Piper just said that the company withdrew from BP Bravo and left us to die. We didn't get the support we needed. The enemy punched through our defenses and is already several kilometers to the east. It's not our fault."

"It's up to you, sir," Piper added sadly. "We don't have much left to fight with. We're down to a few rounds of ammo and only a few canteens of water."

Davis looked at the tired, dirty, bruised men in front of him. Others, wounded and exhausted, lay among the rocks.

"The men will follow you either way," Piper announced slowly.

Davis sat in silence for a long while.

If Davis decides to surrender, go to Section 70.

If Davis decides to fight his way back to friendly lines, go to Section 71.

Section 69

Davis fired an AT4 antitank rocket at the halted tank.

The missile flew short. It exploded against a rock in front of the enemy tank. The tank quickly slewed its turret toward Davis and showered his position with machine-gun bullets.

Davis dove for cover. A 7.62mm bullet ripped through his left arm, shattering the bone. He winced in pain. His arm hung limp, the open wound gushing blood.

"I've got one more missile!" Chambers screamed as the 7.62mm bullets riddled the ground around their positions.

"Chambers, fire! Now!" Davis yelled as he painfully tried to apply direct pressure on his wound to stop the bleeding.

Chambers jumped up and fired. The Javelin exploded, sending the high-explosive warhead toward the enemy tank. Chambers immediately saw that the Javelin was away and jumped for cover.

The Javelin missile hit the enemy tank on top of the turret. The tank shuddered and stopped firing. Thick clouds of black smoke escaped through the open hatches.

The immediate battlefield grew quiet. Davis heard the shouts of enemy infantry. He heard the distant blasts of tank cannon and artillery fire to the north.

"One-Six, this is OP North. They've had it! The tanks and most of the BMPs that are left are held up west of the trails. They're sending infantry forward to clear you out before they risk any more armor."

Davis breathed a sigh of relief. He lay down on his back, clasping the rush of blood from his open wound. Cowper crawled over to his lieutenant, took the first-aid dressing from the lieutenant's medical pouch, and ripped open the plastic bag with his teeth. Kneeling over his wounded officer, Cowper quickly covered the wound with the field dressing. Davis paused as Cowper tied the knot in the bandage. He waited a few moments to catch his breath.

"One-Six, this is OP North. Did you understand?"

"Affirmative, OP North," Cowper answered.

"Cowper, give me the handset," Davis said weakly.

"We're going to try to break contact now, before the infantry closes on us," Davis announced slowly, the pain of his wound evident in the tone of his voice.

"It looks like two BMPs are staying to support their infantry," OP North reported.

Davis hesitated, as if searching for words to say to his small command.

"Roger, OP North," Davis answered sternly, biting back the pain from his wound. "Your mission is over. Lay low and get out when you can. Meet us two kilometers southeast of BP Bravo, in the narrow pass there. Do you understand?"

"Wilco, One-Six. We'll be there before midnight," OP North responded bravely. "Wait for us. We'll be there."

"We'll wait," Davis reassured him. "Stay clear of the enemy. Break. One-Three, did you monitor?"

"Roger, One-Six," Mizogouchi replied. "Any word from One-Four?"

"Negative. We'll stay here for five more minutes, then we're heading east. I'll meet you at the rally point. Good luck. Out."

We stopped the enemy from breaking through, Davis reflected. We accomplished our mission. But at what cost?

Davis gave Cowper the radio handset. Suddenly he felt very weak. The world began to spin and he blacked out.

Go to Section 81.

Section 70

Davis stared at his tired, battered men. They'd done all that was possible, he thought. Nobody ever had to fight against such odds as his platoon had.

"OK," Davis said, sitting down and resigning himself to his fate. He suddenly felt very tired. "How do we go about doing this?"

"I'll rig up a white flag and fly it from the top of this big rock. Sooner or later, the enemy is bound to see it."

Suddenly the valley was filled with the sound of helicopters.

"Hinds!" somebody shouted. Sergeant Mark ran to the top of the rock formation, waving a white rag.

Section 70

> It makes little difference how clearly the circumstances say that the fault was not one's own. The shock which comes of seeing one's own men or comrades killed and of pondering one's own hand in the making of their fate leads almost inevitably to a mood of self-accusation and bitterness—the tokens of moral defeat. The more able and conscientious the commander, the more likely it becomes that he will react in this way. It is only the bloody fool who remains wholly insensitive to his own losses . . . The darkest hours for the novice in war comes with the recoil after the unit has been badly hit . . .
>
> Gen. S. L. A. Marshall

"Mark, no!" Davis shouted.

Two Hind-D helicopters turned toward the platoon, then circled to the north. They turned completely around and began a gun run on the platoon.

"Hit the dirt!" Piper screamed. The Hinds let loose with 12.7mm miniguns and a volley of air-to-ground fragmentation rockets.

"Take cover. Everyone get down!" Davis yelled. Sergeant Mark was hit in the first salvo and blown off the rock. Panic gripped the small band of survivors. The soldiers tried to sprint for cover, but there was nowhere to hide from the Hinds. The helicopter's air-to-ground rockets blasted the target area, killing several of the men running away. Then, slowly banking toward the remaining survivors, the dark-colored Hinds closed in for the kill, their miniguns blazing away.

Davis realized that there wasn't time to run. He picked up a SAW and aimed it at the lead helicopter, shooting off a continuous burst. The tracers ripped into the front of one of the helicopters, but the big ugly bird kept coming. The Hind's miniguns blasted away at Davis. The ground erupted in geysers of dirt all around him, but he kept firing until his ammunition was expended. Then, as he looked for another box of 5.56mm ammunition, the Hind's miniguns found their mark. Davis was riddled with machine-gun bullets. He fell to his knees, then collapsed face first to the ground. For Davis and the men of 1st Platoon, this desperate defiance was their final act.

* * *

Napoleon once said, "Great extremities require extraordinary resolution. The more obstinate the resistance of an army, the greater the chances of assistance or of success. How many seeming impossibilities have been accomplished by men whose only resource was death!"

Another famous general, Maj. Gen. Paul von Lettow-Vorbeck, who commanded the German forces in East Africa during the First World War, put it this way: "There is almost always a way out, even of an apparently hopeless position, if the leader makes up his mind to face the risks."

By surrendering, you failed in your mission and lost your force.

Go back to Section 3 and start again.

Section 71

Davis remembered the words of the historian-strategist, Sir Basil Liddell Hart: "Helplessness induces hopelessness, and history attests that loss of hope and not loss of life is what decides the issue of war."

"We're not surrendering," Davis said, grimly determined to carry on. "Our lines can't be that far away. We have to try."

"But, sir—" Sergeant Mark protested.

"Can it, Mark! That's an order," Davis said, raising his finger in the sergeant's face. He was white hot with anger. The loss of his men stung his soul. He wasn't going to have their sacrifice go for nothing. "You're too good a soldier for that. It's been tough, but we're all better than that. I'm not going to let you get shot or rot in an enemy POW camp—not while we still have a chance to make it back to our lines."

"You're right," Piper said. "We'll make it. In battle there are no prizes for second place. We've got to make it back to our own lines.

First Brigade of the 1st Infantry Division is supposed to be to the southeast. All we have to do now is get there."

The discussion was interrupted by the sudden sound of helicopters.

"Hinds!" somebody shouted. "Enemy helicopters!"

Two Hind-D helicopters flew slowly east, down the valley of Wadi Al Sirree. The big, dangerous birds looked like fat vultures searching for prey.

"Take cover! Everybody get low. Freeze!" Davis ordered.

The battered, tired soldiers obeyed and clung to the rocks like lizards hiding from the crows. The enemy helicopters continued their flight to the east. The sound of the rotor blades slowly faded away.

Davis looked up and searched to the north. The enemy war birds flew harmlessly out of sight.

"That was close," Piper said with a sigh.

"Too close," Davis replied. "Check on our supplies. Reallocate ammunition. Ration the water with priority to the wounded. Throw away anything we don't need. I promised we'd wait at the rally point until 2100. Maybe Tyler and Gerber will show up. We'll wait until then."

Davis planned his move. Tyler and his two men from OP North arrived just before 2000. Nothing was heard from Specialist Gerber and Fetterman.

Davis now had twenty-seven men, four of them wounded. He planned to take the platoon down a narrow pass to the southeast, toward friendly lines. He would have to move in a column, and eight men would carry the four wounded men on makeshift stretchers. That left him only nineteen men who could fight.

Security was provided by a three-man point team, led by Sergeant Mizogouchi. He advanced two hundred meters in front of the platoon. Armed with a squad radio and the last remaining pair of PVS-7 night-vision goggles, he moved slowly, fearful of enemy ambush. Two riflemen trailed closely behind him.

The platoon moved out at 2130, waiting as long as they could for any possible stragglers to arrive. The platoon cautiously snaked its way down a narrow trail that led to the southeast. Davis kept in constant communication with Mizogouchi. The movement was tortuously slow. Mizogouchi took no chances and stopped the column's movement to check out suspicious areas. The wounded got worse.

"Sir, Carlson is in bad shape," Specialist Eisler, the platoon medic, whispered to Davis. Leading the column, Davis signaled a halt. As soon as the column stopped, he talked quietly into the radio transmitter to halt Mizogouchi and the point team.

"How's it look?" Davis asked as Piper came forward from the rear of the column.

"Not good, sir," Eisler said. "Carlson got shot in the gut. I've done all I can, but he's in shock. We're losing him."

"We can't stop," Davis said grimly, shaking his head. "His only chance is for us to get back to our lines. He won't get any better here. We have to keep moving."

The platoon resumed its march. Davis suddenly realized how tired he was. His body ached, and he had cuts and bruises everywhere. He thought about Carlson.

Will we ever make it? Did I make the right decision?

"One-Six, this is Point. We're out of the pass," Mizogouchi whispered. "I can see the big basalt mountain to the southeast, about six kilometers away. That's where you said the friendlies are supposed to be."

Davis looked at his watch. It was 0200. They had been traveling for five slow, agonizing hours.

"Roger, Point. Stay in position. We'll come to you."

The column of exhausted infantrymen closed in on the point team's position. Davis formed them in a tight perimeter while Piper made sure everyone was accounted for.

"Mizogouchi, Mark, Piper—over here," Davis whispered.

"Carlson died," Piper said quietly as he joined the lieutenant. "Everyone else who started with us is accounted for. The other wounded will die if we don't get them some help soon."

Davis stared to the south, trying to see through the dark and trying to close his mind to Carlson's death.

"Cowper, go through the frequencies and try to find someone to talk to. Put up your long antenna."

"Wilco," Cowper replied.

Davis spread his map out before them. He unfolded his poncho, climbed under it to block the flashlight beam from enemy observation, and reviewed the map.

"We have six kilometers to go to reach friendly lines and only three hours of night left. If we can get somebody to answer us, we can try to enter our lines tonight. If that doesn't work, we'll follow the rough ground to the south."

Sergeant Mark moved over to the lieutenant's position and sat down. He took off his Kevlar helmet and dropped it to the ground near his feet. "Sir, the men are beat. We can't go any farther," he said.

"Cowper, any luck?" Davis pleaded.

"Nothing, sir. Just a lot of gibberish on the radio. The enemy must be all over this place."

"Don't give up," Davis ordered, ignoring the odds against them.

"Lieutenant, we can't go on," Mark insisted. "We don't know how far away our lines are. We might just be walking into an ambush."

"He's got a point," Piper added. "We still don't know for sure that 1st Brigade ever made it to the second line of defense. Hell, for all we know they could be headed away from the fighting. What if they're not there? Do you think we can make another six klicks tonight?"

Davis must decide. Rest and wait for tomorrow night, or try to make the linkup tonight?

**If Davis decides to rest and try tomorrow night,
go to Section 73.**

If Davis decides to press on, go to Section 74.

Section 72

"The best landing zone is LZ1, according to the aerial photos," Cromwell advised. "It's the safest and offers the greatest chance of getting behind enemy lines undetected."

"Yes, ma'am," Davis said, "but it's four kilometers away. It'll take me several hours to move my men, extra Javelin rounds, and GLDs across that open desert. My men will be exhausted by the time we get there. LZ2 offers us surprise and places us right on the objective."

"A bold choice," Cromwell announced. "If they're ready for you, they'll blow you out of the sky. How are we going to maintain surprise?"

Who can surprise well must conquer.

John Paul Jones, 1778

"Surprise is everything. We'll surprise them if we land at LZ2. We'll come in from the southwest and pop up over the western trails before they even know we're there. By the time they turn their guns around, our artillery will plaster them."

Captain Cromwell nodded her approval. "The brigade wants you to attack at 0430. That gives you thirty minutes before BMNT. You have to be in position then."

"We must land at LZ2 not later than 0410," Davis replied. "That gives us twenty minutes to be in position. We'll seize a defensive position that overlooks the mouth of Wadi Al Sirree, near NK386080. From there we can block everyone coming in or out."

"What about our artillery?" Cromwell asked. "How do we keep from getting creamed by our own fire?"

"I'll have my fire support officer establish a five-hundred-meter-square no-fire area centered on NK386080.

Section 72

Davis had a total of eighty-four men. His company carried six Javelins (with three rounds each), forty AT4s, six M60 machine guns, and twenty-five antitank mines. He divided his company into three platoons. Sergeant Piper led 1st Platoon, Sergeant Jordan 2d Platoon, and Sergeant Mizogouchi 3d Platoon. Davis organized a makeshift weapons platoon with the six Javelin gunners and their ammo bearers.

By 1800 that evening, every platoon had rehearsed the mission. Team Davis was ready.

The night was quiet. The waning moon gave just enough light for the helicopter pilots to fly with night-vision goggles. Davis watched the bright desert floor speed past as he sat in the fast-moving, low-flying helicopter.

The helicopters popped up the ridge into the mouth of Wadi Al Sirree. Davis saw the flash of enemy artillery guns firing in the opposite direction, toward the American lines in the east.

"We've surprised them," Davis announced over the helicopter's intercom system. "Radio brigade that we're going to set down on LZ2, continuing the mission."

Suddenly the air was filled with green tracers as enemy machine guns opened up on the approaching aircraft.

Roll the dice.

If you roll 2–5, go to Section 79.

If you roll 6–12, go to Section 80.

Section 73

Davis listened to the low moan of one of the wounded. The men are beat, he realized. The enemy is probably just as tired and confused as we are. Maybe we can stay here.

"OK," Davis said, resigned to his fate. "What do you recommend?"

"We could—" began Mark. Piper silenced the forward observer by putting his hand on Mark's shoulder.

"We only have two more hours of darkness. I recommend we pull into a tight defensive perimeter," Piper interjected. "We'll post some security, let Eisler work on the wounded, and camouflage our positions. We'll sleep during the day and then wait until night to get to our lines."

"I guess you're right," Davis answered. "We'll set our backs against the hill to our west. I'll send Mizogouchi to find a wadi to hide in."

Orders were issued. Mizogouchi departed with his security team and found a wadi big enough to hide the entire platoon. The tired soldiers moved into position shortly before first light. Piper set security and everyone else fell asleep. Sergeant Piper took the first watch.

"Lieutenant!" Piper shouted. "Wake up. We've got BMPs headed our way!"

Three BMPs lined up on top of a rise and pointed their cannon at the American position.

"What . . ." Davis stumbled out of exhaustion. "Where?"

"Four hundred meters, along the trail." The wadi suddenly erupted with the detonation of 30mm high-explosive shells.

"Man your positions!" Davis yelled. "Return fire!" More 30mm shells fell against the rocks in front of and behind the wadi. Enemy machine-gun bullets whizzed over the wadi, kicking up the dirt on both sides. Several men screamed as the 30mm projectiles exploded, showering the wadi with deadly shrapnel and rock fragments.

"Open fire! Keep them buttoned up. Use grenades!" Piper yelled.

Private Keller, an M203 gunner, lay dead, drilled by the BMP's machine gun. He fell on top of his M203. Piper raced over to Keller, rolled him over, and grabbed the grenade launcher. The veteran sergeant quickly aimed and fired a 40mm grenade at the nearest BMP.

The BMP shuddered from the impact of the grenade, but after a few seconds continued to fire. Davis aimed his M16 at the enemy vehicle, hoping in vain to draw its fire away from Piper.

"Get all the grenades you can find!" Piper screamed, still pumping 40mm grenades at the advancing armored vehicle. All around Piper's position, 30mm rounds detonated. When the smoke cleared, Piper's mangled body had rolled down to the bottom of the wadi.

"We're all going to die!" Mark shouted as he climbed the far wall of the wadi and tried to sprint for cover.

Davis turned around just in time to see the BMP's machine gun riddle Mark with bullets. The bloody corpse of the forward observer slid to the bottom of a ditch. The lieutenant quickly ducked down below the crest of the wadi to avoid incoming fire.

Mizogouchi crawled over to Piper's lifeless body, then to Mark's. "Piper's dead, sir! So is Mark," the squad leader shouted above the noise of the fighting.

Davis crawled to the bottom of the ditch. Machine-gun bullets riddled the crest of the wadi. Shrapnel flew everywhere. The survivors huddled in the bottom of the wadi. There were only six men left.

"Anyone have grenades left?" Davis asked, crouching against the side of the ditch.

No one answered. Mizogouchi and Cowper changed the magazines in their M16s. The platoon had only small-arms ammunition.

"Look out!" Cowper shouted. A BMP had moved forward and straddled the ditch. Its cannon and guns aimed in perfect enfilade. Davis and the survivors didn't have time to react. The enemy 30mm cannon rounds, fired at point-blank range, detonated into the small group of men cowering at the bottom of the wadi. When the firing stopped, no one could tell the bloody torsos apart.

Go to Section 46.

Section 74

Davis listened to the low moan of one of the wounded. The men are beat, he realized. Still, the enemy is probably just as tired and confused as we are, Davis thought. We must press on. Luck in the long run is given only to those who persist.

> We will either find a way or make one.
>
> Hannibal

"No, we can't quit now. We have to find a way out of this before daylight. I have an idea," Davis said, trying to squeeze one more ounce of strength out of his depleted soldiers. "Mizogouchi, Cowper, and I will move forward to higher ground and try to establish radio contact. If we can reach someone on the radio, maybe we can get help."

"It's worth a try, sir," Piper commented quickly, supporting his lieutenant. "I'll keep everyone here, ready to move on your order."

Piper organized the survivors for defense in a nearby wadi. Mizogouchi, Cowper, and Davis headed southeast through the rough terrain. With every step they took, the small group moved to higher ground. After twenty minutes of travel, Cowper set up his long-distance antenna and tried the radio again.

"Sir, I've got a company command net from 1st Brigade!" Cowper screamed, exuberant.

"Bravo One-Six, this is Whiskey Two-Niner, authenticate Kilo-Uniform."

Davis quickly took the handset. Cowper read his wrist coder and whispered the proper authentication reply to Davis. "This is Bravo One-Six. I authenticate Victor. Over."

There was a pregnant pause.

Davis held his breath. Had they reached an enemy station trying to deceive them? Did the armored brigade have a different set of authentications?

Section 74

"Roger, One-Six. Where are you guys? How can we help get you out?"

Davis sighed in relief. It was going to work! After several radio calls he established a plan to have his team picked up by helicopter. One UH-60 Black Hawk helicopter, stripped down to allow for only the door gunners, would fly to the platoon's position and pick up everyone. A ten-minute artillery prep, called a SEAD (suppression of enemy air defenses), would fire in support of the pickup. The helicopter would land just before sunrise.

Using his handheld GPS, Davis led Cowper and Mizogouchi back to the wadi in less than fifteen minutes.

American artillery shells fell to the north. The SEAD fired right on time. The sky grew lighter with the flashes of artillery fire. As the shells fell, a helicopter radioed Davis that they were inbound.

Davis signaled the advancing helicopters with his blue-filtered flashlight. First an armed OH-68 Warrior buzzed low overhead, searching for enemy opposition. Then a big, dark UH-60 landed on a flat plateau near Davis's position. The wounded were loaded first, then everyone else scurried aboard. Davis insisted on taking Carlson's body with them. He vowed not to leave any more dead soldiers behind.

The OH-68 Warrior buzzed angrily to the north. Suddenly the early-morning sky was lit from the fire of a Hellfire missile from the Warrior. Davis watched as the missile traveled north and ignited against the dark silhouette of a distant BMP.

Davis was the last man to get into the UH-60. Jammed with men, the helicopter quickly took off and raced to the south.

Go to Section 76.

Section 75

"I think you're right," Davis said calmly, passing the aerial photo back to Captain Cromwell. "Our mission is to block the enemy from getting into or out of the trails. I don't have to land right on top of the pass to do that."

Cromwell remained silent, looking at the map.

"We'll land at LZ1 and march to an attack position just short of the trails. Once we've got everyone assembled, we'll move up Trail 4, the most southern trail, and attack to secure the mouth of Wadi Al Sirree, near Grid NK386080. From that location we can block everyone coming in or out and use the GLDs."

Captain Cromwell nodded her approval. "Colonel Hall expects you to attack at 0430. That gives you only thirty minutes before BMNT. Can you be in position by then?"

"Yes," Davis replied. "Assuming a movement rate of two kilometers an hour, we'll have to land at LZ1 not later than 0200. That will give us an hour and a half after landing at the LZ to be in position."

The first helicopter landed at LZ1 at exactly 0200. The moon was waning, but it provided enough light to make navigation easy. The helicopters came in two lifts, four in the first and three in the second. Each chopper carried ten to fourteen men.

"Everybody out, now!" Davis yelled. The men jumped from both sides of the low, hovering Black Hawk helicopter, ran twenty paces, and dove for cover. They pointed their weapons outward, toward the darkness, from the hasty perimeter formed around the helicopter. As soon as all the soldiers and equipment were unloaded, the helicopter quickly lifted off.

"Let's go," Davis shouted as he rushed to occupy the northern perimeter of the LZ. "Follow me!" Cowper, Davis's trusted RTO, was close by his lieutenant.

Davis had divided his company into three platoons. Sergeant Piper led 1st Platoon, Sergeant Jordan 2d Platoon, and Sergeant Mizogouchi

3d Platoon. In addition he had six Javelin teams. The company's total strength was eighty-four men. They carried six Javelins, with three rounds per Javelin, thirty AT4s, six M60 machine guns, and twenty antitank mines. What Davis lacked in firepower he hoped to make up for by taking advantage of the element of surprise.

The rumble of distant cannon fire filled the air. Davis could hear the enemy artillery battalions in Wadi Al Sirree firing at the Americans.

The last helicopter left the LZ. Davis put on his PVS-7s, broke open a small infrared chemical light, and waved it to the south.

In a few minutes Piper, Jordan, and Mizogouchi were kneeling at his side. Davis took off his night-vision goggles. "Piper, are we ready?" he asked.

"Affirmative," Piper answered. "Everyone's accounted for. We're ready to move out as planned."

"OK, from this point on, no talking. No lights. Use your night-vision goggles," Davis reminded the soldiers. "Company wedge. Mizogouchi, you lead. I'll be right behind you. Piper's platoon to the right. Jordan's to the left. Just like we rehearsed."

"Roger, sir," Piper answered.

"It's 0210. Captain Cromwell, I suggest you stick with me," Davis announced and then paused to see if there were any further questions. Cromwell nodded. "OK, get back to your platoons and move out when I give the signal."

The leaders returned to their platoons. In a few minutes Davis whispered the order to advance and the soldiers silently moved forward. Mizogouchi's platoon led the way, sending reconnaissance teams ahead of the main body.

Except for the steady rumble of the enemy's guns firing from Wadi Al Sirree, the desert was quiet. Davis marched quickly, followed closely by Cromwell, Cowper, and Mark. Trailing Sergeant Mark were three soldiers carrying handheld ground laser designators. Three Javelin gunners and their ammo bearers followed close behind Sergeant Mark, within earshot of their company commander. The other three Javelin teams were assigned one to each platoon.

The men struggled forward under the weight of their heavy loads. They had traveled for twenty minutes when a single rifle shot interrupted the advance. The Americans hit the ground, pointed their weapons to the north, and searched the horizon.

"Lieutenant!" Cowper whispered. "Mizogouchi reports—"

A bright explosion of sparks and flame cut off Cowper's sentence. Someone up front had fired an AT4. Davis crawled over to his RTO and grabbed the radio handset. The sound of small-arms and machine-gun fire echoed in the night.

"Three-Six, this is Six-Six," Davis shouted into the transmitter. The battle intensified up ahead. Davis could see the explosions. Two enemy vehicles were on fire. Green and red tracers filled the air.

"Six-Six, this is Three-Six," Mizogouchi replied. His words were spaced as he gasped for air. "We ran into an enemy platoon. Tanks and BMPs. At least five vehicles."

Another explosion illuminated the early-morning sky.

Flares popped overhead and slowly descended over the battle area. A Javelin fired, then another volley of AT4s. Two tanks and two BMPs were burning furiously. In the bright light Davis could see a BMP moving away from the firefight.

"Three-Six, don't let them get away!" Davis screamed over the radio. But it was too late. The BMP and an enemy tank roared off to the north, safely out of range of Mizogouchi's weapons.

"Lieutenant, what the hell happened?" Captain Cromwell demanded.

Davis paused as he exchanged information with Sergeant Mizogouchi over the radio. Cromwell waited patiently as Davis listened to Mizogouchi's report.

"Mizogouchi's men were surprised by an enemy sentry. They had no choice but to fight. When they got into the wadi they found an enemy combined-arms platoon asleep in their vehicles. Mizogouchi managed to destroy two tanks and two BMPs, but it looks like a BMP and a tank got away. One of our men is wounded."

"Great. What are we going to do now?" Cromwell demanded.

Davis reviewed the tactical situation. The enemy now knew that a dismounted force was in their rear. Davis had lost the element of surprise, and his force was moving in relatively open ground. If the enemy counterattacked him with armor, he could be slaughtered. It would be daylight soon and his small force, without the cover of darkness, would be an easy target for the enemy's cannons. Should he continue, or find some good ground to set up a defense right where he was?

His first obligation was to protect his force. The mission was compromised. He couldn't expect to infiltrate Wadi Al Sirree without surprise. Colonel Hall had pointed this out himself in the mission briefing. If Davis found some good ground to defend from, he might be able to keep his company alive and wait for support from 1st Brigade.

On the other hand, if he continued the attack he would have to change his plan. Without surprise, he knew he couldn't make it to the planned blocking position inside Wadi Al Sirree. But he might be able to move to a position near Trail 4 and form a blocking position that could fire enfilade across the tank ditch. This course of action was not without its risks. The enemy would fight like hell to control the western edges of the trails to Wadi Al Sirree.

"Davis, what are you going to do?" Captain Cromwell asked.

Davis has to decide!

If Davis decides to continue the mission, go to Section 77.

If Davis decides to form a defensive position, go to Section 78.

Section 76

Davis sat in a folding metal chair next to a long table that was covered with a plastic-coated 1:50,000-scale map of the area of operations. He looked at his watch and noted that it was already 1330. Alone in 1st Brigade's main command post briefing tent, he waited patiently for orders from his new commander.

The tent flap opened and two officers entered the tent. The first officer was a lean, broad-shouldered colonel with gray hair and silver-rimmed glasses. The colonel was wearing an olive-drab Nomex tanker's uniform and the tank-and-crossed-sabers insignia of the U.S. Armor branch. He wore a shoulder-holstered 9mm automatic pistol on his left side and carried binoculars slung around his neck. A female captain, in desert-camouflaged uniform, holding her helmet under her right arm, walked a few paces behind the colonel. The female officer wore the same load-bearing equipment as any infantry soldier. She had short cropped blond hair and the slender physique of a long-distance runner. She was also armed with a pistol.

Davis stood up and slung his rifle over his shoulder as the colonel approached.

"Lieutenant, how are you feeling?" the tough-looking colonel asked kindly as he shook hands with Davis.

"I could be better, sir," Davis responded, returning the handshake. The rumble of distant artillery fire shook the ground from a battle going on to the north.

"I'm Colonel Hall, commander of 1st Brigade, 1st Infantry Division. This is Captain Cromwell, from the joint task force headquarters," the colonel said, motioning for Davis to move with him to the map table. His voice was confident and strong. "My brigade just arrived in sector yesterday. Tomorrow, we intend to counterattack in zone and pay the bastards back for the rough time they gave you all."

"I understand you led the platoon at Wadi Al Sirree," said Captain Cromwell.

"Yes," Davis said sadly, thinking about the men he had lost in the battle. Most of the soldiers of his battalion had been killed or captured. About a hundred soldiers had fought their way out to reach friendly lines. Few of the members of Bravo Company survived. Davis was the only officer who had not been killed, wounded, or captured.

"You did one helluva job, Lieutenant," the woman said, sensing his loss. "Your men bought us valuable time. Because of your battalion's effort, the enemy has paused to reinforce his lead formations before he tries for a final push to drive us out of the country."

Davis nodded. He wondered what had happened to Lt. Jeff Sandburg, who was still missing in action. Captain Bludgell, Sergeant

Rossetti, and Lieutenant Wilcox had been listed as killed in action. He wondered if their sacrifice was worth the hours they had purchased.

"I studied the aerial photos of your battle in Wadi Al Sirree," the colonel continued. "Captain Cromwell's right. You put up quite a fight there two days ago. You destroyed nine tanks and thirteen BMPs, not to mention the enemy infantry you fought."

Davis stood in silence. He hadn't had time to tabulate their kills. 1st Platoon had destroyed more than half a battalion. He looked at the map and stared at Wadi Al Sirree.

"Have you assembled the survivors of your battalion into a fighting company?" Colonel Hall asked sympathetically.

"Yes, sir," Davis answered, looking into the colonel's hard green eyes. "I have eighty-four men fit to fight. I've organized them into three platoons and a weapons platoon."

"Good," the colonel continued, perceiving the lieutenant's emotion. "Your battalion's defense slowed the enemy for two days. We needed that time to finish drawing our equipment and to plan our counterattack. The counterattack is why I've asked you here. If you feel up to it, I have a mission for you."

Davis leaned forward, a fire flickering in his eyes. "I'm listening, sir." The rumble of artillery grew louder. "My men and I would like to even the score."

"First, let's get the formalities over with." The colonel searched in his pocket and pulled out a shiny silver first lieutenant's bar. He pinned the bar on the collar of Davis's desert-camouflaged uniform. "I don't have a subdued bar, so this one will have to do. Now you're a first lieutenant. Congratulations."

Davis remained silent. The shiny silver bar on his collar glistened in the tent's artificial light.

"I've moved my brigade within striking distance of the enemy. We're well concealed by this line of hills," the colonel briefed, pointing to the map with his index finger, "and there is no indication that the enemy knows we're preparing to strike. Our ally has massed another brigade that will attack the enemy's southern flank. Tomorrow morning we will attack and trap their lead division."

"We believe that we have just enough force to cut off and destroy his lead division, but only if we can even the odds by taking out the enemy's artillery," Captain Cromwell added, talking as if she was reading a checklist. "The staff has determined that the enemy's artillery is the center of gravity of the lead division. The enemy has concentrated his artillery battalions in Wadi Al Sirree."

Davis was beginning to get the picture. The enemy artillery was deployed in Wadi Al Sirree. It was a perfect target for a bold raiding force.

"This is where you come in, Davis," the colonel said. "We need some light infantry to knock out the enemy's guns. I want you to lead your company back to Wadi Al Sirree. I want you to get behind enemy lines, designate artillery targets, and block the enemy from entering or leaving the valley."

There was an odd silence as the colonel stopped talking. Davis stared at the map. Visions of the trails in Wadi Al Sirree filled his mind.

"You know the terrain better than anyone," Captain Cromwell added, breaking the quiet. "With you leading the attack, the staff feels the mission has a very good chance of success."

Davis listened intently as the brigade commander explained the mission. His men were expected to air assault into Wadi Al Sirree and block the trails long enough to destroy the enemy's guns with Apache attack helicopters and U.S. artillery.

"Look, Davis," the colonel said, searching for the right words. "Those artillery battalions are the key. If they're knocked out, I can save a lot of lives and probably win the battle. I don't have enough artillery or close air support to take them out without you."

Davis nodded. His mission was a desperate but classic air assault.

When the larger force concentrates its combat power on a narrow front to break through enemy defenses, the air assault task force may bypass main defenses to destroy artillery positions, command posts, logistics and communications facilities and to secure key terrain in the enemy's rear.

FM 90-4, *Air Assault Operations,* March 1987

"The three GLD teams that we will attach to your company are central to our plan," Cromwell added. "These ground laser designators will mark targets for the laser-guided munitions. We have a few

Apache and Warrior helicopters and a couple hundred laser-guided artillery shells. You must get the GLDs close enough to designate the enemy guns for these assets."

"I understand," Davis answered. "Do we know what's in Wadi Al Sirree right now?"

"Approximately three battalions," Cromwell replied quickly, pulling out a computer-printed report from a notebook she held in her left hand. The captain studied the report for a moment. "We have identified two battalions of towed 130mms and one battalion of self-propelled 122mm. No sign of tanks or infantry in the valley or indications of defensive preparations."

Captain Cromwell displayed intelligence photos that revealed the enemy artillery battalions in Wadi Al Sirree. Davis looked up at the colonel. "You want me to take a company to attack three battalions?"

"Negative," the colonel said seriously. "Your objective is to secure the trails on the western approach to Wadi Al Sirree. Your mission is to position the ground laser designator teams to lase for our artillery and the attack helicopters to take out the enemy's artillery. If you can accomplish this, we will have a great advantage. If you can't get in, I won't be able to use the Apaches and I'll have to fire my artillery blind. The success of your attack will decide whether we win or lose."

"It's now or never," Cromwell added. "It's a desperate mission because we're trying to fight this guy on a shoestring. There just isn't enough stuff in-theater to hit him with anything else. Your infantry will make the difference."

"You know how few forces the United States has in this country," the colonel continued. "Reinforcements are on their way, but most of the heavy stuff won't arrive for weeks. We don't have that much time. I must use everything I have. I can't hold anything back. If we don't win this one, we won't get a second chance."

Davis looked at the map.

"Do you think you can do it?" Hall asked.

"Sir, we lost some good men out there while we bought time for the rest of you to get here," Davis answered proudly. "My men are all fighting mad. I'm sure the rest of the men in the battalion feel the same way. I know they want a chance to even the score."

The colonel nodded thoughtfully, noting the determination in the young lieutenant's voice. "I know I'm asking a lot. Anything can happen. If you run into too much opposition, it's your call on how to act. I don't expect you to sacrifice your men if you can't accomplish the mission."

Davis nodded. He knew that he would have to act independently. It might take several hours after they landed before Colonel Hall's tanks would arrive.

"You'll be resupplied tonight," Colonel Hall added. "You won't have any mortars, but I can get you some Javelins and AT4s. Captain Cromwell will accompany you."

Davis shot a worried look at the armor colonel.

"Don't worry. You're in charge, Lieutenant. She'll be there with an RTO to maintain contact with the brigade when the attacking forces draw within radio range. I want her there to assist the linkup when my tanks get close to you."

Davis nodded. "When do we attack?"

"0430 tomorrow," the colonel answered. "You have to be in position and ready to attack by then. Well, I've got to visit my battalions. Captain Cromwell will fill you in on anything else you require. Good luck, Davis."

"Thank you, sir," Davis answered. The two men shook hands, and Colonel Hall turned and left the tent.

"Even though the bastards outnumber us, we still have some tricks up our sleeve," Captain Cromwell said, passing a glossy black and white photograph to Davis as the colonel exited the tent. "Our satellite and aerial surveillance is one ace in the hole that can give us an advantage."

Davis paused as he studied the two helicopter landing zones that were depicted on the map. Landing Zone 1 was three kilometers to the southwest of the trails of Wadi Al Sirree. Landing Zone 2 was just east of the trails. Davis looked at the photos again.

"Any signs of enemy reserves in this area?" Davis asked, pointing to the area west of the trails.

"Negative," Cromwell said definitively. "But these photos are six hours old. Things could change by tomorrow morning. The enemy's main effort is in the valley to the north, positioning for another attack. Every gun in these photos is facing east."

Davis contemplated his options. The odds looked pretty steep, but he was getting used to that. He could probably land safely at LZ1, but then he would have to move his company three kilometers across

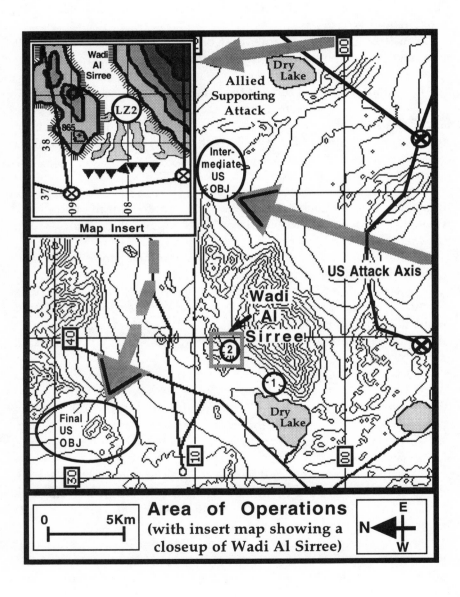

Map Insert

Area of Operations
(with insert map showing a
closeup of Wadi Al Sirree)

0   5Km

open ground to get to the trails. If he landed at LZ2 he would be conducting an assault landing right on top of the objective but within sight of the enemy.

"Which landing zone do you recommend?" Cromwell asked. "We have to tell the pilots within the next hour."

Davis looked at the picture of Wadi Al Sirree. He saw the burned-out hulls of the tanks and BMPs that he had destroyed. He has to decide!

If you choose LZ1, go to Section 75.

If you choose LZ2, go to Section 72.

Section 77

The platoon leaders assembled in front of their company commander. Captain Cromwell knelt next to Davis.

"We can still make it," Davis said confidently. He unsheathed his bayonet and drew a crude diagram on the ground. The moonlight, reflecting off the white sand, was just strong enough for the soldiers to see the lieutenant's hasty sketch. "Jordan, your platoon sets up a blocking position to the southwest to stop any enemy coming from the west. Take all the antitank mines and four Javelins with you. Piper, you'll take a squad with an M60 machine gun and all the GLD teams except one and infiltrate to the high ground south of Wadi Al Sirree. Find a position to lase from and call me as soon as you're ready to use the GLDs. The rest of your platoon and Mizogouchi's platoon will move with me to a position just south of the old tank ditch."

Davis looked up at his platoon leaders. Piper smiled. Mizogouchi, Jordan, and Mark listened with the quiet confidence of veterans.

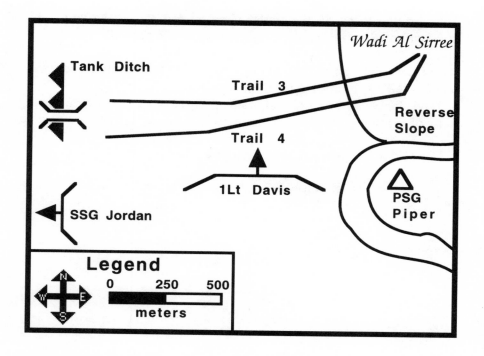

"Piper, I trust you to get the three GLDs up high enough to see into Wadi Al Sirree," the lieutenant said. "Your mission is to target everything in the valley for the attack helicopters and artillery. Mark, is the angle OK to lase from the south wall?"

"Stand by, sir, I'll check," Mark said as he looked at his map and plotted the angle from the laser designators to the location of the guns.

"I'll take the rest of the company just south of the tank ditch, near NK375075," Davis continued. "I'll have one of the artillery ground laser designator teams and two Javelins and cut off all east-west movement along the trails."

"Sir, angle T's OK," Mark announced, explaining that the GLDs would be able to lase safely from their proposed position on the high ground of the south wall of Wadi Al Sirree.

"Roger," Davis said, nodding to Mark. "Well, that's it. Any questions?"

There were none. The platoon leaders departed, issued quick orders to their units, and moved out. It was 0415 when Davis finally got in position. He set up his command post in the center of the firing line that the company formed perpendicular to the tank ditch. Hutchinson and Cowper erected their large antennas and made contact with 1st Brigade. Mizogouchi commanded the platoon to the east. Sergeant Piper called on the radio that he was in position at 0420. The Americans waited.

> The principal problem in almost every attack on every battlefield is to maintain momentum. Every instinct, especially among inexperienced soldiers, is to take cover under fire. Instinct is reinforced when the bodies of others who have failed to do so lie all around. It requires a considerable act of will to persuade limbs to act which have suddenly acquired an immobility of their own. Inexperienced troops find it notoriously difficult to assess the extent of resistance and risk.
>
> Max Hastings

The company, minus Pipe's and Jordan's groups, occupied a firing line along the ridge of a shallow wadi overlooking the exit to the trails of Wadi Al Sirree. Davis lay prone, busy with the radio, getting reports from Piper and Jordan. Sergeant Mark lay a few meters to his right, and Cowper was on his left. The soldiers quickly dug shallow fighting positions with their entrenching tools.

"Sir, it's Piper," Cowper said as he gave Davis the radio handset.

"The enemy is all over the place, camping out," a gleeful Piper reported. "I can see about thirty cannons and twenty trucks. This will be like shooting fish in a barrel."

"Roger. Just stay safe and lase when I call you," Davis ordered. "Wait for my signal."

An earsplitting explosion suddenly detonated from the southwest as a firefight erupted near Jordan's blocking position. An enemy tank burned ferociously, apparently the victim of one of the antitank mines. Davis looked to his left rear and saw the eerie glow of a burning enemy vehicle and a BMP that had fallen prey to Sergeant Jordan's Javelin gunners. Other enemy vehicles returned fire, lighting up the desert with tracers and the flash of cannon fires.

Hold on, Jordan, Davis thought. Hold on!

"Sir, there's a bunch of vehicles moving toward the trails," Cowper announced.

Davis turned to observe to the front. Cowper pointed to a column of trucks heading toward Trail 4. The trucks came to the entrance of the trail and stopped. Davis flashed a savage grin and scanned the oncoming vehicles with his binoculars. Ten fat, defenseless trucks were sitting in Davis's kill zone. "Lovely, just lovely."

"They're sitting ducks. Do you want me to take them out?" Mark asked.

"Call in the fire, on my command," Davis said slowly. He took the handset from Cowper and called Mizogouchi, who was positioned at the western edge of the company firing line. "Three-Six, this is Six-Six. Do you see them? Over."

"Roger, Six-Six," Mizogouchi reported. "They're at max range for AT4s, but I could hit them with my machine gun."

"Negative, hold your fire. I want to get them all. We'll wait a few minutes and use the glids to hit them with artillery," Davis answered, pronouncing the acronym for the man-carried ground laser designators.

"OK, we'll wait for your order to fire," Mizogouchi said.

"Sir, I've got the artillery on the line. They'll be firing soon," Sergeant Mark reported.

Davis looked at his watch: it was 0429. Flashes to the west and the hard sound of the detonation of antitank mines told Davis that Jordan's flank guard was still in business.

"Designate now, all GLDs!" Davis shouted.

"Affirmative, the artillery's firing Copperhead now," Mark answered.

Suddenly the trails to the west of Wadi Al Sirree shook with the terrible roar of incoming artillery. At the same time, American 155mm shells struck the enemy artillery positions at the eastern end of Wadi Al Sirree.

Davis watched the enemy ammunition carriers explode one by one as they were struck by laser-guided artillery shells. Silently working in concert with the artillery, Sergeant Piper's laser designator painted the targets with invisible light. The heavy 155mm artillery shells picked up the designation and were guided toward the target with pinpoint accuracy. Enemy trucks and jeeps were blown apart by the blasts.

"Sir, Piper says the artillery is destroying them in the valley. He's designating their self-propelled artillery and ammo trucks first. He says there's a bunch of towed artillery trying to escape down the trails," Cowper reported.

Davis scanned the area with his binoculars, the light from the burning vehicles and the crash of the artillery rounds illuminating the scene. A series of trucks, towing cannons behind them, started to jostle down Trail 4, headed west. The trucks were moving right into the range of Davis's machine guns.

"Cowper, tell Mizogouchi to get those trucks," Davis ordered. "Fire! Everybody fire!"

The trucks were greeted by the surprise fire of M60 machine guns, SAWs, AT4s, M203 grenades, and rifles. Not a single enemy vehicle escaped. A series of tremendous explosions lit up the early-morning sky as the ammunition trucks accompanying the guns caught fire.

The U.S. artillery suddenly lifted as American attack helicopters arrived. Guided by the fierce explosions, the helicopters used their cannons and antitank missiles to finish off the enemy artillery.

The enemy artillery battalions in Wadi Al Sirree were on the horns of a dilemma, Davis thought. If they stay in the valley, they'll die to artillery and antitank missiles. If they run to the west, my machine gunners, Javelin teams, and laser-designated artillery will search them out and destroy them as they try to escape.

The sun rose. Wadi Al Sirree burned bright with the littered remains of the enemy's artillery regiment.

Go to Section 82.

Section 78

The platoon leaders assembled in front of their company commander. Captain Cromwell knelt next to Davis.

"We can't make it now," Davis said laconically. "Without surprise, we'll never reach Wadi Al Sirree."

"What are you going to do?" Captain Cromwell asked.

"We'll have to defend here," Davis said.

Davis explained the plan, drew a quick diagram on a piece of paper, and illumined the sketch with his blue-filtered flashlight for all to see. The company would form a perimeter defense: Jordan would take his platoon and two Javelins to the left and face west, Mizogouchi would be in the center facing north, and Piper's platoon would deploy on the right, facing east.

The Americans occupied the defensive perimeter and quickly began to dig in. Davis used his PVS-7 night-vision goggles to search the ground to the north.

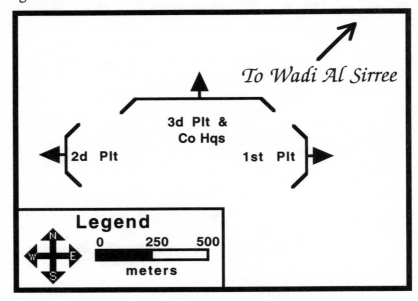

"Lieutenant!" Cowper whispered. "Jordan reports BMPs moving toward him from the west."

"Two-Six, this is Six-Six," Davis shouted into the transmitter. "What's your situation?"

Green and red tracers filled the night air. "Six-Six, this is Two-Six," Jordan replied, his words spaced as he gasped for air. "I've got tanks and BMPs attacking. They've set up a firing line."

A Javelin missile fired. Davis watched as the fast-moving rocket raced to the west and exploded, turning an enemy tank into a brilliant fireball. The flames illuminated the early-morning sky.

Flares popped overhead and burned brightly as they descended over the battlefield, swinging slowly in the wind from their parachutes. A BMP was hit by a Javelin missile.

Davis looked at his watch. It was 0430.

Suddenly the sky above Wadi Al Sirree flashed with the explosion of hundreds of American artillery shells. The detonating artillery crashed into the valley.

"Sir, I've got the fire direction center on the radio. They want to fire Copperhead on the enemy artillery."

"Damn it!" Davis shouted. "Tell them we're not in position. Can they fire Copperhead for us here?"

"Negative. We're too far away to designate targets in the valley, and we have the wrong angle T to lase on the enemy armor to the west," Mark reported. "We can get HE or DPICM."

"Get me DPICM, now," Davis ordered, annoyed that his options were so limited. "Hit those armored vehicles coming at us."

The American artillery fire continued, but without Davis's GLDs to designate the fires, the accuracy was very poor. Mark shifted the aimed wrath of the American fire at the advancing enemy armor. The DPICM burst above the enemy and kept the tanks and BMPs from getting too close to Davis's men. Only a few enemy vehicles were hit by the artillery.

The BMPs moved on line and fired machine guns and 30mm cannon toward the American positions. Fearful of the deadly Javelins, and unwilling to attack across open desert in the dark, the enemy armored vehicles stayed out of range of Jordan's missiles.

"Mark, I need air support," Davis said. "As soon as it's daylight, those bastards are going to try to run us down."

Sergeant Mark nodded and started talking into his transmitter with renewed vigor.

Davis watched as the enemy artillery escaped from Wadi Al Sirree. There was little he could do. The enemy cannons were too far away to designate with GLDs. The American artillery, unable to use their laser rounds, shifted to targets that were designated by helicopters to the north of Wadi Al Sirree.

The sun rose. A few of the enemy's artillery trucks smoldered near the exits of the trails of Wadi Al Sirree. Off to the northwest, the sky turned bright as day as the rush of a hundred rockets filled the air, heading east.

"Shit!" Mark screamed. "Enemy rockets. They must be targeting our guns."

The American artillery stopped firing. Davis watched with dread as half a dozen enemy vehicles moved across the desert toward his company. Cowper gave the handset to Davis.

"Six-Six, this is Two-Six. Spot report!" Jordan reported frantically. "I can't hold them. A couple of tanks and BMPs are coming your way."

"Two-Six, this is Six-Six. Keep engaging them when they get into range," Davis said into the handset. Then he turned toward Sergeant Mark. "Where's the artillery?" Davis yelled.

"Sir, it had to move. They were receiving heavy counterbattery fire. I'm still trying to get air support."

"Lieutenant," Captain Cromwell shouted as she searched for the company commander.

"Over here, captain," Davis shouted. Stooping low, Captain Cromwell and her RTO ran over to the company commander's position.

"I've received word from brigade," Cromwell said, crouching next to Davis. "They've been held up by stiff opposition and heavy artillery fire. We'll have to hold on for a bit longer than we had expected."

"How long?" Davis asked.

The sound of firing erupted. "Lieutenant! BMPs!" Cowper shouted as he fired an M203 grenade in the enemy's direction.

Three BMPs lined up on top of a rise and pointed their cannon at the American position. The wadi suddenly erupted with the detonation of 30mm high-explosive shells.

Davis yelled, "Get down!" Shells smashed into the rocks in front of and behind the wadi. Enemy machine-gun bullets whizzed by, kicking up the dirt on both sides of the wadi and bouncing off the rocks in front of Davis.

Davis looked to his right and saw a Javelin gunner fumbling with his command launch unit. "Fire!" Davis shouted.

The Javelin gunner made a final check and popped up over a pile of rocks to fire. He quickly acquired a target and fired. The missile exploded from the launcher and detonated in a bright flash against the right front track of the BMP. The vehicle jerked to a halt, then continued to fire its 30mm gun at the Americans.

Cannon rounds from the BMP's quick-firing 30mm gun detonated all around Davis's position. Another BMP pushed past its stalled partner and churned the sand in its tracks as it raced to higher ground to get a better firing position at Davis's men.

Davis quickly reached for an AT4. He armed it, put the weapon on his shoulder, and aimed at the advancing BMP. The vehicle fired a long burst from its 7.62mm machine gun. The bullets kicked up the dirt in small geysers that led to where Davis was kneeling. He was hit and fell back, landing on his side.

The BMP continued up the hill, raking the American line with machine-gun fire. One after another of Davis's men were killed or wounded. The uneven battle against the enemy armor was turning against them.

Davis saw that the AT4 was lying next to him. He grabbed it with his right hand and struggled to a kneeling position. In spite of his wounds he placed the antitank rocket on his right shoulder, aimed, and fired at the BMP. The missile hit just below the turret, shattering the vehicle with the impact of the warhead. The firing stopped. Davis fell to the ground, rolled down into the wadi, and died.

Brigadier General S. L. A. Marshall once said, "On the field there is no substitute for courage, no other binding influence toward unity of action. Troops will excuse almost any stupidity; excessive timidity is simply unforgivable."

General George S. Patton put the same idea this way: "There is only one tactical principle which is not subject to change. It is to use the means at hand to inflict the maximum amount of wounds, death and destruction on the enemy in minimal time."

The first basic concept in tactics is to achieve a decision. It is not easy. It requires that the tactical leader think through his situation to see what can be done to make the engagement decisive. To be decisive, an engagement must lead directly to the success of the larger battle.

Davis chose to protect his force instead of trying to continue the mission and focus on producing a result that would lead directly to winning the battle as a whole. In Patton's terms he did not inflict maximum damage on the enemy. The attack of the U.S. armored brigade failed because Davis did not assist in the destruction of the enemy artillery and did not block its movement out of Wadi Al Sirree. This mistake killed him and doomed his command because it delayed the arrival of friendly forces that were to relieve his infantry.

A study of history shows that winning in combat requires many things, not the least of which is battlefield judgment. This is the commander's ability to visualize how he intends to fight the battle and what the results of his actions will accomplish. The leader must continuously ask himself if his combat actions will be decisive and if they will support winning the battle as a whole.

Go to Section 76 and try again!

Section 79

Davis's UH-60 Black Hawk helicopter exploded in a terrible fireball. The burning, twisted wreckage crashed to the ground.

Davis never knew what hit him.

Davis gambled and lost. His selection of the landing zone was the major factor in his defeat. The selection of an air assault landing zone is the critical decision in air assault operations. If there are options available in choosing LZs, the ones that best facilitate mission accomplishment should be selected. The choice usually involves whether to land on or near the objective, or to land away from the objective and maneuver forces on the ground to it. Factors to be considered in making that determination include:

• **Combat Power.** How much combat power can be introduced into the LZ area at one time?

• **Enemy.** What are the enemy's strength and disposition around the objective areas? In particular, what air defense systems does he possess?

• **Surprise.** This is a goal that may be attained by careful use of terrain, cover and concealment, darkness, or reduced visibility created by weather or smoke. Surprise is sometimes achieved by landing on the objective, but this must be weighed carefully against enemy capabilities.

• **Time.** How much time is available for mission accomplishment? Limited time to complete the mission usually favors landing on or near the objective.

It is my experience that bold decisions give the best promise of success. But one must differentiate between strategical or tactical boldness and military gamble. A bold operation is one in which success is not a certainty but which in case of failure leaves one with sufficient forces in hand to cope with whatever situation may arise. A gamble, on the other hand, is an operation which can lead either to victory or to the complete destruction of one's forces. Situations arise where even a gamble may be justified—as, for instance, when in the normal course of events defeat is merely a matter of time, when the gaining of time is therefore pointless and the only chance lies in an operation of great risk.

Field Marshal Erwin Rommel

Davis made a bold decision and lost. Prior to the historic battle of Zama, where Scipio Africanus defeated the great Carthaginian general Hannibal, Scipio said, "Go, therefore, to meet the foe with two objects before you, either victory or death. For men animated by such a spirit must always overcome their adversaries, since they go into battle ready to throw away their lives."

Go to Section 76 and try again!

Section 80

The aircraft behind Davis exploded in a terrible fireball, the victim of an alert enemy SA-14 gunner. The Black Hawk crashed to the ground. The crew and passengers never had a chance.

An Apache attack helicopter, escorting the UH-60 transports, plastered the landing zone with 30mm cannon fire in retaliation. The Apache's cannon killed the enemy antiaircraft gunners and scattered enemy soldiers in all directions. Mayhem erupted in the enemy positions when an Apache drilled a fuel truck with cannon fire. The five-thousand-gallon tanker truck ignited in a surge of fire, splattering burning diesel over panicked enemy soldiers in the center of Wadi Al Sirree.

Davis's helicopter landed at LZ2 exactly as scheduled at 0410.

"Everybody out, now!" Davis yelled. The men jumped from both sides of the low-hovering Black Hawk helicopter, ran ten paces, and dove to the ground. The helicopter quickly lifted off as the door gunners sprayed the confused enemy soldiers with machine-gun fire.

"Let's go, follow me!" Davis shouted as he rushed to occupy the northern perimeter of the LZ. The helicopters came in two lifts, four in the first and three in the second. Each chopper carried ten to fourteen men. The platoons moved out toward their assigned objectives. The waning moon and the burning enemy vehicles provided enough light for the Americans to move without night-vision goggles. Sergeant Piper led 1st Platoon to the right flank and oriented east. Sergeant Jordan led the 2d Platoon, with Davis and the antiarmor section, to the center to block movement into the valley from the trails. Sergeant Mizogouchi led his platoon to the left flank, oriented west to block Trail 4. Each platoon had a GLD attached to designate targets for laser-guided artillery shells.

The rumble of cannon fire stopped as the enemy artillery tried to turn their guns to the west to meet the new threat. Then, like hovering angels, the Apache attack helicopters swept their fire east along the length of Wadi Al Sirree. The valley was filled with the light of burning trucks and enemy artillery vehicles that were unlucky enough to find themselves in the sights of the fast-flying Apaches. The enemy defense dissolved. Any thought of turning the guns ceased as the Apaches made their attacks. The enemy, gripped by panic, ran away in all directions.

The last helicopter left the LZ. Everyone was running at once. Davis rushed with his men to the south of Wadi Al Sirree. The platoon leaders, handpicked by Davis because they had fought with him

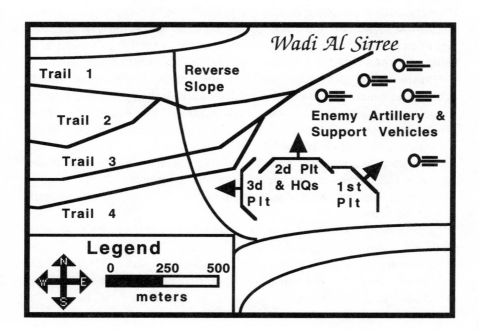

in these same positions two days before, quickly led their units to occupy their assigned positions.

The enemy finally organized a force and pushed a squad forward to oppose the Americans. Rifle tracers filled the night sky. The Americans returned fire with a volley that overwhelmed the confused attackers. Enemy artillerymen crumpled to the ground, cut down by Davis's riflemen.

Davis lay prone against a small pile of rocks, observing the fighting. Cowper, kneeling immediately to Davis's right, extended the long antenna of his precious radio. Sergeant Mark and Specialist Hutchinson were also busy with their radio in a shallow position just a few meters to the lieutenant's left.

"Look at all those targets!" Sergeant Mark screamed with glee, then began calling in coordinates to the U.S. artillery battalions fifteen kilometers to the southeast. "This will be a slaughter."

Davis's men fired at everything within range, adding to the pandemonium of burning trucks and exploding ammunition. Panicked drivers started their vehicles and raced about trying to avoid the machine guns and antitank rockets of the air assault force. As they rushed east they ran into the killing zone of the American helicopters.

Completing their mission to escort the air assault force, the Apaches left the area. Davis knew that the angels of death were hovering just outside of artillery range and would return shortly.

Explosions rippled from one burning ammunition carrier to another. The battle area was covered by lethal flying metal. One of Piper's men was killed and two were wounded by shrapnel from exploding enemy vehicles. The company medics quickly rushed to the wounded and applied immediate first aid.

"Sergeant Mark, make sure the artillery knows we're in position and to activate the no-fire area!" Davis screamed.

"Wilco," Mark answered matter-of-factly. "I'm calling in the artillery strike now."

"Lieutenant!" Cowper yelled. "Mizogouchi reports he's in position. Piper is in position also—"

An explosion, bursting in a bright shower of sparks and flame, cut off the rest of Cowper's sentence. Someone had fired an AT4. Davis crawled over to his RTO and grabbed the radio hand mike.

"Three-Six, this is Six-Six," Davis shouted into the transmitter as the battle intensified up ahead. Wadi Al Sirree was lit up from the explosions. Two more enemy vehicles were on fire. Green and red tracers filled the air.

"Six-Six, this is Three-Six," Mizogouchi replied. "We destroyed two BMPs trying to get into the valley up Trail 4. They didn't see us until we hit them."

Flares popped and, suspended by small parachutes, slowly drifted overhead. Another explosion shook the earth and illuminated the early-morning sky with columns of flame. A BRDM armored car and two BMPs burned furiously. Their onboard ammunition exploded and lit the heavens with shooting sparks and tracers.

In the bright illumination, Davis could see the enemy artillery hitching their guns to their trucks in an attempt to get out of the valley. The enemy gunners frantically gathered trucks and support vehicles into hasty, unorganized clumps.

Davis looked at his watch. It was 0430—time for the American artillery to strike. "Everybody take cover!" he shouted.

The sky above Wadi Al Sirree reverberated with the explosion of dozens of American artillery shells. The first salvo scattered fields of detonating DPICM submunitions across the valley. The valley became an inferno as half a dozen ammunition trucks and artillery vehicles disintegrated.

"Sir, I've got the fire direction center on the radio. I called in the initial barrage of DPICM. Now I've requested laser-guided shells. They're firing Copperhead now."

"Designate now, all GLDs!" Davis shouted. "Fire at the self-propelled howitzers. Leave the towed stuff for the DPICM."

"Wilco," Mark answered and quickly relayed the order to his GLD teams over his radio. Sergeant Mark and the other laser designators painted the targets with invisible laser light.

The second volley of American artillery crashed accurately into the crowded assembly of enemy vehicles, smashing 2S1 self-propelled howitzers with pinpoint accuracy. Each projectile hit a vehicle. Smoke and flames billowed to the heavens.

Davis watched as the enemy ammunition carriers exploded one by one at the strike of laser-guided artillery shells. Trucks and jeeps were blown apart by the accurate blasts. A string of trucks, towing cannons behind them, tried to escape to the west but were greeted instead by the full force of Davis's Javelins, AT4s, machine guns, and rifles. Not a single vehicle escaped.

American attack helicopters arrived, guided by the fierce explosions, to finish off the enemy artillery. As the sun rose, Wadi Al Sirree burned bright with the shattered remains of the enemy's artillery.

"Six-Six, this is Three-Six," Mizogouchi replied, his words spaced as he gasped for air. "I've got tanks heading up into the valley along Trail 4. I've got two killed and two wounded. I've only got a few more AT4s. I won't hold them for long."

"Lieutenant," Captain Cromwell shouted, searching for the company commander.

"Over here, Captain," Davis called.

"Brigade says that the Apaches have to break station," the captain said. "What's the situation?"

"Mizogouchi's men are blocking an enemy counterattack up Trail 4. He doesn't know how long he can hold them. We lost fourteen men killed in Bird 2. I've got two wounded here, and Mizogouchi reports two dead and two wounded."

"Hold on," Cromwell ordered. "You're doing great. Now we have to block those trails long enough for the Apaches to return."

The sun began to rise. The sound of tank cannon and machine-gun fire, the explosions of AT4s, and the detonation of artillery ammunition in burning artillery carriers filled the early morning.

"Six-Six, this is Three-Six," reported Mizogouchi. "Three enemy tanks at NK381067. I can't hold them any longer. They're going to break through on Trail 4."

"That must be the enemy's combined-arms reserve. Mark, get me some artillery, fast," Davis ordered.

"OK, but that's dangerously close. If I fire it, our artillery could hit Mizogouchi's men."

Davis hesitated. "Three-Six, this is Six-Six. I can't fire DPICM. You're danger close. We're calling for Copperhead. Let them come up Trail 4. Take cover, protect your men, and have your GLD paint them with laser light."

"Wilco, Six-Six."

Mark nodded, recognizing what he had to do to make Davis's orders happen. "On the way," Mark shouted. The sound of artillery arcing overhead added to the noise of exploding enemy vehicles in Wadi Al Sirree.

"You're hitting them. Keep firing," Mizogouchi shouted through Davis's radio receiver. "I've fired my last AT4. Two tanks and a BMP are headed your way."

Davis could see black smoke rising high in the sky from the impact of the rounds.

"Javelin gunners, stand by," Davis ordered.

"Here they are!" someone shouted as an enemy tank poked its nose up the crest of Wadi Al Sirree.

Enemy machine-gun bullets bounced off the rocks in front of Davis. "Fire!"

Two Javelin gunners fired at the same time. One missile flew an erratic path to a tank that was frantically firing at Davis's men on the hill. The missile touched the turret and exploded in a bright orange ball of flame. The tank jerked to a tortured halt. Thick black smoke billowed from the turret to the sky.

The second missile struck the trailing tank and tore it apart too. Pieces of its turret flew into the air and then fell back down onto the stalled, burning wreck.

Davis's men cheered.

The BMP pushed past the smoldering tanks, set on avenging the death of its comrades. Its turret swung toward Davis.

Roll the dice.

If you roll 2–9, go to Section 83.

If you roll 10–12, go to Section 84.

Section 81

"Lieutenant, how ya feelin?" asked an exhausted-looking man wearing a light blue apron, cap, and mask.

"Uh . . . where am I?" Davis responded, slowly regaining consciousness. The rumble of artillery fire shook the ground. Davis could sense that a distant battle was going on.

He was in a tent, lying on a stretcher. A lieutenant colonel, wearing the blood-splattered light blue smock of a surgeon, his black oak leaf rank insignia protruding from the collar of his smock, looked down at him. A woman in a desert-camouflaged uniform, a captain, with close-cut blond hair, stood next to the doctor.

"You did one helluva job, Lieutenant," the woman said.

"Who are you?" Davis mumbled.

"I'm Captain Cromwell, from the joint task force staff," she said. "We just arrived today to conduct a counterattack in this zone." Davis blinked his eyes.

"Did you command the platoon at Wadi Al Sirree?" the woman asked.

"Yes," Davis said sadly.

"I studied the aerial photos of that battle," Cromwell continued. "You gave the enemy quite a beating there. If you feel up to it, I have a couple of questions I need to ask you. They're very important."

Davis nodded and tried to get up. He moved his head a few inches, then fell back against the towel that served as a makeshift pillow.

"Take it easy, son. You're going to be fine. In a few hours we'll have you on a hospital ship," the lieutenant colonel said. "You've lost a lot of blood, and they just brought you in a few hours ago." The rumble of artillery grew louder.

"First I have to know what's happening," Davis pleaded.

"We're counterattacking," Cromwell explained. "Your stand two days ago in Wadi Al Sirree made that possible."

"Two days? My platoon . . ." Davis said, grimacing in pain. "How many—"

"You and three others made it back," the captain said sadly. "It's been bad all over."

Davis closed his eyes.

Only three!

He lay his head to the side, away from the officers questioning him. The pain returned. He fought to remain alert, but his wounds were too serious. Slowly he blacked out.

We must never forget our mission is to kill, even though being killed ourselves. We must not shut our eyes to this fact. To make war—to kill without being killed—is an illusion. To fight—to be killed without killing—that is clumsy, inept. One must know how to kill while being ready to be killed oneself. The man who is dedicated to death is terrible. Nothing can stop him if he is not shot down on the way.

Gen. Mikhail I. Dragomirov

Davis accomplished his mission, but his victory was Pyrrhic. He accepted the risk of decisive engagement with no option to withdraw. The defense he chose allowed no margin for error.

Go to Section 3 and try again.

Section 82

Colonel Hall surveyed the scene. Enemy artillery vehicles lay smashed and smoldering throughout Wadi Al Sirree. Burned tanks, wrecked BMPs, and the dead remains of enemy soldiers littered the landscape.

Section 82

Lieutenant Davis, Captain Cromwell, and Sergeant Piper stood by the colonel's HMMWV at the western edge of the valley.

> In choosing their centurions the Romans look not so much for the daring fire-eater type, but rather for men who are natural leaders and possess a stable and imperturbable temperament, not men who will open the battle and launch attacks, but those who will stand their ground even when worsted or hard-pressed, and will die in defense of their posts.
>
> Polybius, 125 B.C.

"Lieutenant Davis deserves all the credit, sir," Cromwell said to Colonel Hall with a wide grin on her face. "We must have taken out at least two battalions and the enemy's combined-arms reserve."

"Yes," Hall said, looking at the burning enemy equipment. "It was a great victory. The brigade destroyed at least an enemy division today. That wouldn't have happened if you hadn't won here."

"Sir, my infantrymen deserve all the credit," Davis said proudly. "But we paid a price for this victory. I only hope we get the rest of our forces here in time to end this damn war." He looked at the six U.S. corpses lying in a neat, solemn line for the graves registration unit.

"Every casualty is a tragedy," Colonel Hall replied. "They are the result of our unpreparedness. The rush to disarm after a conflict is so typically American. As soon as we win a war, we tear down the military. Before this war our army had too few units and too many commitments. Now the bastards at home are calling in the reserves and the recently retired veterans to fill the ranks!"

Davis listened carefully, tired and saddened by the death of his men but proud of the victory his soldiers had won.

"Every time America goes to war it has to learn the same lesson over and over," the colonel continued, his voice growing with anger. "In traditional American fashion we outdid ourselves. We cut down our forces in a world that required more commitments than ever before."

Davis nodded slowly. He understood their sacrifice, even if he didn't understand national policy and geopolitics. All he knew was that he had trained to be a soldier, to fight his nation's wars, and to join the proud legions of her military.

"Davis, I just got permission from the corps commander to make you a captain," Hall said.

"What? Another promotion?" declared Piper. "By God, sir, this will go to his head!"

"I've no choice," Hall said with a grin. "I'm getting in some infantry replacements, and I don't have a company to put them in. I asked the joint task force commander to have you assigned to my brigade for the next few weeks until your battalion gets reorganized."

"Congratulations, Bruce," Cromwell said with a smile as she shook his hand. "Well deserved."

"And since you don't have any officers, I'm making Sergeant Piper a second lieutenant."

"Sir, you can't do that!" Piper protested. "No, sir!"

"You don't have a choice, Lieutenant." The colonel pinned a shiny second lieutenant's bar on Piper's collar. "Now, Captain Davis, get your company ready to move out. We still have a lot of work to do."

Go to Section 98.

Section 83

The BMP fired its cannon at a Javelin team in the process of arming a new missile. The 30mm explosions killed both Americans and destroyed the launcher. One of the M60 machine guns opened up on the advancing enemy vehicle, distracting its attention.

Davis armed an AT4, put the weapon on his shoulder, and aimed at the advancing BMP. The vehicle fired a long burst from its 7.62mm machine gun. The bullets kicked up the dirt in small geysers in front of Davis. Two bullets burned into his left shoulder. He spun out of his hole and fell on his side.

The BMP continued inexorably toward its prey, raking 2d Platoon with machine-gun fire. Tracers tore into the position, bouncing and ricocheting in all directions. The enemy was right on top of Davis's men. A few got up to run and avoid the deadly fire of the BMP. One American after another was hit.

Davis struggled to his knees and grabbed the AT4. His left arm hung limp by his side. In spite of the pain he placed the antitank rocket launcher on his right shoulder, sighted on the BMP, and fired.

The rocket exploded, surged forward, and smashed into the side of the vehicle. The BMP jerked to an abrupt halt and the hatches opened. Smoke billowed from the interior as a burning soldier fell out of the back door.

An American machine gun splattered the BMP with lead, ensuring that anyone exiting the burning wreck was put out of his misery.

Davis tried to get up, failed, rolled back into the wadi, and died.

Colonel Hall observed the wreckage of the enemy artillery battalions in Wadi Al Sirree. Smoldering 2S1 self-propelled howitzers, smoking trucks, and the corpses of enemy soldiers littered the valley.

"His men accomplished the mission," Cromwell said to Colonel Hall, looking down at the body of 1st Lt. Bruce Winfield Davis. "He was a hell of a soldier."

Hall nodded and looked down at the row of twenty-six U.S. corpses lying in a neat line. "We had to take risks to win. He took the risk and paid the price. I only hope that our reinforcements arrive in time for us to finish this damn war."

Go to Section 95.

Section 84

The BMP charged forward, churning up the sand and firing as it advanced. Davis lay prone, facing the advancing enemy armored vehicle. He reached for an AT4 and armed it. The BMP rapidly closed on Davis as he put the weapon on his shoulder and aimed.

The BMP, like a hunter searching for its quarry, fired a long burst from its 7.62mm machine gun. The bullets kicked up the dirt in small geysers that led to where Davis was lying. He was hit. He dropped the AT4 and fell behind the wadi. The BMP continued toward the Americans, enfilading 2d Platoon with machine-gun fire. One American after another was hit.

Captain Cromwell crawled over to Davis and pulled him down inside the wadi. She reached for the AT4 and crawled to the top of the gully. The BMP moved slowly now as its deadly cannon singled out individual defenders and gunned them down. Cromwell placed the AT4 on her right shoulder. The BMP was only eighty meters away. She aimed and fired.

The rocket detonated against the BMP's hull, forcing it to an abrupt halt. The door burst open and the dazed occupants staggered out.

Cromwell grabbed Davis's M16 lying on the ridge, charged the weapon, and fired at the enemy infantry stumbling out of the BMP. "Get the bastards!" she screamed.

An M60 opened up on the same target. The firing continued for several minutes until all the enemy soldiers stopped moving. Then, except for the sounds of fighting in the next valley, five kilometers to the north, it was quiet.

Colonel Hall surveyed the scene. Burned tanks, wrecked BMPs, and the dead remains of enemy soldiers littered the landscape. Enemy artillery vehicles lay wrecked and smoking throughout the length of Wadi Al Sirree.

"He's a hell of a soldier," Cromwell said to Colonel Hall, looking down at 1st Lt. Bruce Winfield Davis as he lay on a stretcher. "We must have taken out at least three battalions of artillery and the enemy's combined-arms reserve."

"Davis, you did a tremendous job," Colonel Hall said as Davis was loaded on an HMMWV ambulance. Four other wounded men were set next to Davis. "The work you did here made our attack a success."

"The men deserve the credit," Davis replied quietly.

"Yes," Hall said, looking at twenty-five U.S. corpses lying in a neat, solemn line for the graves registration unit. "We paid a terrible price for this victory. I only hope we get the rest of our forces here in time to end this damn war."

"Well, Davis, at least your war is over," Cromwell added. "The medics tell me they'll have you on board the hospital ship by this evening."

"Good luck, sir," Piper said, saluting. "You've been a great commander."

Davis winced at the pain streaking through his shoulder. "I'll get back if I can."

"OK, sir, we're on our way," the ambulance driver announced to Colonel Hall. The medic checked the straps that held down Davis's stretcher.

The engine started and the ambulance headed through Wadi Al Sirree to the east.

Go to Section 95.

Section 85

"Dead soldiers don't fight well either," Davis replied curtly. "The enemy will be on us by this time tomorrow. The more mines we get in place, the better our chances. Continue to let two men from each squad rest. Put everyone else to work."

"Right, Lieutenant. I'll check the positions. We'll complete the minefields at M2 and M4 this morning. This afternoon we'll lay wire along M4. At the same time I'll get the squad leaders to complete overhead cover on each position."

Piper kept the platoon working. The soldiers cursed and mumbled under their breath, but they obeyed. Men stretched pained muscles and cramped joints. Sluggishly, they left their fighting positions to lay wire, place and arm antitank mines, and fill sandbags. Piper enforced the sleep plan and made sure that those infantrymen who were resting did so in the shade of their ponchos.

They worked all day. The effort was backbreaking. The sweat-stained men moved about the position like zombies. The desert sun bore down on them, making every task a challenge of endurance.

Piper was everywhere, checking, inspecting, cajoling. He verified the overhead cover by making two men jump on the roof of each fighting position. If the position didn't hold the weight of two men, it wouldn't be much protection against enemy artillery.

Before sunset the platoon had prepared two-man fighting positions in BPs Yankee and X-Ray. Each position was three to four feet deep with heavy overhead cover. The corrugated steel roofs were reinforced by rock and four layers of sandbags. Each position provided its occupants protection to the front and overhead, and offered open firing positions to each side.

Evening fell. The squad on security at BP Alamo left and occupied its positions at BP X-Ray, carefully avoiding the mines that had been laid in each trail. The observation posts reported in, ready for another night of vigil. Sergeant Piper continued the sleep plan, rotating duties between sleeping and security. Each squad was required to have two men up and alert to provide security at all times. At 2200 the platoon occupied BPs Yankee and X-Ray, ready for action.

Maybe they'll try to sneak through some reconnaissance at midnight tonight, Davis thought. Yes, they'll probably come at midnight. Night fighting will be tricky business. Are we ready? Davis thought as he sat down in his bunker on BP Yankee. He pressed the radio receiver to his ear, waiting for the first report of contact that he was sure would occur.

The company radio net was filled with routine reports, interrupted by a few intelligence updates from battalion that were passed over

Section 85

the command net by the company XO. Around midnight, the sky to the west was lit up by the bright flash of explosions and the eerie glow of artillery flares. In spite of the apparent activity to the west, the OPs continued to send negative reports.

"One-Six, this is OP South. Over," an excited soldier announced over the radio, interrupting the otherwise boring night.

"This is One-Six. Send it. Over," Davis replied, glancing at his watch. It was two in the morning. A steady far-off beating sound, growing closer by the minute, indicated the swirl of helicopter rotors.

"Helicopters, just off to the west, headed our way!"

Davis didn't reply. The bright moonlight illuminated the Russian-made transport helicopters as they popped up over the reverse-slope intervisibility line and flew along the south wall. Flying low to the ground, four helicopters sped past 1st Platoon's positions before anyone could react.

Davis stood up in his fighting position and observed the helicopters with his night-vision goggles. He watched as the aircraft landed somewhere to the southeast of Captain Bludgell's Battle Position Bravo.

"Cowper, change the radio freq!" Davis ordered, his voice tinged with urgency. "Company net!"

Cowper quickly struggled with the radio, then gave his platoon leader the handset. "Sir, I hear more choppers coming our way."

Davis nodded. "Bravo Six, this is One-Six. Enemy helicopters have landed southeast of BP Bravo. It looks like four choppers. They were past us before we could engage them. We hear another group approaching. I will take them under fire."

"Roger, One-Six," Bludgell replied over the company command net. "For God's sake, try to stop them. I'll deal with the group that has already landed. You stay in position and continue the mission."

Cowper watched in awe as the second group of helicopters came into range.

"Cowper, now, platoon net," Davis ordered.

Cowper changed the frequency to let Davis talk to his squad leaders.

"This is One-Six. I want all small arms fired in front of the helicopters as soon as they're in range. Direction southwest. I'll initiate fires. Watch my tracer," Davis said into the handset.

Davis got out of his bunker and scanned to the west. "Are the machine guns ready?"

"Ready! Just bring on the targets," Specialist Gerber, the senior machine gunner, shouted confidently.

One soldier stood erect and held the bipod legs of the M60 machine gun, supporting the weapon for its antiaircraft role. Gerber stood behind him and cradled the machine gun on his shoulder, waiting to fire.

Davis put down the hand mike. He searched the western sky with his night-vision goggles.

The enemy is using every trick in the book, he thought to himself. He has landed a company behind me and now he's trying to reinforce them with a second lift. The bastards obviously want Wadi Al Sirree.

"Here they come!" a voice shouted.

Davis watched the horizon with his PVS-7s. He pointed his M16 rifle toward the southwest and fired a full magazine of bullets in the air. Gerber opened up with his own stream of 7.62mm bullets, following the platoon leader's tracers.

Pandemonium broke out. Every rifle and machine gun in the platoon opened up at once on the advancing helicopters. Men were screaming directions and yelling encouragement to each other as the bullets wildly tore into the night sky. Tracers flew through the air, making brilliant sparks as they hit the rocks on the sides of the south wall.

The lead enemy aircraft exploded in midair from a lucky strike to its fuel cells. The rest of the enemy aircraft scattered, breaking formation and flying lower to the ground to avoid the incoming tracers. The trailing aircraft veered violently south. As it maneuvered to avoid the tracers, it hit the mountain that Davis had labeled the south wall. The fireball lit up the night sky like a small sun, illuminating the rocky landscape. The wreckage of twisted metal and burning flesh slid down the side of the mountain like a lava flow.

The men of 1st Platoon continued firing at the fleeing helicopters. Three of the enemy birds swerved south and then flew west, abandoning their attempt to land in the valley.

Davis smiled in silent satisfaction. Two enemy helicopters destroyed. I sure am glad I established an OP high on the south wall, he thought. The sharp thud of distant mortar fire drew his attention to the east.

"One-Six, this is One-Four. That must be Bludgell trying to hit the enemy's air assault troops," Piper yelled over his radio. "If they have troops in our rear, maybe we'd better put out a squad on security."

Davis considered the possibilities. War was often a choice between difficult options. Position Zulu was oriented in the right direction. He could place an M60 machine gun on Zulu to cover the platoon's rear, but that would weaken his defense of the forward areas. His other option was to keep everyone where they were. If he reoriented a couple of machine guns, he could defend a perimeter on BP Yankee that looked both east and west.

Davis has to decide! Should he send a machine-gun team to Zulu or keep everyone in position?

If Davis decides to move a machine-gun team to Position Zulu, go to Section 30.

If Davis decides to keep everyone in place, go to Section 88.

Section 86

Davis settled into his position, hoping for a few minutes' rest.

"Sir, it's Sergeant Mizogouchi on the radio," Cowper said in a zombielike voice.

"One-Six, this is One-Three. Over," Sergeant Mizogouchi announced over a squad radio to the platoon leader.

"This is One-Six. Send it. Over," Davis replied.

"I hear an engine. I can't see anything, but I hear it," Mizogouchi reported.

"Roger, I'll alert the rest of the platoon. It could be an allied armored car. They're supposed to be in front of us, to the west. Keep observing and call me as soon as you see anything."

"Roger, One-Six."

The night passed slowly. Davis checked his watch and waited, searching to the west with his PVS-7 night-vision goggles. He had always been told that the hardest part of any battle was the waiting. Now he realized that it wasn't so much the waiting as it was the thinking. Your mind plays out all of your fears when you're sitting in a foxhole peering out at the dark, expecting any minute to be in mortal combat.

Davis thought over his preparations and his concept of how the battle would unfold. Am I sure my men can stop the enemy from infiltrating into my sector? Can I block the enemy tanks and BMPs in Wadi Al Sirree if he decides to attack down Axis Cobra? Have I put up enough mines and wire? What have I forgotten?

Thus by a rough approximation: 60 percent of the art of command is the ability to anticipate; 40 percent of the art of command is the ability to improvise, to reject the preconceived idea that has been tested and proved wrong in the crucible of operations, and so rule by action instead of acting by rules.

Gen. S. L. A. Marshall

A thousand questions circulated in Davis's head. He looked at his watch. It was now 0340. He lay down with the receiver pressed to his ear and immediately fell into a deep sleep.

"Wake up, Lieutenant," Sergeant Piper said as he nudged his platoon leader.

"Huh? What the hell?" Davis replied, groggy from lack of sleep. Davis was sitting in a two-man fighting position, in Battle Position Alamo. He had a poncho liner pulled over most of his body to keep warm in the cold desert air.

Section 86

"Sir, it's already 0640. Time to inspect our positions," Piper replied, passing a brown MRE ration into his platoon leader's foxhole. "You must have nodded off right before stand-to."

"Shit! Sergeant, why didn't you get me up?" Davis protested feebly.

"Don't worry, sir. I reported to the commander on time. Everything was going fine. You worked your butt off last night. You needed a couple of hours' sleep. We'll all need it tomorrow if the enemy attacks."

Davis rubbed his tired eyes, then reached for the MRE that the sergeant had thrown at his feet. Now that it was daylight he would have to double-check each position.

"What about Mizogouchi's report of an enemy vehicle last night?" Davis questioned.

"Relax, nothing got into our sector," Piper said. "If he did hear an enemy reconnaissance patrol, I doubt whether they discovered anything. Our reverse-slope positions are too well concealed."

"Heard anything from company headquarters?" Davis asked.

"Yes, sir," Piper said as he pulled out a bag of chewing tobacco from his camouflage pants pocket. "Battalion did hit several BMPs last night, and Alpha Company destroyed a BRDM along Axis Viper."

"Alpha Company, huh?" Davis said, finally gaining full consciousness. "Maybe Bludgell is right. Maybe they're going to come straight down the road, just as he expected."

"Sir, that wouldn't break my heart any," Piper said with a grin as he put a large wad of black chewing tobacco into his mouth. "I'm going to start setting Minefield M4 in thirty minutes. After that I'm going to let as many men sleep as I can spare. They'll be exhausted by dark if we don't. I'll keep some security posted on BP Alamo."

"Good job, Sergeant," Davis answered. "I'll walk the terrain from the enemy's perspective this morning and see what he can observe when he enters our engagement areas."

"Good idea," Piper replied. "By the way, the XO came by a few minutes ago and dropped off twenty antitank mines, about six hundred sandbags, ten additional AT4s, and thirty-five gallons of water."

"I'll never say another bad thing about company headquarters," Davis commented with a smile.

"The latest intel from battalion is that the enemy overran an allied

296

reconnaissance company that was screening to the west about forty klicks from here. Things should get exciting very soon."

"So, did our allies fight or did they just turn tail?" Davis asked.

"They fought a bit," Piper said after spitting a wad of chewing tobacco juice on the dust. "But it'll be up to us to do the real fighting. Let the bastards come. We'll be ready."

"The men are beat, sir," Piper protested, anticipating Davis's need to act. "I know you want patrols sent out, but that means we'll be busy for at least three hours climbing the north and south walls rather than preparing our defenses. We'll be wasting precious time looking for an enemy that probably isn't there. Tired soldiers won't fight well."

Davis yawned. He knew how tired everyone was. Conservation of his soldiers' strength was critical, but was Piper right? Would they be wasting time patrolling an area that was already declared clear? Bravo Company had already reported that no enemy were in the area.

"We've got to keep preparing our defenses no matter how tired we are," Davis said quietly.

"No argument there," Piper answered. "But I'm just not sure we can do both, especially since the patrols may not be needed."

"If we don't patrol," Davis said, stroking the stubble on his chin, "we'll have more time to prepare our positions, and you and I could take a leader's recon to Hill 865 and look around."

"OK," Piper said with a grin. "What do you want to do?"

Davis has to decide!

If Davis decides to go with Piper to conduct a leader's reconnaissance on Hill 865, go to Section 10.

If Davis decides to send out patrols, go to Section 91.

Section 87

"Look, Sergeant, I'm tired too," Davis said with a yawn.

"Sir, these men need a few hours' rest," Piper interjected, a strong note of concern coloring his words. "If they don't sleep, there may not be anyone awake to defend our position tonight. It's been a tough week."

Davis understood Piper's objections. The hard work and the fear had worn the men ragged. The company commander had said that the enemy wouldn't be doing anything in this sector until tomorrow. Maybe Piper was right.

Continuous combat exhausts soldiers and reduces their ability to perform tasks as quickly or effectively as necessary. Even during the first night of combat, normal sleeping habits and routines are upset. The soldier feels the effects of fatigue and the pressure of stress from noise, disrupted sleep time, and threat to life. Sheer determination, while essential for endurance, cannot offset the mounting effects of adverse conditions. Cognitive degradation involving poor decision making begins during and after the first 24 hours of sleep deprivation.

FM 22-9, *Soldier Performance in Continuous Operations,*
1991

"OK. A couple of hours won't hurt us," Davis answered. "Let everyone but a few guards sack out for three hours. You post the security. Wake up everyone at 1200."

"Good decision, sir," Piper said with a bleak smile. "We need the sleep. After we rest we can finish our holes and put up the overhead cover."

The tired infantrymen pulled ponchos over their fighting positions to provide shade from the rising sun. Knowing their buddies were standing guard, they quickly fell asleep. Sergeant Piper and a few men pulled perimeter security.

Battle Position Alamo lay quiet as a graveyard.

At 1200 Piper got everyone up. The soldiers stretched pained muscles and cramped joints as they struggled out of their diminutive fighting positions. A two-man fighting position makes a poor bedroom.

The infantrymen worked, sweat stained and thirsty, in the hot desert sun. They laid wire, placed and armed antitank mines, and filled sandbags. In spite of their best efforts, they didn't have time to place all the minefields or get enough overhead protection on each fighting position. As a stopgap measure the soldiers laid single rows of concertina wire, instead of the standard triple strand, on the west side of the tank ditch.

Evening fell. The squads rotated duties between sleeping, working, and security. Even though Davis's defenses were not complete, he felt confident. The platoon had worked well, and he was satisfied that the relationship he and Piper were developing would blossom.

The reverse-slope positions were his ace in the hole. Even though the overhead cover was not finished, Davis felt that his positions on the reverse slope would protect him.

Tense hours passed as the night wore on. The company radio net was filled with routine reports, interrupted by a few intelligence updates from battalion that were passed over the command net by the company XO. Maybe they'll attack at midnight tonight. Yes, the enemy will probably come at midnight, Davis thought.

The sky to the west was lit up around midnight by the bright flash of explosions and the eerie glow of artillery flares, The noise of the artillery fire became more discernible as the night wore on.

"One-Four, this is One-Six," Davis whispered into the handset of his radio. "Do you see anything?"

"Negative. I'll call you as soon as I have a report," Piper replied with the quiet confidence of a veteran soldier.

You're scaring yourself for nothing, Davis thought. Maybe Piper's right. Maybe they won't attack tonight. Hell, once the enemy finds out he's up against the United States, he'll probably head for home.

"Sir, OP North says he sees something," Cowper reported, giving the handset to Davis.

"Helicopters, flying just above the ground, headed our way. Fast!" OP North reported as Davis listened to the radio receiver.

Davis didn't reply.

The full moon highlighted the Russian-made transport helicopters as they flew along the south wall of Wadi Al Sirree. The flight of four helicopters was headed east, toward Captain Bludgell's Battle Position Bravo. Flying low to the ground, the helicopters sped past 1st Platoon's positions before the Americans could react.

Davis jumped out of his fighting position and scanned to the east, following the flight of the enemy helicopters. Soon he recognized the swirl of more helicopter rotors, growing closer by the minute, approaching his position.

"Cowper, change the radio freq," Davis shouted. "Company net!"

Cowper quickly struggled with the radio, climbed out of his position, and gave Davis the handset.

"Bravo Six, this is One-Six. I've spotted four enemy helicopters headed east toward your position. I hear another group of helicopters approaching my position. I'll take them under fire."

"One-Six," Bludgell replied over the company command net, "stop them. I'll handle the group that has already landed. You stay in your positions and continue the mission."

Cowper took off his helmet and listened for the second group of helicopters.

"Cowper, switch to the platoon net," Davis ordered. Cowper changed the frequency to let Davis talk to his squad leaders.

"This is One-Six. I want all our small arms fired in front of the helicopters as soon as they fly into range. I'll initiate the fires. Watch my tracer," Davis declared into the hand mike.

Davis looked to his left. "Are the machine guns ready?"

"Ready, just bring on the targets," reported Specialist Gerber, the senior machine gunner.

One soldier stood erect and held the bipod legs of the M60 machine gun, supporting the gun for its antiaircraft role. Gerber stood behind him and cradled the machine gun on his shoulder, waiting to fire. Davis put down the handset.

The enemy is using every trick in the book, Davis thought to himself. Landing air assault infantry behind the American positions was a bold move. The enemy obviously wanted Wadi Al Sirree. The main attack must be coming this way.

"Here they come!" a voice shouted.

Davis watched the horizon with his PVS-7s. He pointed his M16 toward the southern flank of the valley and fired a full magazine of 5.56mm bullets a half a football field length in front of the lead helicopter.

Gerber opened up with a stream of 7.62mm bullets. His tracers followed the lieutenant's arc of fire.

Following Gerber's lead, every rifle and machine gun in the platoon opened up at once on the advancing helicopters. Pandemonium erupted as tracers flew through the night sky, sparking off the rocks on the sides of the south wall.

The enemy aircraft scattered, breaking formation and flying lower to the ground to avoid the incoming arc of tracers. The lead aircraft veered violently south in an attempt to miss the oncoming fire.

As the fleeing helicopters flew east, 1st Platoon continued firing. Unscathed, the helicopters were quickly out of range.

"Damn it! Didn't even get close!" Davis yelled.

Our positions on BP Alamo are designed to stop an enemy from the west, not from the east, Davis thought. Now the enemy has landed in my rear. Should I move to our reverse-slope positions?

The sound of mortar fire began to the southeast.

"That must be the company mortars trying to hit the helicopter landing zone," Piper yelled over his radio. "If the enemy's landed to the east, we better put a squad out to secure our rear."

The actor in war constantly finds things different from his expectations; and this cannot fail to have an influence on his plans, or at least on the presumptions connected with these plans. If this influence is so great as to render the predetermined plan completely nugatory, then, as a rule, a new one must be substituted in its place; but at the moment the necessary data are often wanting for this, because in the course of action circumstances press for immediate decision, and allow no time to look about for fresh data, often not enough for mature consideration.

Carl von Clausewitz

Davis considered the possibilities. Position Yankee offered a good position to fire to the east. He hadn't planned on fighting from Yankee to the east, but surprise is the nature of war.

I wish I knew more about what was happening! Do I move now or risk waiting until just before daylight? Davis questioned himself.

"Orders Group at my position. Now!" Davis shouted into the radio transmitter.

Go to Section 89.

Section 88

The gray sky turned light blue as the dark receded into dawn. Billows of black smoke could be seen on the western horizon. The rumble of artillery and the high-pitched screech of hundreds of rocket shells filled the early morning with sounds of death.

Davis put down his night-vision goggles; he looked at his map and studied the ground over which he expected the enemy armor to advance. The terrain to the northwest of Wadi Al Sirree sloped downward for four kilometers, then gradually rose for an additional four kilometers to a jagged ridge on the western horizon. Between the valley and this ridge was nothing but empty desert. As the enemy approached from the west, he would have to cross this open space against the brigade's deep fires.

Unfortunately, Davis knew how weak those deep fires were: only one battalion of 155mm artillery and a few sorties from navy F/A-18s and air force A-10s. The carrier-based F/A-18s had a short loiter time because of the distance of the battlefield from the aircraft carrier they called home. The A-10s, on the other hand, could stay longer because they were from an allied air base forty kilometers to the south. The A-10s, potent tank killers, had the disadvantage of being old, big, and slow. With the improvements in air defense systems in the past years, the A-10's survivability was always a matter of pilot skill and luck.

Maybe the enemy won't attack through my valley, Davis thought.

A flight of F/A-18s screamed overhead, flying low over Wadi Al Sirree. The aircraft headed west to attack the advancing enemy columns.

"Sir, I've been eavesdropping on the artillery net," Sergeant Mark reported. "All the long-range stuff is engaging the enemy. We'll be in battle with the main force soon."

The sound of outgoing 155mm artillery shells punctuated Mark's words. The rounds arced high overhead and exploded to the west, detonating with a rumble that shook the ground in Wadi Al Sirree. A pair of F/A-18s roared across the sky to the north, dropping cluster bombs on the advancing enemy armor.

I hope the brigade punches the hell out of them, thought Davis. We need every chance we can to even these odds.

In offensive and defensive tactical actions, commanders fight the enemy throughout the depth of his disposition with fires and with attacks on his flanks and rear. They attack committed and uncommitted forces and synchronize the attack of enemy artillery in depth with close operations. Such in-depth operations degrade the enemy's freedom of action, reduce his flexibility and endurance, and upset his plans and coordination.

FM 100-5, *Operations,* 1993

The sound of multiple explosions resonated from the area beyond the jagged ridge to the northwest.

"That's our stuff," Davis shouted to his men. "Get ready. The enemy will be on us in about twenty minutes."

Davis focused his binoculars on the exits of the jagged ridge, eight kilometers to the northwest. The passes were filled with dust and smoke. Suddenly, dark objects began racing out of each pass. Scores of vehicles, moving in high-speed columns, emerged from the passes. The vehicles quickly exited the narrow defiles and raced east across the broken desert terrain.

"There they are," Davis declared, pointing to the distant ridge. Sergeant Mark gave Davis a worried look, then put the radio receiver back to his ear and continued eavesdropping on the artillery radio frequency.

The rumble of explosions increased. The detonations sounded like the strike of a huge hammer, pounding the earth to the northwest. Davis watched with silent satisfaction as one of the lead enemy columns was blanketed with the impact of CBU-87 cluster bombs and 155mm artillery shells. A number of vehicles in this column lurched to a halt and burst into flame. More vehicles, however, bypassed the wreckage and continued on their determined path to the east.

American planes darted above the advancing enemy formations. A volley of antiaircraft missiles greeted the attacking planes. A fiery explosion registered the midair destruction of one of the F/A-18s. Several other aircraft, having already dropped their ordnance, ignited their afterburners and roared back to the east, attempting to outrun the enemy's effective missile defenses.

The sound of outgoing artillery shells suddenly died away. The battlefield grew ominously quiet. Our deep operation is over, Davis thought. Now it's the enemy's turn.

"That's it, sir," Mark announced, the radio receiver still pressed against his ear. "The F/A-18s are heading home. We may get some A-10s later. We can call for fire whenever we have a formation of armored vehicles to shoot at."

Davis's radio crackled. "One-Six, this is Six-Five," the company XO called, sounding calm and in control. "The enemy is attacking. We haven't identified their main effort yet. Our artillery is giving them hell."

Good, thought Davis. Maybe the attack will pass by us.

"Roger, Six-Five. Anything sighted along Axis Cobra?" Davis asked.

"We have no reports . . . Shit, we're being attacked! Infantry!"

The XO's transmission was abruptly cut off.

"Six-Five, this is One-Six," Davis shouted into the handset. "Six-Five, this is One-Six!"

Tense seconds ticked by. The radio remained silent. There would be no help from Bravo Company.

Davis gave the handset to Cowper and faced to the west, watching the enemy columns get closer with each passing minute. The sound of bursting artillery, pounding a steady path from west to east, interrupted this short interlude of quiet. The explosions moved with precision in an inexorable wall of exploding steel toward the American positions.

Balls of orange flame erupted in the openings to the trails on the western edge of Wadi Al Sirree. The earth shook under the thunder of the enemy's 152mm guns. The men dove into their fighting positions.

"Shit, here it comes. Take cover, incoming!" Cowper yelled as he dove for the bottom of his fighting position.

The earth in front of the tank ditch exploded in fire and smoke. Davis took one last look before he fell to the bottom of his hole, landing on top of his RTO.

The bursting artillery shells showered the American positions with rocks and dirt. The position was engulfed in a turmoil of fire and swirling steel, as if the enemy knew the precise location of every American position.

Roll the dice.

If you roll 2–4, go to Section 48.

If you roll 5–12, go to Section 58.

Section 89

"OP North, this is One-Six," Davis said slowly into the microphone of his radio transmitter. "Did any of those helicopters land near Position Yankee?"

"Negative, One-Six," OP North announced calmly. "They all landed in the valley somewhere south of BP Bravo."

Piper and the squad leaders scrambled over to Davis's fighting position. They listened to Davis's exchange with OP North.

"Good job, OP North. Keep looking both ways and report to me as soon as you see anything."

Davis gave the handset to Cowper. Piper and the squad leaders huddled around their platoon leader.

"We've got enemy infantry in our rear, probably attacking the company right now. If we're lucky, they won't come our way," Davis said grimly. "But we can't count on that, so we have to move to our reverse-slope positions now. I'll occupy Position Yankee looking both ways. You all know the plan. Any questions?"

Everyone remained silent. The huddled soldiers looked at each other with a finality that expressed the gravity of their predicament.

"OK. Keep calm and execute as we have planned. Call me when you're in position."

The group dispersed. Each squad leader shouted orders and the platoon quickly left BP Alamo for their designated positions.

Davis assembled his machine gunners, Javelin teams, Cowper, Mark, and Hutchinson and hurried due east along the ridge. By taking the ridge, where only infantry could walk, they avoided the lethal tank and personnel mines that they had placed along every possible mounted avenue of approach into Wadi Al Sirree.

In thirty minutes Davis's tired soldiers reached BP Yankee. After a quick reconnaissance to make sure the area was clear of the enemy, they occupied their positions and made ready for battle.

"Gerber, you and Spellman set up your machine guns facing east, toward BP Bravo," Davis ordered. "Javelin gunners, set up to fire along Trails 1 and 2."

The machine-gun teams hustled to their new positions and waited. One by one each squad radioed a report to Davis that they had occupied their positions. The platoon was ready to fight.

Davis turned his attention to the din of battle to the east. He could hear the sound of small-arms fire, the thump of grenades, and the crash of muffled explosions emanating from BP Bravo.

"One-Six, this is OP South. There's a battle going on at BP Bravo."

"Roger, OP South," Davis answered. "There's nothing we can do about it now. Just keep an eye out for any enemy that may come our way down the valley from the east."

The clamor of the battle at BP Bravo echoed through the valley. The bright full moon slowly arced across the sky, turning the night into a world of half-lit shadows. Slowly the sounds of fighting from the east diminished, then stopped altogether.

Davis worried about an attack from the rear. What if the enemy destroyed Bludgell and is now turning on me? he thought. Can I stop their attack with two M60 machine guns?

"One-Six, this is OP North," the radio cackled, interrupting Davis's ponderings. "I've got infantry heading up into Trail 4."

This is it, Davis thought. A night infiltration of my position from the east while an air assault confronts BP Bravo is the worst possible scenario. The enemy's actions are now beginning to make sense. He launched an air assault to hold the north end of Wadi Al Sirree, the exit. Now he's launching a dismounted attack to secure the western entrance.

"One-Six, this is OP North," a voice whispered on the other end of the radio. "I see enemy infantry moving at Bravo One-Zero-Six. They're coming right up Trail 4 along the south wall."

"Roger, OP North. I'll call for fires. You adjust," Davis calmly ordered over his radio.

Davis nodded to Sergeant Mark, who was already on the radio with the artillery fire direction center. He had been trying to reach the mortars. Frustrated by the attempt, he switched frequencies.

"Sir, I can't reach anyone at company, but I've got the 105mm FDC on the line," Mark reported.

"Yes, damn it! Anything."

"105mm VT," Mark said, the hand mike close to his mouth. "On the way, sir."

"Stand by, OP North," Davis ordered over his radio.

"One-Six, they've stopped to get organized before pushing farther up the trail. Hurry up, One-Six."

"Shot!" Mark screamed to Davis, indicating that a round was in the air, heading toward its target.

"Shot!" Davis relayed over the radio to OP North.

Suddenly the southwest entrance to the valley was lit by bright flashes. The scream of incoming artillery filled the air. Bright orange and yellow bursts of VT—variable-time-fused 105mm shells—fell among the attacking enemy infantry.

"One-Six, this is OP North. Repeat. You're right on target. Keep pouring it on."

The unmistakable sound of exploding 105mm VT shells filled the air. Mark stayed glued to his transmitter, relaying the firing information as fast as he received it. Davis exchanged firing adjustments from OP North to Sergeant Mark.

The U.S. shells burst high overhead, detonating eighteen feet above the ground and sending a deadly array of white hot metal fragments over the target.

"The rounds are right on target," OP North reported excitedly. "The enemy has nowhere to hide. Repeat."

"Roger, OP North," Sergeant Mark said as calmly as if he were on a firing exercise back on an artillery range at Fort Sill. "I'll have 105mm HE and illumination falling one hundred meters west of Bravo One-Zero-Six in a few minutes."

"One-Six, this is OP North, observing artillery at Bravo One-Zero-Six now. Good effects."

The shelling lasted for ten minutes, but to Davis it seemed like a matter of seconds. Finally, there was silence. The quiet was suddenly more unusual than the noise of the artillery.

Did the enemy get through? Davis wondered.

"One-Six, this is OP North. We stopped them. I don't see anything moving."

"Sir, I can't get anyone on the company fire net," Sergeant Mark announced. Davis put up his hand, silencing Mark. Davis's radio receiver cackled.

"Break, break! One-Six, this is OP South, flash spot report. I see enemy infantry moving east along the north wall. They're almost on top of you!"

"There! At five o'clock!" one of the machine gunners shouted.

Davis looked to the east. "Cowper, Mark, come with me," he said, then rushed to the east side of BP Yankee without looking back to see if the two men were following. Davis ran twenty meters, then plopped into a prone position next to Gerber's machine gun. The lieutenant raised his PVS-7 night-vision goggles to his eyes.

Enemy infantry was moving along the north wall toward Position Yankee. Davis could see fifteen to twenty men moving slowly forward.

"OK, they're coming along the north wall," Davis called in a hushed voice. "Chambers, Montoya, grab your M16s and get over here. Mark, try to get me some artillery."

The enemy moved forward, unaware of the location of BP Yankee. They were walking slowly east, toward the mouth of Trail 1, about two hundred meters away from Davis.

"Fire on my command," Davis ordered quietly. "Gerber, you shoot at the lead of the formation. Spellman, you hit the trailing party."

The enemy switched direction slightly and headed toward BP Yankee. They were now only one hundred meters away.

"Fire!" Davis screamed. Machine guns and rifles opened up. A steady stream of red and green tracer bullets ripped through the air. Half a dozen enemy soldiers crumpled to the ground with the first volley from the machine guns. The enemy immediately returned fire and began to move south, to avoid the effects of Davis's guns.

Suddenly Gerber's gun jammed. He pulled open the cover and frantically tried to clear the stoppage. At the same time an enemy light machine gun blazed away, pelting BP Yankee with fire. A shout came up from the enemy infantry as they rose to rush Davis's position.

Smoke and the smell of cordite filled the air. Shadows raced toward Davis, firing as they advanced. Davis lowered his weapon and dropped two enemy soldiers. Gerber still struggled with his M60.

Two soldiers rushed Davis's position from the right front. Davis hit one who was carrying a grenade. The man fell backward, dropping the grenade. Cowper swung to his side and stopped the other attacker with well-aimed rifle fire.

Davis looked at the hissing grenade lying in front of him.

Roll the dice.

If you roll 2–8, go to Section 26.

If you roll 9–12, go to Section 56.

Section 90

Davis assembled his machine gunners, Javelin teams, Cowper, Mark, and Hutchinson and scurried along the ridge that led due east to Position Yankee. The ridge avoided the lethal tank and personnel mines that they had placed along every possible mounted avenue of approach into Wadi Al Sirree.

In thirty minutes Davis and his men reached Battle Position Yankee. Before occupying Yankee, Davis sent a reconnaissance team to check out the position.

"It's OK, sir," Gerber announced. "No sign of the enemy."

"Gerber, you and Spellman set up your machine guns facing east, toward BP Bravo," Davis ordered. "Javelin gunners, set up to fire along Trails 1 and 2."

Davis's team quickly occupied Position Yankee, splitting the sectors of fire as ordered, and waited. One by one each squad reported set in position.

The sounds of fighting from the east diminished. The bright full moon slowly arced across the night sky, turning the night into a world of half-lit shadows.

"One-Six, this is OP North. I see something moving southwest of Trail 4 again, possibly more infantry."

"Roger, OP North. I'll call for fires. You adjust," Davis calmly ordered over his radio.

Davis nodded to Sergeant Mark, who was already on the radio trying to reach the fire direction center.

"Stand by, OP North," Davis ordered over his radio. "We're trying to get the artillery now."

Mark worked furiously at the radio. "Lima Seven-One, this is Charlie Five-Five. Over."

"Alert, they're behind us!" Gerber shouted as he opened up with a full blast of his M60 machine gun at these attackers.

Suddenly BP Yankee was lit by bright flashes. Incoming rocket-propelled grenades screamed in the night. Enemy infantry was attacking from the east.

"What the hell!" Davis yelled. "What's happening?"

Davis looked to the east and saw the firefight that had started. "Cowper, Mark, come with me," he said, then rushed to the east side of BP Yankee. After racing twenty meters he plopped into a prone position near Gerber's machine-gun team. The lieutenant raised his PVS-7 night-vision goggles and scanned the battlefield.

How the hell did they get behind us? Davis thought. Then he suddenly understood. The enemy had launched an air assault against BP Bravo to seize the eastern exit of Wadi Al Sirree. They must have sent an element to link up with their friends who were coming up Trail 4.

Bullets streaked all around. Mark stayed glued to his transmitter, trying to reach somebody—anybody. Gerber fired furiously toward the east. The two Javelin gunners and their ammo bearers hugged the earth of their fighting positions.

An enemy rocket burst behind them, showering the position with rocks and sparks and sending a deadly array of white hot metal fragments into Position Yankee.

"Sir, I can't get anyone on the company net!" Mark complained. "I've tried all our frequencies."

Davis took the radio handset to try to get help. A stream of bullets cut into Position Yankee. Cowper was hit; he spun backward and collapsed, blood gushing from his torn chest. The spin jerked the mike out of Davis's hand.

Suddenly Gerber's gun jammed. He pulled open the cover and frantically tried to clear the stoppage. At the same time, an enemy light machine gun blazed away, pelting BP Yankee with fire. A shout came up from the enemy infantry as they rose to rush Davis's position.

Smoke and the smell of cordite filled the air. Shadows raced toward Davis, firing as they advanced. He lowered his weapon and dropped two enemy soldiers. Gerber still struggled with his M60.

Davis reached for Cowper's M203 and fired a volley at the advancing Threat infantry. The enemy dashed toward Davis's position in short rushes. Two light machine guns, tucked into shallow wadis, provided covering fire for the advancing enemy.

Gerber's machine gun remained silent, the gunner hit in the head by an enemy slug as he tried to clear the stoppage in his gun. The assistant gunner grabbed the weapon, cleared it, and began firing.

"They're all over the place, sir!" Fetterman yelled. An RPG exploded five meters to the right of his position. Metal shards knocked him off his feet and hurled his lifeless body over his gun.

A loud shout came again as the enemy rushed into BP Yankee. In the smoke all was confusion and terror. Davis dropped an enemy soldier with his M203, then two more rushed forward. Davis fired again, then felt his left side go numb.

Why can't I move? he wondered.

He lay on his back, looking up at the dark, smoke-filled, early-morning sky. The last thing Davis saw was the face of the enemy soldier who fired a full burst into his chest.

Davis failed in his mission to block the enemy from seizing and moving through Wadi Al Sirree. The enemy used an air assault force to secure the key terrain in Davis's sector, forcing Davis to fight both east and west. He never even got a chance to see if his defense of the trails would work.

In 1939 the U.S. Army Infantry School produced a publication entitled *Infantry in Battle*. This classic book on infantry tactics is still worth studying today. A quote from this excellent treatise is applicable here: "It requires perfect performance by a leader to insure that his unit is committed to action according to a clear, workable plan and under favorable conditions. Indeed, it may require extreme energy and forethought to insure that his command is engaged according to any plan at all." In short, leading an infantry platoon isn't easy.

Sometimes the best plans turn out wrong. Davis did many things right. He planned for security using an observation post on Hill 865, and he used his reserve extremely well. In this situation he just ran out of luck. But as the great German general Field Marshal Helmuth Graf von Moltke once said, "Luck in the long run is given only to the efficient."

Go to Section 3 and start again.

Section 91

"We have to patrol the high ground on our flank," Davis said, completely in charge of the situation. The lieutenant unfolded his map and beckoned for the platoon sergeant to bend down to see as he pointed out key terrain on the map.

Piper, his mouth full of chewing tobacco, spat a thin dark brown string into the dust.

"Send Tyler's squad to check out the high ground on the north wall," said Davis. "I want everyone else working on putting in minefields and completing positions. Mark and I will use the time to complete the artillery plan."

"Wilco," Piper said with a grin, happy to see that the lieutenant was firmly in control and making some smart tactical moves. "While you're doing that, I'll get to work on BP Yankee."

The patrol departed. Piper put one M60 machine-gun team on security in the positions overlooking the tank ditch. He took the other machine-gun team and the attached Javelin gunners to dig positions on Yankee.

Davis and Sergeant Mark had nearly completed their artillery plan when suddenly the sound of firing on the north wall interrupted their work.

"Sir, it's Sergeant Tyler on the radio for you," Cowper announced.

"One-Six, this is One-Two," Tyler reported. "We found two enemy soldiers in an observation post on top of Hill 865. We killed them both. We tried to capture them but no dice. No friendly casualties. We captured an AM radio and a map. There's no marks on the map."

"Good work, One-Two. Bring anything you think will help the intel guys with you. I'll report it to higher."

Davis reported the incident to Captain Bludgell. As a result of the enemy contact, Davis decided to have Sergeant Tyler establish two observation posts. The one in the north, with the call sign of OP North, would be positioned on Hill 865. The one in the south, with a call sign of OP South, would be positioned on the south wall.

"Well, sir, maybe now we can grab some sleep," Piper announced. "The men are beat. Tired soldiers don't fight well."

Go to Section 87.

Section 92

"Cowper, get Piper on the radio," Davis ordered.

Cowper fidgeted with his equipment for several moments, calling to Sergeant Piper. "Sir, no answer. I've tried all the frequencies he might be on. I can't reach him."

There isn't a moment to lose, Davis thought. I have to reach Piper. If the enemy is attempting a night infiltration, Piper has to man the forward defenses as we planned. He's not far from here. I'd better meet with him on the ground.

"Sergeant Mark, you're in charge. I'm going to take Cowper and go to Piper's position. He must be having radio problems. I'll call you when I get there."

Davis and Cowper headed off toward Piper's position. Davis led and Cowper trailed several paces behind.

"Keep trying to reach him," Davis ordered. Cowper, the handset of the radio pressed against his face, called repeatedly. The two men paced cautiously toward Position X-Ray.

"It's over there," Davis said, gesturing to Cowper. "Two hundred meters that way."

Suddenly, the quiet night was interrupted by the bark of several M16s. Tracers erupted from Position X-Ray, and Davis was hit in the shoulder and the chest. The lieutenant spun backward and staggered a few steps.

"Cease fire, damn it!" the familiar voice of Sergeant Piper screamed.

Cowper hit the ground and pointed his weapon toward the flash of the rifle that fired at them. Another round struck the platoon leader. Davis fell to his knees, then face first onto the desert floor.

"God damn it! Stop shooting, you son of a bitch!" Piper yelled, trying to get control of his excited and inexperienced soldiers.

"Don't shoot!" Cowper yelled. "Don't shoot! We're Americans! It's me, Cowper and Lieutenant Davis. The lieutenant is hit!"

Davis lay on the desert sand, his lifeblood oozing out of his shattered body. In a few moments he was dead.

Go to Section 37.

Section 93

"Fire! Get the bastard!"

The Javelin gunner, his eye pressed against the command launch unit sight, depressed the firing trigger. The missile burst out of the tube in a loud roar and flew a jumping, erratic path to the stationary tank.

The missile hit the turret and shot a molten stream of energy inside. The tank ignited in a billow of smoke and flame as its ammunition exploded.

A second tank behind the exploding hulk turned its turret toward Davis's position, eager to avenge the death of the lead vehicle. The tank fired its machine guns in a wide, wild arc as the turret turned. Machine-gun bullets ripped through the sandbags of Davis's fighting position.

Davis watched as the Javelin gunner tried to jump to cover. A stream of bullets from the enemy tank cut the American down.

Davis reached down inside his position and armed an AT4 antitank rocket. Quickly, while bullets whizzed by and splattered on his fighting position, he fired. The missile flew short and exploded against a rock, missing the intended target. The tank jerked to a halt, aimed its turret at Davis, and plastered his position with machine-gun bullets.

Davis dove for cover. Several 7.62mm bullets pierced his left arm as he ducked, tearing the flesh and shattering the bone. Davis winced in pain. His arm hung limp, the open wounds gushing blood. He fought to get up, but the effort was futile. With his good arm he reached for the green bandanna he kept in the cargo pocket of his trousers and improvised a hasty tourniquet. He suddenly felt weak. The world began to spin, and in a few seconds Davis fell unconscious.

The hot sun glared down on Davis as he opened his eyes. He felt pain all over, especially his left arm.

He realized that he was in the back of an open truck, moving quickly down a bumpy desert road. He lay on the cold metal bed of the truck. Eisler was doing everything he could to hold his lieutenant down.

"Hold on, sir," pleaded Specialist Eisler, the platoon medic.

"What . . . what happened?" Davis asked, realizing that something was wrong. Eisler wasn't wearing his helmet.

"We've been captured," Eisler reported with tears in his eyes. "There's only a few of us left. They shot most of the wounded. They kept you alive when they found out you were an officer."

Davis closed his eyes in pain.

Go back to Section 3 and try again.

Section 94

The high-caliber enemy artillery shells kicked up huge geysers of dirt and rock. The rounds struck the area west of BP Yankee, far enough away to be harmless. Davis knew that it was only a matter of time until the enemy guns found their range.

Rumbling like a furious thunderstorm, a new volley of artillery shells smashed into the trails that led into Wadi Al Sirree. Many of the enemy rounds were now smoke shells, spreading their haze to obscure the openings of the trails into the wadi. Several shells fell close to BP Yankee. Then, just as suddenly, the fire slackened, rolled over them, and marched east.

Davis and Cowper picked themselves up from the bottom of their fighting position. Davis scanned the position, searching for each familiar face. The Javelin gunners waved that they were all right. Davis received similar assurances from the rest of the men on BP Yankee. Luckily, no one had been hurt in this new volley of fire.

"Sir, it's OP North," Cowper announced. "He says it's hard to see with all the smoke, but he thinks they've got a tank and four BMPs moving up Trail 1."

"Get that Javelin ready," Davis shouted to Specialist Chambers, in the next position to the left. Chambers knelt, with the Javelin on his shoulder, facing the oncoming enemy vehicle. He sent a worried glance back to Lieutenant Davis. Davis coolly stood up in his foxhole and looked to the two antiarmor gunners in positions on the left and right sides of Position Yankee.

"Javelin gunners, stand by," Davis shouted in a cracked voice. "They'll be here in a few seconds. Chambers, make your first shot count!"

The soldiers gave the lieutenant a thumbs-up. Their thermal sights were firmly attached to the Javelin missiles. The gunners were in position, scanning.

The smoke got thicker at the openings of the trails into Wadi Al Sirree. Suddenly a tank crashed through the smoke at high speed, firing its machine guns erratically as it raced by. Chambers fired, his launcher shooting exhaust smoke, flame, and debris to the rear of BP Yankee. The missile darted up and down as it accelerated toward the fast-moving target.

The Javelin missile smashed into the top of the tank. The Javelin warhead tore through the thin top armor, burned into the turret, and ignited the ammunition in the tank's autoloader carousel, right below the breech of the main gun. The explosion sent pieces of the turret into the air.

A BMP jerked to a halt right behind the destroyed tank. Montoya fired his Javelin just as the BMP stopped. The missile struck the BMP in a shower of sparks, forcing the vehicle sideways and exposing the rear doors to the Americans. The doors burst open, but raging flames devoured the life that had once been inside.

A third BMP raced by the scene of devastation. A tremendous explosion stopped this BMP. Fire gushed out of the ground as it hit a well-concealed antitank mine. The mine sent a stream of fire up into the belly of the vehicle. Exploding from inside out, it disintegrated in a burst of black smoke.

More BMPs pushed forward, determined to gain the reverse slope. Davis's men continued to fire at the advancing armored vehicles. Machine guns rattled and scraped the sides of the vehicles. A flurry of American AT4 antitank rockets greeted the advancing enemy, who was unaware that he had entered a well-constructed killing zone. Two BMPs were stopped by AT4s. Two others were destroyed by antitank mines.

Observing through gaps in the smoke, OP North reported that the lead company of the enemy advance guard continued along Cobra. The entire area of Wadi Al Sirree filled with smoke from vehicle exhaust, smoke generators, blazing vehicles, and burning smoke pots. Bypassing the burning vehicles at the end of Trail 1, enemy plow tanks cleared the mines and headed toward Battle Position Bravo.

A tank broke through the smoke and pelted BP Yankee with machine-gun fire. Several of Davis's men were hit. One soldier, Private Winder, lay on his back, clutching his head with both hands and kicking up the ground inside his blood-soaked position. His anguished screams filled the air in between the roar of exploding vehicles and flying lead. After a few seconds, Winder stopped kicking and lay still.

The tank rushed toward BP Yankee, apparently eager to finish off the rest of the defenders. Suddenly the tank disintegrated in a powerful explosion caused by another mine. At the same time, Chambers fired another Javelin and reduced a BMP to a flaming mass of burning metal. The engagement area was now crowded with burning vehicles.

"One-Six, this is OP South. You've bottled them up along Trail 1. A tank is working its way toward you from Trail 3. Watch your left flank."

Before Davis could answer, the tank charged through the smoke and leveled its gun at BP Yankee.

Roll the dice.

If you roll 2 or 3, go to Section 58.

If you roll 4–8, go to Section 64.

If you roll 9–12, go to Section 69.

Section 95

The great victories of the United States have pivoted on the acts of courage and intelligence of a very few individuals. The time always comes in battle when the decisions of statesmen and of generals can no longer affect the issue and when it is not within the power of our national wealth to change the balance decisively. Victory is never achieved prior to that point; it can be won only after the battle has been delivered into the hands of men who move in imminent danger of death. I think that we in the United States need to consider well that point, for we have made a habit of believing that national security lies at the end of a production line. This may be an excusable conceit, though I have yet to see a Sherman tank or Browning gun that added anything to the national defense until it came into the hands of men who willingly risked their own lives. Further than that, I have too often seen the tide of battle turn around the high action of a few unhelped men to believe that the final problem of the battlefield can ever be solved by the machine. . . . And so the final and greatest reality, the national strength, lies only in the hearts and spirit of men.

Gen. S. L. A. Marshall

As a leader of combat infantrymen, you are responsible for the results of battle. The most important result is decisive victory. You have fought well and earned victory, but you could have won with fewer casualties. Marshal Foch of First World War fame once said, "No study is possible on the battlefield; one does there simply what one can in order to apply what one knows. Therefore, in order to do even a little, one has already to know a great deal and know it well."

Now that you know the situation well, go back and decide again.

Go to Section 76 and try again!

Section 96

"OK," Davis said. "I could use the walk."

The two men grabbed their gear and headed north. Davis led. Piper, his M16 held at the ready, followed close behind.

"Why'd you join the army, Lieutenant?" Piper asked as the two strode forward.

"Why? What the hell kind of question is that, Sergeant?"

"Just curious," Piper said. "You come from a military family?"

"Yes, I do. The Davises have always been soldiers or marines. It's in our blood. I have a brother in the marines and another in the army. It's what we do."

"Not me," said Piper. "I joined to earn a college degree. Once I got in, I found out I liked it. Never got around to finishing college."

The two men climbed up a trail that led to the top of Hill 865. Nearing the crest, Davis stopped and raised his hand to Piper, signaling to get down. The lieutenant raised his binoculars to search the ground to their front.

"I could have sworn I saw something moving," Davis said in a whisper. "I don't see anything now."

"Where?"

"Over there, on top of the rise," Davis said, pointing. The two men waited for several minutes. Davis continued to scan the area with his binoculars.

"It was probably an animal," Piper replied. "We haven't had any reports that the enemy is in our area."

"Maybe so, but let's keep alert," Davis said as he switched off the safety on his M16 rifle. "I'd feel like an idiot if something happened to us."

The two men continued walking up the hill. Davis paced ahead steadily, carrying his M16 facing forward. The sound of distant artillery, almost like the rumble of a thunderstorm off on the horizon, emanated from the west.

Section 96

They finally reached the top of the hill. Davis scanned the area to the west. "It sounds like somebody is catching hell up front."

Piper nodded phlegmatically. "I'm sure our allies will be running our way soon. I never worked with these guys before, but from what I saw of Desert Storm, they won't hold out long."

"Maybe so," Davis replied, praying silently that Piper was wrong. "At least our air force will have a chance to soften up the enemy before he hits us."

"Don't count on it," Piper said with a shrug. "In the infantry you've got to take care of yourself. We can't count on any help, other than our own company and battalion."

As if to dispute Piper's comments, the far-off hum of helicopter rotors filled the air to the east. An OH-68 Warrior helicopter, followed by an AH-64 Apache attack helicopter, flew several kilometers off to the north. The friendly helicopters were heading west, toward the sounds of the artillery fire.

"Well, it looks like somebody decided to help. Those babies will sure give 'em hell."

Piper didn't answer. Davis climbed up on top of a large boulder to get a better view.

Just as Davis brought the binoculars to his eyes, a bullet ricocheted inches in front of him. Hit by the terrible impact, he dropped his binoculars and M16 and slid down the hill toward the wall of the pass.

"Lieutenant!" Piper yelled, throwing himself on the ground.

Davis felt a burning sensation in his chest. He was confused, lightheaded. What was happening?

Piper jumped up and fired a few rounds in the direction of their attacker. He then climbed down to grab his stunned lieutenant and draw him out of the field of fire.

Another shot ripped through the air and hit Piper in the neck. He fell backward next to his lieutenant. Davis, lying on his back, searched for his M16. Finally he found his weapon and leveled it in the direction of the incoming fire. He blasted off a full magazine of ammunition.

Time hung in the air, still, frozen. Davis looked up at the clear blue sky. He felt his heart beating fast. He was dizzy.

It had all happened so quickly.

"Piper, are you all right?"

Piper didn't reply.

Davis felt terribly cold and suddenly very, very tired. He wanted to close his eyes and sleep. A thousand questions boiled in his mind. Why couldn't he move or turn his head?

It was difficult to breathe. The air was filled with smoke and dust. His mouth tasted of blood and sand. Suddenly the world went black.

The sounds of battle drifted over him. The last thing he heard was the short, sharp burst from the enemy's sniper rifle.

Davis stopped breathing and died.

Go to Section 37.

Section 97

The familiar voice of Sergeant Piper whispered over the radio. Davis could hear it over the small receiver of his radio's hand mike.

Cowper handed the mike to his platoon leader.

"One-Six, this is One-Four," Sergeant Piper radioed to his platoon leader from the other end of the position. "We got someone in the wire just west of the ditch. We need some illumination."

"Roger, One-Four," Davis whispered into the transmitter. "I'll get Charlie Five-Five working on it." Charlie Five-Five was Sergeant Mark's call sign.

Someone might be trying to infiltrate through our perimeter, Davis thought. He looked at Cowper. The young private's eyes were as big as silver dollars.

Davis realized that it was a mistake not to have made a four-man position so that he could have immediate access to Sergeant Mark, his forward observer. Sergeant Mark was in the next hole, twenty feet to the south of Davis's fighting position. In a firefight, twenty feet might as well be twenty miles.

"Mark! Sergeant Mark!" Davis whispered in a hushed voice.

No answer.

Davis cursed beneath his breath. "Cowper, I'm going to have to crawl to Sergeant Mark's hole. You stay here. I'll bring Mark and his RTO back with me."

"That'll be a tight fit, Lieutenant."

"We'll manage," Davis replied, attempting a courageous smile.

"Sir, couldn't we just call him on the radio?"

"He's on a different frequency—the FDC net," Davis explained. "I can't be changing frequencies every time I need artillery. Next time I'll be sure to put him in my fighting position."

Davis checked his equipment. He crouched low, with his back to the wall of the fighting position. After a few moments of deliberation he jumped up and slithered out of the hole. Crawling on all fours, he slowly made his way toward the artillery forward observer's foxhole.

"Mark, it's me, Lieutenant Davis. I'm coming in to join you."

"Come on in, Lieutenant," Mark whispered.

Mark looked up at the platoon leader as the officer slid into the two-man position.

"You think there's anybody out there?" Mark whispered.

"Maybe . . ." Davis paused, trying to sound confident. The sound of an M16 firing in the night filled the air.

"Hold your fire!" Sergeant Piper screamed. Another M16 fired toward the tank ditch.

"Damn it, I said, hold your friggin' fire!" Piper roared. "Ward, if that's you shooting, I'll bust your ass! Wait for the illumination."

"Mark, give me illum on the tank ditch. Right now," Davis ordered.

"Roger, sir. I'll get battalion mortars," Mark exclaimed as he picked up the transmitter and radioed his request to the fire direction center.

The wait seemed to last forever. Davis heard more muffled noises. It sounded like digging. Davis poked his head up over the rim of Mark's fighting position and scanned the tank ditch with his night-vision goggles. Even with a full moon, it was difficult to distinguish a man from a desert bush or a pile of rocks.

"See anything, sir?" Mark asked.

"Negative. Nothing. Where's that illum?"

"They're working on it, sir."

Finally, two rounds of illumination—two white parachute flares—fell to the east of 1st Platoon's position.

"They're short, damn it!" Davis screamed.

"Adjust fire!" Mark replied instantaneously into his handset. "Add three hundred."

The parachute flares, falling slowly behind the platoon, lit up the landscape with an eerie whitish glow. Finally the two flares hit the ground and burned into small embers.

Davis scanned again with his night-vision goggles. This time the mortar illumination fell in exactly the right spot.

Everyone in the platoon looked toward the tank ditch, searching for signs of the enemy. The night sky lit up with the glare from the two mortar rounds. The burning flares drifted slowly to the ground on their small white parachutes.

"Do you see anything?" Davis shouted, feeling bolder now that the mortars were supporting his platoon. "Piper, what do you see?"

"Not a damn thing," Piper yelled back. "The men are jumpy. Must have been a critter."

Darkness increases fear, Davis thought. Is there somebody out there, or are the men just imagining enemy infiltrators? If I don't control that fear, it could turn into panic. I have to figure out a way to funnel this fear into constructive action. But what can I do now?

Davis looked to the west, scanning with careful eyes for any sign of movement. The flares slowly descended to the desert floor and burned themselves out. As the embers cooled Davis sank back into Mark's hole.

I should have put out some observation posts on Hill 865, and possibly placed some illumination booby traps near the tank ditch, Davis thought.

"First Platoon," Davis yelled, "hold your fire until you've identified a target. Don't shoot at shadows." Half an hour went by. Nothing appeared.

"OK, Mark, you and your RTO, come back with me to my position," Davis ordered.

"Sir, I don't think it's a good idea to put all four of us in the same fighting position," Mark volunteered.

A threat rasped in Davis's voice as he answered. "You got a better idea?"

"You know we can't all fit in one hole," Mark answered. "What if I listen to your platoon net and switch when you want me to call for fires?"

"I guess that would work," Davis said, returning to a more controlled tone. "Switch now and let me talk to Cowper to make sure we're on the same frequency."

Sergeant Mark's RTO, Specialist Hutchinson, turned on his red-filtered flashlight to check his notebook for the frequency. Quickly, Hutchinson changed frequencies and made a radio check with Private First Class Cowper.

"We're OK, Lieutenant," Hutchinson replied.

"All right, stay alert and keep on the radio. I'll head back to my own position. Tell Cowper I'm on my way."

Davis climbed out of the hole and crawled to his fighting position. It's going to be a long night, he thought.

Go to Section 27.

Section 98

In the Gafsa area, east of El Guettar, an enemy armored division launched several attacks from the southeast which were repulsed by American troops who held their position firmly. A number of enemy tanks were destroyed and over 200 German prisoners were captured.

Communiqué 138, March 24, 1943

During World War II the infantry often found itself facing attacks by heavy armored forces. A month after the disastrous rout of U.S. forces at Kasserine Pass, the infantrymen of Patton's III Corps were spoiling for a rematch. They got their chance on March 24, 1943. K Company of 3d Battalion, 18th Infantry, defended the hills east of El Guettar and demonstrated to the vaunted Afrika Korps what a platoon of determined infantrymen could do.

El Guettar was a typical date-palm oasis in the Tunisian desert. Steep, rocky hills covered the major routes of advance into the area. Elsewhere the valley floor was crisscrossed with deep wadis. On March 24, 1943, K Company was deployed as the right flank of 3d Battalion and controlled the main road through its defensive sector. The commander of K Company was ordered that, if attacked, he was to block the enemy and defend until armored forces could arrive.

The company deployed with 1st Platoon in a reverse-slope defense on a ridgeline that ran down toward the road. The 2d and 3d Platoons were located on the counterslope to the rear. There was a wadi on the reverse slope about fifteen meters below and parallel to the crest of the ridgeline.

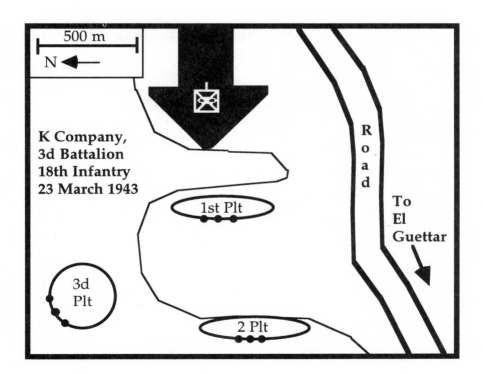

500 m

N

K Company,
3d Battalion
18th Infantry
23 March 1943

1st Plt

3d Plt

2 Plt

Road

To El Guettar

1st Platoon moved into position on March 22 and prepared positions behind the ridge. Browning .30-caliber light machine guns and grenadiers were positioned on each flank. Squad machine guns—Browning automatic rifles (BARs)—were posted to cover the crest of the ridge to plaster anyone coming over the top. A two-man observation post was established five hundred meters forward of the company line.

Once it got dark the platoon moved to the top of the ridge and occupied positions on the forward slope to defend against enemy infiltration. By midnight the defense was ready. At 0600 the observation post alerted 1st Platoon of the approach of a German tank column. Since no supporting infantry was observed with the advancing tanks, the K Company commander ordered his men to let the tanks pass down the road unmolested.

Thirty minutes later the observation post reported a line of half-tracks approaching from the east. German mechanized infantry would soon be opposing 1st Platoon. The platoon immediately moved to its reverse-slope defensive positions. The Germans moved short of the ridge, dismounted their infantry from their half-tracks, and assaulted the crest. The fire from the Americans was so effective that the enemy was unable to take the crest, in spite of repeated attempts. The Germans, determined to take the ridge and drive off the Americans, continued the attack all day.

Eight hours later 1st Platoon still stubbornly held its position on the reverse slope. The enemy finally launched a dismounted attack around the left flank but was hammered back by the deadly fire of the platoon's Browning light machine guns. By 1700 the battle was over and the Germans withdrew, leaving behind five hundred dead and wounded and five destroyed half-tracks. 1st Platoon, K Company, 3d Battalion, 18th Infantry, lost one dead and seven wounded.

This example illustrates the importance of preparation, security, and the intelligent use of terrain to conduct a defense with light infantry against an armored opponent. The positioning of the platoon's key weapons and the flexibility of the defense to respond to different threats (day versus night positions) was a critical ingredient for their success. The platoon's use of concentrated fires, delivered from positions that were undetected on the reverse slope of the ridge, surprised the enemy and disrupted his combined-arms synchronization.

*   *   *

Conventional military forces remain the decisive means of winning war. The unthinkable technological alternative is to nuclear weapons, a resort that did not occur even when the United States possessed a monopoly on nuclear weapons in the decade after the Second World War. The historical truth remains that airpower alone, short of turning the landscape into glass through the use of nuclear bombs, cannot singlehandedly win regional, conventional wars.

This lesson was learned during Operation Desert Storm. It took the execution of a combined-arms ground assault to decisively defeat the Iraqis. Historian and theorist Trevor N. Dupuy defined combined arms as "coordinated action by elements of different combat arms. The term is usually used in relation to combat activities at the tactical level, up to and including the division. The main characteristics of combined arms combat are fire and movement. Effective employment of combined arms is assured by allocation of tasks in combat, as well as by training and education of personnel."*

The combined-arms concept involves the use of different arms and weapons systems, working in concert so that each will maximize the protection and destructive capability of the other. It is the simultaneous application of several elements as an integrated whole in order to produce overwhelming combat power. Combined arms involves the combination of maneuver, organic fires, and supporting arms in such a way that the moves the enemy takes to avoid one threat make him more vulnerable to another. Different arms, such as infantry, mechanized infantry, armor, artillery, aviation, and a host of other supporting arms, work together as a combat team under one commander. The intent is to force the enemy on the horns of a dilemma that results in his decisive defeat.

The concept of combined-arms warfare has existed for centuries, but the nature of the combination and the organizational level at which armies have produced combined arms has varied greatly. This situation occurs because combined arms is characterized by the

*Trevor N. Dupuy, ed., *International Military and Defense Encyclopedia,* 6 vols. (McLean, Va.: Brassey's [US], 1993), 3: 574.

combat means employed: weapons, supporting devices, and organization. The means change rapidly, developing new combinations and methods as technology advances. Combat leaders in the past have increased the effectiveness of their combined-arms organizations by discovering the optimum combination of firepower and mobility and integrating this into their command and control system. The trend in recent military history has been to combine the arms at progressively lower levels of the organization.

To employ combined arms effectively requires a thorough knowledge of the different weapon systems and techniques of the various branches. The combined-arms team works together to conduct operations fully integrated in time, space, and method. When put together deftly, combined-arms warfare paralyzes the enemy and opens the way to quick, decisive victory. This is what occurred during Operation Desert Storm. Each part of the combined-arms team played an essential role. One-handed punchers seldom knock out their opponents. Combined-arms fighters bob and weave and use a one-two punch attack compared to a continuous jab.

If the history of the twentieth century offers any clues to the future, soldiers will continue to face challenges similar to those experienced by the platoon that fought at El Guettar. You have experienced these ideas through the decisions you have made in this book. The tactical decision game of the battle at Wadi Al Sirree is just an example of what soldiers could encounter on future battlefields. It is a battle that is fought in training situations at the U.S. Army's National Training Center almost every month.

Because this situation may have to be faced again, the United States must be prepared to project overwhelming military force to distant battlefields, to fight and win decisively. Decisive victory requires trained and superbly equipped ground forces capable of executing combined-arms warfare. While air- and sea power are vitally important, they alone are not decisive. People do not live in the air or on the sea. Man lives on the land. To control the land you must be willing to put your young soldiers in the mud and force the issue to a decisive conclusion. It always comes down to the infantry. As Niccolò Machiavelli once said: "The infantry must ever be regarded as the very foundation and nerve of an army."

America must never forget the lesson so eloquently recorded by historian T. R. Fehrenbach in his book *This Kind of War** concerning a similar situation that America faced during the Korean War:

If the United States ground forces had not eventually held Korea, Americans would have been faced with two choices: holocaust or humiliation. General, atomic war, in a last desperate attempt to save the game, would have gained Americans none of the things they seek in this world; humiliating defeat and withdrawal from Korea would have inevitably surrendered Asia to a Communist surge, destroying forever American hopes for a free and ordered society across the world.

A nation that does not prepare for all the forms of war should then renounce the use of war in national policy. A people that does not prepare to fight should then be morally prepared to surrender. To fail to prepare soldiers and citizens for limited, bloody ground action, and then to engage in it, is folly verging on the criminal. . . . If liberal, decent societies cannot discipline themselves to do all these things, they may have nothing to offer the world. They may not last long enough.

For Davis, the first major battle of the war was won. In spite of the initial setbacks, the United States and its ally bought precious time. That time was paid for in blood. The aggressor was checked, but he still had plenty of divisions left to fight with. Davis knew that he would be severely tested in the battles that lay ahead.

You have won. I congratulate you on your tactical prowess. Davis must now reorganize the remnants of his shattered battalion for tomorrow's mission. The war is not over yet, but that is another story.

*T. R. Fehrenbach, *This Kind of War* (New York: Macmillan, 1963), 656.

Section 99

No, I'm committed now, Davis thought. I don't have enough force to counterattack against an enemy infantry company. If I move out of my positions here at Yankee, I could lose the entire platoon. Wadi Al Sirree would be open for the enemy to race through and hit the brigade in the flank. Then the enemy will win. I can still accomplish my mission to block this valley. We have to be stubborn today.

"No, we're staying here," Davis announced.

The flashes and firing from the area near BP Bravo slowly faded away. The battle in the east quieted.

Every man faced around to the west, watching the enemy columns get closer with each passing minute. The sound of bursting artillery, pounding a steady path from west to east, interrupted this short interlude of quiet. The ground trembled as the explosions of the enemy shells thundered their way toward the friendly positions.

The explosions grew louder. Balls of orange flame erupted in the openings to the trails on the western edge of Wadi Al Sirree. The earth shook under the thunder of the enemy's 152mm guns. The bursting artillery shells moved slowly up the valley like a wall of exploding death.

The earth along the western trails to Wadi Al Sirree suddenly erupted in a flash of fire and steel. The artillery shells exploded several hundred meters away, marking an inexorable trail of detonations that were slowly marching east.

Rocks and flying steel pelted the sides and tops of the fighting position. The ground rocked and heaved with the impact of each shell. The enemy was doing his best to obliterate BP Yankee.

Davis watched in horror as one of the foxholes on Position Yankee took a direct hit from a Threat 152mm artillery shell. The heavy artillery sliced through the position as if it were made of butter. Spellman's M60 machine-gun teams had been blown to hell.

Roll the dice.

332

If you roll 2–7, go to Section 24.

If you roll 8 or 9, go to Section 58.

If roll 10–12, go to Section 63.

Section 100

A stream of bullets suddenly cut into BP Yankee. Cowper was hit. He spun backward and collapsed, a pool of blood gushing from his torn chest. The radio was still strapped to his back. His sudden spin jerked the mike out of Davis's hand.

Gerber fired furiously. Bullets streaked all around him. The two Javelin gunners and their ammo bearers hugged the earth of their fighting positions. Davis reached for Cowper's M203 and fired a 40mm grenade in the direction of the Threat. The grenade exploded with a flash and a black puff of smoke that was distinguished through the thick white smoke that blanketed the battlefield.

"I can see 'em. Here they come!" Gerber shouted. Chambers and Montoya put down their Javelins and fired their M16s in the direction of the enemy fire.

The enemy advanced toward Yankee in short rushes. Davis could see black shapes about fifty meters away, crouching in the smoke.

Davis chambered another 40mm grenade and aimed it at the nearest enemy infantry. The grenade arced to its target and exploded in the middle of an advancing enemy squad, knocking over three attackers.

A volley of enemy machine-gun fire scythed into Yankee. Gerber's machine gun suddenly fell silent, the gunner hit in the head by an enemy slug. Private Fetterman, the assistant gunner, pushed aside Gerber's lifeless body and charged the weapon to continue firing.

Section 100

"They're all over the place, sir!" Fetterman screamed. "We've got to pull back."

In the smoke all was confusion and terror. Davis dropped an enemy soldier with his rifle, then two more rushed forward. He fired again, and another black shape hit the ground. Suddenly he felt his left side go numb.

Why can't I move? Davis wondered.

He lay on his back, looking up at the smoke-filled early-morning sky. The last thing he saw was the face of the enemy soldier who thrust a bayonet into his neck.

Davis failed in his mission to block the enemy from seizing and moving through Wadi Al Sirree. The enemy used an air assault force to secure the key terrain in Davis's sector, forcing him to fight both east and west.

Security in the defense requires the leaders to consider adjacent key terrain as they plan the defense. Light infantry leaders should look for terrain that will protect them from enemy observation and fires and at the same time provide observation and fires into the area where they intend to destroy the enemy or defeat his attack. Leaders consider adjacent key terrain that threatens the security of their positions. They secure this terrain with observation posts and by cover with direct and indirect fires. Finally they establish observation posts along the most likely enemy approaches into the position or sector to provide early warning.

Once Davis knew that the enemy was behind him, he should have established an observation post to provide early warning. This was a difficult proposition during the fast-paced move back to Yankee. A better option would have been to provide for more observation posts when he first created his plan. Had he done this, he might have survived the enemy infantry attack.

Major General Sir James Wolfe, the victor of the Battle of Quebec in 1759, declared that, "War is an option of difficulties." Sometimes, however, the best decisions turn out wrong and the difficulties win out. Was Davis a poor planner or just unlucky? Could he have used his time to provide more security for his position? Return to Section 3, choose a different answer, and find out.

Go to Section 3 and start again.

Section 101

"One-Six, this is OP North. I see enemy infantry moving behind you. They're coming along the north wall."

"Roger, OP North. We're taking them under direct fire now. I'll call for artillery fires. You adjust," Davis shouted over his radio, the sound of Gerber's machine gun punctuating every word.

"Sir, I've got the 105mm FDC on the line," Mark screamed as the two M60 machine guns blazed away in the direction of the enemy infantry. A steady stream of red tracers slowed the enemy advance.

"Get them now or we won't need them!" Davis yelled.

"I'm getting fires now," Sergeant Mark shouted. "We'll get 105mm HE and illumination falling one hundred meters west of Grid NK395073 in a few minutes. Danger close. Take cover."

"Two o'clock. There, I see them!" Cowper screamed as he fired an M203 grenade at a group of advancing enemy figures.

"Everyone get down!" Davis tried to shout above the firing. "Danger close."

The M60 machine guns poured round after round into the northeast portion of Wadi Al Sirree, catching the enemy infantry in a terrible dilemma of death to direct or indirect fire.

The shells crashed into the ground close to BP Yankee. Davis hugged the dirt. The shelling lasted for eight minutes. The ground trembled and the sound of flying steel filled the air. Finally the artillery stopped.

An eerie silence pervaded the smoking desert east of Position Yankee. Davis scanned the area. Nothing moved.

"Good job, Mark. Chambers, get a status report, men and ammunition," Davis ordered.

For a few moments a deathlike stillness settled in the valley. Chambers ran from one position to another on BP Yankee, checking the status of personnel and ammunition. Davis wondered, Will they still try to come through here with armor?

The silence was suddenly replaced by the rumble of distant artillery. The noise became more discernible. Big guns and rockets pounded the ground to the west in a steady, rhythmic hammering of steel against rock.

"Sir, I've got OP North on the line," Cowper declared, handing Davis the receiver-transmitter.

"One-Six, I can see their armor leaving the passes to the west!" the OP reported. "I figure we have about fifteen minutes before they hit the area on top of you. There's a column of vehicles . . . hundreds of them, coming out of the pass at Grid NK353154."

Apparently, OP North wasn't the only one to see the enemy column. Scores of 155mm artillery shells screamed through the air, filling the early morning with an incredible sound of death. The rounds arced high overhead and exploded to the west, detonating with a rumble that shook the ground in Wadi Al Sirree. Davis's brigade was executing a deep operation before the enemy closed within direct fire range. The brigade hoped to attrit the advancing enemy with artillery and air support.

"One-Six, this is OP North. I see three . . . no . . . five burning vehicles. The lead of the column appears to be heading southeast. At least twenty vehicles. The rest of the column, probably one hundred plus, is headed east." OP North paused for a few minutes, as if he was confirming what he saw. "I say again. One column appears to be attacking along Cobra. Over."

"Roger, OP North. Good report," Davis answered, trying to sound calm. "Continue to report once you confirm that they're in the trails, then call in the targets. Over."

"Wilco, One-Six."

The enemy is sending a separate detachment of tanks and BMPs to attack through Wadi Al Sirree, Davis thought. If they take the valley, they'll have a clear road into the battalion's flank.

"Sergeant Mark, if I ever needed air support, it will be when the enemy is in the trails," Davis proclaimed to his FO, pointing to the map. "Relay the report we just got from OP North. Maybe it'll be juicy enough to get us some support."

"Right—uh—I'm working on it, sir," Mark responded hesitantly. "It looks like all the CAS is going in for the deep operation."

Unfortunately, Davis knew how weak those deep fires were: only one battalion of 155mm artillery and a few sorties from navy F/A-18s and air force A-10s. The carrier-based F/A-18s had a short loiter time because of the distance of the battlefield from the aircraft carrier they called home. The A-10s, on the other hand, could stay longer because they came from an allied air base forty kilometers to the south. The A-10s, potent tank killers, had the disadvantage of being old, big, and slow. With the improvements in enemy air defense systems in the past years, the A-10's survivability was mostly a matter of pilot skill and luck.

A flight of F/A-18s screamed overhead, flying low over Wadi Al Sirree. The aircraft headed west to attack the advancing enemy columns. A pair of F/A-18s roared across the sky to the north, dropping cluster bombs on the advancing enemy armor.

I hope the brigade punches the hell out of them, Davis thought. We need every chance we can to even these odds.

In offensive and defensive tactical actions, commanders fight the enemy throughout the depth of his disposition with fires and with attacks on his flanks and rear. They attack committed and uncommitted forces and synchronize the attack of enemy artillery in depth with close operations. Such in-depth operations degrade the enemy's freedom of action, reduce his flexibility and endurance, and upset his plans and coordination.

FM 100-5, *Operations,* 1993

The sound of multiple explosions resonated from the area beyond the jagged ridge to the northwest.

"That's our stuff," Davis shouted to his men. "Get ready. The enemy will be on us soon."

The rumble of explosions increased. The detonations sounded like the strike of a huge hammer, pounding the earth to the northwest. American and allied planes darted across the sky; a volley of antiaircraft missiles greeted the attackers. A fiery explosion registered the midair destruction of one of the F/A-18s. Several other aircraft, having already dropped their ordnance, ignited their afterburners and roared back to the east, attempting to outrun the enemy's effective missile defenses.

The sound of outgoing artillery shells suddenly died away. The battlefield grew ominously quiet. Our deep operation is over, Davis thought. Now it's the enemy's turn.

"That's it, sir," Mark announced, the radio receiver still pressed against his ear. "The F/A-18s are heading home. We may get some A-10s later. We can call for fire whenever we have a formation of armored vehicles to shoot at."

Suddenly OP North reported, "I see another column heading to the east, just coming out of the passes now. I can't tell if it will follow the lead column. There's too much smoke and dust now. Request permission to pull back!"

If Davis decides to order OP North to withdraw,
go to Section 34.

If Davis decides to leave OP North in position,
go to Section 35.

Section 102

"All stations, this is One-Six," Davis said slowly into the radio handset. "Withdraw now to BP Yankee. Take everyone with you. Bravo Six-Six needs our help."

"One-Six, this is OP North. Do you want OP's personnel to withdraw too?"

"Affirmative. Move to Yankee now. Out," Davis ordered. "Orders Group at my position as soon as possible."

Davis and his men waited. It took forty minutes for everyone to move from their positions to BP Yankee. The Orders Group—Piper and the squad leaders—huddled around their platoon leader.

"Enemy infantry has attacked the company and we have to go and help them," Davis said grimly.

"I understand, sir," Mizogouchi responded. Everyone else remained silent. The huddled soldiers knew how difficult a night attack toward BP Bravo would be.

"OK. Here's what we'll do. We'll follow the north wall east until we come to BP Bravo. We'll move in a modified wedge formation. Mizogouchi, your squad leads. I'll follow you with the rest of 1st and 2d Squads. Piper, you're to my right. We'll get to Bravo, assess the situation, and support the company or retake the position."

Piper and the others nodded.

"Once we leave here we have to move fast. Everybody ready?" Davis asked, his voice edged with determination.

"Damn it, sir," Piper said savagely, "let's get those bastards."

There was nothing more to say and the group dispersed. Each squad leader shouted orders and the platoon quickly left BP Yankee, in the prescribed formation, for BP Bravo. Davis assembled his machine gunners, Javelin teams, Cowper, Mark, and Hutchinson and hurried east down Wadi Al Sirree.

Mizogouchi advanced two hundred meters in front of the platoon. Armed with a squad radio and a pair of PVS-7 night-vision goggles, he moved quickly as Davis had ordered. Two riflemen trailed closely behind him. Davis kept in constant communication with Mizogouchi. The movement was fast, and Davis kept up the pace.

"There! At nine o'clock!" Mizogouchi screamed as he fired his M16 toward the advancing silhouettes. "Enemy patrol one hundred meters, left front."

"Piper, move right, set up a firing line!" Davis ordered as he ran forward. "Mark, try to get me some fires. We need artillery ASAP!"

"I'm working on it, sir," Mark shouted.

Davis and his men hit the dirt, rolled into hasty firing positions, and fired at the enemy. Machine guns and rifles opened fire and tracers flew wildly through the dark desert air. A steady stream of red tracer bullets ripped forward, toward the enemy. The enemy infantry reacted quickly, lying down to avoid the fire from Davis's guns.

Gerber fired furiously. Bullets streaked all around him. Cowper fired a 40mm grenade in the direction of the threat. The grenade arced to its target and exploded in the middle of an advancing enemy squad, silencing several attackers.

"I can see 'em. Here they come!" Gerber shouted. The enemy advanced in short rushes. One group would fire while another moved. Davis could see black shapes advancing about fifty meters away, crouching in the dark.

A volley of enemy machine-gun fire scythed into the American line. Gerber's machine gun suddenly fell silent, the gunner hit in the head by an enemy slug. Private Fetterman, the assistant gunner, pushed Gerber's lifeless body aside and charged the weapon to continue firing.

"They're all over the place, sir!" Fetterman screamed. "We've got to pull back." In the smoke all was confusion and terror. A whistle blew. The enemy infantry advanced rapidly in groups of threes and fours.

"Mark, where's my artillery fire?" Davis shouted.

Suddenly Davis's men were fired on from the right flank. The enemy had worked their way around the Americans and set up a light machine gun to catch them in enfilade.

Bullets ripped through the night, striking several Americans.

"They got Hutchinson. They killed him!" Mark screamed in panic, throwing down his radio handset and falling to the ground to avoid enemy fire. Enemy soldiers rushed forward.

Davis fired his M16 at a moving shadow to his front. The shadow fell.

Tracers lit up the position, bouncing and ricocheting in all directions. Gerber's machine gun opened up again, with Fetterman behind the trigger, but the enemy was right on top of them now.

Cowper fired his M203 again, then fell backward, dead. Incensed, Davis aimed his weapon and blasted off the remaining rounds from his thirty-round magazine. An explosion erupted to Davis's right. Fetterman's M60 machine gun stopped firing. Smoke and the smell of cordite filled the air. Enemy soldiers were moving all over the place.

Davis aimed his weapon and dropped two of the attackers.

"Mark, are you OK?" Davis shouted. "Report! Who's left?"

Two attackers rushed Davis's position from the front. Davis hit one. The man fell backward, dropping his grenade. The other hit the ground and sailed his potato masher grenade in front of the lieutenant.

The grenade exploded right in front of Davis, sending him reeling from the shock of the blast. He felt numb all over, then he opened his eyes. He tried to move but soon discovered that his legs were crushed and bleeding from the blast of the grenade.

Cowper's bloodied and mangled body was lying inches from him. Suddenly Davis was surrounded by moving enemy soldiers. He grabbed his M16 and fired, hitting the nearest attacker. Two more moved forward and blasted him with their assault rifles. Davis felt the searing metal penetrate his chest and neck, and then, rolling to his left side, he died.

Go back to Section 3 and try again.

Appendix A: Light Infantry Weapons

To succeed in combat, infantrymen must be experts in employing their organic and supporting weapons and in employing mines. Organic weapons are weapons that are assigned to the platoon over which the platoon leader has direct control. Supporting weapons provide the platoon and squad leaders additional firepower and are found outside the platoon.

Organic Weapons

Infantry platoons carry a variety of organic weapons. The most critical of these are the M60 machine gun, the M249 squad automatic weapon (SAW), the M203 grenade launcher, and the M16A2 rifle. In addition the infantry platoon will routinely use antiarmor weapons, hand grenades, and mines. The rifle platoon is equipped with two M60 machine guns, six squad automatic weapons, and six M203 grenade launchers. A full discussion of these weapons follows.

M60 machine gun

The M60 machine gun is the only crew-served weapon in the platoon. It is also the most important. The employment of the M60 machine gun is often the most critical decision of the platoon leader. The platoon has two of these guns, each manned by a gunner and an ammunition bearer. The M60 is a belt-fed, gas-operated 7.62mm automatic weapon. It is heavy, weighing twenty-three pounds, and has a maximum effective range of eleven hundred meters against an area target and six hundred meters against a point target. It can fire ball and tracer ammunition.

M249 squad automatic weapon (SAW)

The M249 squad automatic weapon, or SAW, is a lightweight, gas-operated, air-cooled, bipod-mounted, one-man-portable 5.56mm machine gun that provides a base of fire for infantry squads. There are two SAWs per squad, adding up to a total of six in the rifle platoon.

The SAW fires the same 5.56mm ammunition as the M16 rifle. It can be belt fed or magazine fed. This feature makes it possible to share ammunition with other riflemen in the platoon. Normally a two-hundred-round canister is attached to the machine gun. The SAW weighs fifteen and a half pounds and has a maximum effective range of eight hundred meters for an area target and six hundred meters for a point target. A standard load of six hundred rounds of 5.56mm ammunition is carried by each SAW gunner.

M203 grenade launcher

The M203 is a 40mm, single-shot, breech-loaded, pump-action grenade launcher. It is attached to an M16A2 rifle. It fires a variety of 40mm grenade ammunition including high explosive, tear gas, illumination, buckshot, and practice. It can suppress targets that are in defilade; suppress or disable armored vehicles, except tanks; penetrate concrete, timber, or sandbagged weapon positions and some buildings; illuminate; and signal. There is one grenadier armed with an M203 in each rifle squad. The M203 weighs eleven pounds and has an average range of 350 meters against an area target and 160 meters against a point target.

M16A2 rifle

The M16A2 rifle is the standard rifle of the U.S. military. The original design has been in service since the early 1960s. The M16A2 is the latest product improvement. It was improved by removing the full-automatic option of the original M16 rifle. Whereas the M16A1 selector lever had safe, semiautomatic, and automatic positions, the M16A2 selector lever has safe, semiautomatic, and burst options. The burst option fires a three-round burst every time the trigger is pulled. In addition the M16A2 has an improved, heavier barrel and a new compensator to reduce muzzle climb. The result is a weapon with range and accuracy superior to that of the original M16. The M16A2 is a 5.56mm, magazine-fed, gas-operated, semiautomatic, and burst automatic shoulder-fired weapon. The M16A2 weighs 8.7 pounds and has a maximum effective range of 800 meters (area target) and 580 meters (point target). The M16 can be fitted with an M7 bayonet. Each M16 can be loaded with a 20- or 30-round magazine. The standard load of 5.56mm ammunition that an infantry-man carries is seven 30-round magazines, or 210 rounds.

M136 AT4 light antitank weapon (LAW)

The M136 AT4, or Carl Gustav, is a self-contained, shoulder-fired antitank weapon. The M136 replaced the older 66mm M72 LAW in the late 1980s. The AT4 consists of an 84mm high-explosive antitank (HEAT) rocket in a disposable, one-piece, watertight, fiberglass and aluminum launcher tube. Its light weight and ability to penetrate more than 15.6 inches of armor make it a weapon that can be used against some enemy armor, bunkers, and other hard targets out to a range of two hundred meters. The warhead of the AT4 is not sufficient to defeat the armor of most main battle tanks. Several hits by an AT4 are required to seriously damage an enemy tank. For this reason the most effective firing technique is to have a pair of AT4s fired in vol-ley at the same target. The AT4 is issued as a round of ammunition, as are grenades; the number required is determined by the unit's mission.

Hand grenades

Each soldier is issued hand grenades as needed for the operation. Normally, each soldier will carry a minimum of two antipersonnel grenades and one smoke grenade (either colored smoke for special marking or white smoke to provide obscuration). The grenades vary in type, size, and shape but are generally round (like the M67 frag-mentation grenade) or cylindrical (like almost all smoke grenades, the M18 colored smoke hand grenade being the most common). The most common fragmentation grenade is the M67. It weighs .9 pound and has a smooth baseball-type shape with yellow markings on an olive-drab body. The maximum effective range of a grenade is as far as the thrower can pitch it, which is usually no more than forty meters. The blast radius of a standard fragmentation grenade is ap-proximately fifteen meters. Grenades, like all other general-use weapons, are issued as required by the unit's mission.

M18A1 antipersonnel or Claymore mine

The M18A1 fragmentation antipersonnel mine, or Claymore, is issued as needed to individual infantrymen. It is an olive-drab, curved, rectangular fiberglass case containing 1.5 pounds of composition C4 explosive and seven hundred small steel balls. Normally, each squad will carry at least two. The mine weighs 3.5 pounds. It is set up by a soldier and can be command detonated by the use of an electric blasting cap triggered by a handheld firing device ("clacker") connected to the mine by thirty feet of wire, or it can be detonated by trip wire. When detonated, the mine scatters the seven hundred steel balls as far as 250 meters forward in a sixty-degree arc. The Claymore is a very lethal weapon against Threat infantry and can also do significant damage to thin-skinned vehicles, such as jeeps or trucks. It is an excellent weapon for close-quarter fighting.

M16A2 antipersonnel mine

The light infantryman reinforces his defensive positions with mines whenever possible. The M16A2 antipersonnel mine, or Bouncing Betty, is a bounding fragmentation-type mine. The M16A2 weighs 7.88 pounds. When detonated, the mine bounds about one meter in the air before exploding. The casualty radius is thirty meters. The mine is detonated by eight to forty-four pounds of pressure applied to one of the three prongs on the fuse or by three to eight pounds of pressure applied to a trip wire. With a fuse installed, the M16A2 is eight inches high and contains one pound of TNT explosive.

M15 heavy antitank mine

Light infantrymen often must establish their own antitank minefields. Usually these minefields consist of a few mines at a carefully selected choke point. These minefields are termed point minefields. The M15 heavy antitank mine is enclosed in a circular steel case that is thirteen inches in diameter and almost five inches high. It weighs thirty pounds and has a main charge of twenty-two pounds of composition B explosive. The main fuse of the M15 is activated by 350 to 750 pounds of pressure on the plate on the top of the mine. The M15 can disable main battle tanks by destroying their tracks or penetrating their lightly armored belly. Although antitank mines are normally laid by combat engineers, in battle there are never enough engineers to go around.

Appendix A

M21 Killer metallic antitank mine

The M21 Killer metallic antitank mine is enclosed in a circular steel case that fires a nine-inch-diameter shaped-charge projectile into the belly of an unsuspecting armored vehicle. The M21 is only four and a half inches high. It weighs eighteen pounds and has a main charge of ten and a half pounds of explosive. The main fuse of the M21 is activated by pressure or by disturbing the tilt rod on the top of the mine twenty degrees. The M21 is capable of destroying all known main battle tanks.

Supporting Weapons

Javelin medium antitank weapon

The Javelin is a lightweight, one-man-portable, fire-and-forget medium antitank weapon. Unlike the M47 Dragon medium antitank weapon, which it is replacing, the Javelin does not require the soldier to guide it by keeping the crosshairs in the optical sight until it reaches its target. This limits the soldier's exposure to enemy counterfire and even enables the soldier to engage a second target while awaiting the first impact. The Javelin weapon system consists of two major elements—the command launch unit (CLU) and the round. The Javelin round is self-guiding and carries two tandem, high-explosive warheads capable of penetrating even the most heavily armored tanks. The 127mm-diameter missile has an imaging infrared seeker and a direct or top-attack selection engagement option. The Javelin CLU has an integrated thermal sight that allows the gunner to see day or night and hit moving targets as far away as two thousand meters. Because the Javelin is a new weapon system, much of the technical data is still classified.

Appendix B: Role, Organization, and Key Personnel of the Light Infantry Platoon

The Role of Light Infantry on the Modern Battlefield

Light infantry units are specifically organized to fight and win on any terrain in the low- to midintensity spectrum of war. They provide the United States with a versatile and strategically mobile military force that can rapidly deploy by air to any battlefield in the world.

Light infantry is strategically mobile. The resupply needs of a light infantry unit are far less than those of a heavy armored force. Because light infantry units have few vehicles, their fuel resupply requirements and ammunition usage are low. Their ability to deploy rapidly, however, comes at a cost in fighting capability and tactical mobility.

To be light enough to deploy rapidly, the light infantry sacrifices much in terms of firepower and combat support. They have limited firepower and are not equipped with heavy weapons. Light infantry units must be reinforced with heavy forces to defeat most mechanized or armored threats. The artillery, provided mainly by 105mm howitzers, cannot range very far or move very quickly. Once strategically deployed, most of the soldiers in light infantry units are reduced in mobility to the rate of foot marching. Against enemy mechanized and armored forces they are at a severe disadvantage. The trick for the light infantry is to avoid enemy tank forces whenever possible.

Against armored threats, light infantry units fight best on terrain that favors their unique abilities. Like any weapon or type of unit, light infantry has advantages as well as weaknesses. Light infantry is particularly suitable for defending areas of constricted terrain, conducting airmobile operations, and fighting in cities and towns. The history of determined infantry defending passes and key choke points is legendary.

Light infantry forces gain more combat capability when working with other forces in combined-arms teams. Combined arms is defined as the coordinated action by elements of different combat arms. The U.S. Marine Corps definition—given in FMFM 1-3, *Tactics*—is "the idea of posing the enemy not just with a problem, but with a dilemma— a no-win situation. You combine your supporting arms, organic fires, and maneuver in such a way that the action which the enemy takes to avoid one threat makes him more vulnerable to another." This is like a two-handed puncher who can employ infantry, artillery, tanks, army aviation, and other combat support assets to force the enemy between a rock and a hard place.

Together with heavier forces, light infantry units can employ combined arms to overpower and defeat the enemy. To do this the light infantry is trained to move where others cannot go, strike hard, and finish rapidly. Infiltration, for example, is one of the light infantry's most effective combat techniques. Understanding this, the U.S. Army's light infantry doctrine emphasizes surprise, clever use of terrain, and the skill of the individual infantryman to win.

Light infantry leaders at platoon level are tacticians. They cannot merely respond mechanically to situations on the battlefield. It takes great skill and mental agility to successfully lead infantrymen in battle. Leaders are expected to think and make decisions. All decisions, however, are expected to conform to the basic goal of the commander. The basic principle of leadership in the U.S. Army, and particularly in light infantry units, is to always try to make decisions at the lowest possible level of command so they can be made as quickly as possible. On the battlefield, hesitation often breeds defeat.

Leaders in the light infantry must employ maneuver to close with the enemy and then fire and movement to destroy him. This places great responsibility on the infantry leader. To win, the infantry leader must know how to use initiative, understand intent, analyze the battlefield, make rapid tactical decisions, and be ready to take independent action as required. The light infantry leader cannot depend on constant direction but must fight independently even when he cannot communicate outside his own zone or sector. He must know the intention of the commander two levels above him, understand the concept of operation of his immediate commander, and know the responsibilities of the units on his flanks and in support of his operations.

The battlefield is a chaotic and lethal environment. Normal rules of civilized societies do not exist here. Leaders must be cunning and ruthless. They must select the correct fire and movement techniques when in contact. While under fire, they must choose whether to use individual movement techniques or bounds and rushes using a support element and whether to bypass resistance and seek soft spots. They must anticipate enemy locations and movements so that, as the lead element in the attack or defense, they do not lose freedom of maneuver. In short, infantry leaders have to depend on their close combat skill and inspiring leadership to kill the enemy and protect their own soldiers. In the light infantry, there is no armor to hide behind.

Light infantry tactics depend upon small-unit leaders who can carry out mission-type orders on a constantly changing battlefield. Decision making, therefore, is the critical task of the light infantry leader. The subordinate leader is guided by his commander's intent. An effective commander's intent must explain the mission's object (desired end result), reason (the desired end result will create a certain situation), and the importance (what will occur if the end result is not achieved and how far to go to achieve it) of the action. The understanding of this definition is vital to the light infantry leader's tactical success where the situation changes and he must make on-the-spot decisions. A clear knowledge of the commander's intent can provide the tactical leader with the implicit understanding that enables him to outthink and act faster than the enemy.

Furthermore, every light infantry leader is required to understand the intent of the commander two echelons above his level of command. This becomes essential in making independent decisions in the heat of battle when senior commanders either cannot be reached or cannot be reached in time. Understanding the intent of the commanders two echelons above enables a subordinate leader to use the senior commander's intent as a guide to action. Guided with this intent, he can make faster and more correct decisions.

Organization of the Light Infantry Company

An infantry battalion is composed of three rifle companies and one headquarters company. The rifle company is the main element within a light infantry battalion. The rifle company is extremely light and foot mobile.

The organization of the light infantry company is austere. It consists of a headquarters platoon and three rifle platoons. The total personnel strength is five officers and approximately 130 riflemen. The headquarters platoon has a headquarters section and an antiarmor section. The medium antiarmor weapons (MAWs) are consolidated under the headquarters platoon. There are also two 60mm mortars organic to the headquarters section. An organizational diagram of a rifle company, without attachments, is shown follows:

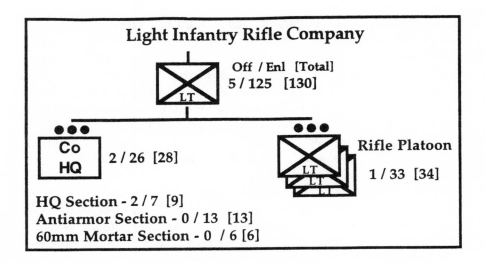

Organization of the Light Infantry Platoon

The rifle platoon is led by a second lieutenant platoon leader. The platoon consists of thirty-three soldiers and the platoon leader. The rifle platoon can operate as a unit or as three separate squads under the control of the platoon headquarters. Each squad contains nine men. The squad can act as a unit or as two teams. An organizational diagram of a rifle platoon, without attachments, is shown below:

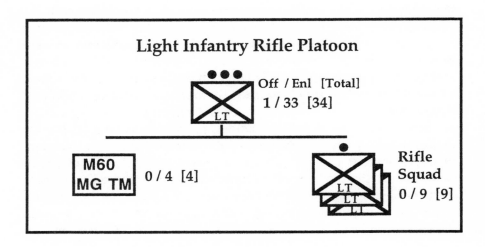

Duties of Key Personnel

Second Lieutenant Davis is the leader of 1st Platoon, B Company. He has a platoon sergeant and three squad leaders. The squad leader and two team leaders lead by example in a "go where I go, shoot where I shoot" mode of operation. Two M60 machine guns are placed in the platoon headquarters. These weapons are the most potent, longest ranging weapons in the platoon. They are controlled and positioned by the platoon leader.

A rifle platoon leader is in charge of thirty-three riflemen, an artillery forward observer team, a medical aidman, and, if the mission requires, Javelin-equipped antiarmor teams. Rifle platoons, however, are seldom at full strength, and soldiers are required to perform a wide range of tasks to compensate for unfilled positions in the rifle platoon. As a general rule, the rifle platoon leader will man his crew-served weapons as his first priority. The duties of the key personnel within a platoon are explained below:

Platoon leader

Leadership is the key to combat power. The platoon leader leads the light infantry platoon. He is responsible for all that the platoon does or fails to do. This includes the tactical deployment, training, administration, personnel management, and logistics of his platoon. He does this by planning, making timely decisions, issuing orders, assigning tasks, supervising platoon activities, and inspiring his soldiers by his personal example. He must know his soldiers and their weapons and how best to use them. He must know how to use supporting weapons such as the M60 machine gun and the 60mm mortar.

The rifle platoon leader leads by example. He employs his platoon to support his company and battalion missions. He commands his platoon through his three squad leaders and platoon sergeant. The platoon leader accomplishes his assigned mission based on the company's mission and the intent of the company and battalion commanders. In the absence of orders, he takes the initiative to accomplish the mission. When this is done he informs his commander of his actions. He makes his plans with the help of his platoon sergeant and squad leaders and the advice of his forward observer. He leads from the front.

Appendix B

Platoon sergeant

The platoon sergeant is normally a sergeant first class with ten to twenty years of experience in the infantry. He is the senior noncommissioned officer in the platoon. He advises and assists the platoon leader in all functions of the platoon. He supervises the administration, logistics, and training of the platoon. He is second in command of the platoon and acts for the platoon leader if the platoon leader is killed or wounded. He is responsible to the platoon leader for the organization and control of the platoon command post (CP), assists in the employment of the platoon's two M60 machine guns, arranges for resupply from the company first sergeant, directs the platoon medic, and takes care of many other details that allow the platoon to fight and win on the battlefield.

Squad leader

The squad leader is normally a staff sergeant with six to ten years of experience in the infantry. He is responsible for all that his squad does or fails to do. He is a tactical leader. He leads by example. He controls the maneuver of the squad and the rate and distribution of its fires. To do this, he controls two fire teams in the offense, selects each fighting position in the defense, and gives the proper commands, codes, and signals to start, stop, and shift fires. He also sees to the total needs of his soldiers and their weapons. He requests and issues ammunition, rations, and special equipment.

Team leader

The team leader is usually a sergeant or a corporal with less than six years of experience in the infantry. He leads his team of three men by example and helps the squad leader as required. His team is called a fire team. He controls the maneuver of his fire team and the rate and placement of fire by leading from the front and using proper commands and signals.

Forward observer

The forward observer is usually a sergeant attached to the platoon from the direct support artillery battalion. The forward observer, or FO, helps the platoon leader to plan for and execute indirect mortar and artillery fires. He passes target information (calls for fire) over his FM radio to either the company mortar section, the battalion mortar platoon, or the direct support artillery battalion. In emergencies he may request and control close air support.

Platoon medic

The platoon medic is a vital part of the platoon. He is attached to the platoon during combat operations. He helps the platoon sergeant to direct medical aid and evacuation. He also monitors the health and hygiene of the soldiers in the platoon.

Radiotelephone operator

The radiotelephone operator (RTO) is a vital part of the platoon headquarters. The RTO is a rifleman who carries an AN/PRC-119—a battery-powered FM radio with a maximum communications range of sixteen kilometers. The RTO's radio is the platoon's only means of radio communications to the company commander. There is one RTO for the platoon leader and one for the forward observer.

Glossary

agility. The mental and organizational ability to act faster than the enemy. Agility is as much a mental as a physical quality.

alternate position. The position given to a weapon, unit, or individual to be occupied when the primary position becomes untenable or unsuitable for carrying out its task. The alternate position is located so that the individual can continue to fulfill his original task.

assembly area. An area in which a force prepares or regroups for further action.

attack. An offensive action characterized by movement supported by fire.

deliberate attack is planned and carefully coordinated with all concerned elements based on thorough reconnaissance, evaluation of all available intelligence and relative combat strength, analysis of various courses of action, and other factors affecting the situation. It generally is conducted against a well-organized defense when a hasty attack is not possible or has failed.

frontal attack is an offensive maneuver in which the main action is directed against the front of the enemy forces and over the most direct approaches.

hasty attack is an offensive operation for which a unit has not made extensive preparations. It is conducted with the resources immediately available in order to maintain momentum or to take advantage of the enemy situation.

main attack is the principal attack or effort into which the commander places the bulk of the offensive capability at his disposal. An attack directed against the chief objective of the battle.

supporting attack is designed to hold the enemy in position, to deceive him as to where the main attack is being made, to prevent him from reinforcing the elements opposing the main effort, and/or to cause him to commit his reserves prematurely at an indecisive location.

attrition (attrit). The reduction of the effectiveness of a force caused by the loss of personnel or materiel.

354

avenue of approach. An air or ground route of an attacking force of a given size leading to its objective or to key terrain in its path.

axis of advance. A general route of advance, assigned for the purposes of control, which extends toward the enemy. An axis of advance symbol graphically portrays a commander's intention, such as avoidance of built-up areas or envelopment of an enemy force. It follows terrain for the size of the force assigned to the axis. A commander may maneuver his forces and supporting fires to either side of an axis of advance, provided the unit remains oriented on the axis and the objective.

base of fire. Fire placed on an enemy force or position to reduce or eliminate the enemy's capability to interfere by fire and/or movement of friendly maneuver elements. It may be provided by a single weapon or a grouping of weapon systems.

block. Deny the enemy access to a given area or prevent enemy advance in a given direction. It may be for a specified time. Units may have to retain terrain and accept decisive engagement.

BMNT. Before morning nautical twilight. The time between night and sunrise when it is light enough to navigate without night-vision devices.

BMP-2. Russian-made infantry fighting vehicle armed with a 30mm cannon, a 7.62mm machine gun, and a missile launcher.

BP (battle position). A defensive location oriented on the most likely enemy avenue of approach from which a unit may defend or attack. Such units can be as large as battalion task forces and as small as platoons. A unit assigned a BP is located within the general outline of the BP.

BRDM. Armored car used for reconnaissance and command and control.

canalize. To restrict operations to a narrow zone by use of existing or reinforcing obstacles, which may interfere with subsequent operations.

CAS (close air support). Air action against hostile targets that are in close proximity to friendly forces and that requires detailed integration of each air mission with the fire and movement of those forces.

checkpoint. A predetermined point on the ground used as a means of coordinating friendly movement. Checkpoints are not used as reference points in reporting enemy locations.

Glossary

clear. To destroy or force the withdrawal of all enemy forces and reduce any obstacles that may interfere with subsequent operations.

combat multiplier. Supporting and subsidiary means that significantly increase the relative combat strength of a force while actual force ratios remain constant. Examples of combat multipliers are economizing in one area to mass in another, surprise, deception, camouflage, electronic warfare, psychological operations, and terrain reinforcement.

commander's guidance. The commander's tool to direct the planning process. Commander's guidance should consist of six elements: the restated mission, the initial concept of the operation, the scheme of maneuver, the time plan, the type of order to be prepared, and the rehearsal technique.

commander's intent. The commander's stated vision of the battle, which defines: the purpose; the end state with respect to the relationship among the force, the enemy, and the terrain; and how the end state will be achieved by the force as a whole. The commander's intent can be explained in terms of the mission's purpose, method and end state.

The purpose is the objective of the action. The mission is the end state with respect to the relationship among the force, the enemy, and the terrain. The importance explains how the end state will be achieved by the force as a whole and how far to go to achieve that end state in terms of combat power.

The acid test of understanding the commander's intent is for the subordinate to act in concert with the commander's desires in a situation where the circumstances are different from those foreseen at the time the plan was issued and the commander cannot be reached for a decision.

company team. A team formed by attachment of one or more nonorganic tank, mechanized infantry, or light infantry platoons to a tank, mechanized infantry, or light infantry company either in exchange for or in addition to organic platoons.

concept of operations. A graphic, verbal, or written statement in broad outline that gives an overall picture of a commander's assumptions or intent in regard to an operation or series of operations; it includes at a minimum the scheme of maneuver and a fire support plan. It is described in sufficient detail for the staff and subordinate commanders to understand what they are to do and how to fight the battle without further instructions.

contain. To stop, hold, or surround the forces of the enemy or to cause the enemy to center activity on a given front and to prevent his withdrawing any part of his forces for use elsewhere.

coordinating point. A control measure that indicates a specific location for the coordination of fires and maneuver between adjacent units. Coordinating points usually are indicated whenever a boundary crosses the forward edge of the battle area (FEBA) and may be indicated when a boundary crosses phase lines (PLs) used to control security forces. In NATO, physical contact between adjacent units is required.

counterattack. Attack by a part or all of a defending force against an enemy attacking force, for such specific purposes as regaining ground lost or cutting off or destroying enemy advance units, and with the general objective of regaining the initiative and denying to the enemy the attainment of his purpose in attacking. In sustained defensive operations, counterattack is undertaken to restore the battle position (BP) and is directed at limited objectives.

cover. Natural or artificial protection from enemy observation.

covered approach. (1) Any route that offers protection against enemy observation or fire. (2) An approach made under the protection furnished by other forces or by natural cover.

CP. Command post.

cross attachment. The exchange of subordinate units between units for a temporary period.

dead space. An area within the maximum effective range of a weapon, surveillance device, or observer that cannot be covered by fire and observation from a given position because of intervening obstacles, the nature of the ground, the characteristics of the trajectory, or the limitations of the pointing capabilities of the systems.

decisive engagement. An engagement in which a unit is considered fully committed and cannot maneuver or extricate itself. In the absence of outside assistance, the action must be fought to a conclusion and either won or lost with the forces at hand.

decisive terrain. Key terrain is decisive terrain if it has an extraordinary impact on the mission. Decisive terrain is rare and will not be present in every mission. To designate terrain as decisive is to recognize that the successful accomplishment of the mission, whether offensive or defensive, depends on seizing or retaining it. The commander designates decisive terrain to communicate its importance in his concept of operations, first to his staff and later to subordinate commanders.

defilade. Protection from hostile observation and fire provided by an obstacle such as a hill, ridge, or bank. To shield from enemy fire or observation by using natural or artificial obstacles.

defile. A narrow passage that tends to constrict the movement of troops.

delay. To trade space for time, inflict maximum damage on the enemy force, and preserve the force within the limits established by the issuing commander.

depth. The extension of operations in space, time, and resources.

destroy. To physically disable or capture an enemy force.

direct fire. Fire directed at a target that is visible to the gunner or firing unit.

direction of attack. A specific direction or route that the main attack or the main body of the force will follow. If used, it is normally at battalion and lower levels. Direction of attack is a more restrictive control measure than axis of advance, and units are not free to maneuver off the assigned route. It is usually associated with infantry units conducting night attacks, or units involved in limited-visibility operations, and in counterattacks. (In NATO, referred to as an attack route.)

direction of fire. The direction on which a cannon or missile is laid. It represents the direction to the most significant threat in the target area.

displace. To leave one position and take another. Forces may be displaced laterally to concentrate combat power in threatened areas.

dominant terrain. Terrain that, because of its elevation, proportions, or location, commands a view of and may offer fields of fire over surrounding terrain.

DPICM (dual purpose improved conventional munitions). Artillery shells that contain submunitions (bomblets) that can damage armored vehicles and devastate unprotected troops.

economy of force. The allocation of minimum-essential combat capability or strength to secondary efforts, so that forces may be concentrated in the area where a decision is sought. A principle of war.

engagement area. An area in which the commander intends to trap and destroy an enemy force with the massed fire of all available weapons. Engagement areas are routinely identified by a target reference point in the center of the trap area or by prominent terrain features around the area. Although engagement areas may also be divided into sectors of fire, it is important to understand that defensive systems are not designed around engagement areas but rather around avenues of approach. Engagement areas and sectors of fire are not intended to restrict fires or cause operations to become static or fixed; they are used only as a tool to concentrate fires and to optimize their effects.

field artillery scatterable minefield (FASCAM). A scatterable minefield, composed of antitank or antipersonnel mines, delivered by artillery.

field of fire. The area that a weapon or a group of weapons may effectively cover with fire from a given location.

fire and movement. The simultaneous moving and firing by men and/or vehicles. This technique is primarily used during the assault of enemy positions.

fire support plan. A plan on how fire support will be used to support an operation. It should include a portion for each means of fire support involved.

fix. Actions taken to prevent the enemy from moving any part of his forces from a specific location within a specific period of time by holding or surrounding them to prevent their withdrawal for use elsewhere.

forward edge of the battle area (FEBA). The forward limit of the main battle area (MBA). Used in the defense.

fragmentary order (FRAGO). An abbreviated form of an operation order (OPORD) used to communicate mission changes to units and to inform them of changes in the tactical situation.

front. The lateral space occupied by an element measured from the extremity of one flank to the extremity of the other flank. The unit may be extended in a combat formation or occupying a position, depending on the type of operation involved.

frontage. The width of the front plus that distance beyond the flanks covered by observation and fire by a unit in combat.

FSO. Fire support officer.

FTX. Field training exercise.

gap. Any break or breach in the continuity of tactical dispositions or formations beyond effective small-arms coverage. A gap is the term to describe a weak spot in the enemy's defenses.

GLD (ground laser designator). A handheld device that paints targets with invisible laser light to direct laser-guided munitions with pinpoint accuracy.

grid coordinates. A set of numbers designating the location of a point in respect to a grid. Coordinates usually are expressed to the nearest 100, 10, or 1 meter in a single expression. Example: NK329378 (nearest 100 meters), NK32943785 (nearest 10 meters), or NK3294837853 (nearest 1 meter). Grid coordinates always consist of pairs of number groups: NK3945, for instance, is read 39 grid line, to the right; and 45 grid line, up. To read grid coordinates on a map, always read right, then up.

HMMWV (highly mobile multipurpose wheeled vehicle). Acronym for the three-quarter-ton truck, also known as a Hummer or a HUMVEE.

initiative. Setting or changing the terms of battle by action. Initiative implies an offensive spirit in the conduct of all operations.

intelligence preparation of the battlefield (IPB). A systematic approach to analyzing the enemy, weather, and terrain in a specific geographic area. It integrates enemy doctrine with the weather and terrain as they relate to the mission and the specific battlefield environment. This is done to determine and evaluate enemy capabilities, vulnerabilities, and probable courses of action.

interdict. To prevent or hinder by any means the enemy's use of any area or route.

intervisibility line. A piece of terrain that blocks direct fire.

key terrain. Any locality or area the seizure, retention, or control of which affords a marked advantage to either combatant.

limit of advance. An easily recognized terrain feature beyond which attacking elements will not advance.

line of contact (LC). A general trace delineating the location where two opposing forces are engaged.

line of departure (LD). A line designated to coordinate the commitment of attacking units or scouting elements at a specified time. A start line.

line of departure is line of contact (LD/LC). The designation of forward friendly positions as the LD when opposing forces are in contact.

LZ. Landing zone.

maneuver. The movement of forces supported by fire to achieve a position of advantage from which to destroy or threaten destruction of the enemy. A principle of war.

mass. (1) The concentration of combat power at the decisive time and place. A principle of war. (2) To concentrate or bring together fires, so as to mass fires of multiple weapons or units. (3) The military formation in which units are spaced at less than normal distances and intervals.

METT-T (mission, enemy, terrain, troops, and time available). The acronym used to describe the factors that must be considered during the planning and execution of a tactical operation. Example considerations are:

    mission. The who, what, when, where, and why of what is to be accomplished.

    enemy. Current information concerning the enemy's strength, location, disposition, activity, equipment, capability, and a determination as to the enemy's probable course of action.

    terrain (includes weather). Information about vegetation, soil type, hydrology, climatic conditions, and light data is analyzed to determine the impact the environment can have on current and future operations for both enemy and friendly operations.

    troops. The quantity, level of training, and psychological state of friendly forces, to include the availability of weapons systems and critical equipment.

    time available. The time available to plan, prepare, and execute operations is considered for both enemy and friendly forces.

minefield. An area of ground containing mines laid with or without a pattern.

MRE. Meals, ready-to-eat field ration.

neutralize. To render ineffective or unusable.

Glossary

objective. (1) The physical object of the action taken (for example, a definite terrain feature, the seizure and/or holding of which is essential to the commander's plan, or the destruction of an enemy force without regard to terrain features). (2) The principle of war that states that every military operation should be directed toward clearly defined, decisive, and attainable objectives.

offense. A combat operation designed primarily to destroy the enemy. Offensive operations may be undertaken to secure key or decisive terrain, to deprive the enemy of resources or decisive terrain, to deceive and/or divert the enemy, to develop intelligence, and to hold the enemy in position. Offensive operations include deliberate attack, hasty attack, movement to contact, exploitation, pursuit, and other limited-objective operations. The offensive is undertaken to seize, retain, and exploit the initiative, and, as such, is a principle of war.

OP. Observation post.

operation order (OPORD). A directive issued by a commander to subordinate commanders for effecting the coordinated execution of an operation; includes tactical movement orders.

operation overlay. Overlay showing the location, size, and scheme of maneuver/fires of friendly forces involved in an operation. As an exception, it may indicate predicted movements and locations of enemy forces.

orders group. A standing group of key personnel requested to be present when a commander at any level issues his concept of the operation and his order.

overwatch. (1) A tactical technique in which one element is positioned to support the movement of another element with immediate direct fire. (2) The tactical role of an element positioned to support the movement of another element with immediate direct fire.

passage of lines. Passing one unit through the positions of another, as when elements of a covering force withdraw through the forward edge of the main battle area, or when an exploiting force moves through the elements of the force that conducted the initial attack. A passage may be designated as a forward or rearward passage of lines.

PGM. Precision guided munition.

phase line (PL). A line used for control and coordination of military operations. It is usually a recognizable terrain feature extending

362

across the zone of action. Units normally report crossing PLs but do not halt unless specifically directed. PLs often are used to prescribe the timing of delay operations.

primary position. A place for a weapon, unit, or individual to fight that provides the best means to accomplish the assigned mission.

priority of fires. Direction to a fire support planner to organize and employ fire support means according to the importance of the supported unit's missions.

priority target. A target on which the delivery of fires takes precedence over all other fires for the designated firing unit/element. The firing unit/element will prepare, to the extent possible, for the engagement of such targets. A firing unit/element may be assigned only one priority target.

PVS-7 night-vision goggles. A lightweight, battery-powered, passive, night-vision device that allows the operator to see in low light (moonlight) levels. The goggles weigh one and a half pounds and offer clear vision on normal nights out to 150 meters.

retain. To occupy and hold a terrain feature to ensure it is free of enemy occupation or use.

reverse slope. A position on the ground not exposed to direct fire or observation. It may be a slope that descends away from the enemy.

reverse-slope defense. A defense area organized on any ground not exposed to direct fire or observation. It may be on a slope that descends away from the enemy.

RTO. Radiotelephone operator.

SAW. Squad automatic weapon.

SEAD. Suppression of enemy air defenses.

sector. An area designated by boundaries within which a unit operates and for which it is responsible. Normally, sectors are used in defensive operations.

secure. To gain possession of a position or terrain feature with or without force, and to deploy in a manner that prevents its destruction or loss to enemy action.

seize. To gain physical possession of a terrain feature from an enemy force.

SOI (signal operating instructions). A pamphlet issued by each unit that contains codes and frequencies for radio operations.

SOP. Standard operating procedures.

Glossary

start point (SP). A clearly defined initial control point on a route at which specified elements of a column of ground vehicles or flight of aircraft come under the control of the commander having responsibility for the movement.

strongpoint. A key point in a defensive position, usually strongly fortified and heavily armed with automatic weapons, around which other positions are grouped for its protection.

support force. Those forces charged with providing intense direct overwatching fires to the assault force.

suppression. Direct and indirect fires, electronic countermeasures (ECM), or smoke brought to bear on enemy personnel, weapons, or equipment to prevent effective fire on friendly forces.

synchronization. The arrangement of battlefield activities in time, space, and purpose to produce maximum relative combat power at the decisive point. Synchronization is both a process and a result. Synchronization need not depend on explicit coordination if all forces involved fully understand the commander's intent and have developed and rehearsed well-conceived standard responses to anticipated contingencies.

tactical operations center (TOC). The element within the main command post (CP) consisting of those staff activities involved in sustaining current operations and in planning future operations. Staff activities are functionally grouped into elements or cells. Units at battalion level and above normally have a TOC.

target overlay. An overlay showing the locations of friendly artillery units, targets, boundaries, and fire support coordination measures.

task organization. A temporary grouping of forces designed to accomplish a particular mission. Task organization involves the distribution of available assets to subordinate control headquarters by attachment or by placing assets in direct support (DS) or under the operational control of the subordinate.

terrain analysis. The process of interpreting a geographic area to determine the effect of the natural and man-made features on military operations.

TRP. Target reference point.

vee. An arrangement of vehicles or personnel in the shape of a V, with two elements up front to provide a heavy volume of fire on contact and one element in the rear to overwatch or maneuver. The point of the V is the trailing element. A V formation may be used when the leader requires firepower to the front and flanks.

warning order. A preliminary notice of an action or order that is to follow. Usually issued as a brief oral or written message. It is designed to give subordinates time to make necessary plans and preparations.

wedge. A formation of vehicles or personnel with one element leading and two elements in the rear to overwatch or maneuver. A wedge (1) permits excellent fire to the front and good fire to each flank, (2) facilitates control, (3) permits sustained effort and provides flank security, (4) lends itself readily to fire and movement, (5) is often used when the enemy situation is vague and contact is imminent.

withdrawal. A retrograde operation in which a force in contact with the enemy frees itself for a new mission.

XO. Executive officer.

zone. The area of responsibility for offensive operations assigned to a unit by the drawing of boundaries.

Decision Chart

Enter each section number as you select it. Victory is the objective, and whatever path achieves it is correct; but obviously it is more efficient to win in a relatively small number of choices without repeatedly having to go back and start over. Consider you choices carefully.

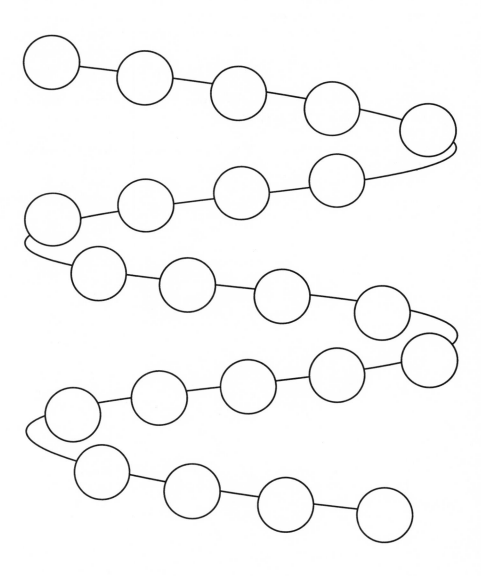

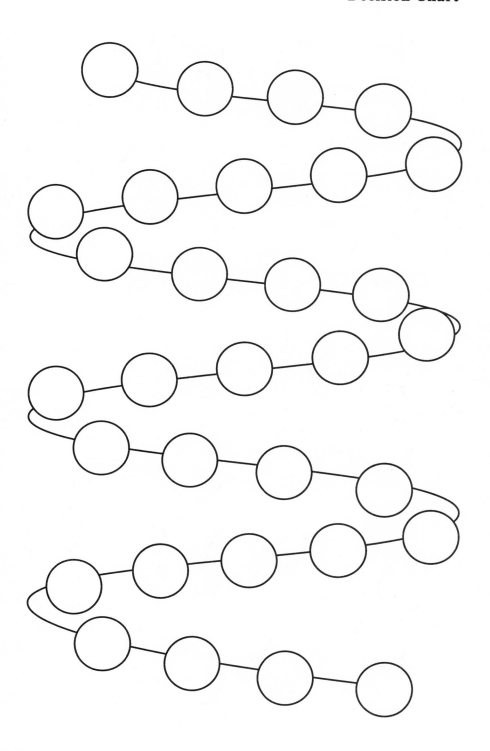

Decision Chart

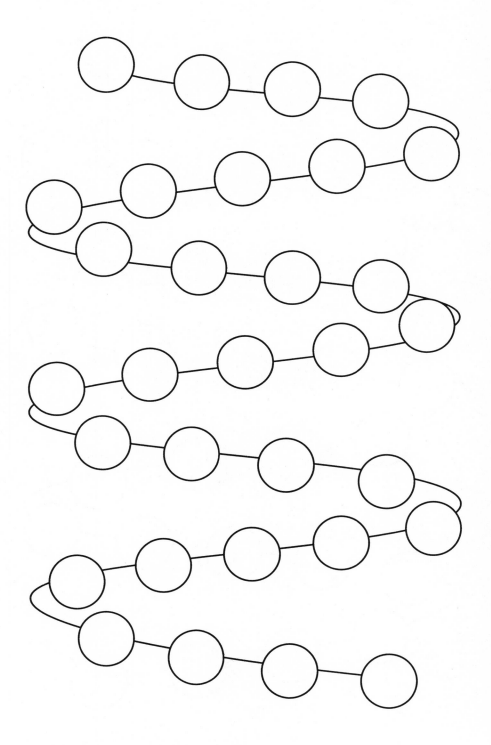

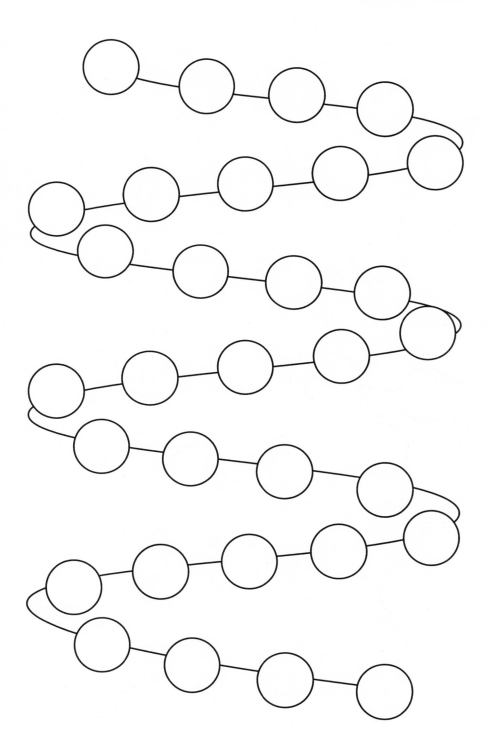

Decision Chart

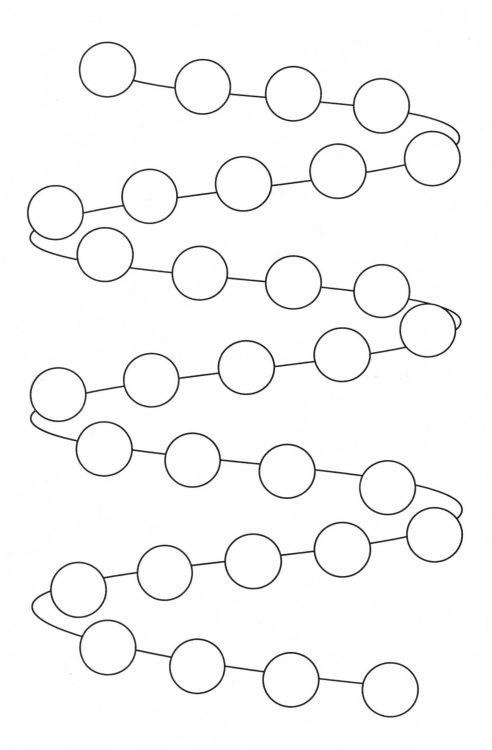